AF411491

The Songs of Johanna Kinkel

The Songs of Johanna Kinkel

Genesis, Reception, Context

Anja Bunzel

THE BOYDELL PRESS

First published 2020
The Boydell Press, Woodbridge

ISBN 978-1-78327-410-9

The Boydell Press is an imprint of Boydell & Brewer Ltd
PO Box 9, Woodbridge, Suffolk IP12 3DF, UK
and of Boydell & Brewer Inc.
668 Mt Hope Avenue, Rochester, NY 14620–2731, USA
website: www.boydellandbrewer.com

The publisher has no responsibility for the continued existence or accuracy of URLs for
external or third-party internet websites referred to in this book, and does not guarantee
that any content on such websites is, or will remain, accurate or appropriate

A catalogue record of this publication is available
from the British Library

This publication is printed on acid-free paper

Typeset in Minion Pro by
Sparks Publishing Services Ltd—www.sparkspublishing.com

To those who make me smile

Contents

List of figures

List of tables

List of music examples

The author and publisher are grateful to all the institutions and individuals listed for permission to reproduce the materials in which they hold copyright. Every effort has been made to trace the copyright holders; apologies are offered for any omission, and the publisher will be pleased to add any necessary acknowledgement in subsequent editions.

Acknowledgements

THIS book's journey from conceptualisation to publication took me to and through a number of challenges, career steps, and countries, and thus memories of the different stages involved in writing this book are manifold. Many people and institutions were involved in this journey – either through administrative advice and/or financial contributions or through professional guidance, collegial encouragement, and friendship. First of all, I thank Professor Lorraine Byrne Bodley for her ongoing support and encouragement. A casual remark at a conference in Maynooth in December 2011 turned into an insightful, incredibly fulfilling and very happy journey as a PhD candidate at Maynooth University. Besides her contextual and administrative advice throughout my PhD and post-doctoral studies, it is Lorraine's trust, quiet but confident encouragement, respect, honesty, patience, understanding, and – by now – her warm friendship for which I thank her most. Furthermore, I am grateful to Professor Fiona Palmer and Professor Christopher Morris, both of whom supported my research beyond their roles as Head of Department during my time at Maynooth University. I thank Professor Harald Krebs and Professor Fiona Palmer for their inspiring remarks regarding Johanna Kinkel's standing in England, aspects of translation and music-analytical observations, as well as the anonymous peer-reviewers of this book for their helpful observations. I thank Dr Patrick Devine, my most reliable lunch-buddy in Maynooth, for generously giving up his time to proofread this entire book, and for pointing me to some unusual aspects of Kinkel's compositions. I gratefully acknowledge the support from all colleagues at the Maynooth University Music Department, the Library, the Graduate Studies and Research Development Offices, as well as the Arts and Humanities Institute (formerly An Foras Feasa). I thank the editorial team at Boydell & Brewer for taking care of me so patiently and professionally and Wendy Baskett for compiling the index. I am grateful to all students whose paths I crossed in Maynooth, Dublin, and Graz for their inspiring remarks and curiosity. In my new home, Prague, I thank my colleagues at the Institute of Art History of the Czech Academy of Sciences for their openness, understanding, patience, humour, and warm welcome – I could not have dreamt of a better start and of a better base for completing this book.

For financial support, I express my sincere gratitude to the Irish Research Council, the Maynooth University Travel Fund, the Society for Musicology in Ireland, Stiftung Preußischer Kulturbesitz, and the Mariann Steegmann Foundation.

Many sources which emerge in this book are archived in different libraries and repositories in Germany and abroad. I would like to thank the staff at the following institutions for their professionalism: Staatsbibliothek zu Berlin – Preußischer Kulturbesitz, Musikabteilung mit Mendelssohn-Archiv; Bodleian Library Oxford; Beethoven-Haus Bonn; Stadtarchiv Bonn; StadtMuseum Bonn; Universitäts- und Landesbibliothek Bonn; Freies Deutsches Hochstift (Frankfurt am Main); Universitätsbibliothek Kassel; Universitätsbibliothek Leipzig; and Stadtbibliothek Lübeck.

The list of further colleagues and friends whose support has been exceptional seems endless, but a few people must be acknowledged individually: Dr Ingrid Bodsch, whose indefatigable enthusiasm for Bonn, Kinkel and Schumann is a pleasure to be around; Professor Bodo Bischoff and Professor Franz Michael Maier, whose long-lasting interests in my research have been both reassuring and inspiring; Dr Petra Dollinger, whose many energetic and knowledgeable e-mails were (and are) both encouraging and fun; Dr Natasha Loges, my 'Retterin in der Not'; Monica Klaus, whose incredible generosity – in terms of knowledge, hospitality and time – is hard to convey and whose friendship I value immensely despite the geographical distance between Bonn and Prague; Dr Henrike Rost, my most loyal conference travel buddy; Dr Katharina Uhde, whose enthusiasm for nineteenth-century music and collegiality are refreshingly contagious; and Professor Harry White, whom I thank for his generosity, warmth and susceptibility towards early-career musicologists in Ireland and abroad. On a similar note, I thank the Council and members of the Society for Musicology in Ireland for welcoming me warmly and making me feel at home within Ireland's musicological landscape.

I sincerely thank my family for their support, trust and understanding from afar, and I thank my canoeing friends in Dublin, Peitz, and Prague for challenging me in non-academic areas of life. Furthermore, I thank Luise Agthe and Dr Maria Agthe, Brigitte Bark, Beate Helfricht, and Marlen Lober whose honest and rewarding friendships I do not want to miss. In Prague, I thank Katarina Fiala, Markéta Kabelková, Hana Kabelková, Veronika Slováčková; Lenka Zavřelová and Jindřich Šedivý with their families for their patience in teaching me Czech, for walks, laughs, and for countless cake and jam samples. More importantly, however, I thank those people for their helpfulness, their genuine curiosity, their generosity and openness, which fulfill me with a sense of complete happiness. Finally, I thank Francis Lomax for sharing with me parts of his life and so much more. I dedicate this book to those who make me smile.

Prague, July 2020

Introduction

THE significance of Johanna Kinkel (1810–1858) as a nineteenth-century female composer, pianist, poet, music pedagogue, writer, journalist, mother to four children, and wife of the German revolutionary, poet, and professor, Gottfried Kinkel (1815–1882), has long been overlooked. Kinkel published seventy-eight Lieder between 1838 and 1851, as well as two singing tutors and a number of music-pedagogical and fictional writings. This book focuses on Kinkel's Lieder and the context within which those Lieder were composed, performed, reviewed, and received.[1] Kinkel's music was performed among her friends and more distant contemporaries, was reviewed in all renowned German nineteenth-century music journals, and was published by a variety of presses. This poses the question why her oeuvre is underrepresented within today's musical and musicological research and performance canons, even though Kinkel was acknowledged in encyclopaedias as early as 1855.[2] Although all of Kinkel's Lieder were published during her lifetime, they were not mentioned in an encyclopaedia until 1911, while her novel *Hans Ibeles in London*, published posthumously in 1860, was recognised by *Pierer's Universal-Lexikon* in the year of publication.[3] It thus seems that – in line with nineteenth-century perceptions of male creative and female reproductive domains – Johanna Kinkel's public image was that of a writer rather than a composer during the second half of the nineteenth century.[4]

---

[1] On aspects of interpreting scores within context see Benjamin Binder, 'The Lied from the Inside Out', in 'Colloquy: Studying the Lied: Hermeneutic Traditions and the Challenge of Performance', convened by Jennifer Ronyak, *Journal of the American Musicological Society*, 67, 2 (2014), 543–82 (553–55); Nicholas Cook, 'Between Process and Product: Music and/as Performance', *The Online Journal of the Society for Music Theory: Music Theory Online*, 7, 2 (2001), 1–31 (31) <http://www.mtosmt.org/issues/mto.01.7.2/mto.01.7.2.cook.html> (accessed 12 June 2019).

[2] The earliest mention of Johanna Kinkel in an encyclopaedia is in *Herders Conversations-Lexikon*, ed. Bartholomä Herder, 5 vols (Freiburg: Herder, 1854–57), iii, 591.

[3] Julius Löbe, 'Kinkel', in *Pierer's Universal-Lexikon*, ed. Julius Löbe, 4th edn, 19 vols (Altenburg: Pierer, 1857–65), ix, 494.

[4] James Deaville, 'This Is (Y)our Life: (Re)Writing Women's Autobiographies in Music in Nineteenth-Century Germany', in *Musical Biography: Towards New*

By contrast, Kinkel was especially respected for her strong-willed personality, her sharp intellect and witty humour, and her brilliance as a composer and pianist among her friends. Malwida von Meysenbug (1816–1903), for instance, described Kinkel as a 'brave fighter for truth and right', while also voicing her fascination for Kinkel's literary, musical, and pedagogical talents.[5] Recalling a holiday with the Kinkels outside of London, von Meysenbug praises Kinkel's pedagogical approach:

> The education of the children was highly organised, and I was especially relieved to be able to put Johanna Kinkel in charge of their musical education, who, although she was a first-class musician herself, had completely devoted herself to direct the initial musical instruction of children.[6]

Another friend, Fanny Lewald (1811–1889), admits that 'one forgot that she was a remarkable poet and a great musician, because one was only able to think about what kind of a woman and what kind of a character she was'.[7] Wilhelm Lübke (1826–1893), a regular visitor at the Kinkels' house and member of the Bonner Gesangverein, reminisces that he enjoyed attending the Gesangverein's rehearsals led by Kinkel because of her vast technical understanding and

---

Paradigms, ed. Jolanta T. Pekacz (Aldershot: Ashgate, 2006), 135–58 (136). This impression is evoked also in the editions of selected letters published in the Preußische Jahrbücher: Marie Goslich, 'Briefe von Johanna Kinkel', Preußische Jahrbücher, 97 (1899), 185–222; Marie Goslich, 'Briefe von Johanna Kinkel: Schluß', Preußische Jahrbücher, 97 (1899), 398–433; Max Pahncke, 'Briefe von Johanna Kinkel an Willibald Beyschlag', Preußische Jahrbücher, 122 (1905), 77–112; Paul Kaufmann, 'Johanna Kinkel: Neue Beiträge zu ihrem Lebensbild', Preußische Jahrbücher, 221 (1930), 290–304; Paul Kaufmann, 'Johanna Kinkel: Neue Beiträge zu ihrem Lebensbild: Schluß', Preußische Jahrbücher, 222 (1930), 48–67; Paul Kaufmann, 'Noch einmal auf Johanna Kinkels Spuren', Preußische Jahrbücher, 229 (1932), 263–68.

[5] Malwida von Meysenbug, Gesammelte Werke, ed. Berta Schleicher, 5 vols (Stuttgart: Deutsche Verlags-Anstalt, 1922), ii, 127, 'unerschrockene Kämpferin für Wahrheit und Recht'.

[6] Ibid., 457. 'Der Unterricht der Kinder wurde auf das reichlichste organisiert, und ganz besonders gereichte es mir zur Beruhigung, seine musikalische Seite in die Hände Johanna Kinkels legen zu können, die, obgleich selbst Musikerin ersten Ranges, es sich doch ganz zur Aufgabe gemacht hatte, den ersten Musikunterricht von Kindern zu leiten.'

[7] Fanny Lewald, Zwölf Bilder nach dem Leben, Erinnerungen von Fanny Lewald (Berlin: Otto Janke, 1888), 3. 'Man vergaß es, daß sie eine bedeutende Dichterin, daß sie eine große Musikerin war, weil man immer nur daran zu denken hatte, welch eine Frau und welch ein Charakter sie sei.'

her ability to introduce the singers to the 'inner structures of the works with brilliant comments'.[8] Lübke also mentions Kinkel's compositions 'in which she glorified primarily her husband's poems'.[9] Among all her Lieder, her settings of Gottfried Kinkel's words must have been performed most frequently during the 1840s, although she also set poems by other authors including herself.

Kinkel's acknowledgement within the field of musicology is a relatively recent phenomenon. Neither the first edition of *Die Musik in Geschichte und Gegenwart* nor that of *Grove's Dictionary of Music and Musicians* includes an entry on Kinkel; the second editions of both works closed this gap and devoted some room to Kinkel's biography and her career as a musician and composer.[10] There have been several attempts to place Johanna Kinkel into her literary and socio-cultural context in special-interest literature, but very few studies focus on her musical personality.[11] There are some publications dealing with Kinkel as a composer, which, however, foreground Kinkel's biographical details rather

[8] Wilhelm Lübke, *Lebenserinnerungen* (Berlin: Fontane, 1891), 106: 'sie verstand es, uns durch geistvolle Bemerkungen in das innere Verständnis der Tonschöpfungen einzuführen'.

[9] Ibid., 105: 'mit denen sie vorzugsweise die Gedichte ihres Mannes verherrlichte'. Lübke mentions as the two Lieder 'Es ist so still geworden' (op. 18, no. 1) and 'Auf einsam hohem Thurme' (op. 17, no. 6).

[10] Sigrid Nieberle, 'Kinkel, Johanna', in *Die Musik in Geschichte und Gegenwart*, ed. Ludwig Finscher and others, 2nd edn, 29 vols (Kassel: Bärenreiter, 1994–2008), x, Personenteil, 131–34; Ann Willison Lemke, 'Kinkel, Johanna', in *The New Grove Dictionary of Music and Musicians*, ed. Stanley Sadie, 2nd edn, 29 vols (London: Macmillan, 2001), xiii, 611.

[11] For instance, Hermann Rösch-Sondermann, 'Johanna Kinkel: Emanzipation und Revolution einer Bonnerin', in *Bonn: 54 Kapitel Stadtgeschichte*, ed. Joseph Matzerath (Bonn: Bouvier, 1989), 179–88; Ruth Whittle, 'Modes of Exile: Revisiting Johanna Kinkel', *Colloquia Germanica*, 34/2 (2001), 97–119; Rosemary Ashton, *Little Germany: Exile and Asylum in Victorian England* (Oxford: Oxford University Press, 1986); Eva Weissweiler, 'Zu Johanna Kinkel und ihrem Chopin-Aufsatz', *dissonanz*, 8 (1986), 4–7; Bettina Brand, '" … wie die Stimme, die aus ihrer innersten Seele spricht": Johanna Kinkels "Vortrag über Beethovens früheste Sonaten inkl. op.10"', in *Maßstab Beethoven?: Komponistinnen im Schatten des Geniekults*, ed. Bettina Brand and Martina Helmig (Munich: TextUndKritik, 2001), 159–74; Marion Freund, *'Mag der Thron in Flammen glühn!': Schriftstellerinnen und die Revolution von 1848/49* (Königstein: Helmer, 2004); Ruth-Ellen Boetcher Joeres, *Respectability and Deviance: Nineteenth-Century German Women Writers and the Ambiguity of Representation* (Chicago: University of Chicago Press, 1998); Carol Diethe, *Towards Emancipation: German Women Writers of the Nineteenth Century* (Oxford: Berghahn, 1998); Ruth Whittle and Debbie Pinfold, *Voices of Rebellion: Political Writings by Malwida von Meysenbug, Fanny Lewald, Johanna Kinkel and Louise Aston* (Bern: Peter Lang, 2005); Klaus Schmidt, *Gerechtigkeit – das Brot des Volkes: Johanna und Gottfried Kinkel* (Stuttgart: Radius, 1996).

than her music.[12] Linda Siegel includes close readings of selected Lieder in the notes to her two edited volumes of Kinkel Lieder.[13] There are a few examinations of Johanna Kinkel's music-pedagogical writings, most importantly Marianne Bröcker's and Linda Siegel's journal articles.[14]

The most notable current contributors to Kinkel research are Monica Klaus and Daniela Glahn. Besides Klaus's letter edition, her volume of selected literary works of Kinkel's (published together with Ingrid Bodsch), and her essay on Kinkel's first published opus, *Die Vogelkantate*, Klaus's Kinkel biography is

[12] The first work on Kinkel's compositions is Else Thalheimer, 'Johanna Kinkel als Musikerin' (unpublished PhD dissertation, University of Bonn, 1922); for later publications see, for instance, Brunhilde Sonntag, *Annäherung an sieben Komponistinnen* (Kassel: Furore, 1997); Ute Büchter-Römer, '"Ein rheinisches Musikfest muß man erlebt haben": Johanna Kinkel, Clara Schumann, Fanny Hensel und die Rheinromantik', in *Romantik, Reisen, Realitäten: Frauenleben am Rhein*, ed. Bettina Bab and Helga Arend (Bonn: Lempertz, 2002); Ann Willison Lemke, 'Robert Schumann und Johanna Kinkel: Musikalische Stimmen der Revolution von 1848/49', in *Internationales Jahrbuch der Bettina-von-Arnim-Gesellschaft*, 11/12 (1999/2000), 179–206; Bettina Brand, 'Johanna Kinkel (1810–1858)', in *Komponistinnen in Berlin*, ed. Bettina Brand and others (Berlin: Bender, 1987), 74–95; Ann Willison Lemke, '"Alles Schaffen ist wohl eine Wechselwirkung von Inspiration und Willen": Johanna Kinkel als Komponistin', in *Annäherung IX – an sieben Komponistinnen: Mit Berichten, Interviews und Selbstdarstellungen*, ed. Clara Mayer (Kassel: Furore, 1998), 53–70.

[13] Linda Siegel, ed., *Johanna Kinkel: Lieder*, 2 vols (Mount Airy: Hildegard, 2002–03), and the author's own articles: Anja Bunzel, 'Johanna Kinkel's *Thurm und Fluth* (Opus 19, No. 6): Revolutionary Ideas and Political Optimism in a 19th-Century Art Song', in *The National Element in Music: Conference Proceedings*, ed. Nikos Maliaras (Athens: Athens University, 2014), 18–25; Anja Bunzel, 'Johanna Kinkel's Political Art Songs as a Contribution to the Socio-Cultural Identity of the German Democratic Movement during the Late 1840s', *Focus on German Studies*, 22 (2015), 1–20; Anja Bunzel and Barbora Kubečková, 'Václav Jan Tomášek (1774–1850): A Versatile Lieder Composer?: A Comparative Analysis of Selected Goethe Settings by Carl Friedrich Zelter, Václav Jan Tomášek and Johanna Kinkel', *Musicologica Olomucensia*, 20 (2014), 15–36. Linda Siegel presented a paper on harmony in Kinkel's Lieder at the *College Music Symposium*'s National Conference in 2004; attempts to find her contact details have been unsuccessful.

[14] Marianne Bröcker, 'Johanna Kinkels schriftstellerische und musikpädagogische Tätigkeit', *Bonner Geschichtsblätter*, 29 (1977), 37–48; Linda Siegel, 'Johanna Kinkel's "Chopin als Komponist" and Other Musical Writings: Untapped Source Readings in the History of Romantic Music Author(s)', *College Music Symposium*, 43 (2003), 105–25. See also the author's own article 'Johanna Kinkel's Pedagogical Approaches as a Socio-Political Mirror of Her Time', *Musicological Explorations*, 14 (2014), 27–58.

a significant resource.[15] Drawing on personal letters, manuscripts, and nine-teenth-century print media, this monograph offers a concise perspective on Kinkel's (psycho)biography in Bonn, Berlin, and London. Daniela Glahn, in her monograph *Johanna Kinkel – Bilder einer Autorschaft*, scrutinises selected music-pedagogical publications, a few of Kinkel's Lieder, and the *Vogelkantate* through the lens of authorship.[16] In her study, Glahn portrays Kinkel as an aesthetically diverse composer who was concerned with the fashionability and marketability of her output.

Taking Klaus's and Glahn's work as a starting point, this book offers an exhaustive close reading and contextualisation of Kinkel's published small-scale vocal music, which includes strophic and through-composed Lieder, duets, and ballads. Besides the literature already published on Kinkel, this study draws on primary sources surrounding Kinkel's artistic oeuvre. Most of these sources are archived at the Universitäts- und Landesbibliothek Bonn (ULB), which, most recently, has also digitised many of Kinkel's published Lieder opus numbers for open access, and the Stadtarchiv Bonn.[17] This study does not analyse in depth Kinkel's published large-scale works, *Hymnus in Coena Domini* (op. 14) and *Die Vogelkantate* (op. 1), nor her unpublished Lieder and duets, Scot-tish songs, and Singspiele, as many of these are incomplete and/or lost.[18] While

---

[15] Monica Klaus and Ingrid Bodsch, eds, *Johanna Kinkel: Eine Auswahl aus ihrem literarischen Werk* (Bonn: StadtMuseum, 2010); Monica Klaus, '"Die Nachtigall hat etwas detoniert!": Johanna Kinkels Vogelkantate – eine Komposition und ihre Geschichte', *Bonner Geschichtsblätter*, 53/54 (2004), 289–300; Monica Klaus, *Johanna Kinkel: Romantik und Revolution* (Cologne: Böhlau, 2008).

[16] Daniela Glahn, *Johanna Kinkel – Bilder einer Autorschaft* (Munich: Allitera, 2017).

[17] See Ulrike Brandt-Schwarze, *Nachlass Gottfried und Johanna Kinkel: Findbuch* (Bonn: n.p., 2001) <https://www.ulb.uni-bonn.de/die-ulb/publikationen/findbuecher-inhaltslisten/kinkel> (accessed 25 November 2018). Digital versions of Kinkel's opus numbers 6, 7, 8, 9, 10, 11, 13, 14, 15, 16, 17, 18, 19, and 21 are available through the ULB online digitalisation project HANS: <http://digitale-sammlungen.ulb.uni-bonn.de/ulbbnhans/content/titleinfo/2148925> (accessed 5 January 2019).

[18] There is a box of sixty-seven sheets of manuscript scores archived in the Stadtarchiv Bonn. The manuscripts include the Lieder; a few sketches; the orchestral part of the overture to *Die Assassinen*; twelve Scottish songs, partly notated in figured bass; six duets for two female voices, without piano accompaniment; a few composition exercises; and a few transcriptions of Charles Glover's compositions. Bonn, Stadtarchiv, SN 098 <http://www.archive.nrw.de/LAV_NRW/jsp/findbuch.jsp?archivNr=20&klassId=20&tektId=115&id=296&expandId=18> (accessed 26 November 2018). I am grateful to the Stadtarchiv Bonn for granting me access to these manuscripts. Furthermore, there is a fragment of a Lieder collection archived at ULB, which includes a few transcriptions of other composers' songs and some of Kinkel's compositions; it originates from Kinkel's own hand and is dated 1856–57 (Johanna Kinkel, *Fragment eines Liederbuchs*, ULB E 4' 756/6 Rara:15). I also found parts of an unpublished Lied ('Vineta' by Wilhelm Müller) on an autograph

the manuscripts of Kinkel's theoretical and music-historical writings are also archived in Bonn, most of her compositions only exist as publications, which do not reveal dates for the individual Lieder they include. Ulrike Brandt-Schwarze and her colleagues' edition of all *Maikäfer* journals is an excellent source here, as it records Kinkel's literary activities with the *Maikäferbund*, and enables us to trace the exact dates of some of the poetry Kinkel set.[19] Some such hints can also be detected in Johanna and Gottfried Kinkel's correspondence, a three-volume edition of which was compiled by Monica Klaus in 2008.[20]

Chapter 1 contextualises Johanna Kinkel's biography and her music-pedagogical approach within her wider private and public circles, as many of Kinkel's Lieder were inspired by her emotional biography and/or socio-cultural surroundings. By way of transition, Chapter 2 provides an overview of Kinkel's productivity, the poets she set, and performers and performance venues, all aspects of which will surface more subtly also in the next four analytical chapters. In Chapter 3, I explore Kinkel's love songs, followed by an examination of Kinkel's political songs in Chapter 4. Chapter 5 is devoted to Kinkel's nature songs. All three of these chapters, I will argue, are autobiographical, while at the same time shedding light on more general socio-cultural phenomena of the time. Kinkel's personality was anchored socio-culturally on different layers, for instance through her own emancipatory views on marriage; her involvement in various social gatherings in Berlin, Bonn, and London; her conversion to the Protestant faith; and her extraordinary artistic standing as a published poet, composer, and writer. Therefore, her vocal repertoire alludes to both her own emotional biography and the problems, challenges, and opportunities she faced as a progressive woman during the first half of the nineteenth century. Kinkel's embedment within her own time surfaces on textual as well as aesthetic levels, the latter of which is demonstrated in a comparative analysis in Chapter 6. Here, I consider the question as to how far Kinkel's compositional style set itself apart from that of her contemporaries. These analytical chapters are

---

archived at Staatsbibliothek zu Berlin, Preußischer Kulturbesitz, Musikabteilung mit Mendelssohn-Archiv (Mus.ms.autogr. Kinkel, J. 1 M.). This proves that Kinkel must have composed more Lieder than she published.

[19] *Der Maikäfer: Zeitschrift für Nichtphilister,* ed. Ulrike Brandt-Schwarze and others, 4 vols (Bonn: Stadtarchiv, 1982–85).

[20] Johanna and Gottfried Kinkel, *Liebe treue Johanna! Liebster Gottit!: Der Briefwechsel zwischen Gottfried und Johanna Kinkel: 1840–1858,* comp. Monica Klaus, 3 vols (Bonn: Stadtarchiv und Stadthistorische Bibliothek, 2008).

geared towards an exploration of musical form and consider such categories as harmony, melody, rhythm, and phrasal structure, depending on each individual piece's aesthetic particularities. While time and space do not allow a comprehensive discussion of every musical aspect in every piece, I focus on observations which help to place Kinkel's music within context.[21] Referring to the potential of poetry to record, express, and evoke emotions and feelings, Lawrence Kramer poses the question whether 'song [is] so intensely [...] expressive because it comes exquisitely close to intoning all those things that we forbid ourselves to say'.[22] The following six chapters are designed to illuminate aspects of Johanna Kinkel's time which she herself did not always voice in writing and which are thus not easily accessible to us through the scrutiny of words in isolation. Kinkel's music illuminates facets of Kinkel's own and her contemporaries' everyday lives. It is being performed and recorded by Kinkel enthusiasts all over the world, and it is my hope that this study will draw further attention to Kinkel's fascinating artistic output, and that it might encourage further performances of her music.[23]

Finally, two practical notes to the reader. First, Johanna Kinkel's surname changed three times over the course of her life. She was born as Johanna Mockel and married Johann Mathieux in 1832. It was not until 1843, when she married Gottfried Kinkel, that her name changed to Johanna Kinkel. In the spirit of consistency and a better flow of reading, I refer to her as Johanna Kinkel throughout this book, although her earlier works were published under the name Johanna Mathieux (and J. Mathieux, respectively). Second, all primary sources are quoted in the original language. While I have kept the original spelling in the music examples, I have followed modern editorial practice for the musical scores for better legibility.

---

[21] For details on the analysis of song as a 'boundless activity' and the need to 'isolate certain dimensions', see Kofi Agawu, 'Theory and Practice in the Analysis of the Nineteenth-Century "Lied"', *Music Analysis,* 11, 1 (1992), 3–36 (13).

[22] Lawrence Kramer, *Music and Poetry: The Nineteenth Century and After* (Berkeley: University of California Press, 1984), 170.

[23] A discography is included at the end of this book; Monica Klaus and Sibylle Wagner revive Kinkel's music in the Bonn area, and Kinkel's music has been performed by Harald and Sharon Krebs (Victoria, Canada), Tammy Hensrud and Korliss Uecker (New York, USA), and the US-based project *Sophie: A Digital Library of Works by German-Speaking Women,* to name but a few.

CHAPTER 1

Johanna Kinkel – mother, musician, revolutionary

❧ *Kinkel's private life*

KINKEL'S education was rather unplanned and was the result of her own eagerness to learn. Born into a Catholic middle-class family in 1810, Johanna Kinkel, traditionally, would have received a basic artistic education in needlework and music, and would have been trained primarily in household tasks including the care of a hard-working husband and numerous children. In contrast to other middle-class girls of her time, however, Kinkel was able to satisfy her hunger for knowledge in her teacher father's library, which comprised books on music, history, literature, theology, and philosophy. Growing up, Kinkel faced the peculiarities of convention when, in order to satisfy her mother's expectations, she took up an apprenticeship as a chef while still playing the piano as a hobby and even teaching others at the Mockels' (Kinkel's) house.[1] In 1832, Kinkel married Johann Paul Mathieux, an educated Catholic bookseller and music dealer. The marriage emerged as a psychological nightmare for Kinkel, as Mathieux expected his wife to give up her musical interests in favour of a frugal Catholic lifestyle.[2] Kinkel became unwell, which prompted her parents to take her back to their house. Shortly after, Kinkel decided to fight for a divorce, which at the time was subject to both the man's and woman's agreement, and she resumed her musical activities with the Bonn musical circle. When Mathieux still had not agreed to a divorce by 1836, Johanna travelled to Frankfurt am Main where she met Felix Mendelssohn (1809–1847) and Georg Brentano (1775–1851). Equipped with references from both, she set out for Berlin. Kinkel's visit to Berlin offered various opportunities. As Berlin was primarily a Protestant centre, Kinkel's social environment was more open-minded than in Catholic Bonn; she also improved her artistic education, as she was introduced to a great number of musical and literary luminaries of Berlin's rich cultural life.[3]

---

[1] Klaus, *Johanna Kinkel*, 8.

[2] Ibid., 15.

[3] Gottfried Kinkel (jun.), ed., 'Aus Johanna Kinkels Memoiren', *Internationales Jahrbuch der Bettina von Arnim-Gesellschaft*, 8/9 (1996/97), 239–71 (241).

In Berlin, Kinkel first lived with Bettina von Arnim (1785–1859), who introduced her to Friedrich Carl von Savigny (1779–1861). There she played the piano at regular gatherings, and a rearranged version of Kinkel's *Vogelkantate,* her op. 1 first conceived for the Bonn musical circle in 1829, was performed on the occasion of Savigny's birthday in 1837.[4] Besides the musical enjoyments at Savigny's, the host, being a renowned jurist, also showed an understanding for Kinkel's desire to get divorced.[5] However, he was not able to push through a prompt divorce, so Kinkel stayed in Berlin until her husband agreed to a divorce in 1839. Besides Bettina von Arnim and Savigny, Kinkel met other cultural protagonists: she attended the *Sonntagsmusiken* (Sunday musical evenings) of Fanny Hensel (1805–1847), she was taught by Wilhelm Taubert (1811–1891) and Karl Böhmer (1799–1884), she befriended Emilie von Henning (1805–1853), a neighbour of Johanna's friend Nanny Müller (1800–?) and the poet Emanuel Geibel (1815–1884), and she visited the painter Carl Begas's circle, the Staegemann salon, as well as a number of smaller, lesser-known gatherings.[6] In 1837, Kinkel moved into her own residence, a decision which increased her independence and compositional productivity. Having gained a reputation as a pianist she was able to make a living from teaching.[7] In Berlin, she thrived professionally and creatively. Nevertheless, she left Berlin in the springtime of 1839, as her parents informed her about Mathieux's acceptance of a divorce. Back in Bonn, she realised that her divorce had not progressed as far as she would have wished and that she had to get used to the Bonn bourgeoisie again, which differed remarkably from the Berlin societies.[8] Due to its huge population, Berlin was much

---

[4] Monica Klaus (*Johanna Kinkel,* 50) depicts the publication date as 1838; Hofmeister announces the publication in January 1839 <http://anno.onb.ac.at/cgi-content/anno-buch?apm=0&aid=1000001&bd=0001839&teil=0203&seite=00000010&zoom=1> (accessed 4 June 2016). See, for instance, [Anon.], review of Johanna Mathieux, *Die Vogelkantate* (1838), *Allgemeiner Musikalischer Anzeiger,* 17 September 1840, 149–50. For further details on Kinkel's *Vogelkantate* see also Klaus, 'Die Nachtigall hat etwas detoniert'.

[5] Kinkel (jun.), 'Aus Johanna Kinkels Memoiren', 242–43.

[6] See Carl Begas to Johanna Kinkel on 2 June 1838 (Stadtarchiv Bonn, SN 98/165); Fanny Hensel to Johanna Kinkel on 2 December 1838 (Stadtarchiv Bonn, SN 98/163); and Kinkel to Fräulein A. Dorn on 31 March 1838 (Stadtarchiv Bonn, SN 98/77); Kinkel to Philipp von Nathusius on 26 February 1841 (UB Kassel, 4° Ms. hist. litt. 15[151]). For details on Berlin salons of the nineteenth century see Petra Wilhelmy, *Der Berliner Salon im 19. Jahrhundert (1780–1914)* (Berlin: de Gruyter, 1989). For full details on Kinkel's social environment in Berlin see Anja Bunzel, 'Johanna Kinkel's Social Life in Berlin (1836–39): Reflections on Historiographical Sources', in *Musical Salon Culture in the Long Nineteenth Century,* ed. Anja Bunzel and Natasha Loges (Woodbridge: Boydell, 2019), 13–26.

[7] Theodor Anton Henseler, *Das musikalische Bonn im 19. Jahrhundert* (Bonn: Universitäts-Buchdruckerei, 1959), 143.

[8] Klaus, *Johanna Kinkel,* 56.

more anonymous than Bonn, and Berlin's cultural life was more diverse with a great number of literary and musical societies, museums and concert venues. Kinkel engaged as much as possible in social activities, through which she met Gottfried Kinkel on 4 May 1839. A former student of Johanna's father, Gottfried had been known to Johanna as a child; however, their relationship was more serious in nature this time around.[9]

Johanna's reputation as a teacher was excellent and she was able to support herself financially through teaching; however, despite her success as a teacher and her positive prospects with Gottfried, the slow proceedings of the divorce and her longing for the metropolitan gatherings in Berlin took their toll on her emotional well-being. Johanna shared her desperate situation with Gottfried, although he was engaged to Sophie Boegehold at the time.[10] The successful completion of Johanna's divorce on 22 May 1840 along with Gottfried's increasing distance to Sophie Boegehold paved the way for a more passionate relationship between Gottfried and Johanna, which was finally settled by a tragic accident on the river Rhine in the summer of 1840.[11] In 1841, Gottfried dissolved his engagement with Sophie Boegehold in favour of Johanna, a decision which cost him his job as a teacher and his position as an assistant sermoniser in Cologne.[12] Johanna's conversion to the Protestant faith in 1842 enabled her and Gottfried to get married on 22 May 1843. Although they had faced disappointments in faithless friends and professional burdens, the following years manifested a diverse cultural life with a remarkable artistic output by both Johanna and Gottfried Kinkel and an increasing engagement with politics, which finally overshadowed all cultural activities.

In 1840, when Johanna's morning concerts at the Mockels' house had become a popular platform for the exchange of recent poetic and prose works, Johanna and Gottfried established the *Maikäferbund* (Maybug Association), a literary association which met regularly and recorded its members' new works and socio-cultural observations in the *Maikäfer*, a handwritten journal. The first volume was issued on 25 June 1840. The members were predominantly male; indeed, Johanna was the only female member throughout the group's history, although Emilie von Binzer (1801–1891) visited the *Maikäferbund* occasionally without joining officially.[13] At an artistic level, both Johanna and Gottfried increased their productivity with the *Maikäfer*, as the regular

---

[9] Ibid., 57.

[10] Ibid., 69.

[11] See letter from Johanna Kinkel to Leopold von Henning dated 11 October 1842, cited in Goslich, 'Briefe von Johanna Kinkel', 212–15.

[12] Johanna and Gottfried Kinkel, *Liebe treue Johanna! Liebster Gottit!*, i, 127; Klaus, *Johanna Kinkel*, 87–97.

[13] Klaus, *Johanna Kinkel*, 105. Kinkel's friendship with Emilie von Binzer is reflected in a letter from Johanna to Gottfried on 8 April 1841, in which Johanna talks about

meetings motivated the members to create new works and enabled a vivid exchange of ideas. It is thus not surprising that Johanna set a great number of poems originating from *Maikäfer* members. Willibald Beyschlag's account of his *Maikäfer* experience reveals that Kinkel also performed her Lieder to the *Maikäfer* audience:

> When she sang her Lieder, the most beautiful, harmonious songs of Geibel or Kinkel, – not with an outstanding voice, but presented in a most thoughtful and soulful performance, then, surrounded by the twilight of the intimate room, she looked youthful and beautiful.[14]

Besides Lieder and poetry, Kinkel produced many of her novellas and her first theoretical writings on contemporary music with the *Maikäfer*.[15]

At a political level, the explosiveness of the *Maikäfer* is reflected especially in the yearbook *Vom Rhein: Leben, Kunst und Dichtung* (About the Rhine: Life, Art and Poetry), edited by Gottfried Kinkel and published in 1847. The political situation of the late 1840s finally led to the closing of the association: some members' works became politically controversial, other members did not want to be associated with revolutionary ideas. The yearbook, while marking the end of the *Maikäfer*, alludes to the Kinkels' desire for a democratic republic. Table 1.1 shows Johanna and Gottfried Kinkel's involvements with politics between 1848 and January 1851.[16]

----

visiting von Binzer in Cologne. Johanna and Gottfried Kinkel, *Liebe treue Johanna! Liebster Gottit!*, i, 169.

[14] Willibald Beyschlag, *Aus meinem Leben: Erinnerungen und Erfahrungen der jüngeren Jahre* (Halle/Saale: Strien, 1896), 114–15. 'Wenn sie ihre Lieder sang, die in Wohlklang verklärten schönsten Lieder von Geibel oder von Kinkel, – nicht mit bedeutender Stimme, aber im durchgebildetsten seelenvollen Vortrag, dann im Dämmerlichte des traulichen Zimmers wurde sie jung und schön.'

[15] Among them were *Dä Hond on dat Eechhorn*, a story for children, written in Bonn dialect; *Lebenslauf des Johannisfünkchens, von ihm selbst verfaßt*, a short biography of a glow-worm which is used as an allegory for the political tension between the aristocracy (the spider) and the people (the small beetles including the glow-worm); *Der Musikant*, a short story about a bourgeois musician who is annoyed by his neighbours who, being of aristocratic origin, play their instruments very badly and thereby distract the musician from his compositional activity; *Musikalische Orthodoxie*, a novella dealing with musical gender conventions, teaching and the superficiality of the aristocracy; 'Über die modernen Liederkomponisten' ('About the Modern Lieder Composers'); and 'Das moderne Klavierspiel' ('Modern Piano Performance').

[16] Table partly taken from Klaus, *Johanna Kinkel*, 342ff.

Table 1.1: Johanna and Gottfried Kinkel's political activities (1848–1851)

Date	Event
1848	
February	In a presentation on the history of art, Gottfried Kinkel advocates a 'state in which the people's will is respected and rules everyone's everyday life'[17]
20 March	Gottfried Kinkel's first democratic speech at Bonn City Hall
27 March	Establishment of a Central-Bürgerversammlung (Central Assembly of the Citizens), including three political branches: Rhine Catholics, Constitutionals, and Democrats, among whom Gottfried Kinkel takes leadership
19 April	Gottfried Kinkel's petition for craftsmen
28 May	Gottfried Kinkel establishes the Handwerkerbildungsverein (Craftsmen's Educational Association)
31 May	Gottfried Kinkel establishes the Demokratischer Verein (Democratic Association)
August	Gottfried Kinkel publishes his work *Handwerk, errette dich!* (Trade, Rescue Yourself!)
6 August	Gottfried Kinkel becomes editor of the *Bonner Zeitung*
15 November	Gottfried Kinkel's public appeal for tax refusal
November	Interruption of Johanna Kinkel's piano lessons by soldier Rosenkranz
6 December	Johanna Kinkel publishes her 'Demokratenlied' in the *Bonner Zeitung*
16 December	Johanna Kinkel's 'Demokratenlied' is published by Sulzbach
1849	
22 January–5 February	Elections for Second Chamber of Prussian Diet; Gottfried Kinkel is elected
24 February	Gottfried Kinkel leaves Bonn in order to join the Prussian Diet in Berlin
February	Carl Schurz, alongside Johanna Kinkel, becomes the leading editor of the *Bonner Zeitung*
8 March	Gottfried Kinkel's first Parliament speech which is published by the *Bonner Zeitung* on 15 March 1849
30 March	Gottfried Kinkel's suspension from Bonn University
12 April	Johanna Kinkel and the children move to Berlin
3 May	The Kinkels move back to Bonn
May	Prussian Diet (Berlin) and German National Assembly (Frankfurt) are dissolved
10 May	'Siegburger Zeughaussturm'; Gottfried Kinkel escapes from military
20 May	Johanna Kinkel takes editorship of the *Bonner Zeitung*

[17] Klaus, *Johanna Kinkel*, 152: 'eine Staatsform, in welcher der Wille des Volkes zur Geltung kommt und zum lebensbeherrschenden Gesetze wird'.

20 June	Gottfried Kinkel joins the Companie Besançon, he fights on the battlefield in Baden
2 July	Gottfried Kinkel is injured during a battle in Küppenheim, near Rastatt, and is arrested
3 July	Johanna visits Gottfried in Rastatt; she writes the Lied 'Der gefangene Freischärler'
12 July	Gottfried Kinkel is unseated as a professor
July	Several appeals for clemency in favour of Gottfried Kinkel
4 August	Gottfried Kinkel's trial at court; sentence is declared invalid on 12 August 1849
12 August	Johanna meets Gottfried in order to discuss guardianship of children; Johanna is appointed the guardian; additionally, Johanna's father and the friends Hermann Schauenburg and Carl Fresenius, or Hermann Velten should the non-Prussian Fresenius not be eligible, are appointed guardians
30 September	Official sentence for Gottfried Kinkel: lifelong imprisonment in a penitentiary, not in a civil prison
8 October	Gottfried Kinkel arrives in Naugard penitentiary
1850	
12 April	Gottfried Kinkel is brought to Cologne for trial for 'Siegburger Zeughaussturm'
29 April–2 May	Gottfried Kinkel's trial; sentence: acquittal for 'Siegburger Zeughaussturm', on the way back he tries to escape, but is caught and relocated to Spandau
6 November	Gottfried Kinkel's escape from Spandau to London
1851	
23 January	Johanna Kinkel and the children arrive in London

As Table 1.1 demonstrates, up until November 1848, Johanna Kinkel had supported her husband's fight for a revolution only passively by looking after the household and the four children, born on 11 July 1844 (Gottfried), 8 August 1845 (Johanna), 12 August 1846 (Adelheid), and 29 July 1848 (Hermann). Her involvement with politics assumed new dimensions when numerous intrigues and aspersions caused the cancellation of all her piano tuition.[18] On 6 December 1848 her 'Demokratenlied' (Democrats' Song), which advocates the fight for a republic, was printed in the *Bonner Zeitung*; shortly after, on 16 December 1848, her song was published by Sulzbach. When Gottfried Kinkel moved to Berlin in February 1849 as a representative of the Zweite Kammer (Second Chamber) of the Preußischer Landtag (Prussian Diet), Johanna Kinkel expanded

---

[18] Ibid., 165–66.

her journalistic activity with the *Bonner Zeitung*.[19] As a link between Berlin and Bonn, she published many of Gottfried's writings in the *Bonner Zeitung*. In April 1849, Johanna, along with the four children and the two housemaids, followed her husband to Berlin.[20] However, they all moved back to Bonn when the Prussian Diet was closed on 3 May 1849.

Out of disappointment Gottfried Kinkel joined the democrats in the 'Siegburger Zeughaussturm' (the storming of the arsenal at Siegburg) on 10 May 1849. The revolutionary attempt failed, and while Gottfried Kinkel managed to escape from the Prussian troops, he did not return home. Johanna, who on 20 May 1849 had taken over the editorship of the *Bonner Zeitung* since Carl Schurz's departure on 9 May, secured some financial income by writing for different newspapers and publishing some of her own and Gottfried's novellas and poems as well as running her singing school for children.[21] On 20 June 1849, Gottfried Kinkel joined the militia Companie Besançon. This decision brought a prompt end to Kinkel's escape from the Prussian troops. On 2 July 1849, he was caught in a fight in Küppenheim near Rastatt.[22] One day later, Johanna visited him in prison in Karlsruhe, after which she composed her Lied 'Der gefangene Freischärler' (The Imprisoned Voluntary Soldier).[23] On 4 August 1849 Gottfried Kinkel's trial opened. It involved a few relocations to different prisons and one failed escape attempt by Gottfried. Numerous friends and associations advocated an appeal for clemency, to be signed and sent to the Prince of Prussia.[24]

---

[19] This was not Johanna Kinkel's first journalistic endeavour. According to Paul Kaufmann ('Johanna Kinkel: Neue Beiträge zu ihrem Lebensbild', 292), she created the *Endenicher Wochenblatt*, a weekly magazine including short literary works, as early as 1830. She also wrote two *Endenicher Modejournale* (Stadtarchiv Bonn, SN 94/253), journals containing small pencil drawings and humorous literary works, in July 1835 and 1839 respectively. Like the *Maikäfer* journals, these journals are handwritten and should therefore be considered semi-public as they were not circulated widely.

[20] See Johanna and Gottfried Kinkel, *Liebe treue Johanna! Liebster Gottit!*, i, 495.

[21] See Klaus, *Johanna Kinkel*, 183. In 1849, Cotta published the novellas in *Erzählungen von Gottfried und Johanna Kinkel* and the poems in *Gedichte von Gottfried Kinkel*; Sulzbach published Johanna's children's story *Dä Hond on dat Eechhorn – ä Verzellcher für Blahge*.

[22] See Klaus, *Johanna Kinkel*, 192.

[23] Johanna Kinkel shared this poem with Gottfried in a letter dated 7 July 1849. Johanna and Gottfried Kinkel, *Liebe treue Johanna! Liebster Gottit!*, ii, 264–65. A score manuscript is not available.

[24] Johanna, too, wrote a petition in which she reminded the Princess of Prussia of their first encounter ten years earlier, when Kinkel had entertained the young

The Kinkels' fate had evoked a great deal of sympathy among friends, acquaintances, and the wider public. The Handwerkerbildungsverein helped out financially, and such friends as Kathinka Zitz (1801–1877), Malwida von Meysenbug (1816–1903), Marie von Bruiningk (1818–1853), Adolf Strodtmann (1829–1879), and Friedrich Althaus (1829–1897) offered financial, moral, and physical support.[25] In an important step towards a return to everyday life, Johanna Kinkel started teaching again in November 1849, which enabled her to make a living less dependent on donations and funds. On 6 November 1849, Johanna wrote to Gottfried that 'besides the childcare, the return to my profession as a teacher has brightened up my days'.[26] At the same time, she planned her husband's escape from prison. In August 1850, Carl Schurz, equipped with money from Johanna, was sent off to Berlin in order to free Gottfried. At the end of September 1850, Schurz met the Spandau prison guard Georg Brune, who agreed to help Schurz.[27] On 6 November, Kinkel was freed with the help of Schurz and a great number of confederates.[28] The escape was conducted via Strelitz and Warnemünde to Rostock, from where Kinkel and Schurz took a ship for Scotland on 17 November 1850. Shortly after, Johanna met them in Paris, where she could finally 'feel like a wife'. She complained that 'here I have been the only man in the household'.[29] Johanna, the children, and Carl Schurz's younger sister Toni set off to London on 19 January 1851. The sailing took four days and the Kinkel family was reunited at the London harbour on 23 January.[30]

In London, Gottfried turned toward politics again. In 1851, he formed the Ausschuss für deutsche Angelegenheiten (Committee for German Affairs). This committee discussed the possibility of a national loan, which set the ball rolling for Gottfried Kinkel's travels to the USA. He left London on 2 September 1851, leaving behind Johanna with the household. Besides Kinkel's voluntary work for friends, mutual friends or like-minded people sent by the party, she gave singing classes and piano lessons in order to make a living, which further

---

princess with piano music while her portrait was being painted. Johanna Kinkel, *Gesuch an die Prinzessin von Preußen*, 4 July 1849, ULB 2407.

[25] Klaus, *Johanna Kinkel*, 205.

[26] Johanna and Gottfried Kinkel, *Liebe treue Johanna! Liebster Gottit!*, ii, 642: 'außer der Kinderpflege ist mir eine tröstliche Tageszeit dadurch geworden, daß ich wieder zu meinem Lehrerberuf zurückgekehrt bin'.

[27] Ibid., 195.

[28] Ibid., 197.

[29] Ibid., 1090. 'Weib fühlen darf. Hier war ich längst der einzige Mann im Hause'.

[30] Klaus, *Johanna Kinkel*, 247.

restricted her spare time.[31] Hoping to concentrate on the children's education, Johanna asked her husband to leave the political stage in favour of a more private life:

> When you come home, is our house going to be like a marketplace again? Am I supposed to be a clothes rail, to represent the Kinkel family on the couch, to entertain visitors on tenterhooks, while *such* children are being neglected?[32]

It must have pleased Johanna that, when Gottfried returned to London on 8 March 1852, the party was quarrelling and many of her friends had decided to emigrate to the USA. Now Johanna and Gottfried were able to enjoy family life. Gottfried taught the children and, in April 1853, he was assigned six presentations on the history of art at the university, which, besides the increasing number of Johanna's piano and singing students, also eased the Kinkels' financial situation.[33] Johanna was now able to turn toward London musical life, on which she commented in several of her writings, such as *Erziehungswesen in London, Musikalisches aus London, Briefe aus London* and *Musikalische Zustände und deutsche Musiker in London,* the last of which summarised the previous three essays and was published in the *Augsburger Allgemeine Zeitung* in June 1853. She also published the English version of her *Anleitung zum Singen* (op. 20) in 1852.[34]

Despite this, the London years were challenging and tiring for Johanna Kinkel, as her decline in physical and mental health, financial struggles and moral disappointment exhausted her. While she only looked after herself and the family in the summertime, numerous visitors occupied her time and leisure during the winters, her disapproval of which she mentioned in a letter to Gottfried on 5 February 1854:

---

[31] Ibid., 260.

[32] Johanna Kinkel in a letter to Gottfried Kinkel dated 10 January 1850, Johanna and Gottfried Kinkel, *Liebe treue Johanna! Liebster Gottit!*, iii, 1245, Italics in original. 'Wenn du wiederkehrst, soll dann wieder unser Haus einem Marktplatz gleichen? Muß ich wieder als Haubenstock dienen, auf dem Sofa repräsentieren, auf glühenden Kohlen Visiten unterhalten, während *solche* Kinder verwahrlosen?'

[33] Klaus, *Johanna Kinkel*, 284–85.

[34] The year 1852 is stated on the original publication, Johanna Kinkel, *Songs for Little Children: English Words Adapted to Madame Kinkel's German "Kindergesangsschule"* (London, 1852).

> If I only had time to tarry a while to focus on myself! But now everything is urgent, everybody who needs me is in a great rush. I speed up and force myself to please the other people, and this only makes things worse.[35]

Gottfried was approached by young women during his lecture tours to Manchester and Edinburgh, which caused distrust within the Kinkels' relationship. Johanna Kinkel remained silent about her disappointment, which she voiced privately in some letters to Gottfried. When, on 15 November 1858, she was found dead under the wide open window of her bedroom, investigators concluded in haste that she must have committed suicide.[36] This assumption, however, was countered by the doctor. The post-mortem showed that her heart was twice the normal size and the official conclusion was that Kinkel was 'killed by an accidental fall from a window forty-eight feet high'.[37]

♫ *Kinkel's approach to music*

Kinkel's love of music was not limited to her Berlin years and is also reflected in her pursuit of a musical career in Bonn, where she attended social gatherings held by others and the meetings of the *Maikäferbund*. The most remarkable musical engagement in Bonn, however, is Kinkel's directorship of the Bonner Gesangverein, the diary of which she wrote down from memory in London during the winter of 1851/52. In 1827, the first initiative was taken by Kinkel's teacher Franz Ries, who invited some of his students to his own or his students' parents' houses in order to have them perform pieces recently learned.[38] After a while, Ries participated only as an audience member, passing on criticism and remarks after each performance. Kinkel became the director of the circle, which eventually grew to a choir of a remarkable size.

The Bonner Gesangverein reached a total of 136 members over the course of twenty years. While Kinkel was in Berlin from 1836 to 1839 the attendance shrank drastically, and the association was nearly decimated by the time Kinkel returned to Bonn.[39] From then on, the choir expanded, partly due to Johanna and Gottfried Kinkel's activities with the *Maikäfer*, as some of the *Maikäfer* members were drawn to music: for instance, Carl Fresenius (1818–1897) joined

---

[35] Johanna and Gottfried Kinkel, *Liebe treue Johanna! Liebster Gottit!*, iii, 1334. 'Hätte ich nur Zeit, einen Moment abzuwarten, mich zu sammeln! Aber nun drängt Alles, jeder Mensch hat die größte Eile, der mich eben braucht. Ich sporne, zwinge mich, es den Leuten recht zu machen, und es wird nur schlimmer dadurch.'

[36] Klaus, *Johanna Kinkel*, 324.

[37] Certificate of Death of the General Register Office, England, cited after Klaus, *Johanna Kinkel*, 325.

[38] Johanna Kinkel, *Notizen den Gesangverein betreffend*, n.d., ULB S2400, 22.

[39] Ibid., 34.

the choir in 1839, and Jacob Burckhardt was accepted in 1843. At the beginning, performances were held in different venues, rotating among a group of families who invited the choir to their houses.[40] When Johanna married Gottfried in 1843, she moved to the Poppelsdorfer Schloss, where Gottfried had been living. This new residence, including the concert room of the Botanical Gardens behind the manor house, was much bigger and enabled an expansion of both choir and audience. It was used for regular performances of the Bonner Gesangverein until 10 October 1846. According to Gottfried Kinkel, the audience of the Bonner Gesangverein's concerts sometimes comprised 140 members.[41] As the choir had grown to a considerable number of members, big venues had to be used for the last two public performances in 1847. Marschner's opera *Hans Heiling* was performed in the Oberer Rathaussaal and Handel's *Israel in Egypt* in the Lesegesellschaftssaal.

The repertoire of the Gesangverein changed over the course of the choir's existence. The first couple of years were filled with light music composed by Hummel, Ries, Auber, Boieldieu and Paer.[42] Throughout the choir's history, excerpts from the operas and oratorios of Beethoven, Gluck, Mozart, Handel, and Carl Maria von Weber formed a solid part of the repertoire. Beethoven's piano sonatas were revived by Kinkel whenever there was an interval to be covered or when rehearsals were attended too poorly. Another composer performed frequently was Kinkel's contemporary Louis Spohr (1784–1859). Spohr's operas mark both the beginning and the end of the choir's history. The first operatic extracts which were ever performed were the second finale from Spohr's *Jessonda* and the quintet from *Zemire und Azor*, and Kinkel decided to disband the choir when the members lacked discipline for rehearsals of Spohr's *Berggeist*. Apart from Spohr, Kinkel did not seem to support contemporary composers through the choir. Mendelssohn was only performed twice – on 13 November 1847, in commemoration of the composer after his death, and on 27 November 1847 when a rehearsal was attended poorly.[43]

The reasons for bad attendance are diverse, as is shown by Kinkel's meticulous list of people who did not attend or arrived late at the final rehearsal of *Israel in Egypt* on 30 July 1847 (Fig. 1.1).

---

[40] In 1843, there were ten such family venues available: Mockel, Schram, Breuer, Haskarl, Freitag, Frowein, Lucas, Müller, Quadt, and Oppenhoff. Furthermore, there were such special concerts as those supporting the Frauenverein in 1835 and 1836, for which such special venues as the Lesegesellschaftssaal or the Ermekeilsche Saal were used.

[41] Gottfried Kinkel, *An die Mitglieder des Gesangvereins unter Leitung der Frau Kinkel*, 1846, ULB S2374, 2.

[42] Kinkel, *Notizen den Gesangverein betreffend*, 25.

[43] Ibid., 75.

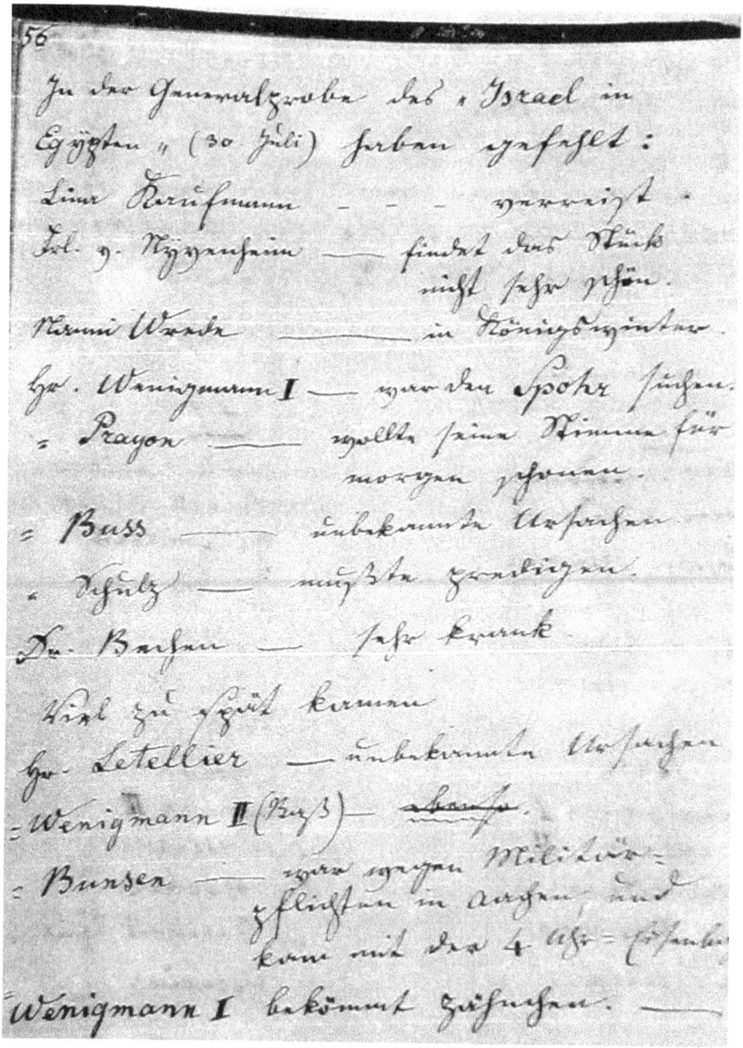

Fig. 1.1: List of people absent or late for choir rehearsal on 30 July 1847[44]

[44] Ibid., 56. 'Rehearsal of *Israel in Egypt*: missing/ Lina Kaufmann – travelling/ Frl. V. Nyvenheim – does not like the piece very much/ Nanni Wrede – in Königswinter/ Hr. Wenigmann – looking for Spohr [visiting Spohr?]/ Hr. Prayon – wanted to preserve his voice for tomorrow/ Hr. Buss – unknown reason/ Hr. Schulz – had to sermonise/ Dr. Bechen – very sick/ arrived way too late/ Hr. Letellier – reason unknown/ Hr. Wenigmann II (bass) – ditto/ Hr. Bunsen – had to go to Aachen for military reasons and came with the 4 o'clock train/ Wenigmann I [*sic*] – is getting teeth.'

However, one day in particular, on 27 November 1847, many of the members stayed at home because they feared contracting scarlet fever. That day only twelve members were present, and some Lieder by Franz Schubert and Fanny Hensel were sung.[45] The vocal miniatures performed were Schubert's 'Gondelfahrer' (private rehearsal on 27 November 1847), Hensel's *Gartenlieder* (performed twice within private rehearsals on 27 November and 11 December 1847), and one of Mendelssohn's hymns.[46] Kinkel did not mention Fanny Hensel's death in her notes on the Gesangverein. However, in her *Lecture on Mendelssohn* she elaborates on the close relationship between Hensel and her brother Felix.[47] It is not surprising, therefore, that Kinkel chose to rehearse some of Hensel's choral compositions shortly after Felix Mendelssohn's death. The Gesangverein performed *Die drei Wünsche* by Carl Loewe (1796–1869) in the very early years of its history but never repeated this opera. Wagner's *Der fliegende Holländer* was discussed as potential material for performance in 1847, but it was never rehearsed, as Kinkel could not get the score and, according to Kinkel, some members had remarked that the piece was ineffective.[48] *Catharina Cornaro* by Franz Lachner (1803–1890) had been proposed, but Kinkel protested against it, because the choral parts were all set in unison.[49] In 1842 and 1843, Kinkel's two Singspiele *Otto der Schütz* and *Die Assassinen* were performed. In her notes she expresses her deep gratitude for the Gesangverein's kindness, willingness and courtesy, which shows that Kinkel was a gentle and modest leader.

Kinkel wanted to 'emancipate the Verein' as she felt that the members possessed a 'remarkably high level of musical discernment, considering that they are dilettantes'.[50] From 1844, new pieces were suggested and discussed in regular meetings and the choir held a vote deciding upon their performances. Kinkel's ambition to practise democracy is also recognisable in the way in which she introduced new members to the choir. If someone new was suggested and a member of the Verein considered this person pretentious or battlesome, the choir would not accept him or her. Although Kinkel tried to educate the singers to be responsible individuals, she also demanded discipline and commitment. Her worries about the lack of discipline are reflected by a list of rules and

---

[45] Ibid., 73.

[46] Ibid., 75.

[47] Johanna Kinkel, *Lecture on Mendelssohn*, n.d., ULB S2398, 20.

[48] Kinkel, *Notizen den Gesangverein betreffend*, 70.

[49] Ibid., 70–71.

[50] Ibid., 43–44. 'Von nun an dünkte es mir besser, einen Verein mehr zu emanzipieren, dessen Mitglieder größtentheils auf einer für Dilettanten bedeutenden Höhe musikalischen Urtheils sich befinden.'

a constitution included in her notes.[51] After the performance of Handel's *Israel in Egypt* on 31 July 1847, for instance, Kinkel noted:

> The piece was too long for the stamina of the singers, who asked for something new before the difficulties of the current job were tackled. As long as the members are so impatient, we should not select a piece of such volume and difficulty.[52]

Despite her focus on democracy, trust, and the choral experience as a whole, the Gesangverein's repertoire included technically challenging choral works and operas. Kinkel's ambitions for the Verein were high, but in general Kinkel rarely referred explicitly to the artistic development of the choir and/or the musical quality of its performances. Perhaps artistic quality stepped into the background, favouring pedagogical and social purposes, although it needs to be noted that she attempted not to engage her singers with political issues. As soon as she sensed a strong political flavour during the choir's meetings, she closed down the Verein. In her notes, Kinkel complained that in 1848/49, 'the revolutionary conversations overshadowed all musical interests', which finally led to the disbanding of the choral association.[53] She recalls that at the end of March 1848, 'there has been more politicising than singing for several Saturdays'.[54] The last piece that was planned to be performed was Louis Spohr's opera *Der Berggeist*. Rehearsals started on 2 October 1847, and the performance was scheduled for mid-February, too. However, it never took place, as Kinkel closed down the choir.[55]

In contrast, Kinkel's pedagogical approach outside of the Gesangverein is marked by many political connotations, as is reflected most notably in her instructive exercises *Anleitung zum Singen* (op. 20, published in 1849; the English version, *Songs for little children*, was published in 1852).[56] Op. 20

---

[51] Ibid., 60–69.

[52] Ibid., 57–58. 'Das Stück ist zu lang im Verhältnis der geringen Ausdauer welche viele der Sänger zeigten, die früher nach etwas Neuem verlangten, als die Schwierigkeiten der gegenwärtigen Aufgabe überwunden waren. Solange diese Ungeduld unter den Mitgliedern herrscht, darf kein Stück von so großer Ausdehnung und Schwierigkeit mehr gewählt werden.'

[53] Ibid., 77. 'später überwucherten die Revolutionsgespräche alle musikalischen Interessen.'

[54] Ibid., 77. 'es wird mehr politisiert als gesungen seit einigen Samstagen.'

[55] Ibid., 79–81.

[56] The date January 1849 is noted in the original German publication; Hofmeister announced the German version for September/October 1849 <http://anno.onb. ac.at/cgi-content/anno-buch?apm=0&aid=1000001&bd=0001849&teil=0203&seite =00000113&zoom=1> (accessed 1 December 2018).

includes twenty-six little pieces for children aged three to seven. With this collection, Kinkel seemingly wanted to help the children of the revolutionary middle class to process psychologically the political circumstances of the time. Furthermore, Kinkel wanted to impart general knowledge about the seasons, nature and good manners, and she aimed to teach virtues, highlighting children's willingness to respect such superiors as parents, grandparents, and the doctor.[57] Such didactic aspects seemed to be more significant to Kinkel than the professional training of the voice, possibly because this exercise book was recommended for mothers who wanted to teach their very young children.[58] Political connotations also surface in the reviews of Kinkel's op. 20. In 1849, shortly after Gottfried Kinkel's imprisonment, the *Neue Zeitschrift für Musik* recommended the purchase and practice of Kinkel's method, stressing that 'the widow of the unfortunate poet [...] will now have to feed her family on her own'.[59]

Kinkel's op. 22 does not allude to any moral aspects but focuses on vocal training through scales and solfeggios.[60] In its preface, Kinkel criticises overly ambitious attempts, which might overstrain the singers' voices and patience:

> There are many talented musical students, who, being very fond of Singing [*sic*], though not gifted with a strong voice, would be happy to commence vocal practise [*sic*], if most Solfeggios published till now, did not require too great an extension of voice.[61]

This statement mirrors Kinkel's business awareness, as she was trying to make a living from teaching when she published this singing school while resident in London. According to her own notes, London was home to many unemployed teachers and untalented but eager students.[62] The structure of the book is clearly comprehensible (Table 1.2); each exercise consists of two parts: a scale and a solfeggio.

---

[57] For further details on political connotations in Kinkel's pedagogical works see Bunzel, 'Johanna Kinkel's Pedagogical Approaches'.

[58] For an examination of this piece through the lens of authorship and the mother's role within this context see Glahn, *Johanna Kinkel*, 192.

[59] C. G., 'Gesangschulen', *Neue Zeitschrift für Musik*, 30 September 1849, 141. 'Die Witwe des unglücklichen Dichters [...] wird nun die alleinige Ernährung ihrer Familie bleiben.'

[60] The publication date, 1852, is printed on the original; Hofmeister announced this opus in August 1853 <http://anno.onb.ac.at/cgi-content/anno-buch?apm=0&aid=10 00001&bd=0001853&teil=0203&seite=00000396&zoom=1> (accessed 1 December 2018).

[61] Johanna Kinkel, *Tonleitern und Solfeggien für die Altstimme/Solfeggios for Contralto-Voice*: Op. 22 (London: Schott, 1852), 1. English quotation in original.

[62] Johanna Kinkel, *Musikalisches aus London*, n.d., ULB S 2391, 6 and 17.

Table 1.2: Overview of Johanna Kinkel's op. 22

	Title	Melody	Key	Metre	Didactic purpose	Tempo
Introduction	Ex.[ercise] I	Scale	A	4/4	counterpoint, basso continuo	Sehr langsam/ Very slow
	Solf.[eggio] I	Scales and triads with their inversions	F	2/4	singing triads and their inversions	Allegretto
Separate intervals	Ex. II	Seconds	B♭	4/4	dynamics, inversions	Adagio
	Solf. II	Seconds, Octaves	d	¾	dynamics, trills	
	Ex. III	Thirds	B	4/4	dynamics	Allegretto
	Solf. III	Thirds	e	2/4	dotted rhythms, pace	
	Ex. IV	Fourths	C	4/4	basso continuo	Andante
	Solf. IV	Fourths, Octaves	C	¾	dotted rhythms, trills, piano accompaniment (Alberti-bass)	
	Ex. V	Fifths	A♭	4/4	dynamics	Moderato
	Solf. V	Fifths, scales	f	¾	dynamics, trills, quintuplets	
	Ex. VI	Sixths	F	4/4	broken triads	Allegretto
	Solf. VI	Cambiata	F	6/8	syncopation, trills	
	Ex. VII	Sevenths	A	4/4	pedal in piano	Adagio
	Solf. VII	chromatic scales	e	4/4	slow, dynamics, triads, cresc., pace	Larghetto
All intervals	Ex. VIII	all intervals (ascending)	C	4/4	basso continuo	Moderato
	Solf. VIII	scales, broken triads	F	4/4	dynamics, accentuation	
	Ex. IX	all intervals (descending)	A	4/4	dynamics	Allegretto
	Solf. IX	all intervals	B♭	6/8	range: minor 7, dynamics, trills	
Synthesis	Solf. X	development of a motive	E♭	¾	triads, distinct development of motif	Allegro
	Solf. XI	all intervals	f	3/8	triads, dynamics, rhythm, long notes (bars 37–40)	Andante
	Solf. XII	development of a motive	C	2/4	rhythm, pace, stacc., trills, dynamics, tempo	Scherzando

Because of its systematic approach, this singing treatise enables a very broad training of musicality, focusing on correct pitching and introducing the student to different types of melodic ornamentation, metres and rhythms, dynamics, accents, tempi, pacing, piano accompaniments, simple contrapuntal constructions, and several harmonic characteristics.

Although many of Kinkel's pedagogical writings focus on descriptive journeys through specific musical works and take the shape of narrative guidebooks of repertoire and music-pedagogical self-help, Kinkel also advocated music-theoretical education and smaller composition exercises in her music treatises.[63] In her *Acht Briefe an eine Freundin über Clavier-Unterricht*, she advises the teacher to 'analyse an excellent composition in front of the students from time to time in order to force them to focus on the inner structure of the composition'.[64] At the same time, Kinkel reminds the teacher to carry out some practical basso continuo exercises at the piano. Akin to such contemporaries as Robert Schumann (1810–1856), Kinkel was rather sceptical of virtuosity, as she states that 'it is more important to educate the student to become a really musical person rather than to increase the number of piano virtuosos, because these are, after bravura singers, the least musical people in the world'.[65]

All of Kinkel's writings reveal a strong awareness of nineteenth-century gender perceptions. For instance, Kinkel stresses that 'everything mathematical naturally constitutes a special difficulty for women', which demanded extraordinary patience, and she reminds teachers that they 'must not disregard the incision that marriage makes in all women's learning'.[66] The socio-cultural rel-

---

[63] For details on concepts of musical writing during the nineteenth century see Leon Botstein, 'Listening through Reading: Musical Literacy and the Concert Audience', *19th-Century Music*, 16, 2 (1992), 129–45 (130).

[64] Johanna Kinkel, *Acht Briefe an eine Freundin über Clavier-Unterricht* (Stuttgart/Tübingen: Cotta, 1852), 9: 'von Zeit zu Zeit eine ganz vorzügliche Composition vor solchen Schülern analysiren und sie nöthigen, ihre Aufmerksamkeit auf deren innern Bau zu richten'.

[65] See Leon Plantinga, 'The Piano and the Nineteenth Century', in *Nineteenth-Century Piano Music*, ed. Larry Todd, 2nd edn (New York/London: Routledge, 2004), 1–15 (9); Johanna Kinkel, *Acht Briefe*, 12: 'daß es wichtiger ist, den Schüler zu einem wirklich musikalischen Menschen zu bilden, als die Zahl der Claviervirtuosen zu vermehren, denn diese sind nächst den Bravoursängern die unmusikalischsten Personen auf der Welt'.

[66] Kinkel, *Acht Briefe*, 13: 'alles Mathematische ist für die weibliche Natur mit einer besonderen Schwierigkeit verknüpft'; ibid., 15: 'aber der Lehrer darf nicht außer Acht lassen, welchen Schnitt in alles Lernen der Frauen die Heirath macht'. This aspect was stressed by the reviewer of the *Neue Wiener Musik-Zeitung*: [Anon.], review of Johanna Kinkel, *Acht Briefe* (1852), *Neue Wiener Musik-Zeitung*, 28 August 1856, 152.

evance of Kinkel's *Acht Briefe* also surfaces when she warns the mother teachers not to 'sacrifice a portion of the child's lifetime for the sake of the mother's addiction to fashion, if the child has neither natural talent nor a great [musical] affinity'.[67] Here, Kinkel refers to the fashion that musical education was considered a necessity for girls by supposedly educated individuals even though not all girls had the same affinities and interests. Contrary to Czerny, who in his *Letters on the Art of Playing the Pianoforte* reminds his female readers of their role as a female part of society, and who asks the young ladies not to neglect their duties in the household for the sake of music, Kinkel criticised the gendered division of male and female activities by tongue-in-cheek comments on gender conventions.[68] She expressed her disapproval of such conventions on many occasions, especially after her successful ending of her first marriage.

Kinkel concludes her *Acht Briefe* with a short excursion into music history, as part of which she praises Mendelssohn, Chopin, Adolf Henselt (1814–1889) and Sigismond Thalberg (1812–1871) for their reformation of piano music toward emotional expression. Chopin impressed Kinkel most, as he attempted to question the division of the tonal corpus by semitones. Kinkel remarks that:

> We, who have become accustomed to the established division in semitones, sense this innovation as eerie and as mere noise; but the next or third generation, once it has ingested the strange sounds with their mothers' milk, might appreciate in it a fresh and doubly-rich art.[69]

During the 1850s, Kinkel gave public lectures on Mendelssohn, Beethoven, Mozart, and Chopin, and produced a substantial analysis on the works of Chopin.[70] Compared to her lectures on Beethoven (40 pages), Mendelssohn (37

---

[67] Ibid., 11. 'aus bloßer Modesucht einen Theil der Lebenszeit ihres Kindes dem Erlernen derselben aufzuopfern, wenn es nicht natürliches Talent oder große Vorliebe dafür äußert'.

[68] On Czerny see Deanna C. Davis, 'The Veil of Fiction: Pedagogy and Rhetorical Strategies in Carl Czerny's *Letters on the Art of Playing the Pianoforte*', in *Beyond the Art of Finger Dexterity: Reassessing Carl Czerny*, ed. David Gramit (New York: University of Rochester Press, 2008), 67–81 (75). Marianne Bröcker points to many such comments also in Kinkel's novel *Hans Ibeles in London*. Bröcker, 'Johanna Kinkels schriftstellerische und musikpädagogische Tätigkeit', 40–41.

[69] Kinkel, *Acht Briefe*, 18. 'Aber uns, die wir an die längst bestandene Einteilung in halbe Töne gewöhnt sind, wird die Neuerung schauerlich und wie ein bloßes Geräusch klingen: doch vielleicht schon begrüßt die nächst- oder drittfolgende Generation, wenn sie erst mit der Muttermilch die fremden Klänge eingesogen hat, in ihnen eine frischerstandene, doppelt so reiche Kunst.'

[70] Johanna Kinkel, *Lecture on Beethoven's Earliest Sonatas, incl. Opus 10*, n.d., ULB 2397, n.p.; Johanna Kinkel, *Lecture on Mozart*, n.d., ULB S 2396; Johanna Kinkel, *Friedrich Chopin als Komponist*, 1855, ULB S 2399, 119.

pages), and Mozart (32 pages), the work on Chopin, containing 195 pages, is much more complex. It is structured by means of different musical genres in Chopin's oeuvre. Bröcker highlights Kinkel's music-practical approach in this work, which shows Kinkel's experience as both a pianist and a pedagogue.[71] Kinkel's other lectures examine the music from a contemporary perspective, geared to the history of compositional thought. Kinkel's critical thinking surfaces also in her *Lecture on Musical History* and her *Lecture on Harmony*, in both of which she challenges the role of Palestrina within the historical discourse of composition. The nineteenth-century Palestrina Renaissance and Baini and von Winterfeld's first monographs on Palestrina, which were published in 1828 and 1832 respectively, reflect an increased interest in Palestrina.[72] Yet Kinkel placed Palestrina in context, stating that:

> He wisely used his excellent position at the pontifical chapel to blaze the trail for the true church style; but some of his lesser-known contemporaries produced works that are of equal, if not superior, beauty to his own compositions.[73]

Another example of Kinkel's courage in contributing new ideas to contemporary music-historical writing is the way in which she organised musical history looking to the emancipation of dissonance. Kinkel's periodisation is the same as that of Raphael Georg Kiesewetter (1773–1850), but their rationales differ. Regarding Monteverdi, for instance, Kiesewetter based his argument solely on Monteverdi's influence on the dramatic opera. Kinkel, on the other hand, also considers Monteverdi's perception that 'the <u>free</u> entry of dissonances is compatible with melodic beauty'.[74]

---

[71] Bröcker, 'Johanna Kinkels schriftstellerische und musikpädagogische Tätigkeit', 43.

[72] See Peter Ackermann, 'Palestrina', in *Die Musik in Geschichte und Gegenwart*, 2nd edn, xiii, Personenteil, 7–46 (41); Giuseppe Baini, *Memorie storico-critiche della vita e delle opere di G. P. da Palestrina*, 2 vols (Rome: Societa Tipografica, 1828); Carl von Winterfeld, *Johannes Pierluigi von Palestrina. Seine Werke und deren Bedeutung für die Geschichte der Tonkunst: Mit Bezug auf Baini's neueste Forschungen* (Wroclaw: Adelholz, 1832).

[73] Johanna Kinkel, *Zur Geschichte der Musik*, n.d., ULB S 2393, 3. 'Er hat gewiß die hervorragende Stellung die er an der päbstlichen [*sic*] Capelle besaß, mit weiser Einsicht benützt, um dem wahren Kirchenstyl die Bahn zu brechen; aber manche seiner minder bekannten Zeitgenossen haben Werke geschaffen die den seinen in Schönheit gleich, wenn nicht überlegen sind.'

[74] Kinkel, *Zur Geschichte der Musik*, 4. 'das <u>freie</u> Eintreten von Dissonanzen mit der melodischen Schönheit für vereinbar hielt'. Underline in original. On Kiesewetter see Thomas Hochradner, 'Probleme der Periodisierung von Musikgeschichte', *Acta Musicologica*, 67, 1 (January–June 1995), 55–70 (60); Herfried Kier, 'Kiesewetter', in *Die Musik in Geschichte und Gegenwart*, 2nd edn, x, Personenteil, 87–91 (90).

On the other hand, it needs to be noted that, despite Kinkel's progressive music-historical approach, her writings reflect analytical, aesthetic and socio-political aspects typical of the nineteenth century. In her analyses of Beethoven sonatas, for instance, Kinkel, like her contemporary Wilhelm von Lenz (1809–1883), uses romanticised metaphors as a means of musical characterisation and employs the notion of a general musical idea (*Idee*), which is also evident in Adolf Bernhard Marx's critical writings.[75] Furthermore, Kinkel's lecture *Zur Geschichte der Musik* (About the History of Music, which differs from Kinkel's English-language *Lecture on Musical History*) reveals typical nineteenth-century national thinking: it praises the discovery of simplified musical notation in the sixteenth century, which enabled composers to interact with the fresh temperament of the people's spirit (*Volksgeist*).[76] Kinkel's fondness for Carl Maria von Weber (1786–1826), supposedly the first composer to have established a German *Nationaloper,* supports this argument.[77]

Despite Kinkel's diverse ways of thinking and the positive reviews in the contemporary print media, her pedagogical works are largely unknown today. Linda Siegel explains that Kinkel's pedagogical writings were published, but that Kinkel's artistic reputation was 'not large enough to warrant an interest in her thoughts about music, as was that of, say, Clara Schumann'.[78] However, Kinkel did publish her most comprehensive writing, *Acht Briefe an eine Freundin über Clavier-Unterricht* in 1852, as well as her two singing treatises, in 1849 and 1852 respectively, in German and English; and she gave public lectures in London. Clara Schumann did not produce any comparable theoretical writings, but the notion that the general public was led primarily by Kinkel's artistic reputation rather than her ideas holds true. Kinkel's pianistic skills were not as highly regarded as those of Clara Schumann, although her piano playing was acknowledged by friends and acquaintances.[79] Kinkel performed publicly only once, on 26 November 1838, in a concert alongside Clara Novello (1818–1908) at the Berlin Königliches Schauspielhaus, where she performed several piano pieces by Chopin.[80] The reviewer of the *Vossische Zeitung* regretted having missed the concert with Kinkel, who 'had distinguished herself in private

---

[75] Kinkel, *Lecture on Beethoven's Earliest Sonatas;* on Marx, see Scott Burnham, 'The Role of Sonata Form in A. B. Marx's Theory of Form', *Journal of Music Theory,* 33, 2 (1989), 247–71 (260).

[76] Kinkel, *Zur Geschichte der Musik,* 1.

[77] See Carl Dahlhaus, *Die Musik des 19. Jahrhunderts* (Laaber: Laaber, 1996), 52.

[78] Siegel, 'Johanna Kinkel's "Chopin als Komponist" and Other Musical Writings', 105.

[79] Carl Schurz cited in Kaufmann, 'Johanna Kinkel: Schluß', 48; von Meysenbug, *Gesammelte Werke,* ii, 88.

[80] [Anon.], concert announcement, *Vossische Zeitung,* 24 November 1838.

circles as an excellent pianist but who has not yet shown her talent in public'.[81] Through reviews Kinkel was known as a pianist, composer, and pedagogue, but her popularity as a pedagogue did not last for long. It might well be the political colouring of Kinkel's pedagogical works which prevented her from a more prominent (posthumous) career as a teacher, especially from the second part of the nineteenth century onwards.

[81] [Anon.], concert review of a concert at Berlin Königliches Schauspielhaus (26 November 1838), *Vossische Zeitung*, 28 November 1838: 'die sich in Privatkreisen als ausgezeichnete Spielerin vielfältige Anerkennung erworben, jedoch ihr Talent noch nicht öffentlich geltend gemacht hat'. The review published in *Iris im Gebiete der Tonkunst* also does not comment in greater depth on Kinkel's playing. [Anon.], concert review of a concert at Berlin Königliches Schauspielhaus (26 November 1838), *Iris im Gebiete der Tonkunst*, 30 November 1838, 192.

CHAPTER 2

Rethinking Kinkel's Lieder

K INKEL'S Lieder cover a wide range of themes: love, longing, searching for the truth of life; political themes including Exoticist plots, mythology, and appraisals of democracy; and such Romantic topoi as watery landscapes, night scenes, and mystical worldviews by self-centred lyrical protagonists. Nineteenth-century poetry can be seen to reflect the cultural and political diversity of contemporary Germany. Such well-known writers and poets as Johann Gottlieb Fichte, Ernst Moritz Arndt, Heinrich Kleist, and Theodor Körner thematised myths of the German past in their works, while others engaged with politics more directly.[1] For instance, Friedrich Schlegel supported Metternich's conservative policies; Joseph von Eichendorff was involved in the Prussian education ministry; and Joseph von Görres stood up for the Catholics in Bavaria. Furthermore, idealism and Romanticism had an impact on the foundation of 'Junges Deutschland' (Young Germany), a politicised literary movement which gathered such influential writers as Georg Büchner, Karl Gutzkow, Heinrich Laube, Ludwig Börne, and Nikolaus Lenau. Another catalyst of politicised literature was the establishment of (literary) salons, which enabled a vivid exchange of ideas during the early decades of the nineteenth century.

In accordance with the increasing bourgeois interest in salonesque gatherings, such cultural institutions as libraries, museums, concert halls, opera houses and theatres emerged during the Biedermeier era and literature and arts were popularised. Salon scholar Andreas Ballstaedt points to the broad cultural, artistic and political opportunities for salon attendees, which developed as a result of the social interaction between intellectuals of different societal strata, regardless of their own backgrounds.[2] However, Barbara Hahn takes an opposing view, positing that this exceptional social constellation in the salon may be a delusion. After all, entry to salons was granted on the basis of invitation or recommendation and only very few salons were fully open to the public.[3]

---

[1] See Karin Friedrich, 'Cultural and intellectual trends', in *Nineteenth-Century Germany: Politics, Culture and Society: 1780–1918*, ed. John Breuilly (London: Arnold, 2001), 96–116 (106).

[2] Andreas Ballstaedt, 'Salonmusik', in *Die Musik in Geschichte und Gegenwart*, 2nd edn, xiii, Sachteil, 854–67 (856).

[3] Barbara Hahn, 'Der Mythos vom Salon', in *Salons der Romantik: Beiträge eines Wiepersdorfer Kolloquiums zu Theorie und Geschichte des Salons*, ed. Hartwig

Hahn's objection is documented by the experience Kinkel gained during her time in Berlin, when references from Mendelssohn and Brentano enabled her to get access to Bettina von Arnim's and Fanny Hensel's social gatherings.

Even though the purposes, structures, and cultural focuses of social gatherings were diverse, Ballstaedt depicts conversation as a central aim of salon culture. Composers and musicians used the salon as a platform to discuss and experiment with unpublished works and to demonstrate their musical skills. In line with Biedermeier ethos, music turned into a means of entertainment. There was a huge demand for so-called *Salonmusik*, defined by the *Allgemeine Musikalische Zeitung* in 1847 as music 'during which one can talk, play and drink tea'.[4] As a result, Ballstaedt and Charles Rosen agree that salon music was considered 'superficial, brilliant and sentimental', although Rosen argues that these characteristics do not distinguish salon music from music performed elsewhere.[5] Although much salon music was criticised for its light and superficial character, two positive consequences of salon culture are worth noting. Firstly, salons enabled young artists to introduce themselves to circles which otherwise would have remained closed to them. Secondly, even though many salons were criticised for their superficial views on aesthetics, these salons must have furthered the course of aesthetic discussion in some way. Moreover, some special-interest salons were the birthplaces of both high-quality musical and literary works and paradigms which influenced cultural output throughout the nineteenth century.

Another important aspect of nineteenth-century cultural practice is the shift of the artist's self-perception from being an employee of the gentry to that of an artistically independent person. Friedrich takes this idea further and alludes to nineteenth-century nationalism when she posits that art acquired the 'function of a substitute religion, to be worshipped together with the genius who produced it and the nation which gave birth to such greatness, the German *Kulturnation*'.[6] This growing national sentiment surfaces in the attempt to create an 'unmistakably' national mythology, which also entered the canon of German Lieder during this time. A new wave of interest in medieval epics, knights, crusaders, folk songs, pagan burial mounds, and the reinterpretation of Nordic gods surfaced in

Schulz (Berlin/New York: de Gruyter, 1997), 213–34 (229).

[4] [Anon.], review of Silphin vom Walde, in *Allgemeine Musikalische Zeitung*, 1 December 1847, 834. 'Salonstücke sind solche, wobei man reden, spielen und Thee trinken kann.'

[5] Charles Rosen, *The Romantic Generation*, paperback edn (London: Fontana, 1999), 383–84. Rosen admits, however, that salon music is a 'useful term' as long as 'we do not [...] attach too limited a meaning' or judge its audience too strictly.

[6] Friedrich, 'Cultural and intellectual trends', 110.

writings of various genres.[7] Rey M. Longyear argues that the return to the medieval past and Exoticism can indicate both a conservative and a progressive direction, as it may point to a longing for an established order on the one hand, or to socio-political criticism by way of disguise on the other.[8] Established in 1819 in the 'Karlsbad Decrees', censorship remained in place until the Berlin March Revolution in 1848, and thus it was less risky to publish music and literature dealing metaphorically with a plot set in a remote place.[9] Other popular revolutionary themes were the German emperor and German geography, especially the Rhine and the North Sea, which were involved in wars over Prussian or foreign hegemony.[10] Besides a strong emphasis on patriotism and nationalism, Western European nineteenth-century literature and music drew on such non-political themes as longing for the infinite, love, pre-industrialised landscapes, and wanderlust.[11] All of these themes surface in both Kinkel's poetry and Lieder.

As Kinkel's compositions are not dated meticulously and there is no record of her opus numbers 2, 3, 4, and 5, it is sometimes difficult to ascertain when particular compositions were conceived, and thus their socio-political anchoring is not always obvious. The appendix provides an overview of all her compositions. As Kinkel's surviving documents do not contain a diary, it is her correspondence which provides chronological clues to the origin of certain songs. The records of the *Maikäferbund* are another fruitful source, as some of Kinkel's Lieder were produced within that context. Kinkel's letters to Angela Oppenhoff reveal a great deal of compositional activity in Berlin. In December 1837, Kinkel told her that 'yesterday was the ceremonious day, at which Trautwein, my publisher, collected the first manuscript; and six Lieder for mezzo-soprano (not alto) will be published in the New Year'.[12] Kinkel then explains that she only used two of the songs already known to Oppenhoff, as 'the others seemed much too immature to be published', and that she included four 'new compositions

---

[7] George S. Williamson, *The Longing for Myth in Germany: Religion and Aesthetic Culture from Romanticism to Nietzsche* (Chicago: University of Chicago Press, 2004), 73–77.

[8] Rey M. Longyear, *Nineteenth-Century Romanticism in Music,* 3rd edn (New Jersey: Prentice Hall, 1988), 10–11.

[9] Norman Manea, *On Clowns: The Dictator and the Artist* (New York: Grove Weidenfeld, 1992), 30.

[10] Williamson, *The Longing for Myth in Germany,* 112.

[11] Friedrich, 'Cultural and intellectual trends', 105–06 and Longyear, *Nineteenth-Century Romanticism,* 12.

[12] Kinkel in a letter to Angela Oppenhoff dated 10 December 1837, cited in Kaufmann, 'Johanna Kinkel: Schluß', 51: 'gestern war der feierliche Tag, wo Trautwein, mein Verleger, das erste Manuskript bei mir abgeholt, und ohngefähr im Neujahr erscheinen 6 Lieder für Mezzo-Sopran (nicht Alt)'.

chosen out of many'.[13] Kinkel's first Lieder opus (op. 7) appeared in 1838 and was dedicated to Bettina von Arnim. It was not until 1839 that she published her op. 6, dedicated to Angela Oppenhoff. Also in 1838, Trautwein published Kinkel's op. 8, which was announced by Gottfried Wilhelm Fink with bewilderment about Kinkel's gender. The review in the *Allgemeine Musikalische Zeitung* reads: 'The eighth album has just been published, and the author is supposed to be a woman'.[14] Kinkel refers to Fink's review and to her own compositional eagerness in a letter to Nanny Müller, an old Bonn friend who had moved to Berlin in 1830. When she got back from a holiday in Gosen, a town on the outskirts of Berlin, Kinkel wrote to Müller on 30 August 1838:

> Since I arrived back, after the Gosen musical famine, I've been composing a lot, mostly Goethe Lieder. I have the correction of the [Lied] 'Runenstein' before me; another review has been published in the Allg[emeine] Musikalische Zeitung as well, in which I am constantly maltreated as *the male composer*.[15]

After her op. 8 Kinkel experimented with different genres. In December 1837, she announced in a letter to Oppenhoff that 'the composition of Lieder will be resting for a long time now, as I am completing a different plan. [...] The prank is half-finished! – A comical opera'.[16] Paul Kaufmann suspects that the comical opera Kinkel mentions might be *Verrückte Komödien aus Berlin* (Crazy Comedies from Berlin, manuscript lost).[17] In the same letter, Kinkel praises an unforgettable evening in Fanny Hensel's *Sonntagsmusiken* and tells her friend that

[13] Ibid. 'Von denen, die Sie schon kennen, konnte ich nur zwei brauchen. [...] Die anderen dünken mir viel zu unreif für die Publikation. [...] Die neuen, die ich aus vielen ausgewählt'.

[14] G. W. Fink, review of Johanna Mathieux, *6 Lieder für eine Singstimme mit Begleitung des Pianoforte: Op. 7* (1838), *Allgemeine Musikalische Zeitung*, 8 August 1838, 525. 'Eben ist das achte Heft erschienen, und der Verfasser soll eine Verfasserin sein'. Kinkel's op. 8 was announced by the *Neue Zeitschrift für Musik* on 13 July 1838 (18).

[15] Kinkel in a letter to Nanny Müller dated 30 August 1838, cited in Kaufmann, 'Johanna Kinkel: Neue Beiträge zu ihrem Lebensbild', 303–04. Italics in original. 'Seit ich wieder hier bin, nach der Gosener musikalischen Hungersnoth, habe ich viel komponiert, meist Göthesche Lieder. Der Runenstein liegt eben in Correktur vor mir, auch ist wieder eine Rezension angelangt aus der Allgem. Musikalischen Zeitung, wo ich immer als der *Herr Verfasser* traktiert werde'.

[16] Kinkel in a letter to Angela Oppenhoff dated 10 December 1837, cited in Kaufmann, 'Johanna Kinkel: Schluß', 51. 'Jetzt ruht das Liederschreiben auf lange Zeit, denn ich vollende einen anderen Plan. [...] Nemlich der Narrenstreich ist schon halb fertig! – Eine komische Oper'.

[17] Ibid.

her 'five senses were idealised throughout the entire week, so I put aside the crazy opera and tried to set for female choir the Singing of the Sirens, Faust II, by Göthe'.[18] Unfortunately, there is no sign of Kinkel's Faust setting among her published or unpublished works. Despite Kinkel's eagerness for compositional experiment, she seemingly placed herself in the public eye as a Lieder composer. The great number of published songs was most likely attributed to Trautwein's specialisation in Lieder and the tremendous public interest in this genre, which mirrors the popularity of Lieder performances in private and semi-public social gatherings.

When Kinkel returned to Bonn in 1839, she focused on her work as a conductor and leader of the Bonner Gesangverein, an activity which might have encouraged her to compose the choral work *Hymnus in Coena Domini*, published as op. 14 in 1843, and dedicated to her first teacher Franz Ries. According to Klaus, Kinkel composed this work as early as 1840, and it was performed by the Bonner Gesangverein in 1842.[19] Like many of Kinkel's Rhineland songs, her setting of Nikolaus Becker's 'Der deutsche Rhein' appeared in 1840. Besides Kinkel's patriotic love for the Rhineland, her compositions between 1841 and 1851 reflect her strong attachment to Gottfried Kinkel and her involvement in the democratic movement of the 1840s. In accordance with Kinkel's social environment during that time, most of her post-1840 Lieder opus numbers were dedicated to Rhineland friends and acquaintances: Emilie von Binzer (op. 16, 1841), Heinrich Dorn (op. 21, 1851), Adele and Emily Thormann (op. 12, 1840), Josephine Hubar (op. 17, 1847), and Bertha Forstheim (op. 18, 1843), the latter four of whom were members of the Bonner Gesangverein.[20]

After the Kinkels' escape to London in 1850/51, Johanna's compositional activity receded into the background in favour of teaching, writing, and general household duties. In a letter to her husband dated 2 October 1851, she regrets that 'I might have to bury my dreams of a higher artistic activity as long as I do not have a single minute to myself'.[21] On 26 October 1854, Kinkel wrote to her friend Gretchen Biesing:

---

[18] Ibid., 52. 'Die ganze Woche durch war mir noch so idealisch um die 5 Sinne herum, und da habe ich dann die verrückte Oper solang liegen lassen, und den Gesang der Sirenen – Faust 2ter Teil, v. Göthe – für Frauenchor zu schreiben versucht.'

[19] Klaus, *Johanna Kinkel*, 117.

[20] Besides the Hofmeister announcement, Kinkel's op. 17 was advertised in the *Neue Zeitschrift für Musik* on 2 December 1847 (270), and by Jul. Weiss. of the *Neue Berliner Musikzeitung* on 29 March 1848 (97). It was reviewed by the *Neue Zeitschrift für Musik* on 19 February 1848 (87–88), but none of the Lieder were discussed individually.

[21] Johanna and Gottfried Kinkel, *Liebe treue Johanna! Liebster Gottit!*, iii, 1161. '[Ich] muß wol meine Träume von einer höhern künstlerischen Tätigkeit begraben, solange ich keine Minute mein eigen nenne.'

The challenges of life increase day by day, and, despite all time management, I barely have time for half of my duties. [...] Compared to our home country, teaching in London does not mean a quiet exchange of thoughts and interaction with a few students, but the teacher's house seems like the head office of a huge trade institution, where people keep coming and going.[22]

Although Kinkel was not able to devote as much time to composition, a fragment manuscript of Lieder in Kinkel's hand and dated 1857/58 reveals that she never fully gave up composing.[23] The collection includes slightly varied copies of 'Kathleen Mavourneen' by Frederick Nicholls Crouch;[24] Franz Schubert's 'Der Musensohn' (set in B-flat major rather than A-flat major or G major, the two keys Schubert chose for his two versions of this Lied) and 'Der Pilgrim' (set in A major rather than E major); Friedrich Silcher's 'Französische Melodie' and 'Matrosenlied';[25] the two Scottish songs 'Mein Herz ist im Hochland' (My Heart Is in the Highlands) and 'The Highland Watch', the latter of which is very similar to Beethoven's setting of the same words but is set in F major rather than B-flat major and includes a shortened piano postlude; a song by Bernhard Klein; Kinkel's own settings of Gottfried's 'Du gabst dem Mann des Schwertes' (from Gottfried's Singspiel *Friedrich in Suza*, set in 1842); and, finally, 'Geistliches Abendlied', which corresponds with Kinkel's earlier published version of this Lied but is set in B-flat major rather than E-flat major.

[22] Johanna Kinkel in a letter to Gretchen Biesing dated 26 October 1854, unpublished, ULB S2424. 'Aber die Anforderungen des Lebens werden täglich mannigfaltiger, und ich finde mit aller Zeitökonomie kaum noch Zeit für die Hälfte meiner Pflichten. [...] Das Unterrichtgeben hat in London nicht wie bei uns in der Heimath den Anstrich eines stillen Gedankenlebens und Wirkens auf ein paar Schüler, sondern eines Lehrers Haus ist wie das Comptoir eines großen Handelsinstituts, wo immer Menschen aus und eingehen.'

[23] Johanna Kinkel, Fragment eines Liederbuchs, ULB E 4' 756/6 Rara:15; Klaus, *Johanna Kinkel*, 310.

[24] Frederick Nicholls Crouch (1808–1896) was a London-born cellist, singer and composer. He composed his most famous tune 'Kathleen Mavourneen' between 1835 and 1838. He also gave lectures on songs and legends of Ireland. See Bruce Carr, 'Crouch, Frederick Nicholls', in *The New Grove Dictionary of Music and Musicians*, 2nd edn, xxiii, 733–34 (733).

[25] Philipp Friedrich Silcher (1789–1860) was a German composer, who, like Hans Georg Nägeli, considered the folk song the most suitable performance genre for the general public. He composed approximately 250 songs, but he also collected and arranged folk songs from Germany and other countries. See Luise Marretta-Schär, 'Silcher, Philipp Friedrich', in *The New Grove Dictionary of Music and Musicians*, 2nd edn, vi, 386.

As regards Kinkel's published oeuvre, the working relationship with Trautwein was the most fruitful cooperation. Its intensity is reflected by the large number of opus numbers Kinkel published with him – the song 'Der Runenstein', her *Vogelkantate* op. 1, and the Lieder collections opp. 7, 8, 9, 10, 11, and 12 appeared there. Her correspondence with Trautwein's partner Ferdinand Mendheim reveals quite personal details and thus underlines the intense nature of the relationship.[26] Despite (or because of) their closeness, Kinkel did not mention any monetary figures in her letters to Mendheim, so it is not known how much money she turned over with her Lieder, but her orders of *Iris im Gebiete der Tonkunst* and of other scores in exchange for her honorarium reveal that the income from her Lieder was sufficient to nourish her intellectual curiosity. On 10 November 1842, Kinkel reminds Mendheim of the honorarium for her *Vogelkantate*. She enquires 'whether and how much money you will give me for this work, which I had produced upon your own request'. She then explains how she relied on 'the earnings of my musical talent in order to meet my small demands'.[27] Kinkel was determined to make money with her compositions, and she was concerned about their marketability. On 16 May 1839, she wrote to Mendheim that she had written quartets for soprano, alto, tenor, and bass without piano accompaniment and asked whether 'the dilettantes ever enquire about something like that'.[28] Despite her financial dependency on publishing, Kinkel displayed modesty and uncertainty to her peers. Referring to her correspondence with Mendheim, she wrote to her friend Emilie von Henning on 8 December 1839:

> Recently I offered Trautwein some new compositions. They responded that they would publish them in the new year, but they prefaced the letter in the following way: They would still have a large stock of manuscripts, but they would [...]

---

[26] For instance, on 9 June 1840 Kinkel informed Mendheim: 'It was not until May that my court case [the divorce], with many difficulties, was completed (as desired), and I am now enjoying complete freedom again" Johanna Kinkel to Ferdinand Mendheim, 9 June 1840, Berlin Staatsbibliothek, Mus.ex. Johanna Kinkel 8. 'Erst zu Ende Mai ist nach vielen Schwierigkeiten hier mein Prozeß (nach Wunsch) beendet worden, und ich erfreue mich wieder vollkommener Freiheit.'

[27] Johanna Kinkel to Ferdinand Mendheim on 10 November 1842, Berlin Staatsbibliothek, Mus.ex. Johanna Kinkel 10: 'ob und wie viel Honorar Sie mir für diese Arbeit, welcher ich mich auf Ihre Bestellung unterzogen hatte, geben können. Wenn ich schon darauf angewiesen bin, von dem Ertrage meines musikalischen Talents meine kleinen Bedürfnisse zu bestreiten'.

[28] Johanna Kinkel to Ferdinand Mendheim, 16 May 1839, Berlin Staatsbibliothek Mus. ex. Johanna Kinkel 5. 'Quartetten für Sopran, Alt, Tenor, Bass ohne Begleitung habe ich auch gemacht; Fragen die Dilettanten wohl zuweilen nach dergeichen?'

publish my music out of special consideration. [...] my works are no longer sell-ing as well as my first works, etc. etc. Now I do not want to publish anything with them anymore, as I do not want to harm my publisher. I am not certain what to think about this. Either Trautwein wants to lower my demands, or my friends are commending me too much when they tell me that my Lieder are being per-formed with enthusiasm. I would give so much if I could only achieve clarity on that matter; Trautwein's letter has paralysed me more than all the flattering mes-sages from you, Arnims, and others who have encouraged me. I have to write; but I do not want to publish too much.[29]

In 1840, Kinkel published her last opus with Trautwein. Nevertheless she retained her contact with Mendheim until 1842, and asked for advice occasion-ally. On 23 September 1840, for instance, she asked for Mendheim's opinions on a church composition but assures him that he 'should not accept it, risking that it might not sell at all, which is indeed quite likely, as I am a complete beginner in this genre, and because one cannot generally trust women to write coun-terpoint'.[30] Mendheim's response to this request is unknown, but Mendheim's business partner Trautwein never published these genres by Kinkel.

The reasons for Kinkel's quite frequent switching of publishers after her return to Bonn are manifold. She did not want to push Trautwein to pub-lish further works once she noticed a decline of interest, and she might have chosen a mix of publishers to promote her output. Her ambition to reach a large

[29] Johanna Kinkel to Emilie von Henning, 8 December 1839, cited after Goslich, 'Briefe von Johanna Kinkel', 192. 'Ich hatte Trautweins neulich einige neue Kompositionen angeboten; sie schrieben zwar zurück, daß sie sie im nächsten Jahre verlegen wollten, machten aber eine lange Vorrede folgenden Inhalts: Sie hätten noch großen Vorrath von Manuskripten, aber aus besonderer Rücksicht … wollten sie dennoch … und meine Sachen gingen nicht mehr so gut, wie die ersten Werke usw. usw. Nun will ich lieber nichts mehr bei ihnen herausgeben, den ich möchte doch meinem Verleger keinen Schaden zufügen.. Ich weiß nicht recht, was ich davon halten soll. Entweder Trautweins wollen nur meine Ansprüche herunterstimmen oder meine Freunde schmeicheln mir zu viel, wenn sie mir sagen, daß meine Lieder mit Beifall gesungen werden. Ich gäbe etwas darum, wenn ich nur in diesem Punkt zur Klarheit kommen könnte; es hat der Trautweinsche Brief mehr meinen Muth gelähmt als alle schmeichelhaften Nachrichten von Euch, Arnims und anderen die mich angespornt hatten. Indeß schreiben muß ich einmal; ich will nur nicht zu viel herausgeben.' Elisions in original.

[30] Johanna Kinkel to Ferdinand Mendheim, 23 September 1840, Berlin Staatsbibliothek Mus.ex. Johanna Kinkel 9. 'dass Sie es nicht auf die Gefahr hin übernehmen sollen, daß es vielleicht durchaus keinen Absatz findet, welches sogar sehr wahrscheinlich ist, da ich in diesem Styl noch völlig Anfängerin bin, und man überhaupt den Damen wenig Contrapunkt zuzutrauen Ursache hat.'

audience surfaces in her letter to Felix Mendelssohn dated 25 February 1843, which reads: 'Please accept indulgently the small, light, very modest church piece, which I am enclosing. I would be honoured and very grateful if you were occasionally able to get it performed and reviewed.'[31] It is likely that this composition was *Hymnus in Coena Domini,* perhaps the same work she introduced to Mendheim in 1840. A similar attitude is revealed in her letter to Schott, with whom she published her op. 20. Dated 13 February 1849, the letter reads:

> I want to abstain from the agio and only demand 50 silver Thaler, even if you insist on lowering the number of [12] free copies, but please consider the following: I would never think of selling those free copies, for these are used in your own interest. I have friends and acquaintances in different regions. I give them each opus I publish with the request to achieve a review and distribute it within their circles.[32]

Kinkel first offered her op. 20 to Schloß, with whom she had previously published her op. 19. Examining Kinkel's correspondence with Schott and Schloß, Glahn concludes that Kinkel's demands to Schloß might have been too ambitious and that her market-orientation must have been very high.[33]

Other factors determining Kinkel's choice of publishers were geographical location and recommendation. Her two political songs, 'Demokratenlied' and 'Hymne auf den Tod des Marco Botzaris', for instance, appeared with Sulzbach in her hometown Bonn. Some of Kinkel's Heine settings were published by Dunst (also Bonn) as part of his Lieder collection. Much like Kinkel's drinking song included in Schumann's supplement to the *Neue Zeitschrift für Musik,* her Heine settings in Dunst's *Rhein-Sagen und Lieder* were most likely requested

[31] Letter from Johanna Kinkel to Felix Mendelssohn, 25 February 1843, Oxford Bodleian Library, GB-Ob, M.D.M.d.43/100–101. 'Die kleine, leichte, sehr anspruchslose Kirchenmusik die ich beilege, nehmen Sie nachsichtig auf. Können Sie es gelegentlich veranlaßen, daß sie irgendwo gesungen oder rezensirt werde, so werden Sie mich sehr ehren und zum Dank verpflichten.'

[32] Johanna Kinkel to Schott, 13 February 1849, cited after Glahn, *Johanna Kinkel,* 211. 'Ich will das Agio ablassen, und nur 50 Thl. Silber ausbedingen, auch, wenn Sie darauf bestehen, auf eine geringere Zahl [12] Frei=Exemplare herunter zu gehn, doch gebe ich Ihnen Eines zu bedenken: Es fällt mir nicht ein diese Freiexempl: zu verkaufen, sondern dieselben dienen vielmehr Ihrem Interesse. Ich habe Freunde u. Bekannte in den verschiedensten Gegenden. Diesen sende ich jedes Opus das von mir erscheint zum Geschenk, mit der Bitte für Rezension und Verbreitung in ihren Kreisen zu wirken.'

[33] For further details on Kinkel's proposals to Schloß and Schott, see Glahn, *Johanna Kinkel,* 208–12.

by the editor, although to date no correspondence between Dunst and Kinkel has been uncovered.

Kinkel's op. 6 was published by Kistner (Leipzig) upon Mendelssohn's recommendation; Kinkel had approached Mendelssohn in 1839.[34] Op. 17 was published by Bote & Bock (Berlin) in 1847, but this cooperation was initiated earlier. On 2 January 1839, Bote & Bock received a letter from Kinkel in which she thanked them for their enquiry, but rejected their offer, as 'the manuscript about which you ask, has been given to Mr Trautwein already, with whom I have no reason to break, as I have been very happy with him so far'.[35] While she was happy with Trautwein then, she might have refreshed her contacts with Bote & Bock once Trautwein had lost interest. The appendix shows that other publishers of Kinkel's include Schlesinger (Berlin), Eck & Lefebvre (Cologne), Eisen (Cologne), and Hofmeister (Leipzig), but, as there is no correspondence between Kinkel and these publishers, the backgrounds of these collaborations remain obscure.

As much as Kinkel was able to familiarise herself with various publishers during her time in Berlin and later in Bonn, she acquainted herself with many different poets during her childhood. As the daughter of a teacher of German, Latin and the sciences, Kinkel must have come across Goethe's poetry at a young age. She might have been inspired by the fashion of her time, as Goethe's poems were an inherent part of nineteenth-century song composition. Additionally, Kinkel's association with Bettina von Arnim must have increased her interest in Goethe. In her memoirs, Kinkel describes her first meeting with von Arnim, during which she 'thoroughly studied [Bettina's] outward appearance and compared it with the picture [she] had in mind after reading the correspondence with Goethe'.[36] Interestingly, five of Kinkel's seven Goethe Lieder are settings of words that were hardly set by any of Kinkel's contemporaries, although Kinkel was familiar with his popular works. In a letter to Oppenhoff

---

[34] Mendelssohn admitted to his mother that he 'talked Kistner into [Kinkel's opus]'. Mendelssohn in a letter to his mother on 2 March 1839, *Felix Mendelssohn Bartholdy: Sämtliche Briefe*, ed. Kadja Grönke and Alexander Staub, 11 vols (Kassel: Bärenreiter, 2008–), vi, 332–33, 'ich habs Kistner aufgeschwatzt'.

[35] Johanna Kinkel in a letter to Bote and Bock, 2 January 1839, Berlin Staatsbibliothek, Mus.ex.Johanna Kinkel 2. 'Das Manuskript, nach welchem Sie sich erkundigen, ist schon Herrn Trautwein übergeben, mit dem ich keine Ursache habe zu brechen, da ich bisher sehr zufrieden mit ihm war.'

[36] See Kinkel (jun.), 'Aus Johanna Kinkels Memoiren', 240. 'Dabei studirte ich ihre äußere Erscheinung auf das Genaueste und verglich sie mit dem Bilde, das ich mir nach dem Briefwechsel mit Goethe von ihr entworfen hatte.' Here, Kinkel alludes to *Goethe's Briefwechsel mit einem Kinde*, published in 1835.

dated November 1838 she expressed her suspicion about the sentimental effects of the Lied 'Wer nie sein Brot mit Thränen aß' from Goethe's *Wilhelm Meister*:

> Recently, a sentimental woman sighed over the lovely song 'He, who never ate his bread with tears, he, who never sat on his bed crying' and she wanted to transfer it to her own silly fates. [...] Please do not imagine that I have forgotten what tragic moods are like, but I agree with Chamisso, who replied to Mrs Quandt when she wanted to discuss Schleiermacher's philosophy over tea that it is better to have biscuits with tea.[37]

Besides Goethe, Kinkel set words by three other poets whom she never met in person: Friedrich Rückert, August von Platen-Hallermünde, and Heinrich Heine. Eva Weissweiler ascertains that Kinkel sympathised with Heine because of their biographical and aesthetic commonalities. Like Kinkel, the Jewish-born Heine was from the Rhineland and converted to the Protestant faith, and, Weissweiler argues, Kinkel must have acknowledged the musical structure of Heine's poetry and shared his fascination for Chopin.[38]

Kinkel's stay in Berlin enabled her to get to know many talented poets from all over Germany and beyond. Adelbert von Chamisso, who, along with his parents, moved to Berlin in 1796, was a frequent visitor of the Berlin salons attended by Kinkel.[39] In Berlin Kinkel also met August Kopisch and Emanuel Geibel, the latter of whom must have been Kinkel's most influential Berlin acquaintance in terms of compositional inspiration. Kinkel published ten Geibel settings, but a letter from Geibel to his mother dated 12 February 1838 reveals that many others remained unpublished. Interestingly, Geibel criticised the prominence of the piano in Kinkel's Lieder in the same letter:

> She inexhaustibly composes Lieder, and she has taken a liking to my poems. I think she has already set about twenty of my poems, and yet there are very few

---

[37] Johanna Kinkel in a letter to Angela Oppenhoff dated 10 November 1838, cited in Kaufmann, 'Johanna Kinkel: Schluß', 58. Italics in original. 'Eine Sentimentale seufzte neulich über das schöne Lied "Wer nie sein Brod [*sic*] mit Thränen aß, wer nie – auf seinem Bette weinend saß" und wollte das auf ihre eigenen dummen Schicksale beziehen. [...] Glauben Sie nicht, daß ich indessen tragische Stimmungen verlernte, aber ich denke mit Chamisso, den Frau Quandt beim Thee über Schleiermachers Dogmatik ausfragen wollte, und der entgegnete: Zwieback *beim Thee* ist besser.'

[38] Eva Weissweiler, 'Die stille Opposition: Heine-Vertonungen von Frauen – Am Beispiel von Johanna Kinkel und Clara Schumann', in *Komponistinnen in Berlin*, ed. Bettina Brand and others (Berlin: Bender, 1987), 96–106 (97).

[39] See Kaufmann, 'Johanna Kinkel: Schluß', 53.

that I *really* like. For my taste, there is usually too little melody and too much accompaniment; and I do not agree at all with her principle that the *accompaniment* should define the mood of the poem.[40]

Kinkel, by contrast, praised Geibel and his talent almost unconditionally in one of her letters to her friend Oppenhoff:

I am surprised that we never got to know Geibel in Bonn as he was studying there when I was there; he is one of the most brilliant and ingenious people that I have ever met. It would be a shame if he were employed at some point as such a valuable visionary is a rarity and should never become a philistine. There are enough philistines (I cannot find a suitable epithet), but very few real poets. When I talk about poets, I do not mean people who write verses (who does not write verses nowadays?), but I mean such people who absorb the sounds with the eyes of a painter and the ears of a singer.[41]

Back in Bonn, Kinkel's social contacts centred on the Bonner Gesangverein and the *Maikäfer*. Kinkel set poems by such *Maikäfer* members as Wolfgang Müller von Königswinter, Wilhelm Seibt, Sebastian Longard, Alexander Kaufmann, and Nikolaus Becker. One of Kaufmann's poems served as the *Maikäfer* anthem, but it was never published.[42] Moreover, many of the Lieder composed between 1839 and 1851 are settings of Johanna's and Gottfried's own poems. Both Johanna

---

[40] *Emanuel Geibels Jugendbriefe: Bonn – Berlin – Griechenland*, ed. Karl Curtius (Berlin: Curtius, 1909), 116. Italics in original. '(Auch) im Liedercomponieren ist sie unerschöpflich, und namentlich hat sie meine Verse in Affektion genommen. Ich glaube, sie hat schon gegen zwanzig meiner Sachen in Musik gesetzt und doch sind wenige darunter, die mir *recht* gefallen. Für meinen Geschmack ist gewöhnlich zu wenig Melodie und zu viel Accompagnement dabei aufgewandt, wie ich denn überhaupt ihren Grundsatz, daß die *Begleitung* eigentlich die Stimmung des Gedichts angeben solle, nicht theilen kann.'

[41] Johanna Kinkel in a letter to Angela Oppenhoff dated 10 December 1837, cited in Kaufmann, 'Johanna Kinkel: Schluß', 52. 'Es wundert mich, daß wir in Bonn nie Geibel kennen lernten, der doch noch zu meiner Zeit da studierte; das ist einer der geistvollsten genialsten Leute, die mir je begegnet sind. Es wäre jammerschade, wenn er je eine Anstellung bekäme, denn ein solcher kostbarer Phantast ist eine Rarität und sollte sich nie einphilistern, denn der Philister (ich finde kein schickliches Beiwort) gibts schon genug, aber wenig ächte Dichter. Auch meine ich unter Dichtern nicht Leute, die Verse machen (denn wer macht heutzutage keine?), sondern so Leute, die mit Augen eines Malers und Ohren eines Sängers alle Töne in sich aufnehmen.'

[42] Johanna Kinkel in a letter to Gottfried on 25 May 1841, Johanna and Gottfried Kinkel, *Liebe treue Johanna! Liebster Gottit!*, i, 192.

and Gottfried Kinkel used the salon-like *Maikäfer* gatherings as a platform for the performance and discussion of their works. The Lied was a popular genre within such gatherings, because it offered 'a wide expressive range with minimal forces'.[43] Carl Schurz's memoirs confirm that Kinkel must have performed Lieder in Bonn:

> She composed just as delightfully as she played the piano. Although her voice was not very strong and she only seemed to whisper when singing, her singing, indeed, had a touching effect. She really understood how to sing without a voice.[44]

Spontaneous *Maikäfer* performances were not documented in Kinkel's precise records of the *Maikäfer* gatherings. However, Kinkel was aware that she was not a very good singer, so it is uncertain if and how frequently she performed her songs before an audience.[45] Several documents tell of Kinkel's virtuosic piano playing, but she is hardly ever mentioned as a singer. In her memoirs, Kinkel describes her first public piano playing in Berlin at an exhibition:

> Although I was used to playing in front of an audience if the occasion was right, I did not enjoy playing here as I did not want to impose my music [upon the other visitors of the exhibition].[46]

That Kinkel was used to playing for an audience becomes evident in her letters to Oppenhoff, in one of which she raves about an unforgettable evening at Fanny Hensel's where Vieuxtemps, Hensel and Gans performed a Beethoven trio:

> I was supposed to play something by Chopin afterwards, but I was not able to play as I was too keyed up, so I asked Hensel to postpone it to the next concert.

---

[43] Donald J. Grout, J. Peter Burkholder and Claude Palisca, *A History of Western Music*, 7th edn (New York: W. W. Norton & Company, 2006), 605.

[44] Carl Schurz, *Lebenserinnerungen bis zum Jahre 1852* (Berlin: Reimer, 1906/11), 106. 'Sie komponierte ebenso reizend, wie sie spielte. Obgleich ihre Stimme kein Klangmetall besaß und sie im Singen die Töne scheinbar nur andeuten konnte, sang sie doch mit ergreifender Wirkung. Sie verstand wirklich die Kunst, ohne Stimme zu singen.'

[45] See Klaus, *Johanna Kinkel*, 209.

[46] Kinkel (jun.), 'Aus Johanna Kinkels Memoiren', 242. 'Zwar daran gewöhnt, vor dem Publikum zu spielen, wenn die Gelegenheit mich dazu berechtigte, war ich dem Aufdringen meiner Musik zu abhold, um mich hier wohl zu fühlen.'

I thought I would put the audience into a state of shock if I played a brilliant Chopin piece after the holy, coruscant, solemnly paced Beethoven.[47]

Kinkel's preference for the piano also surfaces in her compositional aesthetics of her early Lieder, as she admits to Oppenhoff in July 1837:

> The Lieder [op. 7] are, of course, beginner's attempts, and as I assumed that nobody would like to sing them except for myself, I turned the piano accompaniment into the main thing, and, so to speak, allowed the alto voice merely to explain the mood that the piece called for through the text.[48]

This quote implies that Kinkel performed her own Lieder in Berlin. In her memoirs, Kinkel recalls that on the occasion of Savigny's birthday, at which her *Vogelkantate* was performed, she took on the role of the magpie.[49] In general, however, she seemed to prefer conducting and playing the piano, which raises the question of who might have performed Kinkel's Lieder and where.

In Berlin, Bettina von Arnim's daughters and singers from their circle of friends performed at smaller gatherings. In Bonn, Kinkel's friends Andreas Simons and Angela Oppenhoff were interested in her Lieder from a performative perspective; the latter received new compositions from Kinkel quite regularly. Kinkel's dedications to Sophie Schloß, Bertha Forstheim, and Josephine Hubar point to a few more singers who must have appreciated (and performed) her Lieder. In London, Kinkel performed piano works as is confirmed by her London acquaintance Malwida von Meysenbug.[50] This, however, does not mean that she did not perform Lieder in London at all. Her manuscript scores include Scottish songs, none of which were published. Furthermore, the songs included in the aforementioned handwritten transcriptions are notated in lower

---

[47] Kinkel in a letter to Angela Oppenhoff dated 16 June 1837, cited in Kaufmann, 'Johanna Kinkel: Schluß', 52. 'Danach sollte ich von Chopin etwas spielen, war aber vor Enthusiasmus nicht im Stande dazu und bat die Hensel, es bis zum nächsten Konzert aufzuschieben. Ich dachte, die Zuhörer müßten wie mit kalt Wasser begossen werden, wenn ich mit einem brillanten Chopin-Stück nach dem heiligen, sternenbekränzten, feierlich schreitenden Beethoven hinterher getanzt hätte.'

[48] Johanna Kinkel in a letter to Angela Oppenhoff dated 31 July 1837, cited in Kaufmann, 'Johanna Kinkel: Schluß', 50. 'Die Lieder sind, versteht sich, Anfängerversuche, und da ich voraussetzte, es werde sie doch niemand singen mögen als ich, so habe ich die Klavierbegleitung zur Hauptsache gemacht, und die Altstimme nur so zu sagen die Empfindung, die das Stück verlangt, durch den Text erklären lassen.'

[49] See Kinkel (jun.), 'Aus Johanna Kinkels Memoiren', 261.

[50] von Meysenbug, *Gesammelte Werke*, ii, 88.

keys – possibly pointing to the possibility that Kinkel, being an alto singer, might have arranged those songs with her own performance in mind. But Kinkel's Lieder were also performed by other (unknown) singers in London. In her unpublished *Briefe aus London* (Letters from London), Kinkel describes how she walked into a music shop and flicked though an album entitled *Juwelen deutscher Melodien* (Gems of German Melody):

> I was flattered to find among them some of my earliest compositions, to which, to my surprise, English words and the initials of an unknown name had been added; and which had also been dedicated to a complete stranger. When I expressed my surprise at this, the publisher replied: 'Well, as you know, melodies are as free as a bird. We have been selling yours for ten years at great profit.'[51]

It is uncertain to which English-language publication Kinkel referred in her anecdote, because Kinkel's 'Nachtlied' was published in 1843 as 'Evening Song' in *Gems of German Song*, vol. 6, no. 3, and Kinkel's authorship was acknowledged there.[52] Perhaps Kinkel came across an earlier edition unknown today, or she created this anecdote in order to give voice to her general suspicion about the commercialisation of music. Glahn suggests that the edition of *Gems of German Song* currently known might have been edited after Kinkel's complaint at a later stage.[53] At any rate, in light of Melanie Unseld's theory that anecdotes are not committed to historical truth but provide valuable insight into the contexts within which certain events are remembered, Kinkel's narration of this event suggests two conclusions.[54] First, Kinkel aimed to promote herself as an exploited but marketable composer. Second, Kinkel's Lieder, whether incognito or not, made their way across the German border long before the Kinkels arrived in London.

---

[51] Johanna Kinkel, *Briefe aus London*, n.d., ULB 2390, n.p. 'Ich war nicht wenig geschmeichelt darunter auch einige meiner eignen frühsten Compositionen wiederzufinden, die aber zu meiner Verwunderung mit einem englischen Text, und mit den Anfangsbuchstaben eines mir fremden Namens versehen, und einer ebenfalls wildfremden Person gewidmet waren. Als ich meine Befremdung darüber ausdrückte, sagte der Verleger: "Nun, Sie wißen, Melodien sind vogelfrei. Wir verkaufen die Ihrigen schon seit 10 Jahren mit großem Vortheil."

[52] Melanie Ayaydin, 'Kinkel, Johanna', *Musik und Gender im Internet*, ed. Beatrix Borchard <http://mugi.hfmt-hamburg.de/artikel/Johanna_Kinkel.pdf> (accessed 18 April 2019).

[53] Glahn, *Johanna Kinkel*, 118.

[54] Melanie Unseld, *Biographie und Musikgeschichte: Wandlungen biographischer Konzepte in Musikkultur und Musikhistoriographie* (Cologne: Böhlau, 2014), 119.

CHAPTER 3

Love songs

O N 20 April 1840, in one of her first letters to Gottfried, Johanna promised not to 'intervene in your (certainly bright mood) with a diminished seventh chord'.[1] A letter from 17 June 1840 reveals more concrete musical links between the Kinkels, when Johanna tells Gottfried that she and some choir members sang '[his] Lieder, of which [she] has also composed a new one again'.[2] These two excerpts demonstrate that music played a crucial part in the Kinkels' relationship, an aspect which confirms Maynard Solomon's concept of interconnected aspects of life and art.[3] Drawing on constructiveness as a commonality between historiography and biography, Unseld warns that autobiographical documents may be particularly prone to (mis)readings as historical sources, because their authenticity and objectivity are questionable.[4] Nevertheless, such documents can be valuable in tracing links between music and life. For Kinkel, music served as a means of self-expression, a way of socialising and relaxation, and an inspirational mediator between herself and her second husband. It should be borne in mind, however, that 'there is no such thing as a biographical truth' and that, according to Unseld, (auto)biographical works bear a dialogical balance of the inventory self ('inventarisches Ich') and inventive self ('inventorisches Ich'), an observation which will also surface in relation to Johanna Kinkel.[5]

---

[1] Johanna and Gottfried Kinkel, *Liebe treue Johanna! Liebster Gottit!*, i, 37: 'in Ihre (jetzt gewiß sonnenhelle Stimmung) mit einem verminderten Septimenakkord einzufallen'.

[2] Ibid., i, 45. Underlining in original: 'auch von <u>Ihren</u> Liedern, deren ich auch <u>wieder</u> ein neues komponiert habe'.

[3] Maynard Solomon, 'Thoughts on Biography', *19th-Century Music*, 5, 3 (Spring 1982), 268–76 (272).

[4] Unseld, *Biographie und Musikgeschichte*, 50 and 62. For further considerations of the constructiveness of autobiographical sources see David Gramit, 'Unremarkable Musical Lives: Autobiographical Narratives, Music, and the Shaping of the Self', in Pekacz, ed., *Musical Biography*, 159–78.

[5] Unseld, *Biographie und Musikgeschichte*, 316 and 437. 'Die biographische Wahrheit ist nicht zu haben.'

✌ *Berlin: Kinkel's attempt to process her first marriage*

Considering Kinkel's own biography and her motivation in moving to Berlin, it is not surprising that all of Kinkel's love songs published during her Berlin time allude to a desperate search for true love. In Kinkel's Lied 'Verlornes Glück' (Lost Happiness, op. 6, no. 5), the words of which originate from Kinkel herself, the lyrical I returns to their favourite place and bemoans their love being over.[6] Although this Lied was not published until 1839, the opus number points to one of Kinkel's earlier compositions (the first published opus was op. 7).

Verlornes Glück (op. 6, no. 5)		**Lost Happiness**[7]
Johanna Kinkel (published 1839)		
Sitze hier an lieber Stelle,	*a*	I am sitting here at a lovely place,
Wo ich einst nicht saß alleine;	*b*	Where I used to sit in company;
Damals klang hier süße Rede,	*c*	Back then, sweet words were voiced,
Wo ich heut' mein Los beweine.	*b*	Now I am weeping over my destiny.
Schön und hell nennt man die Erde,	*d*	Beautiful and bright they call the world,
Voller Lust und voller Freuden;	*e*	Full of happiness and joy;
Doch ist mir sie ewig dunkel,	*f*	But for me, the world is dark forever
Weil ich soll ihr Schönstes meiden.	*e*	Because I miss its greatest joy.
Von den vielen duft'gen Kräutern,	*g*	Of these aromatic herbs
Die in diesem Garten stehen,	*h*	Which grow in this garden,
Wird kein einz'ges, ach, mich heilen;	*i*	Not a single one, alas, will cure me,
Ich muss qualvoll untergehen.	*h*	I will have to cease in pain.

This Lied's timing and structure are interesting – perhaps one of the reasons why the reviewer of the *Allgemeine Musikalische Zeitung* thought it was one of the most beautiful Lieder within this collection.[8] The two-quaver upbeat in the vocal line is preceded by a cadence-like crotchet progression in the piano accompaniment. The cadential character of those two crotchets is confirmed when they re-sound in the last bar as a means of concluding this song (Ex. 3.1).

In Kinkel's Geibel Lied 'Abreise' (Departure, op. 8, no. 6), also one of her first Lieder compositions, the lyrical protagonist enters a boat departing from his home place. Table 3.1 shows that Kinkel does not, as usual, divide the Lied into phrases of four bars each. In accordance with the unusual rhyme scheme,

---

[6] Throughout this book, I name the lyrical protagonist's gender where it is obvious, based on the bipolar order of sexes, because this is the interpretation of gender which reflects Kinkel's own mindset. When it is not obvious, I refer to the lyrical I as 'they' or s/he.

[7] Unless otherwise noted, all translations are my own.

[8] [Anon.], review of Johanna Mathieux, *Opus 6* (1839), *Allgemeine Musikalische Zeitung*, 8 December 1841, 1044.

Ex. 3.1   Final phrase and piano coda of 'Verlornes Glück' (bars 8–16)

she inserts two two-bar phrases ('B', bars 5–6; and 'B$_{prolongation}$', bars 11–12), which embrace the expected four-bar phrase B (here: 'B$_{mirror+prolongation}$', bars 7–10). Based on the melodic and harmonic features, an alternative interpretation would be a tripartite structure (4+4+4+chorus rather than 4+2+4+2+chorus).

| **Abreise (op. 8, no. 6)** | | **Departure** |
| Emanuel Geibel (published 1838) | | |

Es kommt ein Schiff gezogen,	*a*	A ship is approaching,
Rot glühen die Segel im Abendschein,	*b*	The sails glow red in the sunset,
Der Wind kommt kosend geflogen,	*a*	The wind blows fondly,
Und leise plätschern die Wogen,	*a*	And the waves dabble softly,
Und Hörnerton schallt drein,	*b*	And the horns sound,
Trarah,		Trarah,
Und Hörnerton schallt drein.	*b*	And the horns sound.
Trarah, trarah, trarah, trarah!		Trarah, trarah, trarah, trarah!
Und an des Schiffleins Rande	*c*	And at the ship's railing
Steht hoch der Knab' und er schwingt das Pokal;	*d*	There stands tall the boy and swings the cup;
Ihr Vöglein, ihr flieget zum Strande,	*c*	Birds, fly to the beach,
O grüßt im heimischen Lande	*c*	Oh greet loved ones at home
Die Lieben viel tausend mal.	*d*	A thousand times.
Trarah,		Trarah,
Die Lieben viel tausend mal.	*d*	A thousand times.
Trarah, trarah, trarah, trarah!		Trarah, trarah, trarah, trarah!

48   THE SONGS OF JOHANNA KINKEL

Table 3.1   Formal design of 'Abreise' (op. 8, no. 6)

Bar	1–2	3–4	5–6	7–8	9–10	11–12	13–16	17–18
Line	a	B	A	A	b	b	Refrain	
Melodic Phrase	A		B	$B_{mirror+prolongation}$		$B_{prolongation}$	Chorus	Piano Coda
Harmony	B♭	B♭⁷-e♭-C⁷-F	F⁷-B♭	G-c^{dim}-F	B♭-F⁷-B♭	g-C⁷-F⁷-B♭	F-B♭-G-c^{dim}-F⁷-B♭	B♭
Function	I	I⁷-iv I⁷-IV vii--V⁷--I	I	VI-ii^{dim} v^{dim}--I	V⁷-I IV—I⁷	vi-II⁷ V⁷---I V⁷---I⁷	IV-I---VI-ii^{dim}-V⁷-I	I

The formal irregularity in bars 5 to 12 and the dynamic change from **_pp_** to _f_
in bar 9 emphasise the lyrical I's imagining of the sea-gulls carrying a thousand
wishes to the loved ones left behind at home.

That Kinkel might have processed psychological burdens in her songs is
reflected in the two-part Lied 'Vorüberfahrt' (Passing Journey, op. 7, no. 3), a
poem of Kinkel's, in which the female lyrical I is reminded of the pain and tor-
ture caused by an unhappy love while passing her home place.

Vorüberfahrt (op. 7, no. 3)
  Johanna Kinkel (published 1838)

Passing Journey

Ihr Liebe flüsternden Linden!	_a_	You linden trees whispering of love!
Am Wege rechter Hand,	_b_	At the right-hand side of the street
Ihr streckt herüber die Zweige	_c_	Your overhanging branches
Und grüßt mich so wohl bekannt!	_b_	Are greeting me as ever!
Ihr zeigt mir rosig beleuchtet	_d_	Rose-lit, you are showing me
Die Türme der freien Stadt,	_e_	The towers of the free town,
Die meine glühendste Liebe	_f_	Which gave birth to my glowing love
Und Qual geboren hat.	_e_	And to my torture.
Es zieht zum gothischen Thore	_h_	Violently, I am pulled into the town
Mich wie mit Gewalt herein,	_i_	Through the Gothic gates,
Vielleicht begegn' ich dem Liebsten,	_k_	Perhaps I will meet my [male] beloved,
Doch ach! Das darf ja nicht sein!	_i_	But alas! It must not happen!
Ich möchte weilen so gerne	_l_	I would love to stay
An dem geliebten Ort;	_m_	At this beloved place;
Doch Alles hat sich verschworen	_n_	But everything has conspired against me
Und reißt mich grausam fort.	_m_	And, cruelly, I am taken away.
Ihr unerbittlichen Räder,	_o_	You adamant wheels,
So steht denn euer Sinn	_p_	Why do you keep rolling,
Zu rollen, immer zu rollen,	_q_	Rolling all the time,
In's ferne Blaue dahin.	_p_	Out into the far unknown.
Die flücht'gen Rosse verstehen	_r_	The escaping horses do not
Mein innres Flehen nicht,	_s_	Understand my inner pleading,
Sie jagen brausend vorüber,	_t_	They continue their rushing journey,
Ob auch das Herz mir bricht.	_s_	No matter whether my heart is breaking.

Kinkel's personal touch surfaces in lengthy piano passages and colourful harmony (Ex. 3.2). Set in C minor, Kinkel employs in 'Vorüberfahrt' the mediants E-flat major and A-flat major, which are reached through the commonly used dominant and subdominant. In addition, a German augmented sixth chord (bar 12, introduced via the upper tonal mediant E-flat major) and the minor

Ex. 3.2   Harmonic symbolism in 'Vorüberfahrt' (bars 11–21)

subdominant (F minor, bar 20) increase the effect of the lyrical I's pain reflected in the last line of each verse. In part B of each stanza (bars 13–20), a brightening passage in C major alludes to the lyrical I's past happiness. However, the return to C minor in bar 20, followed by an eight-bar piano coda in C minor, restores the desperate mood established initially.

In the Heine setting 'Die Sprache der Sterne' (The Language of the Stars, also known as 'For Many Thousand Ages', op. 6, no. 6), the stars serve as an allegory for two lovers whose affection for each other cannot be understood by anyone else. This varied two-part Lied contains no major compositional complexities.

Die Sprache der Sterne (op. 6, no. 6) Heinrich Heine (published 1839)		**For Many Thousand Ages**[9] Translation by James Thomson
Es stehen unbeweglich	*a*	For many thousand ages
Die Sterne in ihrer Höh',[10]	*b*	The steadfast stars above
Viel tausend Jahr, und schauen	*c*	Have gazed upon each other
Sich an mit Liebesweh.	*b*	With ever mournful love.
Sie sprechen eine Sprache,	*d*	They speak a certain language,
Die ist so reich, so schön;	*e*	So beautiful, so grand,
Doch keiner der Philologen	*f*	Which none of the philologians
Kann diese Sprache verstehn.	*e*	Could ever understand.
Ich aber hab sie gelernet,	*g*	But I have learned it, learned it
Und ich vergesse sie nicht;	*h*	For ever, by the grace
Mir diente als Grammatik	*i*	Of studying the grammar of
Der Herzallerliebsten Gesicht.	*h*	My heart's own darling's face.

The deep-rooted desire to spend time with the beloved is also expressed in August Kopisch's 'Wunsch' (Desire, op. 7, no. 2), in which the lyrical I hopes to be stranded with their beloved on a lonely island.

---

[9] *The LiederNet Archive*, hosted by Emily Ezust <http://www.lieder.net/lieder/get_text.html?TextId=27076> (accessed 3 May 2019). Translations accessed at *The LiederNet Archive* are hereafter referenced by way of URL only.

[10] Heine's original reads 'in der Höh' rather than 'in ihrer Höh'. Heinrich Heine, 'Es stehen unbeweglich', in *Buch der Lieder von Heinrich Heine* (Hamburg: Hoffmann und Campe, 1827), 116, cited after *Heinrich Heine: Historisch-Kritische Gesamtausgabe*, ed. Manfred Winfuhr <http://hhp.uni-trier.de/Projekte/HHP/Projekte/HHP/searchengine/werke/baende/D01/enterdha?pageid=D01S0138&bookid=D01&lineref=Z25&mode=2&textpattern=es%20stehen%20unbeweglich&firsttid=0&widthgiven=30> (accessed 3 May 2019).

Wunsch (op. 7, no. 2)		**Desire**
August Kopisch (published 1838)		
Im Meere möchte' ich fahren	*a*	I want to travel on the sea
Mit dir, mit dir allein,	*b*	With you, with you alone.
Möcht auf einsamem Eiland	*c*	I want to be stranded
Mit dir verschlagen sein.	*b*	With you on a lonely island.
Da wären nicht Muhmen und Basen,	*d*	There would be no relations,
Nur du und ich allein,	*e*	Just you and me alone,
Da würdest du nicht so spröde,	*f*	You would not be so tough,
Nicht hart und grausam sein.	*e*	So hard and cruel.
Da schlängst du die Lilienarme	*g*	Lovingly, you would put your lily arms
Mir liebend um Hals und Brust,	*h*	Around my neck and chest,
Und ich, ich dürfte dich küssen	*i*	And I, I would be able to kiss you
Nach meines Herzens Lust.	*h*	To my heart's content.
Wir säßen und strickten uns Netze	*k*	We would sit there and knit nets,
Und fingen uns Fische im Meer,	*l*	We would catch the fish in the sea.
Und Gast wär allein die Liebe	*m*	Our only visitor would be love
Und weiter niemand mehr.	*l*	And nobody else.
Im Meere möchte ich fahren,	*a*	I want to travel on the sea
Mit dir, mit dir allein,	*b*	With you, with you alone.
Möcht auf einsamem Eiland	*c*	I want to be stranded
Mit dir verschlagen sein.	*b*	With you on a lonely island.

In a similar way to 'Vorüberfahrt' and 'Die Sprache der Sterne', the piano in 'Wunsch' takes priority. The Lied includes a lengthy piano prelude and postlude, and the accompaniment is foregrounded by way of a distinct rhythm imitating the moving sea. The unusual tonic key of F-sharp minor is surrounded by diverse harmonies including the mediants and parallel major keys. While their entrances are prepared by way of conventional progressions, their presence attests to Kinkel's ambition to widen her harmonic scope.

In the Geibel setting 'Gondellied' (Gondola Song, op. 8, no. 3) the lyrical I imagines being outside under a clear sky with his/her beloved. The poem, whose words originate from Geibel's translation of Thomas Moore's 'When Daylight Sets', was set by numerous nineteenth-century composers.[11] Besides fashionability, the theme centring on love might have inspired Kinkel personally.

[11] For instance, Clara Schumann, Fanny Hensel, Friedrich Kücken (1810–1882), Joseph Joachim Raff (1822–1882), and Johann Wenzeslaus Kalliwoda (1801–1866).

Gondellied (op. 8, no. 3)
    Emanuel Geibel (published 1838)

When Daylight Sets[12]
    Original poem by Thomas Moore

O komm zu mir, wenn durch die Nacht	*a*	Oh, come to me when daylight sets;	
Wandelt das Sternenheer,	*b*	Sweet! then come to me,	
Dann schwebt mit uns in Mondespracht	*a*	When smoothly go our gondolets	
Die Gondel übers Meer.	*b*	O'er the moonlit sea.	
Die Lieb erwacht, der Scherz beginnt[13]	*c*	When Mirth's awake, and Love begins,	
Im gold'nen Zauberlicht.	*d*	Beneath that glancing ray,	
Die Zither lockt so sanft, so lind,	*c*	With sound of lutes and mandolins,	
Du widerstehst ihr nicht.	*d*	To steal young hearts away.	
O komm zu mir, wenn durch die Nacht	*a*	Then, come to me when daylight sets;	
Wandelt das Sternenheer,	*b*	Sweet! then come to me,	
Dann schwebt mit uns in Mondespracht	*a*	When smoothly go our gondolets	
Die Gondel übers Meer.	*b*	O'er the moonlit sea.	
Das ist für Liebende die Stund',	*e*	Oh, then's the hour for those who love,	
Liebchen, wie ich und du;	*f*	Sweet, like thee and me;	
So friedlich blaut des Himmels Rund,	*e*	When all's so calm below, above,	
Es schläft das Meer in Ruh.	*f*	In Heaven and o'er the sea.	
Die Mädchen singen Liebeslust,[14]	*g*	When maidens sing sweet barcarolles,	
Das Echo hallt von fern,	*h*	And Echo sings again	
Da drängt sich klopfend Brust an Brust,	*g*	So sweet, that all with ears and souls	
Schließt Mund an Mund sich gern.	*h*	Should love and listen then.	
O komm zu mir, wenn durch die Nacht	*a*	So, come to me when daylight sets;	
Wandelt das Sternenheer,	*b*	Sweet! then come to me,	
Dann schwebt mit uns in Mondespracht	*a*	When smoothly go our gondolets	
Die Gondel übers Meer.	*b*	O'er the moonlit sea.	

A similar motivation might have driven Kinkel to set Geibel's 'Trennung' (Separation, op. 8, no. 5), in which a heartbroken lyrical I bemoans that their beloved has left them. Like 'Gondellied', this poem was set by many nineteenth-century composers, but Kinkel's setting was one of the first.[15]

---

[12] <http://www.lieder.net/lieder/get_text.html?TextId=22989> (accessed 3 May 2019).

[13] This verse differs from Geibel's published version. It is uncertain whether Kinkel changed the verse or whether she used one of Geibel's previous unpublished versions. Emanuel Geibel, 'Gondoliera', in *Gedichte*, ed. Emanuel Geibel, 39th edn (Berlin: Duncker, 1855), 89.

[14] Geibel's original reads: 'Und wie es schläft, da sagt der Blick | Was keine Zunge spricht | Die Lippe zieht sich nicht zurück | Und wehrt dem Kusse nicht.'

[15] For instance, Wilhelm Baumgartner (1820–1867), Franz Commer (1813–1887), Robert Franz (1815–1892), Wilhelm Bernhard Molique (1802–1869), Karl Heinrich Carsten Reinecke, and Robert Schumann.

| Trennung (op. 8, no. 5) | | Separation[16] | |
| Emanuel Geibel (published 1838) | | Translation adapted from Linda Godry | |

In meinem Garten die Nelken	*a*	The carnations in my garden
Mit ihrem Purpurstern	*b*	With their crimson centre-star
Müssen nun alle verwelken,	*a*	They all must wilt away now,
Denn du bist fern.	*b*	Because you are afar.
Auf meinem Herde die Flammen	*c*	The flames in my hearth
Die ich bewacht so gern,	*b*	Which I so loved to watch,
Sanken in Asche zusammen,	*c*	Crumbled to ashes,
Denn du bist fern.	*b*	Because you are afar.
Die Welt ist mir verdorben,	*d*	The world went sour,
Mich grüßt nicht Blume nicht Stern,	*b*	With neither flower greeting me nor star,
Mein Herz ist lange gestorben,	*d*	My heart died away long ago,
Denn du bist fern.	*b*	Because you are afar.

Kinkel's two-part Lied is characterised by dense harmonic progressions and an elaborate piano part, which stresses the line 'denn du bist fern' (because you are afar, bars 8 ff., Ex. 3.3).

Ex. 3.3   Harmonic progression in 'Trennung' (bars 7–13)

[16] <http://www.lieder.net/lieder/get_text.html?TextId=24997> (accessed 4 May 2019).

The same compositional features apply to the Heine setting 'Die Geister haben's vernommen' (The Ghosts Have Heard My Desire, op. 6, no. 3). Here, the lyrical I wishes to see the beloved in order to kiss her even just once. Although the two-part form is simple, the Lied can be characterised as one of Kinkel's more challenging compositions on account of its harmonic density and the piano's expansiveness (Ex. 3.4). Set in C minor, this Lied features a tritone progression (C-flat major–F major) at the words 'nicht mehr weichen | Zurück in die alte Nacht' (They do not want to despair | Back into the old night, first musical stanza, bars 10–13).

Die Geister haben's vernommen (op. 6, no. 3) Heinrich Heine (published 1839)		**The Ghosts Have Heard My Desire**
Da hab ich viel blasse Leichen	*a*	I have charmed many pale corpses
Beschworen mit Wortesmacht;	*b*	With the power of my words;
Die wollen nun nicht mehr weichen	*a*	Now they do not want to disappear
Zurück in die alte Nacht.	*b*	Back into the old night.
Das zähmende Sprüchlein vom Meister	*c*	The magician's taming verse
Vergaß ich vor Schauer und Graus;	*d*	I forgot out of fear and terror,
Nun ziehn die eignen Geister	*c*	Now, my own ghosts
Mich selber ins neblichte Haus.	*d*	Pull me into the foggy house.
Laßt ab, ihr finstern Dämonen!	*e*	Let go, you dark demons!
Laßt ab, und drängt mich nicht!	*f*	Let go, and do not push me!
Noch manche Freude mag wohnen	*e*	Some pleasure may still live
Hier oben im Rosenlicht.	*f*	Up here in the rosy light.
Ich muß ja immer streben	*g*	I always have to strive
Nach der Blume wunderhold;	*h*	For the lovely flower;
Was bedeutet' mein ganzes Leben,	*g*	What is my whole life worth,
Wenn ich dich nicht lieben sollt?[17]	*h*	If I am not allowed to love you?
Ich möcht sie nur einmal umfangen	*i*	I only want to embrace her once,
Und pressen ans glühende Herz!	*k*	And press her to my glowing heart!
Nur einmal die Lippen und Wangen	*i*	I only once want to kiss her lips and cheeks
Küssen mit seel'gem Schmerz!	*k*	Kiss her, laced with blessed pain.

---

[17] Heine's original reads 'sie'(her) rather than 'dich' (you). Heinrich Heine, 'Das Erwachen', in *Buch der Lieder von Heinrich Heine* (Hamburg: Hoffmann und Campe, 1827), 36, cited after *Heinrich Heine: Historisch-Kritische Gesamtausgabe*.

Nur einmal aus ihrem Munde	*l*	I only want to hear a loving word
Möcht ich hören ein liebendes Wort –	*m*	Just once out of her mouth –
Alsdann wollt ich folgen zur Stunde	*l*	Then I would follow you,
Euch, Geister, zum finsteren Ort.	*m*	Ghosts, follow you to the dark place.
Die Geister habens vernommen,	*n*	The ghosts have heard my desire
Und nicken schauerlich.	*o*	And nodded gruesomely.
Feins Liebchen, nun bin ich gekommen;	*n*	My love, now I have arrived,
Feins Liebchen, liebst du mich?	*o*	My dearest, do you love me?

Ex. 3.4   Expansive coda in 'Die Geister haben's vernommen' (bars 31–36)

Despite its desperate mood, this Lied closes in C major, reflecting the lyrical protagonist's hopes to meet his beloved. Kinkel's change of words in the fourth poetic strophe – she replaced the word 'sie' (her) with 'dich' (you) – encourages a reading of this poem through the lens of autobiography.

The two settings 'Nachgefühl' and 'Der Kuss' (both op. 10, published in 1839) tie in with this thematic scope. In both settings, the male lyrical protagonist expresses a sentimental longing for a former beloved. In the Goethe Lied 'Nachgefühl' (Emotional Retrospect, op. 10, no. 1), the extensive use of the pedal as well as broken triads in the piano accompaniment support the melancholic mood evoked by the lyrical I's memories.

| Nachgefühl[18] (op. 10, no. 1) | | Emotional Retrospect |
| Johann Wolfgang von Goethe
(published 1839) | | |

Wenn die Reben wieder blühen,	*a*	When the grapes are again in blossom,
Rühret sich der Wein im Fasse,	*b*	The wine is stirring in the barrel,
Wenn die Rosen wieder glühen,	*a*	When the roses glow once more,
Weiß ich nicht, wie mir geschieht.	*c*	Then I do not know what is happening to me.

Tränen rinnen von den Wangen,	*d*	Tears run down my cheeks,
Was ich tue, was ich lasse,	*b*	No matter what I do,
Nur ein unbestimmt Verlangen	*d*	I only feel an uncertain desire
Fühl ich, das die Brust durchglüht.	*c*	Which burns in my heart.

Und zuletzt muß ich mir sagen,	*e*	Finally, I remember,
Wenn ich mich bedenk und fasse,	*b*	When I take a moment to think,
Daß in solchen schönen Tagen	*e*	That on such lovely days,
Doris einst für mich geglüht.	*c*	Doris once loved me.

The Heine setting 'Der Kuss' (The Kiss, op. 10, no. 2) features an interesting harmonic concept (Ex. 3.5). A through-composed piece at first glance, it comprises four varied musical stanzas, the first phrase of which is especially remarkable for its prominence of the note 'c²' and its melodic progression in very small steps, mostly minor and major seconds. Kinkel varies the individual stanzas by lowering single notes in each first phrase, which causes a change of mood through different harmonic contexts.

| Der Kuss (op. 10, no. 2) | | The Kiss[19] |
| Heinrich Heine (published 1839) | | Translation by Paul Hindemith |

Ich will meine Seele tauchen	*a*	I want to delve my soul
In den Kelch der Lilie hinein.	*b*	Into the cup of the lily;
Die Lilie soll klingend hauchen	*a*	The lily should give resoundingly
Ein Lied von der Liebsten mein.	*b*	A song belonging to my beloved.

Das Lied soll schauern und beben	*c*	The song should shudder and tremble
Wie der Kuss von ihrem Mund	*d*	Like the kiss from her lips
Den sie mir einst gegeben	*c*	That she once gave me
In wunderbar süßer Stund.	*d*	In a wonderfully sweet hour.

---

[18] Goethe wrote this poem on 24 May 1797 and first titled it 'Erinnerung' (Memory). Its title was changed to 'Nachgefühl' in later publications. *Johann Wolfgang Goethe: Sämtliche Werke nach Epochen seines Schaffens (Münchner Ausgabe)*, ed. Karl Richter and others, 33 vols (Munich: Hanser, 1985–98), iv.i, 1230.

[19] <http://www.lieder.net/lieder/get_text.html?TextId=7695> (accessed 5 May 2019).

Ex. 3.5   'Der Kuss' (op. 10, no. 2)[20]

[20] The first 'g¹' in bar 6 of the vocal line is originally notated as 'a¹'; however,
considering the harmonic framework and the motivic relationship with bar 30, this
is most likely supposed to be 'g¹'.

Ex. 3.5 (*continued*)

Contrary to the songs discussed thus far, the loyalty oath voiced in the Rückert setting 'So wahr die Sonne scheinet' (As Truly as the Sun Shines, op. 10, no. 3) creates positive and hopeful emotions. The composition seems to prioritise the textual content, as its form is straightforward.

So wahr die Sonne scheinet
  (op. 10, no. 3)
  Friedrich Rückert (published 1839)

As Truly as the Sun Shines[21]
  Translation adapted from Emily Ezust

So wahr die Sonne scheinet,	*a*	As truly as the sun shines,
So wahr die Wolke weinet,	*a*	As truly as the clouds weep,
So wahr die Flamme sprüht,	*b*	As truly as the flames spark,
So wahr der Frühling blüht;	*b*	As truly as Spring blooms,
So wahr hab' ich empfunden,	*c*	So truly I felt,
Wie ich dich halt' umwunden:	*c*	As I held you in my embrace:
Du liebst mich, wie ich dich,	*d*	You love me, as I love you,
Dich lieb' ich, wie du mich.	*d*	I love you, as you love me.
Die Sonne mag verscheinen,	*a'*	The sun may stop shining,
Die Wolke nicht mehr weinen,	*a'*	The clouds may weep no more,
Die Flamme nicht mehr sprüh'n,[22]	*b'*	The flames may die down,
Der Frühling nimmer blühn![23]	*b'*	Spring may blossom no more!
Wir wollen uns umwinden	*c'*	But let us embrace
Und immer so empfinden;	*c'*	And feel this way forever;
Du liebst mich, wie ich dich,	*d*	You love me, as I love you,
Dich lieb' ich, wie du mich.	*d*	I love you, as you love me.

Adelbert von Chamisso's 'Der Müllerin Nachbar' (The Mill-Maid's Neighbour, op. 10, no. 6) takes on a humorous tone. Here, the lyrical I, the mill-maid's neighbour, fancies the miller's widowed wife. However, the mill-maid does not reciprocate these feelings and, instead, favours the servant.

---

[21] <http://www.lieder.net/lieder/get_text.html?TextId=14129> (accessed 6 June 2019).

[22] Rückert's original publication reads 'mag versprühn' rather than 'nicht mehr sprüh'n'. Friedrich Rückert, 'So wahr die Sonne scheinet', in *Friedrich Rückert's gesammelte poetische Werke in zwölf Bänden: neue Ausgabe*, ed. Heinrich Rückert, 12 vols (Frankfurt: Sauerländer, 1882), i, 378.

[23] Rückert's original publication reads 'nicht mehr' rather than 'nimmer'.

Der Müllerin Nachbar (op. 10, no. 6)
Adelbert von Chamisso
(published 1839)

The Mill-Maid's Neighbour

Die Mühle, die dreht ihre Flügel,	*a*	The windmill turns its blades,
Der Wind, der sauset darin,	*b*	The wind, it roars within.
Ich wollt' ich wäre der Müller,	*c*	I wish I were the miller,
Von wegen der Müllerin.	*b*	Because of the mill-maid.
Der Müller ist gestorben,	*d*	The miller has died,
Gott schenk' ihm die ewige Ruh.	*e*	May he rest in peace.
Ich wollte es holte der Henker	*f*	I wish the executioner took
Den Flegel von Knecht dazu.[24]	*e*	That lout of a servant as well.
Am Sonntag in der Kirche,	*g*	On Sunday, in the church,
Da glaubt' ich sie schiele nach mir.	*h*	I thought she glanced at me.
Sie schielte an mir nur vorüber,	*i*	But she overlooked me,
Der Knecht der stand an der Thür.	*h*	The servant was at the door.
Und als es ging zum Tanze,	*k*	And when the dance opened,
Da kam sie mir eben recht.	*l*	I luckily bumped into her.
Sie grüsste mich freundlich und fragte,	*m*	She greeted me cordially and asked,
Und fragte mich gar nach dem Knecht.	*l*	And asked about the servant.
Der Knecht, der Knecht, ich wollte …,	*n*	The servant, the servant, I want to …,
Mir kocht in den Adern das Blut,	*o*	The blood is boiling in my veins,
Ich wollte an ihm mich rächen,	*p*	I want to get back at him,
Ich wollt ich hätte den Mut.	*o*	I wish I had the courage.
Ich wollte nun … was weiss ich,	*q*	I want to … what do I know,
Ich weiss nicht wo ich bin.	*b*	I do not know where I am.
Die Mühle die dreht ihre Flügel,	*r*	The windmill turns its blades,
Der Wind der sauset darin.	*b*	The wind, it roars within.

At an *Allegro vivace* tempo, the semi-quavers in the right-hand piano part
stress the lyrical I's inner disturbance caused by the mill-maid's behaviour. The
fast pace imitates the tireless moves of the windmill's blades, which symbolises
passing time – the time the mill-maid's neighbour loses in his attempt to win
over the mill-maid. As can be seen, Kinkel's oeuvre during her Berlin time was
thematically diverse, ranging from desperate to humorous themes, some of
which can be attributed to her awareness of the music market. Her relocation to
Bonn in 1839 resulted in a biographical turn which also emerges in her Lieder.

---

[24] Chamisso's original publication includes the word 'noch' before 'dazu'. *Gedichte von Adelbert von Chamisso*, ed. Wilhelm Rauschenbusch (Berlin: Grote, 1874), 128–29.

🪲 *Early Bonn years: approaching Gottfried Kinkel and the* Maikäfer

Although not published until 1841, the Lied 'Du nah'st' (You Are Approaching, op. 15, no. 2) was composed at the very beginning of Johanna's and Gottfried's relationship.[25] It is a love song in which the beloved neither realises nor reciprocates the lyrical I's affection for him/her.

Du nah'st! (op. 15, no. 2)
  Johanna Kinkel (published 1841)

You Are Approaching!

Du nah'st! Und wie Morgenröthe	*a*	You are approaching! And my cheeks
Bebt's über die Wangen mein;	*b*	Become aurora-red;
Du gehst, und ein Thränengewölke	*a*	You are leaving, and my eyes
Dunkelt des Auges Schein!	*b*	Fill with tears.
Ich denke an dich,	*c*	When I am thinking of you,
Da steigen die Flammen hoch und licht	*d*	The flames climb up, high and bright,
Empor aus Herzens Tiefen,	*e*	From the depths of my heart,
Aber du siehst es nicht!	*d*	But you do not see it!
Melodische Seufzer tönen	*f*	Melodic sighs are sounding,
Herauf, ein voller Chor;	*g*	A full choir,
Als dir geweihete Lieder	*h*	My lips are whispering [them]
Haucht sie die Lippe hervor.	*g*	As if they were songs devoted to you.
Im Herzen, da wohnt eine Stimme	*i*	In my heart, there is a voice
Die deinen Namen spricht;	*d*	That calls your name;
Sie ruft ihn so laut, so flehend,	*k*	It calls it out loudly, pleadingly –
Ach, du vernimmst es nicht.	*d*	Alas, you do not hear it.
Der stolze Muth ist gebrochen,	*l*	My proud courage is broken,
Und Hoffnung und Lebenslust;	*m*	And so are my hope and my joy in life;
Aus tief unheilbarer Wunde	*n*	In my chest the heart is bleeding
Blutet das Herz in der Brust.	*m*	From an incurable wound.
Viel Schmerzen noch muss es erdulden,	*o*	It will have to put up with a great deal of pain
Bis Tod mitleidig es bricht.	*d*	Until it is mercifully broken by death.
Viel namenlose Schmerzen,	*p*	Nameless pain,
Wehe, du fühlst es nicht.	*d*	Woe betide, you do not feel it!

Compositionally a simple two-part Lied in G minor, this song prioritises textual content over musical craft (Ex. 3.6).

Gottfried and Johanna Kinkel's correspondence begins in March 1840. Despite an increase of affectionate feelings, the letters reveal emotional uncertainty and constant inner contradiction. Although Johanna's divorce was

[25] Klaus, *Johanna Kinkel*, 74–75; Adolf Strodtmann, *Gottfried Kinkel: Wahrheit ohne Dichtung*, 2 vols (Hamburg: Hoffmann und Campe, 1850/51), I, 230.

Ex. 3.6   'Du nah'st' (op. 15, no. 2)

* Die Fermate gilt nur für die erste Strophe

completed on 22 May 1840, the difference in religious confession and Gottfried's engagement to Sophie Boegehold put a strain on the Kinkels' relationship.

Both Johanna and Gottfried were doubtful that they could overcome socio-cultural hurdles. Kinkel had codified such doubts four months earlier in her Lied 'Die Gefangenen' (The Convicts, op. 16, no. 1), in which she set her own words (the poem was included in the *Maikäfer* journal dated 25 August 1840).[26]

Die Gefangenen (op. 16, no. 1) Johanna Kinkel (published 1841)		**The Convicts**
Der erste Tagesschimmer	*a*	The first ray of sunlight
Hellt unsres Kerkers Raum[27]	*b*	Brightens up our prison cell
Und webt um die düstern Stirnen[28]	*c*	And weaves around sorrowful foreheads
Lieblichen Morgentraum.	*b*	A morning dream of love.
Ein stiller Garten winket	*d*	A silent garden beckons
Daheim am lieben Rhein;	*e*	At home by the beloved river Rhine,
Die sinkende Sonne grüßt ihn	*f*	The setting sun greets it
Lachend mit rotem Schein.[29]	*e*	With a smiling red shine.
Und ich, und du, wir wandeln[30]	*g*	And I, and you, we ramble
Darinnen Hand in Hand,	*h*	Hand in hand in the red sunlight,
Und schau'n von der hohen Terrasse[31]	*i*	And we look down from the high terrace
Weit in das goldne Land;	*h*	Into the wide golden land,
Und Kinder sind wir wieder,	*k*	And we are like children again,
So schuldlos, glücklich und frei,	*l*	Innocent, happy, and free,
Und wissen noch nicht was Scheiden,[32]	*m*	As if we had not learnt yet
Ach, und Entsagen sei.	*l*	What parting, alas, what renouncing means.
Die fernen Segel ziehen[33]	*o*	The sails are moving past
Am blauen Ufersaum;	*b*	The blue river bank,
Wir schauen uns an voll Sehnsucht –	*p*	We look at each other full of longing –
Weh, da zerfließet der Traum.	*b*	Woe – the dream melts away.
Wir sind ja beid' gefangen,[34]	*q*	We both are imprisoned,
In Ketten sind wir ja beid';	*r*	We are both kept in chains;
Und nur im Wechselgesange	*s*	And only in our anthem
Einen wir ewiges Leid.	*r*	We unify our suffering.

[26] Johanna Kinkel, 'Der erste Tagesschimmer', in Brandt-Schwarze and others, *Der Maikäfer*, i, 94.

[27] Kinkel's original reads 'erhellt' rather than 'hellt'.

[28] Kinkel's original reads 'düstre Stirne'.

[29] Kinkel's original reads 'lächelnd' (smiling) rather than 'lachend' (laughing).

[30] The original reads 'du und ich' rather than 'ich und du'.

[31] The original does not include the word 'hohen'.

[32] The original reads 'Und wissen nicht was Entbehren | Ach, und was Scheiden sei'.

[33] The original reads 'Es ziehen die fernen Segel'.

[34] The original reads 'Im fremden Land gefangen | In Ketten sind wir Beid' (In the strange country | We are kept in chains).

In 'Die Gefangenen', the lyrical protagonist regrets that s/he cannot be with their beloved due to external circumstances. Johanna tells Gottfried about this song in a letter on 17 December 1840:

['Die Gefangenen'] is a nice song, too. Once, after a Wednesday evening, when I was still awake after midnight, a great riff tore my heart, and the song arose from its flaming wellspring. I stayed by the window on my own until late and did not stop crying.[35]

Set in A minor, this two-part Lied uses harmony as a means of semantic expression. The interplay between minor and major keys portrays the emotional turmoil expressed in the poem, and Kinkel employs an enharmonic reinterpretation before the last phrase, which embraces three significant aspects within her own biography: the river Rhine, freedom, and togetherness (bar 12, Ex. 3.7).

Ex. 3.7: Enharmonic reinterpretation in 'Die Gefangenen' (bars 10–13)

Daniela Glahn interprets Kinkel's decision to circulate this Lied in a published Lieder collection as a step towards shaping her own identity as a lovesick composer.[36] Kinkel did not publish this song immediately, but she first circulated it among her closer circle of the *Maikäferbund* in August 1840, which supports the idea that this Lied received Kinkel's thorough consideration.

---

[35] Johanna and Gottfried Kinkel, *Liebe treue Johanna! Liebster Gottit!*, i, 61. 'Es ist auch ein schönes Lied. Einmal nach einem Mittwoch Abend, wo ich um Mitternacht noch wachte, riß ein großer Spalt in mein Herz, und da sprang aus dem heißen Quell das Lied hervor. Ich blieb bis spät allein beim Fenster und weinte ohne Ende.'
[36] Glahn, *Johanna Kinkel*, 45–49.

Kinkel's duet of Wolfgang Müller von Königswinter's 'Die Fischerkinder' (The Fisherman's Children, op. 12, no. 1) refers to two lyrical protagonists who, as children, drift out to the sea and never return.

Die Fischerkinder (op. 12, no. 1) Wolfgang Müller von Königswinter (published 1840)		The Fisherman's Children[37] Translation by Sharon Krebs
Hast du von den Fischerkindern	*a*	Have you heard the old fairy tale
Das alte Märchen vernommen,	*b*	About the fisherman's children?
Die auf dem schwanken Kahne	*c*	The ones who went out to sea
Allein ins Meer geschwommen?	*b*	Alone in a rickety boat?
Sie pflückten sich Wasserrosen	*d*	They picked water-lilies for each other,
Sie sangen sich Lieder viele,	*e*	They sang each other many songs,
Sie herzten und küßten einander	*f*	They embraced and kissed each other
Im süßen Wechselspiele.	*e*	In sweet exchange.
Sie hatten den Strand verloren,	*g*	They had lost sight of the shore
Als sich der Tag entschwungen,	*h*	When the day departed,
Sie kehrten nimmer wieder,	*i*	They never returned,
Ihr Name ist verklungen.	*h*	Their names have been forgotten.
Und weißt du: wir sind die Kinder,	*k*	And do you know: we are the children,
Die Maid bin ich, du der Knabe;[38]	*l*	I am the maiden, you the lad,
Das Meer ist unsre Liebe,	*m*	The sea is our love,
Die wird uns wohl zum Grabe!	*l*	It shall likely become our grave!

This duet is characterised by frequent changes between minor and major chords, a means which the reviewer of the *Allgemeine Musikalische Zeitung* described as interplay between 'happiness and pain'.[39] While this depiction is plausible the reviewer's interpretation of it as a 'carefree interplay of the lovers' hearts' is questionable.[40] It is possible that Kinkel wanted to portray musically the unsettled emotional state of her own and her beloved Gottfried Kinkel's

---

[37] <http://www.lieder.net/lieder/get_text.html?TextId=108746> (accessed 14 March 2019).

[38] The original reads 'Die Maid Du, ich der Knabe' (You are the maid, I am the lad). Wolfgang Müller von Königswinter, 'Von den Fischerkindern', in *Dichtungen eines rheinischen Poeten*, ed. Wolfgang Müller von Königswinter, 4th edn, 6 vols (Leipzig: Brockhaus, 1871–76), i, 82.

[39] [Anon.], review of Johanna Mathieux, *Drei Duetten für weibliche Stimmen: Opus 12*, *Allgemeine Musikalische Zeitung*, 28 October 1840, 904: 'wie zwischen Freud und Leid'.

[40] Ibid., 904: 'unbesorgten Spiele der Herzen'.

minds, which was by no means 'carefree'. Her change of the gender constellation in the words encourages this reading: the original poem reads 'die Maid du, ich der Knabe' (You are the maiden, I am the lad) while Kinkel turned this line into 'Die Maid bin ich, du der Knabe' (I am the maiden, you the lad). Monica Klaus suggests that Kinkel refers to this Lied when she writes to Gottfried:

> Who feels this torture, who is able to see into the deep pit of suffering, where songs cover the bottom of the sea, and which reflects our own story. 'Ach, Die Gefangenen, Die Gefangenen', Longard shouted. But I thought of the afternoon in Obercassel, where the other Lied by C. W. Müller ended in tears, and [while improvising] I was looking for suitable harmonies.[41]

Gottfried's cancellation of his engagement with Sophie Boegehold on 19 February 1841 improved the Kinkels' future prospects, which is also reflected in Kinkel's poetry. On 23 March 1841, for example, the *Maikäfer* journal includes two optimistic poems by her, both of which draw on the beauty of life and the lyrical I's strong power of attraction to the beloved.[42] The Kinkels' marriage on 22 May 1843 marked an important cornerstone towards a secure relationship. In light of this, it is not surprising that op. 18, published in May 1843, only comprises settings of Johanna and Gottfried Kinkel as well as of Emanuel Geibel, who was the Kinkels' best man. Johanna's and Gottfried's joint work 'Am Ufer' (At the River Bank, op. 18, no. 2), was published in 1843, but the *Maikäfer* journals reveal that the words were produced only a few weeks after 'Die Gefangenen', on 29 September 1840.[43] The first verse, which was written by Johanna Kinkel, portrays the lyrical I's memories of a river bank and a tree, under which s/he used to meet his/her beloved. The second verse, written by Gottfried, foresees a positive influence on future couples because the lovers' silent songs will live on even when they have died. This *vivace* three-part setting expresses hopefulness through *ff* passages, a lively piano accompaniment, and many arpeggios.

---

[41] Johanna and Gottfried Kinkel, *Liebe treue Johanna! Liebster Gottit!*, i, 61. 'Wer fühlt diese Qual, wer sieht je in den Abgrund von Leid hinein, wo die Liedesgaben den Grund jenes Meeres bedecken, und das unser Lied ist (Lied von C. M. M.). "Ach die Gefangenen die Gefangenen" rief Longard. Aber ich dachte an den Nachmittag in Obercassel wo das andre bezeichnete Lied von C. W. M. sich in Tränen auflöste, und suchte nach vermittelnden Akkorden.'

[42] Johanna Kinkel, 'Ein träumerisch dunkles Schweigen' and 'Ich fand schon so viele Schmerzen', in Brandt-Schwarze and others, *Der Maikäfer*, i, 384–85.

[43] Johanna and Gottfried Kinkel, 'Erblick ich dort', in Brandt-Schwarze and others, *Der Maikäfer*, i, 137–38.

Am Ufer (op. 18, no. 2)
   Johanna and Gottfried Kinkel
   (published 1843)

At the River Bank

Erblick' ich dort am Ufer jene Stelle,	*a*	When I see that place at the river bank,
So dringt es bis an's Herz mir warm und helle;	*a*	My heart feels warm and bright;
Ein Liebeshauch weht über allen Lüften,[44]	*b*	The breeze of love is blowing everywhere,
Ein Liebesruf hallt wieder aus den Klüften.	*b*	A call of love echoes from the cliffs.
Mit dir einst stand ich unter jenen Bäumen,[45]	*c*	Once I stood with you under those trees,
In ihre Wipfel auf stieg unser Träumen;	*c*	Our dreams rose up to their tree tops;
Und tönet nun wie Aeolsharfen-Lieder	*d*	And now, they sound like Aeolian harp songs
Harmonisch säuselnd aus den Wipfeln wieder.[46]	*d*	And whisper harmoniously from the tree tops.
Die Bäume werden stolz nach oben streben,[47]	*e*	Proudly, the trees will grow into the air,
Wenn längst zu Staub gesunken unser Leben.	*e*	When our lives have long turned into dust.
Mit jedem Lenzgeweckten jungen Triebe,[48]	*f*	Each sapling awakening in the spring time
Leis' rauschen sie die Botschaft unsrer Liebe.	*f*	Will softly whisper the message of our love.
Daß stürmender in weicher Dämmerstunde,	*g*	May the boy and the girl kiss each other
Der Mund des Knaben häng' an Liebchens Munde	*g*	More passionately, in soft dawning hours,
Und heilig weihend ihre Brust durchfluten	*h*	May, in holy consecration, the secret fires of the long forgotten
Verscholl'nen Sängerpaars verschwieg'ne Gluten.	*h*	Singing couple flood through their hearts.

This opus number's second *vivace* setting, 'Seelige Nacht' to Johanna's words (Blessed Night, op. 18, no. 4), portrays a concrete nocturnal event, in which a loving couple bobs up and down in a boat on the river Rhine (strophes 4 and 5 were not set).[49]

[44] The original reads 'schwebt' (is floating) rather than 'weht' (is blowing).

[45] The original reads 'diesen' (these) rather than 'jenen' (those).

[46] The original reads 'Blätter' (leaves) rather than 'Wipfeln' (tree tops).

[47] The original reads 'noch aufwärts' (further up) rather than 'nach oben' (up, i.e. into the air).

[48] The original reads 'langgeranckten' (long) rather than 'Lenzgeweckten' (awoken by the spring time).

[49] Johanna Mockel, 'Noch einmal erklinget', in Brandt-Schwarze and others, *Der Maikäfer*, i, 419–20.

Seelige Nacht (op. 18, no. 4)
  Johanna Kinkel (published 1843)

Blessed Night

Noch einmal erklingt ihr Gläser,[50]	*a*	Once again, clink the glasses,
Durchglüht von dem purpurnen Wein!	*b*	Full of glowing red wine!
Ein Lied der Kraft und der Freude	*c*	A song of strength and happiness
Soll hell noch gesungen sein.	*b*	Shall be sung brightly.
Da unten vom dunkeln Strande	*d*	Down there, at the dark bank
Der Schiffer schon ruft: habt Acht,	*e*	The captain already shouts: Watch out,
Nun auf, aus dem schimmernden Saale[51]	*f*	From the gleaming hall
In die hehre, die seelige Nacht.	*e*	Let us go into the noble, blessed night.
Da liegt, wie im blauen Mantel[52]	*g*	There lies the river Rhine,
Ein schlafender König der Rhein;	*h*	Blue-coated, like a sleeping king;
Vom Himmelsgewölbe giessen	*i*	From the canopy there sparkle
Die Sterne den milden Schein.	*h*	The stars with a mild shine.
Wohl schweigen Wort und Gesänge,	*k*	No words and no singing, all silent,
Doch tief in der Seele erwacht	*e*	But this great secret of love awakens
Das hohe Geheimniß der Liebe	*l*	Deep in the soul
In der heiligen, seeligen Nacht.	*e*	During the sacred, blessed night.
So sanft auf den Spiegelfluthen[53]	*m*	The floating punt cradles us gently
Wiegt uns der schwebende Kahn;	*n*	Over the reflective floods;
Mir war, gelehnet an den Liebsten[54]	*o*	I felt, leaning against my beloved,
Als schifft' er uns himmelan.[55]	*n*	As if he shipped us skywards.
So nah dem geliebtesten Herzen	*p*	So close to the beloved's heart,
Behorcht' ich, was still es gedacht;	*e*	I listened to what it contemplated quietly;
Es schlug voll unendlicher Treue	*q*	A beat full of eternal faith
In der trauten, holdseeligen Nacht.	*e*	During the intimate, blessed night.
[not set]		[not set]
Da hob sich über die Berge	*r*	The moon arose over the hills
Der Mond, und schaut' in den Fluß;	*s*	And looked at the river;
Ihm sandten die tausend Gestirne	*t*	Thousands of stars sent
Entgegen den Liebesgruß.	*s*	Towards him the loving message.
Dem nächtlichen Freund erbebten	*u*	The waves trembled for my nocturnal friend;
Die Wellen, umspielten ihn sacht	*e*	They gently rippled about,
Wo wiederstrahlte sein Bildniß	*v*	His image that beamed from the water,
Aus der blauen, der seeligen Nacht.	*e*	During the blue, blessed night.

[50] The original reads 'erklinget' rather than 'erklingt'.

[51] The original does not include the word 'nun'.

[52] The original reads 'in' (in) rather than 'wie' (like).

[53] The original reads 'so sanft auf den spiegelnden Fluthen'.

[54] The original reads 'Theuren' (dear) rather than 'Liebsten' (beloved).

[55] The song publication reads 'schiff'', which is most likely an editorial error and has
  been corrected to 'schifft'', as is also suggested by Kinkel's original poem.

[not set]

Nun hell die Thürme am Ufer	*w*	The towers at the river bank
Der Mond mit Golde ummalt,	*x*	Were contoured by the golden moonlight,
Und manche liebliche Stelle	*y*	And many a lovely place
Von holder Erinn'rung umstrahlt.	*x*	Was illuminated by graceful memories.
Da wandtest auch du dein Auge	*z*	Then you too turned your eye
Zum Licht, und in stolzer Macht	*e*	To the light, and proudly
Erglänzten die edlen Züge	*A*	Shone your noble traits
In der hohen, der seeligen Nacht.	*e*	During the great, blessed night.

Fest Hand in Hand geschlossen,	*B*	Hand in hand,
Tief Seele der Seele vereint! – [56]	*C*	Having united our souls! –
Da fallen zwei Sterne vom Himmel,[57]	*D*	Two stars fall from the sky
Als ob es ein Engel beweint'	*C*	As if an angel had cried a
Mit leuchtenden Himmelsthränen	*E*	Bright heavenly tear about the fact that
Daß irdischen Glückes Pracht	*e*	The glory of earthly joy
Ach, immer zu bald uns entschwebet[58]	*F*	Ah, only too soon drifts away from us,
Wie die seelige, seelige Nacht.	*e*	Like the blessed, blessed night.

A similar event is thematised in the three-part setting of Kinkel's poem 'Nächtliche Fahrt' (Nocturnal Journey, op. 16, no. 2), in which the female speaker remembers a nocturnal boat journey on the river Rhine. Like Johanna and Gottfried on 4 September 1840, the couple in the poem are fascinated by the silence of the night and the gleaming river bank. While the Kinkels' boat journey ended with a dramatic crash into a ship, the Lied's 'magical punt' takes the lovers to a remote beach.

Nächtliche Fahrt (op. 16, no. 2)   Nocturnal Journey
   Johanna Kinkel (published 1841)

Wenn über Wellen und Land	*a*	When the stars shed their light
Sich giesset der Sternenschein,	*b*	Over the water and land
Dann möcht' ich fliehen zum Strand	*a*	Then I want to escape to the beach
Mit Dir, o Geliebter mein.	*b*	With you, my beloved.
Wir fänden den Nachen dort,	*c*	There, we would find the punt,
Wir stiegen vertrauend hinein;	*b*	We would step into it full of trust;
Er schaukelt uns fort und fort	*c*	It will cradle us away
Hinunter den kühlen Rhein;	*b*	Down the cool river Rhine;
Verhallt der menschliche Laut,	*d*	The human sound would trail off
Und über uns milde Ruh';	*e*	Gentle silence would settle above us;
An deinem Herzen traut,	*d*	Leaning against your dear chest,
Da schlöss' ich die Augen zu,	*e*	I would close my eyes,
Da schlöss' ich die Augen zu.	*e*	Then I would close my eyes.

[56] The original reads 'geeint' rather than 'vereint'.

[57] The original reads 'herunter' (down) rather than 'vom Himmel' (from the sky).

[58] The original reads 'immer im Flug entschwebet' (always in haste).

Bis endlich ich staunend erwacht	*f*	Until I finally wake up astonished
Im funkelnden Morgenlicht;	*g*	In the sparkling morning light;
Vorüber schon manche Nacht,	*f*	Some nights slipped by, so did
Viel Tages, ich merkt' es nicht.	*g*	Many a day, I did not notice.
Auf blauer Meeresbahn,	*h*	Down the blue water road
Vorüber manch' schimmerndem Land,	*i*	Past many a gleaming land,
Uns trägt der verzauberte Kahn	*h*	The magical punt carries us
Zum fernsten Inselstrand.	*i*	To the remote island beach.
Da steht ein Purpurgezelt,	*k*	There is a crimson shelter,
Zwei Harfen, zwei Becher Wein,	*b*	Two harps, two glasses of wine,
Verschollen die ganze Welt,	*k*	The whole world is forgotten,
Verschollen auch wir und allein,	*b*	We are lost, and alone,
Verschollen auch wir und allein.	*b*	We are lost, and alone.

A similar account of the mystic Rhineland is given in Kinkel's setting of Sebastian Longard's poem 'Rheinfahrt' (Rhine Journey, op. 16, no. 5). Kinkel's decision to set this poem testifies to her close friendship with the *Maikäfer* member Longard (1817–1892) and her fascination for Rhineland-themed poetry. Thus, it is not surprising that 'Rheinfahrt', like 'Nächtliche Fahrt', prioritises the words over compositional complexity. The song is set in F major, and the only compositional irregularities occur in bar 11: an Italian sixth chord and a melodic tritone progression in the right-hand piano part ('f'–'b''). These are reached via the tonic's submediant, D-flat major and, following conventional voice-leading rules, dissolve into the dominant chord of C major. Perhaps Kinkel wanted to emphasise the associations with the river Rhine expressed in the corresponding lines (line 6 of each verse).

Rheinfahrt (op. 16, no. 5)   **Rhine Journey**
   Sebastian Longard (published 1841)

Die Nacht kommt still gezogen	*a*	The night approaches quietly
Mit ihrem dunkeln Haar;	*b*	With its dark hair;
Es kommt ihr nachgeflogen	*a*	A host of colourful dreams
Der Träume bunte Schaar.	*b*	Follows the night.
Ich steure mit meiner Süßen	*c*	I steer with my beloved,
In die blaue Fluth hinein.	*d*	Into the blue flood.
Die Abendwinde grüßen	*c*	The evening breeze greets us
Still flüsternd im blauen Rhein.	*d*	And whispers calmly on the blue river Rhine.
Die Weidenbäume schwanken	*e*	The willow trees sway
Am Strand in stiller Ruh'.	*f*	Peacefully at the beach.
Und raunen duft'ge Gedanken	*e*	And they murmur sweet thoughts
Der spielenden Woge zu.	*f*	To the rustling wave.
Am Himmel die Sternlein gaukeln	*g*	The stars shine in the sky
Wie glänzendes Edelgestein,	*d*	Like brilliant jewels,
Die träumenden Wellen schaukeln	*g*	The dreaming waves cause
Den leuchtenden Wiederschein.	*d*	Their luminous reflection to tremble.

Da steigt in seinem Glanze	*h*	Then, the pale moon rises
Der bleiche Mond herauf,	*i*	In its lustre,
Hinter dem Bergeskranze	*h*	Behind the mountains
In heimlich stillem Lauf.	*i*	Secretly and quietly.
Hui wie er schwelgt und leuchtet	*k*	Hui, how the moon basks and shines
In seinem Zauberschein	*d*	In its magical brilliance,
Und glühende Liebe beichtet	*k*	And glowing love is confessed
Dem frischen blauen Rhein.	*d*	To the fresh blue river Rhine.

Ein treuer Buhle grüßt er	*l*	The loyal mate [the moon] greets
So recht aus vollem Muth,	*m*	Full of courage,
Und sanft erröthend küsst er	*l*	Gently blushing, he kisses
Die spiegelhelle Fluth.	*m*	The bright reflective water.
Wir aber im Traum zerflossen,	*n*	But we, dissolving in our dreams,
Schaukeln in seeliger Lust	*o*	Swing happily on the water
Und halten uns liebumschlossen,	*n*	And we embrace each other with love
Und lehnen Brust an Brust.	*o*	And we lean against each other.

Despite the Kinkels' marriage, their relationship was still characterised by a dichotomy between happiness and desperation. This is revealed in a number of Lieder which were produced within the context of the *Maikäferbund*. For instance, Kinkel set Longard's poem 'Klage' (Lamentation, op. 16, no. 6), a simple three-part Lied which deals with the lyrical I's disappointment in his/her beloved's unfaithfulness.[59] As a means of expressive emphasis, Kinkel uses contrasting dynamics and a rhythmic augmentation in this composition. While dotted rhythms are applied throughout the Lied, the second part of the third line of each verse, which – in the song – occurs three times, is set in steady and calm slurred minims and crotchets (Ex. 3.8).

Klage (op. 16, no. 6)   **Lamentation**
   Sebastian Longard (published 1841)

Ach dass du doch so ferne bist,	*a*	Alas, that you are so far away,
Dass ich dich nimmer seh',	*b*	That I cannot see you anymore,
Und dass du dort so gerne bist,	*a*	And that you like being so far away,
Tut mir im Herzen weh,	*b*	That makes my heart ache.
Tut mir im Herzen weh.	*b*	That makes my heart ache.

Als du mir gabst dein heilig Wort,	*c*	When you pledged loyalty to me,
Mir ewig treu zu sein,	*d*	When you promised to be with me forever,
Wohl war es nur ein eilig Wort	*c*	It must have been a hasty word,
So bald vorbei zu sein.	*d*	It was forgotten so soon,
So bald vorbei zu sein.	*d*	It was forgotten so soon.

[59] Sebastian Longard, 'Ach! daß du doch so ferne bist', in Brandt-Schwarze and others, *Der Maikäfer*, i, 44.

Was war ich ein unvorsichtig Kind,	*e*	What a careless child I was,
Dass ich nicht bei dir blieb!	*f*	That I did not stay with you!
Doch dass auch Schwüre flüchtig sind,	*e*	But that oaths are fleeting,
Das wusst' ich nicht, mein Lieb,	*f*	That I did not know, my love,
Das wusst' ich nicht, mein Lieb.	*f*	That I did not know, my love.

Ex. 3.8: Prolonged rhythms in the melodic line of 'Klage' (bars 8–23)

In the Geibel Lied 'Wolle keiner mich fragen' (Does Nobody Want to Ask Me, op. 18, no. 5), the lyrical I regrets his/her own desperate state of mind, as their love is not reciprocated.

Wolle keiner mich fragen (op. 18, no. 5)		**Does Nobody Want to Ask Me**
Emanuel Geibel (published 1843)		

Wolle Keiner mich fragen,	*a*	Does nobody want to ask me,
Warum mein Herz so schlägt,	*b*	Why my heart beats so fast,
Ich kann's nicht fassen, nicht sagen,	*a*	I cannot comprehend it, I cannot tell
Was mich bewegt.	*b*	What it is that moves me.
Als wie im Traume schwanken	*c*	Like drunk dreams
Trunken die Sinne mir;	*d*	My senses spin around;
Alle meine Gedanken	*c*	All my thoughts
Sind nur bei dir.	*d*	Are only concerned with you.

Ich habe die Welt vergessen,	*e*	I have forgotten about the world
Seit ich dein Auge gesehn;	*f*	Since I saw your eyes;
Ich möchte dich an mich pressen	*e*	I want to hold you to me
Und still im Kuß vergehn.	*f*	And die quietly on your kisses.
Mein Leben möcht' ich lassen,	*g*	I want to die,
Ach, um ein Lächeln vor dir,[60]	*d*	Alas, for the sake of one smile from you,
Und du – ich kann's nicht fassen –	*g*	And you – I cannot comprehend it –
Versagst es mir.	*d*	Refuse it [the smile] to me.
Ist's Schicksal, ist's dein Wille?	*h*	Is it fate? Is it your will?
Du siehst mich nicht.	*i*	You do not see me.
Nun wein' ich stille, stille,	*h*	Now I will cry quietly, quietly,
Bis das Herz mir zerbricht.	*i*	Until my heart breaks.

The two-part Lied is set in A minor. An unexpected harmonic turn occurs at the beginning of part B, which temporarily establishes the remote key of B-flat major, introduced via the tonic's submediant F major. In order to conclude the Lied with its original tonic, A minor, the last line of each verse is harmonised with a tritone progression involving the Neapolitan sixth (B-flat major–E major), which stresses the lyrical I's sorrows (Ex. 3.9).

Ex. 3.9: Harmonic progression in 'Wolle keiner mich fragen' (bars /10–13)

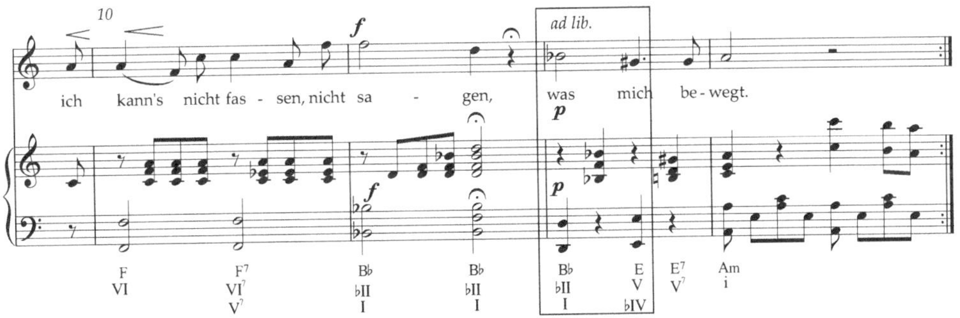

The strophic setting 'Welt, o Welt! Wie liegst du so weit!' (World, oh World! You Are so Wide!, op. 17, no. 6) to words by Gottfried Kinkel deals with a lonesome lyrical I that regrets his love not being reciprocated. Typically for a Romantic setting, such themes as magic and nature are combined with the lyrical I's heartache.[61]

---

[60] The word 'ach' (alas) is not included in the original poem. Emanuel Geibel, 'Wolle keiner mich fragen', in Geibel, *Gedichte*, 94.

[61] The composition date of this Lied is obscure, although its publication was announced in December 1847. However, it must have been composed before then,

Welt! o Welt! Wie liegst du so weit![62]
   (op. 17, no. 6)
   Gottfried Kinkel (published 1847)

World, oh World! You Are so Wide!

Auf einsam hohem Thurme	*a*	On the lonely high tower
In trüber Nebelnacht,	*b*	In the dark foggy night
Umbraust vom Wintersturme	*a*	Surrounded by blustery winter storms
Halt ich die stille Wacht.	*b*	I keep watch.
Des Lebens Sturm Gebrause	*c*	The storm of life
Berührt nicht meine Klause	*c*	Does not touch my cell,
Mit Lust und Sorg' und Leid,[63]	*d*	With happiness, sorrow and pain.
Mit Lust und Sorg' und Leid.	*d*	With happiness, sorrow and pain.

Refrain

Chorus

O sonst in wilden Strudel	*e*	Once, impatience
Riss mich die Ungeduld;	*f*	Drew me into a wild torrent;
Mir quoll des Lebens Sprudel,	*e*	Life's wellspring flowed for me,
Mich lockte Frauenhuld.	*f*	I was attracted by women's charm.
Das alles ist verdorben	*g*	This is all over now
Seit ich vor Liebe gestorben	*g*	Since I have died from heartache
In träumender Einsamkeit,	*d*	In loneliness lost in reverie,
In träumender Einsamkeit.	*d*	In loneliness lost in reverie.

Refrain

Chorus

Merlin ist fest gebunden	*h*	Merlin is bound tightly
Durch grauses Zauberwort,	*i*	By an evil spell,
Von Minnespruch umwunden	*h*	Entwined by a spell of love
In Waldes stillstem Ort.	*i*	In the quiet forest.
Es zeugt, dass er noch lebet,	*k*	The only sign of his being alive,
Sein Lied nur das durchschwebet	*k*	Is his song, which soars
Die Forsten weit und breit,	*d*	Through the forests everywhere,
Die Forsten weit und breit.	*d*	Through the forests everywhere.

Refrain: Welt, o Welt!	Chorus: World, oh World!
Wie liegst du so weit!	You are so wide!
Welt, o Welt!	World, oh World!
Wie liegst du so weit, so weit,	You are so wide, so wide,
Wie liegst du so weit!	You are so wide!

---

as Wilhelm Lübke, who left Bonn in 1846, praised Kinkel's performance of this Lied in his memoirs. 'Lübke, Wilhelm', in *Deutsches Literatur-Lexikon*, 3rd edn, x, 61.

[62] The original title of Gottfried Kinkel's poem is 'In der Winternacht' (In a Winter's Night). Gottfried Kinkel, *Gedichte* (Stuttgart/Tübingen: Cotta, 1843), 125.

[63] The original reads 'Angst' (fear) rather than 'Sorg' (sorrow).

In the stirring farewell song 'Abschied von Italien' to words by Gottfried Kinkel (Farewell from Italy, op. 16, no. 3), the lyrical I regrets having to leave Italy. The second line 'Ich weiß, du magst nicht eilen' (I know you do not want to rush) in bar 2 is contrasted with a fast-paced preceding bar, thus portraying the lyrical protagonist's inner turmoil.

Abschied von Italien (op. 16, no. 3)		**Farewell from Italy**
Gottfried Kinkel (published 1841)		
Fort nun, o Schiff!	*a*	Begone, oh ship!
Ich weiß, du magst nicht eilen,	*b*	I know you do not want to rush,
Von diesen Ufern scheidet sich's so schwer.	*c*	It is so hard to leave these shores.
Ihr Segel auf! Ich weiß, ihr wollt noch weilen,	*b*	Unfurl the sails! I know you would like to stay,
Bald schwellt euch ja des Südens Hauch nicht mehr.	*c*	The Southern breeze will fill you no more.
Aufwinde, Anker, dich an straffen Seilen,	*b*	Raise the anchor on the ropes,
Ob lau und blau dich auch umspielt das Meer,	*c*	Although the mild and blue sea plays with you,
Ach, schwerer banger Weh als ihr erleidet	*d*	Alas, the heart which has to leave Italy
Das Herz, das blutend von Italien scheidet.	*d*	Suffers badly.
Fort nun, o Schiff![64]	*a*	Begone, oh ship!
Hinauf zum rauhen Norden!	*e*	Northwards to the rough North!
Zum letzten Male glänzt des Südens Nacht.	*f*	The Southern night gleams for the last time.
Der Mond tritt hoch hervor aus Ostens Pforten,	*e*	The moon rises high from the East
Dem ewig klar die Flut entgegen lacht.	*f*	Reflected clearly in the ever-lasting smile of the sea.
Laut rauscht die See, es flammt an Schiffes Borden	*e*	The sea soughs loudly; against the ship's hull
Des Meeresleuchtens zauberhafte Pracht;	*f*	The magical shine of the sea is flaming;
Der Morgen hebt sich über Wogenschäume,	*g*	The morning rises over the foam of the waves;
Vorbei! Ach fern schon liegt das Land der Träume.	*g*	Gone! Alas, already far behind is the land of dreams.

Exhibiting the constant dualism between Johanna Kinkel's desperation and happiness, 'Allegretto: War hinaus gezogen' (Allegretto: I Went on a Ramble, op. 15, no. 6) is rather light-hearted. It is a setting of her own words.

[64] From here on, Gottfried Kinkel's published original poem differs to a great extent. It is uncertain whether Johanna Kinkel wrote the words to the second musical stanza herself, or whether she set an unpublished version of Gottfried's poem. Kinkel, *Gedichte*, 97–100.

War hinaus gezogen (op. 15, no. 6)		**I Went on a Ramble**
Johanna Kinkel (published 1841)		

War hinaus gezogen,	*a*	I went on a ramble,
Lustig singend, wälderwärts;	*b*	Happily singing, towards the woods;
Kam ein Pfeil geflogen,	*a*	An arrow came flying
Von dem schönst' gewölbten Bogen,	*a*	From the most beautifully arched bow,
Traf mir in der Brust das Herz.	*b*	It hit my heart in my chest.
Er spaltet es wohl bis zum tiefsten Grund.	*c*	It split it to its very depths.
Nie, ach, nie mehr wird's gesund.	*c*	Never, alas, never shall it recover.
Wollt' von dannen fliehen,	*d*	I wanted to escape,
Doch in Schlingen fiel der Fuß,	*e*	But my foot was caught in snares,
Die mich rückwärts ziehen.	*d*	Which pulled me backwards.
Ach vergebens ist mein Mühen,	*d*	Alas, my resolution, all in vain,
Ach vergebens mein Entschluss.	*e*	Alas, my courage, all in vain.
O Ketten der Liebe, wer reißt euch entzwei!	*f*	Oh chains of love, who would ever tear you apart!
Nie, ach, nie mehr wird ich frei.	*f*	Never, alas, never will I be free.

The playful melody and constant harmonic changes evoke an amusing tone, which helps to portray musically the lyrical I's ironic description of how s/he fell in love and cannot escape anymore.

Op. 15 also includes the humorous Goethe setting 'Lust und Qual' (Joy and Agony, op. 15, no. 4), which is about a fisherman who is unsuccessful in his attempt at winning over a young woman.

Lust und Qual[65] **(op. 15, no. 4)**		**Joy and Agony**[66]
Johann Wolfgang von Goethe (published 1841)		Translation by Sharon Krebs

Knabe saß ich, Fischerknabe,	*a*	A lad I sat, a fisher lad,
Auf dem schwarzen Fels im Meer,	*b*	Upon the black rock in the sea,
Und, bereitend falsche Gabe,	*a*	And, preparing a deceptive gift,
Sang ich lauschend rings umher.	*b*	I sang listening round about me.
Angel schwebte lockend nieder;	*c*	My fishing rod wafted temptingly downward;
Gleich ein Fischlein streift und schnappt,	*d*	Immediately a little fish darted up and snapped,
Schadenfrohe Schelmenlieder –	*c*	Gleeful, roguish songs –
Und das Fischlein war ertappt.	*d*	And the little fish was caught.

---

[65] This poem was first published in 1820. *Johann Wolfgang Goethe: Sämtliche Werke nach Epochen seines Schaffens (Münchner Ausgabe)*, xi.1.1, 478.

[66] <http://www.lieder.net/lieder/get_text.html?TextId=105850> (accessed 5 May 2019).

Ach! am Ufer, durch die Fluren,	*e*	Ah! upon the shore, through the meadows,
Ins Geklüfte bis zum Hain,[67]	*f*	Into the chasms of he grove,
Folgt' ich einer Sohle Spuren,	*e*	I followed the footsteps of a shoe,
Und die Hirtin war allein.	*f*	And the shepherdess was alone.
Blicke sinken, Worte stocken! –	*g*	Gazes fall, words fail! –
Wie ein Taschenmesser schnappt	*d*	As a pocket knife snaps shut,
Faßte sie mich in die Locken	*g*	She grasped my curls
Und das Bübchen war ertappt.	*d*	And the little lad was caught.

Weiß doch Gott mit welchem Hirten	*h*	Only God knows with which shepherd
Sie auf's neue sich ergeht!	*k*	She is sporting anew!
Muß ich in das Meer mich gürten,	*h*	I must gird myself with the sea,
Wie es sauset, wie es weht.	*i*	No matter how it roars, how it blows.
Wenn mich oft im Netze jammert	*k*	When often now I feel pity for the seething mass
Das Gewimmel groß und klein,	*f*	Of creatures, great and small, in my net,
Immer möcht' ich noch umklammert	*k*	Always I would like to be,
Ach von ihrer Armen sein![68]	*f*	Ah, clasped in her arms!

Despite a few melodic ornaments (grace notes in bars 1, 6, and 18; triplet in bar 7; and trill in bar 24), the musical interpretation of the words seems less jocular. The *Andante con moto* tempo, a skilful piano introduction and a coda including a number of arpeggios and dynamic contrasts, as well as the harmonic complexity incorporating a shift from C minor to C major, grant the Lied a serious tone.

A more positive impression is gained in 'Blaue Augen' (Blue Eyes, op. 17, no. 1, by Gottfried Kinkel) and 'Schwarze Augen' (Dark Eyes, op. 17, no. 2, by Sebastian Longard). Both Lieder were inspired by a *Maikäfer* discussion about whether blue eyes or dark eyes are more beautiful.[69] Besides the thematic and inspirational common ground, both settings feature a challenging piano accompaniment with arpeggios and ornamentation.

Blaue Augen (op. 17, no. 1)   Blue Eyes
Gottfried Kinkel (published 1847)

In ahnungsvollem Glanze	*a*	Surrounded by ominous brightness
Ruht still Neapels tiefes Meer,	*b*	Naples's deep sea rests quietly,
Es ziehn im dunklen Kranze	*a*	The dark mountain range
Die Berge schweigend rings umher.	*b*	Embraces the sea silently.

[67] The original reads 'tief' (deep) rather than 'bis' (into).

[68] The original reads 'Noch' (still) rather than 'Ach'.

[69] Brandt-Schwarze and others, *Der Maikäfer*, i, 14 and 21–23.

Drin liegt, so sagt die Kunde,	*c*	According to mythology,
Ein unbekannter Edelstein,	*d*	An unknown jewel lies in the sea,
Drum bricht aus seinem Grunde	*c*	That's why a magic bright light
Ein zauberhafter heller Schein.	*d*	Is reflected from its ground.
Und wenn du scheidest	*e*	And if you leave
Von dem süßen Lande,	*f*	The sweet land,
Bleibt dir das Herz, ach,[70]	*g*	Your heart is caught, oh,
Gefesselt dort am Strande.	*f*	And kept at the beach.
Doch mich riß los vom Wehe	*h*	But my beloved's eyes
Der Liebsten Auge wunderbar,	*i*	Pulled me away from the pain,
Und wenn hinein ich spähe,[71]	*h*	And if I look into her eyes,
Wird mir der große Zauber klar:	*i*	Then I understand the powerful magic:
Es strahlt, als ob drin schliefe,	*k*	Her eye is as bright as if
Des Zauberdemants Wunderschau,	*l*	The magic jewel slept in it,
Und wie des Meeres Tiefe,	*k*	And the graceful woman's eye
Blau ist das Aug' der holden Frau.	*l*	Is as blue as the depth of the sea.

Schwarze Augen (op. 17, no. 2)
   Sebastian Longard (published 1847)

Dark Eyes

Ach, in dem funkelnden,	*a*	O, in the bright
träumerisch dunkelnden	*a*	Dreaming dark
Aug' meiner Holden,	*b*	Eye of my beloved
Da lacht mir die herzliche	*c*	Love smiles
Liebe entgegen.	*d*	At me.
In freudiger Gluht,	*e*	With a joyous glow
Winkt mir die Sehnsucht,	*f*	The longing is waving at me,
Die bange, die schmerzliche,	*c*	Fearful, painful longing,
Und doch in schwellendem,[72]	*h*	And yet with increasing
Quellendem Muth.	*e*	Courage.
Und die unsäglichen,	*i*	And the unspeakable,
Immer beweglichen	*i*	Always active
Träume der Jugend,	*k*	Dreams of youth,
Die frischen, die prächtigen	*l*	The fresh and splendid dreams
Blühn wie im Maien	*m*	Blossom like the fragrant meadow
Die duftige Au;	*n*	In the springtime.
Ach! Und die Thränen,	*o*	Ah! And the tears,
Die heissen, die mächtigen	*l*	The hot and powerful tears
Giessen darüber	*p*	Pour over it
Den glänzenden Thau.	*n*	The glossy dew.

[70] The original does not include the word 'ach'.

[71] The original reads 'wann' rather than 'wenn'.

[72] The original reads 'voll' (full of) rather than 'in' (in/with).

Und in dem lebenden,	*q*	And in this lively,
Wonnig erbebenden	*q*	Richly trembling
Bild ihrer Augen,	*r*	Image of her eyes,
Dem wundergestaltigen,	*s*	In those fascinating eyes,
Lern ich den Zauber	*t*	I learn to understand
Der Liebe versteh'n;	*u*	The magic of love;
Wie in der Freude,	*v*	I see both fresh and powerful
Der frischen, gewaltigen,	*s*	Happiness,
So in dem Schmerz	*w*	And pain,
Und unendlichen Weh'n.	*u*	Eternal pain.

However, the major difference between the two songs is that 'Schwarze Augen' is a strophic setting with a simple formal structure, while 'Blaue Augen' is through-composed. The latter's vocal line includes ornamentation and ranges from 'c¹' to 'f²', an unusually wide range compared to other Lieder of Kinkel's. Along with many metric changes between the two parts, it points to the high standard Kinkel attributed to the dedicatee Josephine Hubar's singing.

Kinkel's Platen setting, 'Die Stimme der Geliebten' (Her Voice, op. 17, no. 4), adds another blissful note to Kinkel's op. 17. It deals with the lyrical protagonist's positive feelings in relation to his beloved.

Die Stimme der Geliebten (op. 17, no. 4)
  August von Platen (published 1847)

Her Voice[73]
  Translation by Sharon Krebs

Laß tief in dir mich lesen,	*a*	Let me read deep within you –
Verhehl' auch dies mir nicht,	*b*	Do not conceal this from me either –
Was für ein Zauberwesen	*a*	What kind of a magical spirit
Aus deiner Stimme spricht!	*b*	Speaks through your voice.
So viele Worte dringen	*c*	So many words assail
Ans Ohr uns ohne Plan,	*d*	Our ears without design
Und während sie verklingen,	*c*	And when they have died away,
Ist alles abgetan!	*d*	Nothing remains!
Doch drängt auch nur von ferne	*e*	But if even from a distance
Dein Ton zu mir sich	*f*	The sound of your voice finds its way
her,		to me,
Behorch' ich ihn so gerne,	*e*	I listen to it so gladly,
Vergess ich ihn so schwer.	*f*	I find it so difficult to forget.
Ich bebe dann, entglimme	*g*	I tremble then, come alight
Von allzu rascher Glut:	*h*	With all too rapid ardour;
Mein Herz und deine Stimme	*g*	My heart and your voice
Verstehn sich gar zu gut!	*h*	Understand each other too well!

[73] <https://www.lieder.net/lieder/get_text.html?TextId=42243> (accessed 27 March 2020).

The arpeggio piano accompaniment and the tempo marking, *Adagio*, enable a thoughtful emphasis of each single word, and the slow-pace instrumental underlay incorporates a dense harmonic rhythm (Ex. 3.10). A French augmented sixth chord occurs as early as in bar 2; bar 13, which introduces the most meaningful line, includes both a German and another French augmented sixth. The *rallentando* in the same bar places further emphasis on this line. Kinkel's affinity for augmented sixth chords resurfaces in bar 18, in which a pre-cadential German augmented sixth prepares the Lied's conclusion.

Ex. 3.10: 'Die Stimme der Geliebten' (op. 17, no. 4)

Later Bonn years: the 1848/49 revolution

Published in 1848, Johanna Kinkel's op. 19 seems to sum up the Kinkels' situation during that time. It includes three political settings to Gottfried Kinkel's words; Heine's farewell song 'Abschied'; 'Die Mandoline' by Wilhelm Seibt; and Kinkel's 'Liebesmacht' (The Power of Love, op. 19, No. 3).[74] One of Kinkel's later works, 'Liebesmacht' reflects her personal development on different levels. The vocal line is unusually challenging with a great deal of ornamentation, and the poetry, containing a great number of internal assonances, seems further developed than Kinkel's earlier poetry. Furthermore, the desperate confusion and playful boldness of Kinkel's earlier settings have been replaced by profound sorrow, as the lyrical I regrets that his/her beloved is not able to love, although, physically, the beloved is able to achieve the most amazing things.

Liebesmacht (op. 19, no. 3) Johanna Kinkel (published 1848)		**The Power of Love**
Das Bächlein magst du dämmen	*a*	You may dam the stream
Wenn überschwillt die Fluth;	*b*	If it is flooded;
Gebietend magst du hemmen	*a*	You may put out
Der Flammen rothe Gluth.	*b*	The red glow of flames.
Den Falken magst du zähmen,	*c*	You may tame the falcon,
Des Adlers Schwinge lähmen;	*c*	You may clip the eagle's wings,
Doch eigen stilles Denken,	*d*	But, to lead your own quiet thoughts
Und Herz und Liebe lenken	*d*	And your heart and love,
Ach, das vermagst du nicht.	*e*	Alas, that you are not able to do.
Dem fernen Thal vertraust du	*f*	You do not entrust the remote valley
Kein Samenstäubchen an;	*g*	With a single grain of seed;
Und doch im Lenze schaust du	*f*	And yet you will look at the meadow full of flowers
Voll Blumen reich den Plan.	*g*	In the springtime.
So keimt aus Herzensgrunde	*h*	Thus, from the depths of your heart,
Die holde Liebeskunde;	*h*	There springs graceful love;
Der Rosen Fülle wecken,	*i*	But to waken the wealth of the roses,
Und dann mit Schnee sie decken,	*i*	And then cover them with snow,
Nein, das vermagst du nicht.	*e*	No, that you are not able to do.

Kinkel's strophic setting of the *Maikäfer* member Wilhelm Seibt's poem 'Die Mandoline' (The Mandolin, op. 19, no. 1) centres on a similar issue. The seemingly female lyrical protagonist feels abandoned by its player, so it keeps its lonesome pain to itself.

---

[74] Wilhelm Seibt (1823–1891) was a teacher at a Frankfurt high school until 1881. In 1843, his prose and theoretical writings were published regularly in the *Maikäfer* journal. *Deutsches Literatur-Lexikon,* 3rd edn, xvii, 339.

Die Mandoline (op. 19, no. 1)		**The Mandolin**	
Wilhelm Seibt (published 1848)			
Ich bin der Mandoline gleich,	*a*	I feel like a mandolin	
Die dort im Saal vergessen steht;	*b*	Which has been left and forgotten in the hall;	
An wunderbaren Klange reich,	*a*	Rich in wonderful sound	
Der tief zu Herzen geht.	*b*	Which goes straight to the heart.	
Doch alles bleibt in ihrer Brust,	*c*	But all the sounds stay in its body,	
Der Lieder reiche Zauberglut,	*d*	The rich magic of the songs,	
Und alles Weh, und alle Lust,	*c*	And all pain, and all pleasure,	
Denn ach, ihr Meister ruht.	*d*	Because, alas, its player rests.	

The Heine setting 'Abschied' (Farewell, op. 19, no. 5) tells the story of a lyrical I who has to leave his home and his beloved. An autobiographical anchoring is not immediately obvious here, although Kinkel's letters reveal that she regretted her husband's absence in the late 1840s.

Abschied (op. 19, no. 5)		**Farewell**[75]	
Heinrich Heine (published 1848)		Adapted from Emily Ezust	
Schöne Wiege meiner Leiden,	*a*	Lovely cradle of my sorrows,	
Schönes Grabmal meiner Ruh',	*b*	Lovely tombstone of my rest,	
Schöne Stadt, wir müssen scheiden, –	*a*	Lovely town, we must part, –	
Lebe wohl! ruf' ich dir zu.	*b*	Farewell! I call to you.	
Lebe wohl, du heil'ge Schwelle,	*c*	Farewell, you holy threshold,	
Wo da wandelt Liebchen traut;	*d*	Across which my darling would tread;	
Lebe wohl! du heil'ge Stelle,	*c*	Farewell! you sacred spot	
Wo ich sie zuerst geschaut.	*d*	Where I first saw her.	
Hätt' ich dich doch nie gesehen,	*e*	I wish I had never seen you,	
Schöne Herzenskönigin!	*f*	Lovely queen of my heart!	
Nimmer wär' es dann geschehen,	*e*	Never would it then have happened,	
Daß ich jetzt so elend bin.	*f*	That I am now so wretched.	
Nie wollt' ich dein Herze rühren,	*g*	I never wished to touch your heart,	
Liebe hab' ich nie erfleht;	*h*	I never begged for love;	
Nur ein stilles Leben führen	*g*	All I wished was to lead a quiet life	
Wollt' ich, wo dein Odem weht.	*h*	Where your breath could stir me.	
Doch du drängst mich selbst von hinnen,	*i*	Yet you yourself pushed me away from you,	
Bittre Worte spricht dein Mund;	*k*	With bitter words at your lips;	
Wahnsinn wühlt in meinen Sinnen,	*i*	Madness fills my senses,	
Und mein Herz ist krank und wund.[76]	*k*	And my heart is sick and wounded.	

[75] <http://www.lieder.net/lieder/get_text.html?TextId=7793> (accessed 29 March 2020).

[76] Heine's original reads 'das' (the) rather than 'mein' (my). Heinrich Heine, 'Lebewohl', in *Buch der Lieder von Heinrich Heine* (Hamburg: Hoffmann und Campe, 1827), 42–43, cited after *Heinrich Heine: Historisch-Kritische Gesamtausgabe*.

Und die Glieder matt und träge	*l*	And my limbs are heavy and sluggish;
Schlepp' ich fort am Wanderstab,	*m*	I'll drag myself forward, leaning on my staff,
Bis mein müdes Haupt ich lege	*l*	Until I can lay my weary head
Ferne in ein kühles Grab.	*m*	In a cool and distant grave.

The reviewer of the *Neue Zeitschrift für Musik* bemoaned that 'Heine's pain of farewell is not noticeable', seemingly ignoring Kinkel's compositional semantics.[77] While Kinkel sets a chromatic descent to the third line of each stanza (bars 17–21), a pedal point on the note 'c' is used to indicate the longing for stability and peace (bars 24–32, Ex. 3.11).

Ex. 3.11: Chromatic descent and pedal point in 'Abschied' (bars 17–32)[78]

[77] [Anon.], review of Johanna Kinkel, *Opus 19* (1848), *Neue Zeitschrift für Musik*, 2 April 1849, 146. 'Vom Abschiedsschmerz eines Heine aber will nichts verlauten.'

[78] In the original publication, the slur in bars 31–32 in the piano right hand is notated from 'd¹' (bar 31) to 'f' (first note, bar 32). However, the voice-leading and melodic flow suggest that this might be an editorial mistake as the slur combining 'f' (first beat, bar 31) and 'f' (first beat, bar 32) would make more sense.

Kinkel's indefatigable support of her husband in spite of her own personal struggles is echoed in her settings of Gottfried's words. Her last Lieder opus, op. 21, only compiles Johanna and Gottfried Kinkel's own poems, among which are 'Lied aus dem "Spessarttraum"' and 'Des Lehnsmanns Abschied' (both by Gottfried Kinkel), and 'Jugenderinn'rung' (by Johanna Kinkel). The poem in 'Lied aus dem "Spessarttraum"' (Song from the 'Spessarttraum', op. 21, no. 1) originates from Gottfried's tale *Spessarttraum* (Dream of the Spessart), which tells the story of a young boy who is raised by a chaplain. The chaplain introduces the boy to literature, which attracts the boy's curiosity and evokes a strong longing to see a female person. He then starts singing this song.

Lied aus dem 'Spessarttraum' (op. 21, no. 1) Gottfried Kinkel (published 1851)		**Song from the 'Spessart Dream'**
Welle, darfst du nimmer weilen,	*a*	Wave, why are you never able to rest,
Nie zu mir in Liebe glühn?	*b*	Why do you never glow with love for me?
Sprich, was zwingt dich fort zu eilen	*a*	Tell me, what is it that forces you to rush
Aus des Waldes trautem Grün?	*b*	Out of the lovely green forest?
Lass in Liebe ungemessen	*c*	In endless and unmeasurable love
An die heiße Brust dich pressen!	*c*	Let me hold you!
Fass' ich dich, lass' ich Dich nimmer von hier.	*d*	If I hold you, I will never let you go.
Wehe, du fliehst und ich lodre nach dir.	*d*	Alas, if you escape I will long for you.
Hindin, braune, holde, schlanke,	*e*	Doe, dark, graceful, slender,
Lockt dich so die Waldesnacht?	*f*	Does the dark forest attract you?
Warum meidest du die Schranke,	*e*	Why do you avoid the gate
Drin mein lieber Garten lacht?[79]	*f*	Behind which my garden smiles at you?
Lass mit holdem Wort dir schmeicheln,	*g*	Let me flatter you with nice words,
Lass dich kosen, lass dich streicheln!	*g*	Let me love you, let me pet you!
Wehe, sie flieht in geflügelter Zier,[80]	*d*	Alas, she escapes gracefully,
Ach, und sie lässt mich, den Einsamen, hier.	*d*	Alas, and she leaves me, the lonesome one, behind.
Keine Wellen, keine Hinden[81]	*h*	No waves, no does
Gleichen doch dem holden Bild,	*i*	Match the graceful image,
Das ich nie vermocht zu finden,	*h*	Which I have never been able to find,
Doch im Herzen steht es mild.	*i*	But I carry it gently in my heart.
Oft wohl mein' ich, aus den weiten	*k*	Often, I think she would walk out of the
Wäldern müsst es grüßend schreiten.	*k*	Wide forest, greeting me.
Selige Schönheit, enthülle dich mir!	*d*	Blessed beauty, reveal yourself to me!
Weh, du zerrinnst und ich lodre nach dir.	*d*	Alas, you dissolve and I long for you.

[79] The original reads 'die' (the) rather than 'drin' (in which).

[80] The original reads 'Wehe Du fliehst in geflügelter Zier | Ach und Du lässest mich Einsamen hier'.

[81] The original reads 'Welle' (wave) rather than 'Wellen' (waves).

Contrary to 'Die Mandoline', in which the lyrical I is longing to be loved by a particular person, 'Lied aus dem "Spessarttraum"' does not refer to a real beloved. Nevertheless, the theme of a lonesome lyrical I's disappointment at not being able to find the perfect partner might reflect Johanna Kinkel's own situation.

A sense of loneliness also surfaces in the other two love songs included in Kinkel's op. 21, 'Des Lehnsmanns Abschied', and 'Jugenderinn'rung'. Kinkel set 'Des Lehnsmanns Abschied' (Soldier's Farewell, op. 21, no. 6) twice – it was also published singly by the Mainz publishing house Schott ('Ritters Abschied').

Des Lehnsmanns Abschied (op. 21, no. 6)
  Gottfried Kinkel (published 1851)

Soldier's Farewell

Weh, dass wir scheiden müssen,	*a*	Alas, that we must part,
Lass dich noch einmal küssen;	*a*	One more parting kiss I give you;
Ich muss an Kaisers Seiten	*b*	I must, at the Emperor's side,
Ins falsche Welschland reiten:	*b*	Ride into treacherous Italy:
Fahr wohl, fahr wohl, mein armes Lieb!	*c*	Farewell, farewell, my poor true love!
Ich werd auf Maienauen	*d*	I will never again
Dich niemals wieder schauen,	*d*	See you on spring meadows,
Der Feinde grimm'ge Scharen[82]	*e*	The troops of the ferocious foe
Sind kommen angefahren:	*e*	Are advancing:
Fahr wohl, fahr wohl, mein armes Lieb!	*c*	Farewell, farewell, my poor true love!
Ich denk an dich mit Sehnen,	*f*	I think of you with longing,
Gedenk an mich mit Tränen;	*f*	Think of me in tears;
Wenn meine Augen brechen,	*g*	When my eyes shut for the last time
Will ich zuletzt noch sprechen:	*g*	I shall whisper once more:
Fahr wohl, fahr wohl, mein armes Lieb![83]	*c*	Farewell, farewell, my poor true love!

Considering Kinkel's inscription *Volkslied* (folk-song) underneath the title within her op. 21, it is not surprising that she published this Lied individually and thus enabled a rapid distribution. Indeed, Kinkel's choral version became an established part of the repertoire for male choral singing during the second half of the nineteenth century.[84] The words were versified by Gottfried Kinkel and originate from his Liederspiel *Friedrich Barbarossa in Suza*.

---

[82] In both of Kinkel's Lieder publications, this line reads 'grimme' rather than 'grimm'ge'.

[83] In the single publication, the word 'armes' (poor) is used rather than 'treues' (faithful).

[84] This is evident when searching for publications of Johanna Kinkel's 'Ritters Abschied' in the Hofmeister catalogue. Especially the years between 1882 and 1900 feature a great number of publications of this Lied. Glahn mentions Melanie

In 'Jugenderinn'rung' (Youthful Memory, op. 21, no. 5), the male lyrical I recalls how he sang forgotten songs with his beloved. The notion of a mature grown-up remembering his/her happy past with their beloved might hint at Johanna Kinkel's own biography. In the last verse, the lyrical protagonist regrets the love being over, whereas a rhythmic adjustment, evoked by a changing piano accompaniment, portrays the lyrical I's new lifestyle. The Lied begins with a flowing left-hand piano part, but, introduced by a linear descent, changes to a sedate, almost melancholic musical texture (Ex. 3.12).

Jugenderinn'rung (op. 21, no. 5)		**Youthful Memory**
Johanna Kinkel (published 1851)		

Alt verscholl'ne Lieder steigen	*a*	Forgotten old songs come to my mind
Mir empor mit frischem Klang;	*b*	With a fresh sound;
Wieder tönt der muntre Reigen	*a*	Again, the carousers' happy roundelay
Und der Zecher Rundgesang.	*b*	Resounds.
Mich fasst es mit Lust und Schmerzengewalt,	*c*	Joy and pain grasp me,
Mit Lust und mit Schmerzengewalt.	*c*	Joy and pain.
O goldene Zeit, o goldene Zeit,	*d*	Oh golden times, oh golden times,
Wie schwandest du bald,	*c*	How swiftly you disappeared,
Wie schwandest du bald.	*c*	How swiftly you disappeared.
Dort bin ich hinausgezogen	*e*	There I went out
Mit der Jäger wildem Schwarm;	*f*	With the swarm of the wild hunters;
Damals spannt' den schweren Bogen	*e*	Back then, my strong arm still
Noch so leicht mein starker Arm.	*f*	Drew the heavy bow so easily.
Des Jagdhorns Ruf umsonst mir erschallt	*c*	Now the hunting call sounds for me,
Umsonst, ach umsonst mir erschallt.	*c*	Ah, in vain it sounds for me.
O goldene Zeit, o goldene Zeit,	*d*	Oh golden times, oh golden times,
Wie schwandest du bald,	*c*	How swiftly you disappeared,
Wie schwandest du bald.	*c*	How swiftly you disappeared.
Dort die Schwelle meiner Lieben,	*h*	There is my beloved's door,
Wo ich nächtliche Lieder sang.	*i*	Where I used to sing nocturnal songs.
Kaum ein Hauch ist mir geblieben	*h*	Barely a breath remains
Von dem reichen Liebesklang.	*i*	Of the rich sounds of love.
Mich grüßt noch im Träumen die holde Gestalt,	*c*	My love is greeting me even in my dreams,
Die holde, die holde Gestalt.	*c*	My love, my graceful love.
O goldene Zeit, o goldene Zeit,	*d*	Oh golden times, oh golden times,
Wie schwandest du bald,	*c*	How swiftly you disappeared,
Wie schwandest du bald.	*c*	How swiftly you disappeared.

Unseld's interpretation of this Lied as a farewell song, mostly sung by male soldiers for their female partners. See Glahn, *Johanna Kinkel*, 280–81, 286 and 295.

Ex. 3.12: Rhythmic change and linear descent in 'Jugenderinn'rung' (bars 23–26)

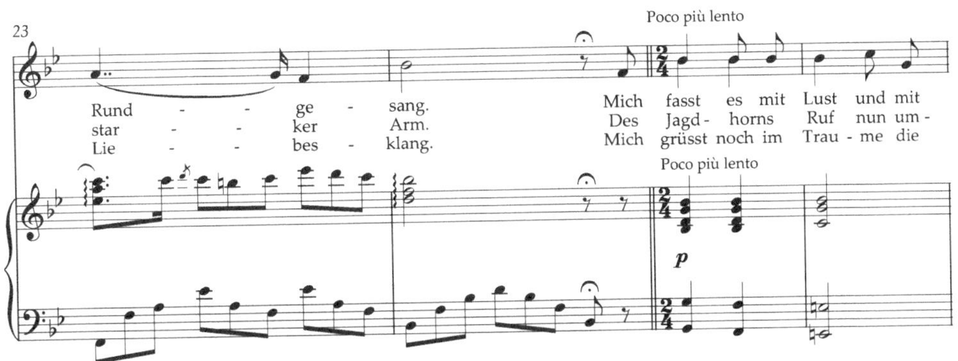

Reminiscent of Kinkel's earlier works, the piano accompaniment takes priority. Interpretatively, this compositional flashback might allude to Kinkel's own memories of her time as a young woman. Kinkel did not publish any further Lieder after op. 21, but the lonesome predictions voiced in 'Jugenderinn'rung' remained valid for one who had to share her husband's time and love with different public strands up until the end of her life.

ఠ *Epilogue: Kinkel's love songs as autobiographical documents*

Autobiographical elements in Kinkel's love songs can be traced on different levels. Kinkel's progression in compositional style reflects her musical development, a biographical indicator, which is also asserted by Sharon Krebs in her study of Kinkel's contemporary Josephine Lang's Köstlin settings.[85] Josephine Lang referred to her songs as her diary, an aspect which led Aisling Kenny to conclude that Lang's songs 'were not created for entertainment but because of a deep-rooted need to create'.[86] In a similar way to Lang's Lieder, Kinkel's love songs arose out of a psychological motivation, although Kinkel never explicitly referred to her songs as a diary. However, her letter to Gottfried, in which she explains how she wrote the song 'Die Gefangenen', reveals strong parallels

---

[85] Sharon Krebs, cited after Aisling Kenny, 'Josephine Lang's Goethe, Heine and Uhland Lieder: Contextualizing her Contribution to Nineteenth-Century German Song' (unpublished PhD dissertation, National University of Ireland, Maynooth, 2010), 196.

[86] Harald and Sharon Krebs, *Josephine Lang: Her Life and Songs* (Oxford: Oxford University Press, 2007), 8; and Kenny, 'Josephine Lang's Goethe', 196.

between her compositions and a diary. Additionally, Gottfried Kinkel's perception of his beloved and her songs ('Du nah'st!') indicates Johanna's deep personal attachment to her own songs. In light of this, Kinkel's love songs are indeed anchored autobiographically. Many of Kinkel's Berlin publications tell of an unhappy partnership or a longing for love. Furthermore, many Lieder dealing with themes centring on water, boat journeys, and the river Rhine ('Nächtliche Fahrt', 'Am Ufer', 'Seelige Nacht', 'Allegretto', 'Rheinfahrt') allude to Kinkel's fascination for her home and the significance of the Kinkels' boating accident in September 1840. Perhaps the blurred boundaries between Kinkel's 'inventive' and 'inventory self' emerge here, as the anecdote of the boating accident might be slightly dramatised in Kinkel's writings. Nevertheless it constitutes a momentous life event, which she also processed in her music. Finally, allusions to Johanna's fears, doubts, and sorrows disclosed in her letters to friends and, later, to Gottfried recur in her Lieder throughout her life (for instance, 'Vorüberfahrt', 'Verlornes Glück', 'Der Kuss', 'Liebesmacht', 'Jugenderinn'rung', 'Des Lehnsmanns Abschied'). In this respect, Kinkel's late love songs reveal emotions whose intensity might have otherwise remained unstated, as Kinkel did not always voice her emotions publicly. More importantly, however, the autobiographical scope of Kinkel's Lieder, and in addition to this their therapeutic value, means that Kinkel's compositional activity might have been the reason why she managed to juggle the many challenges she faced until her death in 1858 – an aspect which points to the biographical importance of Kinkel's compositions even to Kinkel herself during her lifetime.

CHAPTER 4

Political songs

↛ *Rhineland settings*

THE publisher J. M. Dunst opens the first volume of his Lieder collection *Rhein-Sagen und Lieder* (Rhine-Myths and Songs) with a patriotic note to the reader:

> Among all German lands, the educated traveller prefers the beautiful Rhineland. The mellow banks of the river Rhine are surrounded by nature's poetic magic. [...] Therefore, the Rhineland has fascinated the greatest poets and singers in all times. Many of these Rhineland myths and song collections [...] have been widely published. However, very little has been done in order to embellish this poetry musically. This publishing company aims to fulfil the desire of many singers by putting together such a Lieder collection. [...] We want to offer to our singers a truly national compilation, which will outlive the flood of novelties and which will be of great value even in the far future. May our collection increase the Rhinelander's love of his homeland, and may it remind the distant Rhinelander of his happy moments at the bright river banks of the Rhine.[1]

The title page promotes different facets of the Rhineland: an old man symbolises wisdom and poetic wealth; a harpist represents the artistic strand; a graceful woman illustrates beauty and skilfulness; a hunter reflects the wide

---

[1] Note to the reader in *Rhein-Sagen und Lieder*, ed. J. M. Dunst (Bonn: Dunst, 1838), 1. 'Vor allen deutschen Ländern wallt der gebildete Reisende gern zum prächtigen Rhein. [...] daher auch die Rheingegend die größten Dichter und Sänger aller Zeiten begeisterte. Viele dieser Rheinsagen und Liedersammlungen [...] sind weit verbreitet und in aller Händen. Die Musik hat indessen wenig getan, diese Poesien zu verschönern, und will die Verlagshandlung den Wünschen so vieler Freunde des Gesanges gerne entgegen kommen, indem sie sich die Aufgabe stellt, eine solche Sammlung zu gestalten. Der Zusage der vorzüglichsten jetzt lebenden Komponisten [...] bereits gewiss, soll hier den Gesangfreunden ein echt nationales Werk angeboten werden, das, unverdrängt durch die Flut der Neuigkeiten, auch in der fernsten Zeit seinen Wert behält. Es möge unsere Sammlung Rheinsagen- und Lieder die Liebe des Rheinländers zum Heimatlande erhöhen, so wie dem frühen Pilger zum Rhein in der Ferne das Andenken der an seinen blühenden Ufern erlebten glücklichen Momente wieder hervorzaubern.'

Fig. 4.1   Title page of *Rhein-Sagen und Lieder*, first volume

landscape; and a ruler demonstrates the Rhinelanders' confidence and pride (Fig. 4.1).

Kinkel's Rhineland Lieder, with their folk-like themes, underline the impression of *Rhein-Sagen und Lieder* as a patriotic collection for the wider public. Alongside such famous nineteenth-century composers as Carl Loewe, Heinrich Marschner, and Felix Mendelssohn, Dunst published in his first volume Kinkel's settings of Heine's 'Der Rheinstrom' (The River Rhine) and 'Kölln' (Cologne). Both Lieder refer to unique Rhineland appearances as an allegory for the lyrical I's beloved. In 'Der Rheinstrom', the lyrical protagonist sees in the river's characteristics his beloved's malice, a tone which points to Heinrich Heine's fondness for ironic turns. The lyrical I in 'Kölln' associates his beloved with the Cologne Cathedral image of the Virgin Mary.[2]

[2] For further elaborations on irony in Heinrich Heine's poems 'Kölln' and 'Rheinstrom' see my own article 'Johanna Kinkel's Political Art Songs'.

Der Rheinstrom
Heinrich Heine (published 1838)

Berg und Burgen schau'n herunter	*a*
In den spiegelhellen Rhein;	*b*
Und mein Schiffchen segelt munter	*a*
Rings umglänzt von Sonnenschein.	*b*

Ruhig seh' ich zu dem Spiele *c*
Goldner Wellen kraus bewegt; *d*
Still erwachen die Gefühle *c*
Die ich tief im Busen hegt. *d*

Freundlich grüßend und verheißend *e*
Lockt hinab des Stromes Pracht; *f*
Doch ich kenn' ihn, oben gleissend *e*
Bringt sein Inn'res Tod und Nacht. *f*

Oben Lust, im Busen Tücken, *g*
Strom, du bist der Liebsten Bild! *h*
Die kann auch so freundlich nicken, *g*
Lächelt auch so fromm und mild. *h*

The River Rhine[3]
Translation by Emily Ezust

a Mountains and castles gaze down
b Into the mirror-bright Rhine,
a And my little boat sails merrily,
b The sunshine glistening around it.

c Calmly I watch the play
d Of golden, ruffled waves surging;
c Silently, feelings awaken in me
d That I have kept deep in my heart.

e With friendly greetings and promises,
f The river's splendor beckons;
e But I know it – gleaming above
f It conceals within itself death and night.

g Above, pleasure; at heart, malice;
h Oh river, you are the very image of my beloved!
g She can nod with just as much friendliness,
h Also smiling so devotedly and gently.

Kölln
Heinrich Heine (published 1838)

Im Rhein, im heiligen[5] Strome, *a*
Da spiegelt sich in den Well'n, *b*
Mit seinem großen Dome *a*
Das große heilige Köln. *b*

Im Dom da steht ein Bildnis, *c*
Auf goldenem Leder gemalt; *d*
In meines Lebens Wildnis *c*
Hat's freundlich hinein gestrahlt. *d*

Es schweben Blumen und Englein *e*
Um unsre liebe Frau; *f*
Die Augen, die Lippen, die Wänglein, *e*
Die gleichen der Liebsten genau. *f*

Cologne[4]
Translation by Paul Hindemith

a In the Rhine, in the holy stream
b Is it mirrored in the waves,
a With its great cathedral,
b That great, holy city Cologne.

c In the cathedral stands an image,
d Painted on golden leather;
c Into the wildness of my life
d Has it shone, friendly.

e Flowers and little cherubs hover
f Around our beloved Lady;
e The eyes, the lips, the cheeks –
f They match my beloved's exactly.

---

[3] <http://www.lieder.net/lieder/get_text.html?TextId=7455> (accessed 20 April 2019).

[4] <http://www.lieder.net/lieder/get_text.html?TextId=7663> (accessed 20 April 2019).

[5] Like Robert Franz and Robert Schumann, Kinkel used the word 'schönen' (beautiful) rather than 'heiligen' (holy). This corresponds with the Gesamtausgabe, while the Hoffmann und Campe edition reads 'heiligen'. Heine, 'Im Rhein, im schönen Strome', in *Buch der Lieder von Heinrich Heine* (Hamburg: Hoffmann und Campe, 1827), 120.

Kinkel's two Lieder 'Der Rheinstrom' and 'Kölln' fulfil two typical Romantic criteria: they combine the themes of Rhineland patriotism and love, and they confirm Dunst's representation of the Rhineland as a friendly, bright and mystic region. Vera Lampert stresses that there are several reasons why folk-like elements were popular among nineteenth-century artists: national feelings (among composers and the target group); the entertainment factor; commissions for certain purposes and occasions; pedagogical purposes; and personal reasons.[6] All these aspects can be related to Kinkel's Rhineland songs. However, did her compositional style conform to Dunst's promised memorability and cultural stamina of these Lieder? Oswald Lorenz, in *Neue Zeitschrift für Musik*, stressed the 'freshness' and 'charm' of Kinkel's two contributions to the first volume. Without providing details, he identifies a 'tender feminine hand' in the piano accompaniment of 'Kölln'.[7] Musically, the greatest challenge in 'Kölln' is its harmonic constitution, which is evoked by chromaticism in both the piano and the vocal line. 'Kölln' also features a change of the piano accompaniment at the third musical stanza when the lyrical I ponders on the similarities between Cologne Cathedral and his beloved. The accompanimental changes are supported by a *decrescendo*, perhaps a feature Lorenz identified in his review as 'feminine'. The review provides no detail on 'Der Rheinstrom'. Both Lieder feature quite complex harmonic designs and challenging piano accompaniments, which question their suitability as popular folk songs. However, their simple melodic progressions and recognisable rhythms increase their memorability.

Dunst's third volume includes Kinkel's varied strophic song 'Die beiden Brüder' (The Two Brothers), another Heine setting, which is based on the myth of the two adjacent Rhineland castles Sternberg and Liebenstein. The Lied tells the story of two brothers who quarrel over a maiden. As the maiden cannot decide whom she would prefer, the two men fight out the courtship. During their fight, they both fall down a mountain and die. According to the myth, the brothers fight in the valley at midnight even many centuries later. The blood-curdling atmosphere is symbolised through an *Andantino* tempo and piano tremolos.

---

[6] Vera Lampert, 'Nationalism, Exoticism, or Concessions to the Audience?: Motivations behind Bartók's Folksong Settings', *Studia Musicologica Academiae Scientiarium Hungaricae*, 47 (2006), 337–43 (343).

[7] Oswald Lorenz, review of *Rhein-Sagen und Lieder*, *Neue Zeitschrift für Musik*, 7 February 1840, 47. '"Der Rheinstrom" und "Köln", welche so wie der im 3ten Hefte befindliche Gesang von dieser Componistin und demselben Dichter, "Die beiden Brüder", durch Frische und Anmuth reizen und von denen namentlich die Begleitung des zweiten die zarte weibliche Hand verräth.'

Die beiden Brüder
  Heinrich Heine (published 1839)

The Two Brothers[8]
  Translation adapted from Emily Ezust

Oben auf der Bergesspitze	*a*	Up on the summit of the mountain
Liegt das Schloß in Nacht gehüllt;	*b*	The castle stands shrouded in night;
Doch im Thale leuchten Blitze,	*a*	But in the valley, lightning blazes
Helle Schwerter klirren wild.	*b*	And bright swords clash savagely.
Das sind Brüder, die dort fechten	*c*	It is brothers fencing
Grimmen Zweikampf, wutentbrannt.	*d*	A grim duel there, enraged with anger.
Sprich, warum die Brüder rechten	*c*	Tell me, why are brothers fighting
Mit dem Schwerte in der Hand?	*d*	With sword in hand.
Gräfin Lauras Augenfunken	*e*	Countess Laura's sparkling eyes
Zündeten den Bruderstreit.[9]	*f*	Ignited the brothers' strife:
Beide glühen liebestrunken	*e*	Both smoulder, intoxicated with love,
Für die adlig holde Maid.	*f*	For the noble, lovely maid.
Aber welchem von den beiden	*g*	But towards which of the two
Wendet sich ihr Herze zu?	*h*	Does her heart lean?
Kein Ergrübeln kann's entscheiden,[10]	*g*	No musing can decide it;
Schwert heraus, entscheide du!	*h*	So out comes the sword – you shall decide!
Und sie fechten kühn verwegen,	*i*	And they fight on keenly, foolhardily,
Hieb auf Hiebe niederkracht's.	*k*	Blow upon blow cracking down.
Hütet euch, ihr wilden Degen.	*i*	Beware, you savage swordsmen.
Grausig Blendwerk schleichet nachts.	*k*	Grisly illusion creeps about at night.
Wehe! Wehe! blut'ge Brüder!	*l*	Woe! Woe! Bloody brothers!
Wehe! Wehe! blut'ges Tal!	*m*	Woe! Woe! Bloody valley!
Beide Kämpfer stürzen nieder,	*l*	Both fighters fall,
Einer in des andern Stahl. –	*m*	Each upon the other's steel.
Viel Jahrhunderte verwehen,	*n*	Many centuries drift past,
Viel Geschlechter deckt das Grab;	*o*	Graves cover many generations;
Traurig von des Berges Höhen	*n*	Mournfully from the heights of the mountain
Schaut das öde Schloß herab.	*o*	The deserted castle looks down.

---

8 <http://www.lieder.net/lieder/get_text.html?TextId=7692> (accessed 6 June 2019).

9 Heine's original poem reads 'Brüderstreit' rather than Bruderstreit; this may be an editorial error in Kinkel's version. Heinrich Heine, 'Zwei Brüder', in *Buch der Lieder von Heinrich Heine*, 52.

10 Kinkel's version reads 'Ergrüblen' rather than 'Ergrübeln', which is most likely an editorial error.

Aber nachts, im Talesgrunde,	*p*	But at night, in the depths of the valley,
Wandelt's heimlich, wunderbar;	*q*	Something is moving secretly, wondrously:
Wenn da kommt die zwölfte Stunde,	*p*	When the twelfth hour strikes,
Kämpfet dort das Brüderpaar.	*q*	The two brothers fight there.

Harmonically, this Lied is diversified by way of a change of mode (G minor to G major) and by adding the flattened supertonic, A-flat major (Table 4.1), the latter of which emphasises the words 'Wehe! Wehe!' (Woe! Woe!) at the beginning of the sixth stanza.

Table 4.1: Tonal relations in 'Die beiden Brüder'

Stanza	1	2	3	4	5	6	7	8	Postlude
Form	A	A	B	B	A'– C	D–C'	E	E	
Tempo	All. feroce	All. fer.	Più lento		All. fer.	Lento-Adagio	Andantino	Andantino	
Key	g–D	g–D	G	G–D	g–A♭	A♭–g–G	e–G	e–G	G–g
Function	i-V	i-V	I	I-V	i-♭II	♭II-i-I	vi-I	vi-I	I-i

Another Heine setting of Kinkel's is 'Der Runenstein' (The Runestone, published in 1838), in which the lyrical protagonist sits at the sea and remembers his/her loved ones who have all disappeared.

| **Der Runenstein** | | **The Runestone**[11] | |
| Heinrich Heine (published 1838) | | Translation by Emily Ezust | |

Es ragt ins Meer der Runenstein,	*a*	The runestone juts into the sea,
Da sitz' ich mit meinen Träumen.	*b*	And I sit there with my dreams.
Es pfeift der Wind, die Möwen schrein,	*a*	The wind whistles and the sea-gulls shriek;
Die Wellen, die wandern und schäumen.	*b*	And the waves, they wander and foam.

Ich habe geliebt manch schönes Kind	*c*	I have loved many a fair girl
Und manchen guten Gesellen –	*d*	And made many good friends –
Wo sind sie hin? Es pfeift der Wind,	*c*	Where have they gone? The wind whistles,
Es wandern und schäumen die Wellen.[12]	*d*	And the waves wander and foam.

---

[11] <https://www.lieder.net/lieder/get_text.html?TextId=7673> (accessed 6 June 2019).

[12] Heine's original poem reads 'Es schäumen und wandern die Wellen'. Heinrich Heine, 'Es ragt ins Meer der Runenstein', in *Heinrich Heine: Historisch-Kritische Gesamtausgabe*.

The Lied is through-composed, although both stanzas share motivic common-alities (Ex. 4.1[13]). The melodic variants constitute a diverse harmonic plan. Another striking feature is Kinkel's use of tremolo, a means which Richard Taruskin interprets as an expression of timeliness in his analysis of Carl Loewe's 'Erlkönig'.[14] That Kinkel knew of Loewe's compositional style is reflected in her essay 'Über die modernen Liederkomponisten' (On the Modern Lieder Composers), in which she praised Loewe's piano accompaniment in 'Erlkönig':

> It is admirable how he [Loewe] uses the most inconspicuous means in order to transport the listener into the mood of his ballad. With a few accompanying notes he expresses the whirring of the leaves, the rushing sea, the fluttering of the birds, and the like; e.g. in 'Erlkönig' (by Goethe), the bare tremolo on the third and the fifth throughout a few bars evoke a really spooky shudder.[15]

Although Kinkel wrote this essay in 1843, she most likely knew Loewe's compositions when she composed 'Der Runenstein' in 1838, as she familiarised herself with the German Lieder œuvre during her Berlin time (1836–1839), although, in general, piano tremolo technique was not as rare towards the late 1830s as in Loewe's time.

The tradition of using runestones as memorials dates back to the fourth to the twelfth centuries and originates in the Northern lands. Historical flashbacks via references to the past were a common theme in nineteenth-century Germa-ny.[16] This aspect is also reflected in Kinkel's Geibel setting 'Rheinsage' (Rhine Legend, op. 8, no. 2). 'Rheinsage' includes Romantic topoi, for instance the

---

[13] A score in a hand other than Kinkel's is archived at Stadtbibliothek Lübeck (Mus. P 1433 Ex. 1). In this manuscript copy, the final chord in the piano left hand (f♯ octave) is notated as a major sixth ('A'–'F♯'); considering the concluding character of this chord and the conventions of the time, the final chord seems to be more correct as an octave rather than a major sixth. Furthermore, the final note in the piano right hand in bar 22 is notated in the manuscript copy as 'e', although it was most likely intended to be 'c'. Both editorial mistakes have been corrected in this example.

[14] Richard Taruskin, *The Oxford History of Western Music: The Nineteenth Century* (New York: Oxford University Press, 2005), 158.

[15] Johanna Kinkel, 'Über die modernen Liederkomponisten', in Brandt-Schwarze and others, *Der Maikäfer*, iii, 28–37 (30). 'Bewunderswert ist es, wie er mit den unscheinbarsten Mitteln den Hörer in die Szenerie seiner Ballade versetzt. Mit ein paar begleitenden Noten bringt er Blättergesäusel, Wellenrauschen, Vögelgeflatter und dergleichen hervor; z.B. im "Erlkönig" (von Göthe) wo ein blosses Tremuliren auf Terz und Quinte durch ein paar Takte hindurch einen wirklich gespenstigen Schauer hervorruft.'

[16] Martin Wehnert, 'Romantik und romantisch', in *Die Musik in Geschichte und Gegenwart*, 2nd edn, viii, Sachteil, 463–507 (483).

Ex. 4.1: 'Der Runenstein'

Ex. 4.1   (*continued*)

night and moonlight, and it praises such Rhineland phenomena as the wine and beautiful landscapes. A further feature is the Kaiser (Emperor), who was often used as a theme identifying nationalism.[17] Ludwig Rellstab considers Geibel a felicitous imitator of Heine, who 'possesses the most peculiar style and energy, and thereby attains the true beauty of ideas and forms'.[18]

Rheinsage (op. 8, no. 2)
  Emanuel Geibel (published 1838)

Rhine Legend

Am Rhein, am grünen Rhein,	*a*	The night is mild
Da ist so mild die Nacht!	*b*	By the green river Rhine!
Die Rebenhügel liegen	*c*	The vineyards lie
In goldner Mondespracht.	*b*	In the golden glory of the moonlight.
Und an den Hügeln wandelt	*d*	And a tall shadow wanders
Ein hoher Schatten her	*e*	Along the hills
Mit Schwert und Purpurmantel,	*f*	With a sword and red coat,
Die Krone von Golde schwer.	*e*	And a heavy golden crown.
Das ist der Carl der Kaiser,	*g*	That is Carl, the Emperor,
Der mit gewalt'ger Hand	*h*	Who used to rule the
Vor vielen hundert Jahren	*i*	German lands with his powerful hands
Geherrscht im deutschen Land.	*h*	Hundreds of years ago.
Er ist herauf gestiegen	*k*	He left his grave
Zu Aachen aus der Gruft	*l*	In Aachen,
Und segnet seine Reben	*m*	He blesses his vine
Und atmet Traubenduft.	*l*	And he breathes the smell of grapes.
Bei Rüdesheim, da funkelt	*n*	At Rüdesheim, the moon shines
Der Mond ins Wasser hinein.	*a*	Into the water.
Und baut eine goldne Brücke	*o*	It builds a golden bridge
Wohl über den grünen Rhein.	*a*	Across the green river Rhine.
Der Kaiser geht hinüber	*p*	The Emperor crosses the river,
Und schreitet langsam fort,	*q*	He walks slowly,
Und segnet längs dem Strome	*r*	He blesses the vine
Die Reben an jedem Ort.	*q*	along the river in each place.

---

[17] Williamson, *The Longing for Myth in Germany*, 112.

[18] Ludwig Rellstab, review of Johanna Mathieux, *Sechs Gedichte von Emanuel Geibel für eine Singstimme mit Begleitung des Pianoforte: Opus 8* (1838), *Iris im Gebiete der Tonkunst*, 3 August 1838, 121–22: 'hat [...] die eigenthümlichste Richtung und Kraft, und erhebt sich eben so zur wahren Schönheit des Gedankens als der Formen'.

Dann kehrt er heim nach Aachen	*s*	Then he returns to Aachen	
Und schläft in seiner Gruft,	*l*	And sleeps in his grave,	
Bis ihn im neuen Jahre	*t*	Until the smell of the grapes	
Erweckt der Trauben Duft.	*l*	Wakes him up in the next year.	
Wir aber füllen die Römer	*u*	But we fill the glasses	
Und trinken im goldnen Saft	*v*	And we drink in the golden juice;	
Uns deutsches Heldenfeuer	*w*	Here's to the German heroic fire,	
Und deutsche Heldenkraft.	*v*	And German heroic strength.	

While Rellstab suggests that the contextual turn in the poem should be reflected by a compositional variation in the last stanza, Kinkel keeps it simple and instructs for the corresponding section to be sung 'in a stronger and livelier manner' (stärker und lebhafter).[19] In these last four lines, the personal pronoun 'wir' (we) consolidates the impression of a coherent German people and culture, an aspect which was by no means to be taken for granted in the light of the German socio-political 'patchwork' of the time. Although the reviewer of *Allgemeine Musikalische Zeitung* regrets the lack of emotionality in Kinkel's op. 8, he considers her 'Rheinsage' the best of the opus.[20] This positive criticism might reflect the political tone of the time, as journalists often situate themselves in agreement with the editorial line of their paper and/or the expectations of their peers and target groups.[21]

In line with with the thematic trends of her time, it is not surprising that Kinkel also set Nikolaus Becker's 'Der deutsche Rhein' (The German Rhine). The poem was set many times during the 1840s, an era which Cecelia Hopkins Porter associates with the Rhinelanders' increased consciousness of their own identity in opposition to their French neighbours.[22] Accordingly, each stanza of 'Der deutsche Rhein' repeats the line 'they shall not have it | The free German Rhine', followed by a list of different circumstances under which the Rhine will remain German. The poem references such Rhineland features as the cliffs, the boats, the fish, and the cathedrals.

---

[19] Ibid.

[20] [Anon.], review of Johanna Mathieux, *Sechs Gedichte von Emanuel Geibel: Opus 8* (1838), *Allgemeine Musikalische Zeitung*, 26 September 1838, 637–38 (638).

[21] For intersections between politics and journalistic review practice see Jann Pasler, *Writing through Music: Essays on Music, Culture, and Politics* (Oxford: Oxford University Press, 2008), 185–96.

[22] Cecelia Hopkins Porter, 'The "Rheinlieder Critics": A Case of Musical Nationalism', *The Musical Quarterly*, 63, 1 (January 1977), 74–98 (75).

Der deutsche Rhein		**The German Rhine**[23]
Nikolaus Becker (published 1840)		Translation by Sharon Krebs

Sie sollen ihn nicht haben,	*a*	They shall not have it,
Den freien deutschen Rhein,	*b*	The free German Rhine,
Ob sie wie gierige Raben,	*a*	Though they like greedy ravens
Sich heiser danach schrein,	*b*	Scream themselves hoarse after it,
So lang er ruhig wallend	*c*	As long as, peacefully flowing,
Sein grünes Kleid noch trägt,	*d*	It still wears its green garb,
So lang ein Ruder schallend	*c*	As long as even one oar resoundingly
In seine Wogen schlägt.	*d*	Strikes into its waves.
Sie sollen ihn nicht haben,	*a*	They shall not have it,
Den freien deutschen Rhein,	*b*	The free German Rhine,
So lang sich Herzen laben	*a*	As long as hearts refresh themselves
An seinem Feuerwein,	*b*	With its fiery wine,
So lang in seinem Strome	*e*	As long as within its current
Noch fest die Felsen stehn,	*f*	The rocks still stand firmly,
So lang sich hohe Dome	*e*	As long as lofty cathedrals
In seinem Spiegel sehn.	*f*	Can see themselves in its mirror.
Sie sollen ihn nicht haben,	*a*	They shall not have it,
Den freien deutschen Rhein,	*b*	The free German Rhine,
So lang dort kühne Knaben	*a*	As long as courageous lads
Um sanfte Mädchen frei'n,[24]	*b*	Court gentle girls,
So lang die Flosse hebet	*g*	As long as a fin is lifted
Ein Fisch auf seinem Grund,	*h*	By a fish within its depths,
So lang ein Lied noch lebet	*g*	As long as a song still lives
In seiner Sänger Mund.	*h*	In the mouths of its singers.
Sie sollen ihn nicht haben,	*a*	They shall not have it,
Den freien deutschen Rhein,	*b*	The free German Rhine,
Bis seine Flut begraben	*a*	Until its floodwaters have buried
Des letzten Manns Gebein!	*b*	The bones of the last man.

Becker's poem was popular and well-known.[25] That the poem was noticed within the *Maikäferbund* is reflected by the *Maikäfer* member Sebastian

---

[23] <http://www.lieder.net/lieder/get_text.html?TextId=97755> (accessed 29 March 2020).

[24] Becker's original reads 'um schlanke Dirnen frei'n' (court slender maidens). <http://www.rheinische-geschichte.lvr.de/persoenlichkeiten/B/Seiten/NikolausBecker.aspx> (accessed 20 April 2019). The translation is adjusted accordingly by the author.

[25] Hopkins Porter, 'The "Rheinlieder Critics"', 78.

Longard's confirmatory response 'Sie wollen ihn dennoch haben' (They Still Want to Have It), which was included in the *Maikäfer* journal of 17 November 1840.[26]

Sie wollen ihn dennoch haben
  Sebastian Longard

They Still Want to Have It

Ihr wollt ihn dennoch haben?	*a*	You still want to have it?
Wohlan! Glück auf den Marsch!	*b*	Now then – good luck on your march!
Nur schreit nicht, wie die Knaben,	*a*	But do not cry like little boys,
So trotzig keck und barsch.	*b*	Boldly and cheekily.
Wir wissen noch zu singen	*c*	We still know how to sing
Den alten Schlachtgesang,	*d*	The old battle song,
Wir wissen noch zu schwingen	*c*	We still know how to swing
Den deutschen Schwerterschwang!	*d*	The German swords!
Ja, kommt nur, ihn zu nehmen,	*e*	Yes, just come and try to take it,
Den grünen Rhein, ja kommt,	*f*	The green Rhine, yes, come,
Wir sollen euch schon zähmen	*e*	We will tame you
Und lehren, was euch frommt.	*f*	And teach you what you deserve.
Zerspalten und zerschnitten,	*g*	We are not split and cut anymore
Wie einst, sind wir nicht mehr,	*h*	As we were long ago,
Ganz Deutschland kommt geritten,	*g*	The whole country of Germany will,
Wenn's Noth ist, uns zur Wehr!	*h*	If needed, come riding to help us!
Wir kennen euer Dürsten, –	*i*	We know your thirst, –
Das laßt ihr wahrlich sein!	*k*	You'll leave that!
Ihr denkt uns hier zu bürsten	*i*	You are planning to take from us
Den frischen, deutschen Wein.	*k*	The fresh, German wine.
Wir schwingen indeß die Becher	*l*	In the meantime, we are toasting
Und singen in wilder Lust	*m*	And we sing happily
Und alle deutschen Zecher	*l*	And all German topers
Antworten aus voller Brust.	*m*	Respond loudly.
Wir kennen euer Schmachten, –	*n*	We know your longing, –
Ihr seid wahrhaftig klug! –	*o*	And you are right! –
Einstmals am Rhein, da lachten	*n*	In days of yore, at the Rhine
Euch frische Mägdlein g'nug.	*o*	Young girls enough were smiling at you.

<hr>

[26] Sebastian Longard, 'Sie wollen ihn dennoch haben', in Brandt-Schwarze and others, *Der Maikäfer*, i, 209–11.

Da mögt ihr euch nur wischen	*p*	You may wipe your
Die brennenden Lippen gleich;	*q*	Burning lips;
Wir schwingen das Schwert dazwischen:	*p*	We will swing the sword in between:
Halt! – Wer da? – Nichts für euch!	*q*	Stop! – Who is there? – Nothing for you!
Wir kennen euer Hoffen:	*r*	We know your hope:
Wär't ihr am Rhein, am Rhein,	*k*	If you were at the Rhine,
Da stände die Welt euch offen,	*r*	The world would lie before you,
Das soll euch nie gedeih'n!	*k*	You should never succeed in this!
Weithin an unsern Marken,	*s*	At all our posts,
Bei Tage, wie bei Nacht,	*t*	By day and night,
Da ragen die trotzigstarken	*s*	Our defiant strong castles
Burgschlösser und halten Wacht.	*t*	Are keeping watch.
Wir selber sind die Mauer	*u*	We ourselves are the wall
Und unser deutsches Schwert,	*v*	And our German sword,
Der Bürger, wie der Bauer	*u*	The citizens and peasants
Jauchzt, wenn er das Kriegshorn hört.	*v*	Cheer when they hear the sounds of war.
Nun sprecht, ihr kühnen Streiter,	*w*	Now, tell us, you brave fighters,
Was wollt ihr noch am Rhein?	*k*	What are you doing at the Rhine?
Was wollt ihr nun noch weiter	*w*	What are you up to
Am Rhein, am grünen Rhein?	*k*	At the Rhine, the green Rhine?

Johanna Kinkel never published a setting of these words, but the poem provides an insight into the themes discussed within the *Maikäfer* association, of which Becker was appointed honorary member in 1841. He contributed a metaphoric poem titled 'Humoristische Bitte' (Humorous Request), which deals with a beaver that asks nature to bestow on him a beautiful fur after the long winter period.[27] It could be interpreted as a request to acknowledge Becker's diverse skills and interests rather than constantly picking on one and the same poem, 'Der deutsche Rhein'.

Humoristische Bitte		**Humorous Request**
Nikolaus Becker		
Mit Sorgfalt weißt du zu bekleiden	*a*	With care, you know to dress
All' deine Kinder, o Natur;	*b*	All your children, oh nature;
Wie's eben kommt, mit Sammt und Seiden,	*a*	As the case may be, with velvet or silk,
Bald auch mit grünem Zeuge nur.	*b*	Soon also in green clothes.

[27] Nikolaus Becker, 'Humoristische Bitte', in Brandt-Schwarze and others, *Der Maikäfer*, i, 271–72.

Die Blumen steh'n in buntem Glanze,	*c*	The flowers are shining colourfully,
Es quillet Grün an Strauch und Stock;	*d*	The bushes and branches are nice and green;
Bedacht hast du die kleinste Pflanze,	*c*	You considered the smallest plant,
Nur mir bescheerst du keinen Rock.	*d*	But you do not give me a coat.
Kannst du es dulden, daß dein Lieber	*e*	Can you accept that your beloved
Im Lenz allein soll schmucklos geh'n;	*f*	Walks around unadorned in springtime;
Daß auf den abgeschabten Biber	*e*	That the humans sneer at
Die Menschen höhnisch niederseh'n?	*f*	The shabby beaver?
Daß mich dies Volk mit eitlen Scherzen	*g*	That the people sneer at me
Den Überrest des Winters schilt,	*h*	As if I were the winter's leftover,
Nicht ahnend, daß in meinem Herzen	*g*	Not knowing that in my heart
Ein reicher Frühlingsleben quillt?	*h*	There swells a rich spring life?
Ich bitte dich, nur etwas Flimmer	*i*	I beg you for just a little bit of glamour
Auf dieses abgenutzte Tuch,	*k*	On top of this worn out coat,
Ein bischen Silber-, Rosenschimmer,	*i*	A bit of silver, some colour of roses,
Du hast ja doch des Zeugs genug.	*k*	You have enough cloth.
Daß, wenn in solchen lichten Fäden	*l*	So that, when, dressed in such bright clothes,
Am Hügel sie mich sitzen seh'n,	*f*	They spot me sitting at the hills
Sie athemlos durch alle Läden	*l*	They breathlessly look in all shops
Nach jenem fremden Stoffe späh'n.	*f*	For this exotic fabric.

As a result of Kinkel's acquaintanceship with Becker, and despite – or because of – the boom 'Der deutsche Rhein' experienced at the beginning of the 1840s, Kinkel published her two-part song singly with the Bonn publisher Bach.

Remaining in the Rhineland, Kinkel also set the popular Heine poem 'Die Lorelei' (The Lorelei, op. 7, no. 4), which tells the story of a beautiful woman sitting on a cliff overlooking the river Rhine where she sings and combs her long blonde hair. The fishermen passing the cliff on the river crash into the cliff and capsize, distracted by the beauty of the woman and her voice. In the legend, both the woman and the cliff are referred to as the 'Lorelei'.

Die Lorelei (op. 7, no. 4)		**The Lorelei**[28]
Heinrich Heine (published 1838)		Translation by Walter Meyer
Ich weiß nicht, was soll es bedeuten	*a*	I'm looking in vain for the reason
Daß ich so traurig bin;	*b*	That I am so sad and distressed;
Ein Märchen aus alten Zeiten	*a*	A tale known for many a season
Das kommt mir nicht aus dem Sinn.	*b*	Will not allow me to rest.

[28] <https://www.lieder.net/lieder/get_text.html?TextId=7601> (accessed 29 March 2020).

Die Luft ist kühl und es dunkelt,	*c*	Cool is the air in the twilight
Und ruhig fließt der Rhein;	*d*	And quietly flows the Rhine;
Der Gipfel des Berges funkelt	*c*	The mountain top glows with a highlight
Im Abendsonnenschein.	*d*	From the evening sun's last shine.
Die schönste Jungfrau sitzet	*e*	The fairest of maiden's reposing
Dort oben wunderbar,	*f*	So wonderously up there.
Ihr goldnes Geschmeide blitzet	*e*	Her golden treasure disclosing;
Sie kämmt ihr goldenes Haar.	*f*	She's combing her golden hair.
Sie kämmt es mit goldenem Kamme	*g*	She combs it with comb of gold
Und singt ein Lied dabei;	*h*	And meanwhile sings a song
Das hat eine wundersame	*g*	With melody strangely bold
Gewaltige Melodei.	*h*	And overpoweringly strong.
Den Schiffer im kleinen Schiffe	*i*	The boatman in his small craft
ergreift es mit wildem Weh,	*k*	Is seized with longings, and sighs.
Er schaut nicht die Felsenriffe,	*i*	He sees not the rocks fore and aft;
Er schaut nur hinauf in die Höh'.	*k*	He looks only up towards the skies.
Ich glaube, am Ende verschlingen	*l*	I fear that, at the end, the waves
Die Wellen Schiffer und Kahn;[29]	*m*	Will fling both vessel and man;
Und das hat mit ihrem Singen	*l*	That must have been what with her singing
Die Lorelei getan.	*m*	The Lorelei did intend.

Contrary to Eva Weissweiler, who bases Kinkel's motivation to set 'Die Lore-lei' on her background as a Rhineland woman, Sanna Iitti doubts that Kinkel read this song through a political lens, because Kinkel published it in 1838 and included it in her op. 7, which does not cover any political subjects.[30] It is true that Kinkel's political interests developed later. However, Kinkel's great number of Rhineland songs during the late 1830s testify to patriotic feelings towards her home. In her analysis of the song, Iitti points to Chopinesque rhythmic features and to the Schubertian harmonic switch from E major to the tonic E minor.[31] Weissweiler, on the other hand, downgrades Kinkel's composition as 'of minor compositional quality […] because of its political background', and concludes that it 'is a creation for consumption – perhaps one should not take

---

[29] Heine's original reads 'Ich glaube, die Wellen verschlingen | am Ende Schiffer und Kahn', but Kinkel changed the word order of the first two lines of the final stanza. Heinrich Heine, 'Die Lorelei', in *Buch der Lieder von Heinrich Heine*, 179. The translation is adjusted accordingly by the author.

[30] Sanna Iitti, *The Feminine in German Song* (New York: Peter Lang, 2006), 115.

[31] Ibid., 118.

it too seriously'.[32] How was Kinkel's 'Lorelei' received by her contemporaries? Ludwig Rellstab criticised the complex juxtaposition of different rhythms in the vocal line and piano accompaniment, as well as the harmonic meandering between minor and major modes. He writes:

> Rather than stressing the effect of a simple setting, the artist has prioritised the musical skill of developing two melodies at the same time. In our opinion, this is a mistake, although we do acknowledge the finesse of her compositional technique. Nevertheless, the Lied has a nice effect, and the problem should easily be resolved if accompanists resign themselves to keeping the difficult accompaniment in the background as much as possible. The e minor chord at the end of the prelude, which recurs significantly during the Lied, exhales the mood of the wonderful Lied. The profound line 'Die Nacht ist kühl, es dunkelt, und ruhig fließt der Rhein', and the thematically contrary line 'Der Gipfel des Berges funkelt' are especially beautiful. Thus the Lied contains enough felicitous elements to become a favourite song.[33]

Similarly, Oswald Lorenz regrets that the accompaniment dominates the vocal line. He refers to 'Die Lorelei', alongside the Geibel setting 'Die Zigeuner', as the 'most distinctive' composition of op. 7. He finds the harmonic return from E major to the tonic E minor awkward and considers the unusual three-bar hypermeter rhythm too difficult. Furthermore, the ending of the Lied is criticised, as 'the melody demands a conclusion with a dominant chord in the last but one bar, but the accompaniment has introduced it [the dominant chord]

[32] Weissweiler, cited after Iitti, ibid., 115.

[33] Ludwig Rellstab, review of Johanna Mathieux, *Sechs Lieder für eine Singstimme mit Begleitung des Pianoforte: Opus 7* (1838), *Iris im Gebiete der Tonkunst*, 12 January 1838, 5–7 (6). 'Die Künstlerin hat hier eine musikalische Geschicklichkeit, zwei Melodien zugleich fortzuführen, höher angeschlagen als die Wirkung einfacher Behandlung. Dies ist nach unsrer Ansicht ein Irrthum, wenngleich wir die Gewandtheit ihres Talentes bei der Ausführung nicht verkennen. Trotz dem aber hat das Lied eine schöne Wirkung, und wenn der Accompagnist das schwere Accompagnement mit der Resignation, sich so wenig geltend zu machen als irgend möglich, ausführt, so dürfte sich der Uebelstand leicht bedecken lassen. Der Emoll-Akkord am Schluß des Vorspiels, was auch im Liede sinnvoll wiederkehrt, haucht die Seele der Stimmung, in der das wunderschöne Lied gedichtet ist, aus. Sehr schön ist hier die in die Tiefe gehende Stelle: "Die Nacht ist kühl, es dunkelt, und ruhig fließt der Rhein," und im Gegensatz dazu die folgende Zeile: "Der Gipfel des Berges funkelt". So behält das Lied doch noch der trefflichen Elemente genug, um ein Lieblingslied werden zu können.'

already 6 bars before and then dwells on the tonic'.[34] Gottfried Wilhelm Fink keeps his account of Kinkel's op. 7 unspecified. He praises the wealth of emotion of all songs and the fresh rhythms, suitable melodies, sensible harmonies, and the stable accompaniment, the latter of which avoids overly virtuosic passages.[35] All three responses reflect the subjective nature of music reviews, especially as most of the critics keep their opinions general and ungrounded. It is only Fink's review that might be associated with female authorship, as it points to the wealth of emotions. Rellstab's and Lorenz's reviews reveal that 'Die Lorelei' was received as a challenging work. Thus, Weissweiler's conclusion that Lieder composed for consumption are of minor compositional complexity might be overhasty.

Also set in the Rhineland, Kinkel's Chamisso ballad 'Das Schloß Boncourt' (The Castle Boncourt, op. 9) touches on such nineteenth-century subjects as the dreamy impression of a vagabond's life and, more generally, the muses as a lonesome traveller's company. The three-part Lied deals with a wanderer who bids farewell to his home. Remembering his ancestors, he visits the chapel and the castle while he is preparing to travel the world with his lyre.

| **Das Schloß Boncourt (op. 9)** | | **The Castle Boncourt**[36] |
| Heinrich Heine (published 1838) | | Translation adapted from Suzanne Summerville |

Ich träume als Kind mich zurücke	*a*	As dreams of childhood overcome me
Und schüttle mein greises Haupt;	*b*	I shake my graying head
Wie sucht ihr mich heim, ihr Bilder,	*c*	How do you engulf me, images,
Die lang ich vergessen geglaubt?	*b*	Which I had long forgotten?
Hoch ragt aus schattigen Gehegen	*d*	A gleaming palace rises
Ein schimmerndes Schloß hervor,	*e*	Out of a shady bank of hedges.
Ich kenne die Türme, die Zinnen,	*f*	I recognize its towers, the battlements
Die steinerne Brücke, das Tor.	*e*	And stone bridge, the gate.

---

[34] Oswald Lorenz, review of Johanna Mathieux, *Sechs Lieder für eine Singstimme mit Begleitung des Pianoforte: Opus 7* (1838), *Neue Zeitschrift für Musik*, 9 March 1838, 77–78 (78). 'im vorletzten Tacte verlangt die Melodie einen Schluss mittelst des Leitaccordes, während ihn die Begleitung schon 6 Tacte früher gemacht hat und dann beim Accord der Tonika beharrt'.

[35] Gottfried Wilhelm Fink, review of Johanna Mathieux, *Sechs Lieder für eine Singstimme mit Begleitung des Pianoforte: Opus 7* (1838), *Allgemeine Musikalische Zeitung*, 8 August 1838, 524–25.

[36] <https://www.lieder.net/lieder/get_text.html?TextId=3731> (accessed 29 March 2020).

Es schau'n von dem Wappenschilde	*g*	From the coat of arms
Die Löwen so traulich mich an,	*h*	The lions look benevolently down on me.
Ich grüße die alten Bekannten	*i*	I greet my old friends
Und eile den Burghof hinan.	*h*	And rush through the courtyard.
Dort liegt die Sphinx an dem Brunnen,	*k*	The sphinx is there beside the fountain
Dort grünt der Feigenbaum,	*l*	And the fig tree is in bloom.
Dort, hinter jenen Fenstern,[37]	*m*	The windows where I dreamed
Verträumt ich den ersten Traum.	*l*	My earliest dreams are still there.
Ich tret in die Burgkapelle	*n*	I enter the chapel
Und suche des Ahnherrn Grab,	*o*	And look for the graves of my ancestor.
Dort ist's, dort hängt von dem Pfeiler	*p*	The old armor
Das alte Gewaffen herab.	*o*	Is hanging there on the pillar.
Noch lesen umflort die Augen	*q*	The gauzed eyes do not yet
Die Züge der Inschrift nicht,	*r*	Read the inscription,
Wie hell durch die bunten Scheiben	*s*	No matter how brightly the colourful glass
Das Licht darüber auch bricht.	*r*	Reflects the light.
So stehst du, o Schloß meiner Väter,	*t*	So you are once again real in my thoughts,
Mir treu und fest in dem Sinn	*u*	Palace of my ancestors.
Und bist von der Erde verschwunden,	*v*	You disappeared from the earth
Der Pflug geht über dich hin.	*u*	And the plough moves over you.
Sei fruchtbar, o teurer Boden,	*w*	Be fruitful, oh dear earth,
Ich segne dich mild und gerührt,	*x*	I give to you my blessings, gently and full of emotion,
Und segn' ihn zwiefach, wer immer	*y*	And doubly bless any
Den Pflug nun über dich führt.	*x*	Who now guide the plough over you.
Ich aber will auf mich raffen,	*z*	However, I must gather up
Mein Saitenspiel in der Hand,	*A*	My lyre
Die Weiten der Erde durchschweifen	*B*	And traverse the wide, wide world
Und singen von Land zu Land.	*A*	Singing from land to land.

In this ballad Kinkel portrays the moving water by means of a barcarole rhythm in the piano, which Hopkins Porter identifies as a 'Rhenish musical idiom fulfilling the ideal of *Volkstümlichkeit* (folk-likeness)'.[38] Despite this folk-like facet,

---

[37] Chamisso's original reads 'hinter diesen Fenstern'. Adelbert von Chamisso, 'Das Schloß Boncourt', in *Adelbert von Chamisso*, i, 192–93. Further differences between the original and Kinkel's version are very minor and only refer to phrasing and metric aspects; for example Kinkel replaced 'am Brunnen' with 'an dem Brunnen' (stanza 4) and 'vom Pfeiler' with 'von dem Pfeiler' (stanza 5).

[38] Linda Siegel, *Johanna Kinkel*, ii, v; Hopkins Peter, 'The "Rheinlieder Critics"', 91.

the harmonic progression is dense and the melodic line includes a great deal of ornamentation. Nevertheless, and although, like Kinkel's op. 7, the work was published by Trautwein, 'Das Schloß Boncourt' was not reviewed publicly.

The same observation applies to Kinkel's Heine ballad 'Don Ramiro' (op. 13), which, besides her unpublished stage works, is one of her longest and most complex compositions. 'Don Ramiro' tells the story of a woman, Donna Clara, who gets married to the knight Don Fernando. However, a different man, Don Ramiro, is in love with her and regrets that she cannot marry him. When Clara asks Ramiro to overcome his own pride and attend the wedding, Ramiro promises to do so. At the wedding dance, Clara dreams of Ramiro wearing a black robe and smelling of death and, in her imagination, she dances with him. When she awakes from her unconsciousness after the fearful dream, she realises that Ramiro was not at the wedding. Her groom asks what had happened to her, whereupon she utters 'And Don Ramiro?'. Fernando replies 'Lady, ask not bloody tiding | Don Ramiro died this morning'.

Don Ramiro (op. 13)
  Heinrich Heine (published 1840)

Donna Clara! Donna Clara!
Heißgeliebte langer Jahre!
Hast beschlossen mein Verderben,
Und beschlossen ohn' Erbarmen.

Donna Clara! Donna Clara!
Ist doch süß die Lebensgabe!
Aber unten ist es grausig,
In dem dunkeln, kalten Grabe.

Donna Clara! Freu' dich, morgen
Wird Fernando, am Altare,
Dich als Ehgemahl begrüßen –
Wirst du mich zur Hochzeit laden?

Don Ramiro! Don Ramiro!
Deine Worte treffen bitter,
Bittrer als der Spruch der Sterne,
Die da spotten meines Willens.

Don Ramiro[39]
  Translation adapted from Emma Lazarus

Donna Clara! Donna Clara!
Hotly-loved through many years!
You have wrought me mine undoing,
And have wrought it without mercy!

Donna Clara! Donna Clara!
Still the gift of life is pleasant.
But beneath the earth 'tis frightful,
In the grave so cold and darksome.

Donna Clara! Laugh, be merry,
For tomorrow shall Fernando
Greet you at the nuptial altar,
Will you invite me to the wedding?

Don Ramiro! Don Ramiro!
Very bitter sounds your language,
Bitterer than the stars' decrees are,
Which bemock my heart's desire.

[39] <https://www.lieder.net/lieder/get_text.html?TextId=37005> (accessed 29 March 2020).

Don Ramiro! Don Ramiro!
Rüttle ab den dumpfen Trübsinn;
Mädchen gibt es viel auf Erden,
Aber uns hat Gott geschieden.

Don Ramiro, Überwinder
Vieler tausend Mohrenritter,
Überwinde nun dich selber –
Komm' auf meine Hochzeit, Lieber.

Donna Clara! Donna Clara!
Ja, ich schwör es, ja ich komme!
Will mit dir den Reihen tanzen; –
Gute Nacht, ich komme morgen.

Gute Nacht! – Das Fenster klirrte.
Seufzend stand Ramiro unten,
Stand noch lange wie versteinert;
Endlich schwand er fort im Dunkeln.

Endlich auch, nach langem Ringen,
Muß die Nacht dem Tage weichen;
Wie ein bunter Blumengarten
Liegt Toledo ausgebreitet.

Prachtgebäude und Paläste
Schimmern hell im Glanz der Sonne;
Und der Kirchen hohe Kuppeln
Leuchten stattlich wie vergoldet.

Dumpfig und wie Bienensummen
Klingt der Glocken Festgeläute,
Lieblich steigen Betgesänge
Aus den frommen Gotteshäusern.

Aber dorten, siehe! siehe!
Dorten aus der Marktkapelle,
Im Gewimmel und Gewoge,[40]
Strömt des Volkes bunte Menge.

Don Ramiro! Don Ramiro!
Cast aside your gloomy temper.
In the world are many maidens,
But the Lord has parted us two.

Don Ramiro, you who bravely
Many and many a moor has conquered,
Conquer now yourself, – tomorrow
Come and greet me at my wedding.

Donna Clara! Donna Clara!
Yes, I swear it. I am coming!
I will dance with you the measure, –
Now good night! I come tomorrow.

So good night! The casement rattled,
Sighing beneath it, stood Ramiro.
Long he stood a stony statue,
Then amidst the darkness vanished.

After long and weary struggling,
Night must yield unto the daylight.
Like a many-coloured garden,
Lies the city of Toledo.

Palaces and stately fabrics
Shimmer in the morning sunshine.
And the lofty domes of churches
Glitter as with gold incrusted.

Humming like a swarm of insects,
Ring the bells their festal carol.
With sweet tones the sacred anthem
Ascends from each house of God.

But behold, behold! beyond there,
Yonder from the market-chapel,
With a billowing and a swaying,
Streams the motley throng of people.

[40] This line corresponds with the Düsseldorf Gesamtausgabe. Heinrich Heine, 'Don Ramiro', cited after *Heinrich Heine: Historisch-Kritische Gesamtausgabe*. The Hoffmann und Campe edition is slightly different. Heinrich Heine, 'Don Ramiro', in *Buch der Lieder von Heinrich Heine*, 62–70, cited after *Heinrich Heine: Historisch-Kritische Gesamtausgabe*.

Blanke Ritter, schmucke Frauen,	Gallant knights and noble ladies,
Hofgesinde, festlich blinkend,[41]	In their holiday apparel;
Und die hellen Glocken läuten,	While the pealing bells ring clearly,
Und die Orgel rauscht dazwischen.	And the deep-voiced organ murmurs.
Doch, mit Ehrfurcht ausgewichen,	But a reverential passage
In des Volkes Mitte wandelt	In the people's midst is opened,
Das geschmückte junge Ehepaar:[42]	For the richly-clad young couple,
Donna Clara, Don Fernando.	Donna Clara, Don Fernando.
Tausend Augen schaun nach ihnen,[43]	A thousand eyes are staring at them,
Tausend frohe Stimmen rufen:	A thousand merry voices are shouting:
Heil Kastiliens Mädchensonne!	Hail bright girl from Castille!
Heil Kastiliens Ritterblume!	Hail knight of Castille!
Bis an Bräutigams Palasttor	To the bridegroom's palace-threshhold,
Wälzet sich das Volksgewühle;	Wind the waving throngs of people;
Dort beginnt die Hochzeitfeier,	There the wedding feast begins,
Prunkhaft und nach alter Sitte.	Pompous in the olden fashion.
Ritterspiel und frohe Tafel	Knightly games and open table,
Wechseln unter lautem Jubel;	Interspersed with joyous laughter,
Rauschend schnell entfliehn die Stunden,	Quickly flying, speed the hours,
Bis die Nacht herabgesunken.	Till the night again has approached.
Und zum Tanze sich versammeln	And the wedding guests assemble
Dort im Saal die Hochzeitgäste;	For the dance within the palace,
Alle funkeln bunt beleuchtet	And their many-coloured raiment
Von dem Lichterheer der Kerzen.	Glitters in the light of tapers.
Don Fernando strahlt wie'n König	Don Fernando smiles like a king
In dem güldnen Purpurmantel;	In his golden coat;
Clara wie die junge Rose,	Clara blooms like a young rose
Blüht im weißen Brautgewande.	In her white bride's dress.
Auf erhobne Ehrensitze	Seated on a lofty dais,
Rings von Dienerschaft umwoget,	Side by side, are bride and bridegroom,
Ließen sich die beiden nieder,	Donna Clara, Don Fernando, –
Und sie tauschten süße Worte.	And they murmur sweet love whispers.

[41] This line corresponds with the Düsseldorf Gesamtausgabe. The Hoffmann und Campe edition is slightly different ('Festlich blinkend Hofgesinde').

[42] This line corresponds with the Düsseldorf Gesamtausgabe. The Hoffmann und Campe version reads 'Donna Clara schwarz verschleiert, Don Fernando waffenglänzend'.

[43] This stanza does not appear in the Gesamtausgabe, but it is included in the 1827 version published by Hoffmann und Campe.

Und im Saale braust es dumpfig,
Wie ein Meer von Sturm beweget!
Und die lauten Pauken wirbeln,
Und es schmettern die Trommeten.

Doch warum, o schöne Herrin,
Sind gerichtet deine Blicke
Dorthin nach der Saalesecke?
So verwundert sprach der Ritter.

Siehst du denn nicht, Don Fernando,
Dort den Mann im schwarzen Mantel?
Und der Ritter lächelt freundlich:
Ach! das ist ja nur ein Schatten.

Doch es nähert sich der Schatten,
Und es war ein Mann im Mantel;
Und Ramiro schnell erkennend,
Grüßt ihn Clara, glutbefangen.

Und der Tanz hat schon begonnen,
Munter drehen sich die Tänzer;
In des Walzers wilden Kreisen,
Und der Boden dröhnt und zittert.[44]

Wahrlich gerne, Don Ramiro,
Will ich dir zum Tanze folgen,
Doch im nächtlich schwarzen Mantel
Hättest du nicht kommen sollen.

Mit durchbohrend stieren Augen
Schaut Ramiro auf die Holde,
Sie umschlingend spricht er düster:
Sprachest ja, ich sollte kommen!

Und ins wirre Tanzgetümmel[45]
Drängen sich die beiden Tänzer;
Und die lauten Pauken wirbeln,
Und es schmettern die Trommeten.

And within the hall wave brightly
All the gay-decked streams of dancers;
And the rolling drums are beaten.
Shrill the clamorous trumpet soundeth.

Why, why, beauteous lady,
Are your lovely glances fastened
Yonder in the hall's far corner?
In amazement asked Fernando.

Do you not see, o Don Fernando,
Yonder man in sable mantle?
And the knight spoke, kindly smiling,
Why, 'tis nothing but a shadow.

But the shadow drew anear them,
'Twas a man in sable mantle,
Clara knows at once Ramiro,
And she greets him, blushing crimson.

And the dance begins already,
Gaily whirl around the dancers
In the waltz's reckless circles,
Till the firm floor creaks and trembles.

Yes, with pleasure, Don Ramiro,
I will dance with you the measure;
But in such a night-black mantle
You should never have come hither.

With fixed, piercing eyes, Ramiro
Gazes on the lovely lady,
Then embracing her, speaks strangely, –
I followed your invitation.

In the wild whirl of the measure,
Press and turn the dancing couple,
And the rolling drums are beaten,
Shrill the clamorous trumpets sound.

[44] This version corresponds with the Gesamtausgabe. The Hoffmann und Campe
version reads 'Und der Boden dröhnt und zittert | Von dem rauschenden Getöse'.

[45] This line corresponds with the Gesamtausgabe. Hoffmann und Campe's version
reads 'wilde' (wild) rather than 'wirre' (whirly).

Sind ja schneeweiß deine Wangen!
Flüstert Clara, heimlich schauernd.
Sprachest ja, ich sollte kommen!
Schallet dumpf Ramiros Stimme.

Und im Saal die Kerzen blinzeln
Durch das flutende Gedränge;
Und die lauten Pauken wirbeln,
Und es schmettern die Trommeten.

Sind ja eiskalt deine Hände!
Flüstert Clara, schauerzuckend.
Sprachest ja, ich sollte kommen!
Und sie treiben fort im Strudel.

Laß mich, laß mich! Don Ramiro!
Leichenduft ist ja dein Odem!
Wiederum dieselbe Antwort:[46]
Sprachest ja, ich sollte kommen!

Und der Boden raucht und glühet,
Lustig fiedeln die Geiger;
Wie ein tolles Zauberweben
Schwindet alles im Gekreisel.[47]

Laß mich, laß mich! Don Ramiro!
Wimmerts immer im Gewoge.
Don Ramiro stets erwidert:
Seine dumpfen dunklen Worte.[48]

Nun, so geh in Gottes Namen!
Clara riefs mit fester Stimme;
Und dies Wort war kaum entfahren,
Und verschwunden war Ramiro.

White as driven snow are your cheeks!
Whispers Clara, inly trembling.
I followed your invitation,
Hollow ring Ramiro's accents.

In the hall the tapers flicker,
With the eddying stream of dancers,
And the rolling drums are beaten,
Shrill the clamorous trumpet soundeth.

Cold as ice I feel your fingers,
Whispers Clara, thrilled with terror.
I followed your invitation.
And they rush on in the vortex.

Leave me, leave me, Don Ramiro!
Your breath is like a corpse's scent.
Once again the gloomy sentence,
I followed your invitation.

And the firm floor glows and smokes,
Merry sound the horns and fiddles;
Like a woof of strange enchantment,
All within the hall is whirling.

Leave me, leave me, Don Ramiro!
All is waving and revolving.
Don Ramiro still repeats,
His hollow dark words.

In the name of God, begone then!
Clara shrieked, with steadfast accent.
And the word was scarcely spoken,
When Ramiro had vanished.

[46] The Gesamtausgabe reads 'Wiederum die dunklen Worte'. The Hoffmann und Campe version reads 'Don Ramiros grause Worte'.

[47] The Gesamtausgabe and Hoffmann und Campe use 'schwindelt' rather than 'schwindet'. It is uncertain whether this is an editorial error or whether Kinkel changed the words.

[48] The Gesamtausgabe and Hoffmann und Campe use the line 'Sprachest ja, ich sollte kommen!'. It is uncertain whether Kinkel had a different version at hand or whether she changed the words.

Clara starret, Tod im Antlitz,	Clara stiffens! deathly pallid,
Kaltumflirret, nachtumwoben;	Numb with cold, with night encompassed.
Ohnmacht hat das lichte Bildnis	In a swoon the lovely creature
In ihr dunkles Reich gezogen.	To the shadowy realm is wafted.
Endlich weicht der Nebelschlummer,	But the misty slumber passes,
Endlich schlägt sie auf die Wimper;	And at last she lifts her eyelids.
Aber Staunen will aufs neue	Then again from sheer amazement
Ihre holden Augen schließen.	Her fair eyes at once she closes.
Denn derweil der Tanz begonnen,	For she sees she has not risen,
War sie nicht vom Sitz gewichen,	Since the dance's first beginning.
Und sie sitzt noch bei dem Bräutgam,	Still she sits beside the bridegroom,
Und der Ritter sorgsam bittet:	And the knight speaks with anxious question.
Sprich, was bleichet deine Wangen?	Say, why are your cheeks so pale?
Warum wird dein Aug so dunkel? –	Why are your eyes filled with shadows?
Und Ramiro? –– stottert Clara,[49]	And Ramiro? stammers Clara,
Und Entsetzen lähmt die Zunge.	And her tongue is glued with horror.
Doch mit tiefen, ernsten Falten	But with deep and serious furrows
Furcht sich jetzt des Bräutgams Stirne;	Is the bridegroom's forehead wrinkled.
Herrin, forsch nicht blutge Kunde –	Lady, ask not bloody tiding –
Heute Mittag starb Ramiro.	Don Ramiro died this morning.

This Heine ballad exhibits many operatic features, echoed in its dedication to the Leipzig singer Sophie Schloß.[50] In fact, the instrumentation for voice and piano is the only obvious Lieder characteristic. Perhaps Kinkel chose this arrangement in the interest of a more feasible performance and an increased market value.[51] A through-composed work, this ballad is virtually divided into different acts and scenes, evoked by changes in tempo, key, metre, and piano accompaniment. An extensive densely textured conclusion in C major suggests the end of the first act (Ex. 4.2).

[49] This line corresponds with the Gesamtausgabe. The Hoffmann und Campe version reads 'schaudert' (shudders) rather than 'stottert' (stammers).

[50] Sophie Schloß performed frequently at the Gewandhaus. Colin Timothy Eatock, *Mendelssohn and Victorian England* (Farnham: Ashgate, 2009), 94, and *Robert Schumann Tagebücher*, ed. Gerd Nauhaus, 4 vols (Basel/Frankfurt: VEB Deutscher Verlag für Musik, 1971–87), ii, 504 and 512.

[51] Glahn draws a similar conclusion in her analysis of Kinkel's self-perception within the marketplace in relation to her musical joke *Die Vogelkantate*. Glahn, *Johanna Kinkel*, 106–08 and 111.

Ex. 4.2: Cadence in C suggesting a conclusion of the first act of 'Don Ramiro' (bars 71 ff.)

More strikingly, the work includes three declamatory recitatives, which are marked 'Recitando' and which have much in common with an opera recitative. Furthermore, the ballad elaborates on musical themes associated with the two main protagonists. Don Ramiro's opening speech, for instance, is introduced through a distinct sighing motif consisting of two linear four-note descents (Ex. 4.3a). This motif recurs in the accompaniment when Clara imagines Ramiro at the wedding (Ex. 4.3b[52]).

[52] The original reads 'nach der Saales Ecke', which is grammatically incorrect. In accordance with nineteenth-century German convention, I have changed this to the genitive 'nach des Saales Ecke' (rather than the compound 'nach der Saalesecke'). Following convention, I divided 'ck' clusters as 'kk' in 'Blik-ke' and 'Ek-ke'.

Ex. 4.3a: Sighing motif introducing Don Ramiro

Ex. 4.3b: Recurring sighing motif at the wedding dance (bars 252 ff.)

The harmonic constitution of the work is diverse. Kinkel uses enharmonic reinterpretations where the atmosphere changes abruptly. For example, at Ramiro's question 'Are you going to invite me to your wedding?', Kinkel employs an enharmonic progression in order to support the dreadful tone of Clara's and Ramiro's final conversation (Ex. 4.4). Depending on the reading, the first chord in bar 25 can be interpreted as a dominant seventh chord in second inversion, a German augmented sixth chord in third inversion, or a decorated B major^7 chord. All three interpretations show that Kinkel must have given some thought to this particular passage in response to the suspenseful lyrics.

Ex. 4.4: Enharmonic progression at Don Ramiro's question (bars 23–26)

In spite of the ballad's aesthetic complexity Kinkel employed more conventional features when depicting different cultural aspects. For example, rhythms and ornaments reminiscent of the Spanish musical heritage sound in the piano at the beginning of the wedding ceremony. When the wedding party leaves the church Kinkel applies a march-like rhythm, and the dance registers a waltz. Kinkel might have used the waltz as a means of cross-cultural identification between her own background and that of the couple featured in Heine's ballad. Furthermore, at the line 'Heil Kastiliens Mädchensonne' (Hail, bright girl from Castille!), the melodic line borrows Figaro's motif of Gioachino Rossini's *The Barber of Seville*, which reads 'Ah, che bel vivere, che bel piacere' (Ah, what a fine life, what fine pleasure, Ex. 4.5). Linda Siegel, too, identifies in this line an operatic touch.[53]

---

[53] Siegel, *Johanna Kinkel*, vol. ii, iii.

Ex. 4.5: Figaro's motif in 'Don Ramiro' and *The Barber of Seville*[54]

The motivic constellation in 'Don Ramiro' reveals Kinkel's ability to respond musically to Heine's use of Romantic irony.[55] This idea is plausible considering Florian Kraemer's concept of irony as a way of 'criticis[ing] the political status quo of the time without voicing criticism directly'.[56] Kinkel may have aimed to criticise her own socio-cultural conventions: when she published this ballad in September 1840, she had just completed her divorce from her first husband. She commented on the light-hearted and simple compositional constitution of Italian opera several times; the most telling impression of her opinion on Italian melodies is revealed in her writing *Notizen zum Klavier- und Gesangsunterricht und zur Ästhetik der Musik*, in which she states that:

> In relation to expressive truthfulness, Scottish national melodies are the most brilliant among all nations, and they lead us to develop a favourable impression of the [Scottish] national character; Italian melodies sound a bit affected; French [melodies sound] frivolous; besides which German *Volksmelodien* sound a bit indolent.[57]

---

[54] Score of *The Barber of Seville: Largo al factotum della città* <http://conquest.imslp.info/files/imglnks/usimg/f/f2/IMSLP25462-PMLP07237-Rossini_Barbiere_No_1--5.pdf> (accessed 5 April 2019).

[55] For further details on Romantic irony see Jean-Pierre Barricelli, 'Musical Forms of Romantic Irony', in *Romantic Irony,* ed. Frederick Garber (Budapest: Akadémiai Kiadó, 1988), 310–22; Beate Julia Perrey, *Schumann's* Dichterliebe *and Early Romantic Poetics* (Cambridge: Cambridge University Press, 2002), 33–34; Lauri Suurpää, 'Schumann, Heine, and Romantic Irony: Music and Poems in the First Five Songs of "Dichterliebe"', *Intégral,* 19 (1996), 93–123 (117); and Florian Kraemer, *Entzauberung der Musik: Beethoven, Schumann und die romantische Ironie* (Munich: Fink, 2014).

[56] Kraemer, *Entzauberung der Musik,* XXX.

[57] Johanna Kinkel, *Notizen zum Klavier- und Gesangsunterricht,* n.d., ULB (S 2394), 21. 'In der Wahrhaftigkeit des Ausdrucks stehen die schottischen Nationalmelodien allen Nationen als ein Meister da, und lassen uns für den Charakter der Nation ein günstiges Vorurtheil fassen; die italienischen Melodien klingen bisschen nach

Her employment of Rossini's motif is ambiguous: on the one hand, it is used in order to symbolise superficiality, and to ironally criticise the marriage conventions of her time. On the other hand, Kinkel must have appreciated the motif's compositional suitability if she felt it was worthwhile to borrow it. Kinkel's thinking in categories of national characteristics reflects the nineteenth-century perception that each nation has certain traits, which are mirrored in their language and culture.[58] It is therefore not surprising that she applies the term *Volksmelodien* (folk melodies) in relation to German song. Kinkel promoted German nationalism through her Rhineland songs and, even more obviously, through her later political settings.

🎵 *Drinking songs*

When, in the summer of 1838, Kinkel sent Robert Schumann a drinking song for male choir as a contribution to his journal *Neue Zeitschrift für Musik*, she made a clear statement as to how she wanted to place herself in public. Complaining about the review previously published in this journal, Kinkel wrote to her friend Oppenhoff on 14 July 1838:

> A group of young Leipzig composers, who had read Rellstab's review, pretended that they would have been able to tell from my compositional style that my compositions were written by a woman. Among others, they stressed humorously (in their review) the fondness for the *soft* and *tender* and they sneered at one of the moonlight songs. All of a sudden they changed their minds; one of them (not the reviewer) is writing extremely flattering letters to me without knowing more than my name and my short songs, and he asks for a composition as a contribution to the musical supplement of a journal. This proved to be a precious chance to show him the *soft* and *tender* of my compositions. I wrote a very prissy letter and included my wildest drinking song for male choir, to which I had versified a real students' text. If I could only see the reactions of my unknown correspondents when they try to sing this piece![59]

Verstellung, die französischen leichtsinnig, die deutschen Volksmelodien etwas indolent daneben.'

[58] Henry Raynor, *Music and Society since 1815* (London: Barry & Jenkins, 1976), 127–28.

[59] Cited in Kaufmann, 'Johanna Kinkel: Schluß', 55. Italics in original. 'Nach dem Erscheinen des ersten [Liederheftes] passierte es, daß eine Confederation junger Liederkomponisten in Leipzig, die Rellstabs Rezension gelesen, sich hinterher die Miene geben wollten, als hätte sie an meinem Styl gleich gemerkt, daß dies eine Damenkomposition sey. Unter anderem hoben sie die Vorliebe für das *Sanfte, Zarte* ein wenig scherzhaft (in ihrer Rezension) heraus, und spöttelten über eins

Kinkel's letter to Oppenhoff reveals that she disagreed with the common nine-teenth-century assessment of music according to the composer's sex. Her 'Trinklied für Männerchor' consists of two stanzas: the first stanza begins with an Anacreontic drinking theme and then turns into a political song, which points to the narrow-mindedness of Kinkel's reception in the *Neue Zeitschrift für Musik* by celebrating liberal views. The second stanza praises wine as a means of imparting and spreading love.[60]

Trinklied für Männerchor		**Drinking Song for Male Choir**
Johanna Kinkel (published 1838)		
Lasst uns trinken, lasst uns singen,	*a*	Let us drink, let us sing,
Und vergessen trägen Harm.	*b*	And let us forget the heavy grief.
Glutgefüllter Gläser Klingen	*a*	The clinging of glowing glasses
Scheucht hinweg der Sorgen Schwarm.	*b*	Drives out the swarm of worries.
Trinkt ihr Philister, bekehret euch doch,	*c*	Drink, Philistines, convert yourselves,
Wer liberal ist, der lebe hoch!	*c*	Long live he who is liberal!
Wein entfesselt Liebesblicke,	*d*	Wine unleashes lovers' glances,
Die sich sonst verbergen scheu;	*e*	Which otherwise hide shyly;
Aug' in Auge eine Brücke	*d*	Eye to eye, wine builds
Baut er, drauf sie wandeln frei.	*e*	A bridge, on which the glances stroll freely.
Darum sei höher der Becher gefüllt,	*f*	May the glass be topped up
Dessen Schaume die Liebe entquillt.	*f*	From whose foam love flows.

Drinking songs were generally associated with male singers, in particular male students.[61] By offering Schumann a drinking song for male choir Kinkel

---

der Mondscheinlieder. Auf einmal sattelten sie um; einer dieses Clubs (nicht der Rezensent) schreibt mir äußerst schmeichelhafte Briefe, ohne mehr als meinen Namen und die Liederchen zu kennen, und bittet mich als Mitarbeiterin bei einer musikalischen Beilage zu einer Zeitung irgend eine Komposition zu liefern. Dies war für mich eine kostbare Gelegenheit, das *Sanfte, Zarte* dem Rezensenten einzutränken. Ich schrieb einen ganz feinen zimperlichen Brief, und schickte dazu mein wildestes Trinklied für Männerchor, zu welchem ich selbst einen rechten Studententext gemacht habe. Dürfte ich doch nur die Gesichter meiner unbekannten Korrespondenten sehn, wenn sie die Bescheerung durchsingen.'

[60] A more elaborate analysis of this work is conducted in the author's own essay 'Johanna Kinkel (1810–1858) within the Context of Nineteenth-Century Music Criticism', in *Nineteenth-Century Music Criticism*, ed. Teresa Cascudo García-Villaraco (Turnhout: Brepols, 2017).

[61] See 'Trinklied', in *Brockhaus Enzyklopädie*, 20th edn, 30 vols (Leipzig/Mannheim: Brockhaus, 1996), xxii, 316; Friedrich, 'Cultural and intellectual trends', 107.

challenged conventions of authorship and political participation, as many of this Lied's contextual, compositional and poetic features are quite harsh and virile.[62]

Kinkel published another drinking song for voice, choir and piano accompaniment, in her op. 6: the Kopisch setting 'Wasser und Wein' (Water and Wine, op. 6, no. 2). It praises different qualities of water but prioritises wine as the most suitable drink. *Neue Zeitschrift für Musik* was in favour of this song, because 'the conclusion, in relation to both the words and the music, convinces the most innocent (listener)'.[63]

Wasser und Wein (op. 6, no. 2) August Kopisch (published 1839)		**Water and Wine[64]** Translation adapted from Gary Bachlund
Freunde sagt was wollt ihr trinken?	*a*	Friends, say what would you drink?
Wein! Wein! Wein!	*b*	Wine! Wine! Wine!
Soll der Knecht nach Wasser hinken?	*a*	Shall the fellow limp to water?
Nein! Nein! Nein!	*b*	No! No! No!
Laß das Wasser Wasser bleiben,	*c*	Let water remain water,
Laß es gehn und Mühlen treiben,	*c*	Let it go and push the water wheel,
Laß es in den Wüstenein	*b*	Let it serve in a desert
Trost den Karavanen sein.	*b*	To quench the thirst of caravans.
Laß die Hügel es beregnen	*d*	Let it sprinkle the hillsides
Daß sie uns mit Trauben segnen,	*d*	So they bless us with grapes,
Laß es seine stolzen Well'n	*e*	Let it be proud waves
Bis hinauf zum Himmel schnell'n.	*e*	That rise to the heavens.
Laß es große Schiffe schwingen,	*f*	Let it carry great ships
Die den Wein von Ferne bringen,	*f*	Which bring wine from afar,
Laß in alle Land' es laufen	*g*	Let it be in all places
Und damit die Heiden taufen;	*g*	Thereby to sprinkle the fields;
Wasser soll belobet sein,	*b*	Water be praised,
Doch wir trinken: Wein Wein Wein!	*b*	But we drink: Wine! Wine! Wine!

---

[62] For further references to drinking songs within the context of the Anacreontic Gesellschaftslied see Hans Ritte, *Das Trinklied in Deutschland und Schweden: Vergleichende Typologie der Motive* (Munich: Fink, 1973), 50.

[63] Oswald Lorenz, review of Johanna Mathieux, *Sechs Lieder: Opus 6* (1839), *Neue Zeitschrift für Musik*, 3 January 1840, 7–8: 'der Schluß, in Musik und Text, überzeugt den Unschuldigsten'.

[64] <http://www.lieder.net/lieder/get_text.html?TextId=48980> (accessed 30 March 2020).

'Wasser und Wein' is through-composed and comprises three stanzas, each of which is set to a different piano accompaniment; the vocal line remains unvaried. Thalheimer identifies traits of Zelter's and Reichardt's folk-like songs in the alternation of solo-performed verse and refrain, sung by the choir, as well as in in the way in which Kinkel uses stereotypical piano figures.[65]

ࣔ *Socio-political criticism under the disguise of religion and nature*

The Lied 'Rette Vater, Dein geliebtes Kind!' (Father, Rescue Your Beloved Child, op. 15, no. 5), which is a setting of Gottfried Kinkel's words, offers a wide range of possible interpretations. The Kinkels' background helps to understand this song. When it was published in 1841, Gottfried and Johanna faced social hurdles, which were caused by the incompatibility of their religious backgrounds. The poem's first line, which is set in a melodic and dynamic contrast to its subsequent lines, reveals that the lyrical I followed a call led by his heart, which is the reason why he is in trouble. Gottfried Kinkel's religious belief surfaces in the lyrical protagonist's cry for help. The second stanza, in which the lyrical I processes an emotional debate between himself and the world, supports the assumption that Kinkel's poem carries an autobiographical element. His increasing interest in the Catholic-born Johanna put a strain on both his romantic relationship with Sophie Boegehold and his professional career.

Rette Vater, Dein geliebtes Kind! (op. 15, no. 5) Gottfried Kinkel (published 1841)		**Father, Rescue Your Beloved Child!**
Einem Ruf hab' ich gelauschet,	*a*	I listened to a call,
Den du mir in's Herz gesendet,	*b*	Which you sent into my heart,
Ew'ger Vater, Quell des Lichts!	*c*	Eternal Father, source of light!
Mein Verderben ist gewendet,	*b*	My ruin has been turned,
Nicht mehr todverkündend rauschet	*a*	The roaring last judgement does not
Mir der Sturm des Weltgerichts.	*c*	Herald death anymore.
Doch wie sie mir Schaden brächten	*d*	But the troop of enemies is always
Stets die Schaar der Feinde sinnt –	*e*	Seeking ways to do me harm –
Rette du aus diesen Nächten,	*d*	Father, rescue your beloved child
Vater, dein geliebtes Kind!	*e*	Out of these nights!

---

[65] Thalheimer, 'Johanna Kinkel als Musikerin', 58. 'In dem fortgesetzten Spiel zwischen unison gehaltener Frage und chorisch gegebener Antwort betritt es die bekannten Wege, die Zelter und Reichardt in ihren volkstümlichen Liedern gegangen sind, auch in den stereotypen Klavierfiguren zeigt sich der Stil der Berliner Liederschule.'

Mag in heil'gem Muth ich streben,	*f*	I may aspire in blessed courage
Ganz die Welt mir zu erkämpfen,	*g*	To conquer the entire world,
Daß sie diene deinem Reich:	*h*	That it may serve your kingdom:
Ach ich kann sie doch nicht dämpfen,	*g*	Alas, I cannot subjugate it,
Oft noch muß ich mich ergeben	*f*	I often have to abandon myself to
Ihrem Locken süß und weich.	*h*	Its sweet and soft luring.
Schau, wie sie mit Zauberflechten	*d*	Look, how, with the magic plaits
Ihrer Schönheit mich umspinnt –	*e*	Of its beauty it enwraps me –
Rette du aus Sündennächten,	*d*	Rescue, out of these sinful nights,
Vater, dein geliebtes Kind!	*e*	Father, your beloved child!
Ja, du nährst die Kraft! Gewaltig	*i*	Yes, you nourish my strength! Powerfully,
Steh' ich in dem Streit als Sieger!	*k*	I will win this battle!
Aber weh, mich trifft ihr Zorn,	*l*	But alas! Its anger hits me,
Und den kühnen Gotteskrieger	*k*	And, in many ways, having been rejected,
Trifft, verschmäht, sie vielgestaltig	*i*	It strikes the keen holy warrior
Mit des bittern Todes Dorn.	*l*	With the thorn of bitter death.
Mit dem letzten Feind zu fechten	*d*	Lord, help me to fight with my last enemy,
Hilf, Herr! meine Kraft verrinnt –	*e*	My strength fades away –
Rette du aus Todesnächten,	*d*	Out of deathly nights,
Vater, dein geliebtes Kind!	*e*	Father, rescue your beloved child!

Despite the differences in Johanna and Gottfried's confession, religion played an important role in their relationship, especially during the first period of their courtship. On 2 July 1840, Johanna wrote to the sermoniser Gottfried:

> Yesterday I had the great intention to travel to Cologne and listen to your sermon; but too many people would know me there so I must deny myself [this trip]. Please send me the promised sermon on my favourite text; surely I will decipher your writing; I have been able to decipher Henning's writing, and there is no theologian or philosopher in the world who would write more unclearly than he.[66]

This letter reflects Johanna's admiration for Gottfried: not only does she praise his preaching style, but she also acknowledges his expertise as a theologian and a philosopher. The latter surfaces in a letter dated 10 July 1840, in which Johanna writes:

[66] Johanna and Gottfried Kinkel, *Liebe treue Johanna! Liebster Gottit!*, i, 48. 'Gestern hatte ich den großartigen Plan, nach Cölln zu reisen, um Sie predigen zu hören; aber auch dort kennen mich zu viele Leute, und so muß ich mir's wohl versagen. Bitte senden Sie mir doch die versprochene Predigt über meinen Lieblingstext; ich werde Sie schon enträthseln; ich habe doch nun Hennings enträthseln müssen, und undeutlicher als der schreibt gewiß nicht Theolog noch Philosoph mehr auf Erden.' Considering that Johanna and Gottfried corresponded over particular sermons he gave on different occasions, one can assume that Johanna had in mind a certain sermon when she asked Gottfried to send her the 'promised sermon on [her] favourite words' and that Gottfried knew which sermon she meant.

I ask you to give me advice. After prolonged struggles, I have come to <u>one</u> conclusion on my own; namely: <u>for years, I have developed false concepts of truth</u>.
[…] Love and hate take in us priority over truth, and it has to be the other way
around; – how will I achieve this? I feel that I have found out what separated me
from my own salvation; once I overcome <u>this</u> self-deception, and I am rescued
and free. The most difficult burdens are: 1) I need to digest that <u>before</u> this illu-
mination I have already written: 'False to oneself, false to the world'. How can I
keep the old view without [my] hindering progress?; I do not want to perceive
myself as being inconsistent. 2) I need to fight against irreconcilability; this is the
most difficult task for me, but I am aware of its necessity and I cannot avoid it,
no matter how much I resist.[67]

Gottfried Kinkel responds on 11 July 1840:

The Lord is trying to lead my friend into truth quickly, which is why He sends
her struggles. 'We need to pass through many tribulations on our way into the
kingdom of God', say the apostles. You, dear friend, will attest before God's throne
that it was not <u>I</u> who pushed forward your development in haste. It is only now
that I am really happy, as the spirit, of whom is written: 'he shall judge and light
a fire', has started his irresistible work in your mind without my personal assis-
tance. I am positive that you are on the right path, because you want to become
forgiving, you no longer want to condemn and reject your brother but only want
to hate the sin that lies within him.[68]

---

[67] Ibid., i, 50–51. Underlining in original. 'Ich rufe Sie an, mir mit Rath beizustehen.
Zu <u>einem</u> Resultat bin ich nach langen Kämpfen schon selbst gekommen;
nämlich: <u>auch in mir sind jahrelang verkehrte Begriffe über Wahrheit
eingewurzelt</u>. […] Liebe und Haß machen sich in uns die Wahrheit unterthan,
und es muss umgekehrt seyn; – wie bringe ich das zu Stande? Mir ist, als hätte ich
nun entdeckt, was zwischen mir und dem Heile stand; über <u>die</u> Selbsttäuschung
hinüber, und ich bin erlöst und frei. Die ärgsten Klippen sind noch: 1) es zu
verdauen, daß ich <u>vor</u> diesem Lichtstrahl schon geschrieben "Unwahr gegen sich
selbst, unwahr gegen die Welt", wie rette ich die alte Ansicht, ohne den Fortschritt
zu hemmen?; ich möchte mir so ungern inkonsequent erscheinen. 2) Nun muß
die Unversöhnlichkeit bekämpft werden; das ist mir das schwerste, aber ich
erkenne es als eine Nothwendigkeit der ich nicht entschlüpfen kann, wie ich mich
auch sträube.'

[68] Ibid., i, 51–52. Underlining in original. 'Der Herr will meine Freundin rasch in
die Wahrheit führen, darum sendet er ihr immer Kämpfe. "Wir müssen durch
viele Trübsale in das Reich Gottes gehen", sagen die Apostel. Sie, theure Freundin,
werden es mir vor Gottes Richterstuhle bezeugen, daß nicht <u>ich</u> Ihre Entwicklung
hastig vorwärts getrieben habe. Jetzt erst kann ich mit reiner Freude mich freuen,
da ohne mein Zuthun der Geist, von dem geschrieben steht: "er wird richten und

These two quotations mark the beginning of an intensive exchange of ideas concerning religious matters. As a result, Johanna converted to the Protestant faith on 10 December 1842.[69] Her new beliefs are summarised in her credo, which reads:

> I believe in One God, who created and reigns over the world; who saturates every human spirit with His life and who established the skill and ambition in the human spirit to aspire to truth and goodness; who presides over all muses with love and justice and who leads the international reputation towards the victory of love and justice over hate and sin. […] I believe that no human authority may dictate to us and demand from us a certain form in which we externally honour and worship Him; that no priestly mediation between Him and the individual soul is necessary; and that He wants to be honoured by means of pure behaviour, holy love towards Him, and brotherly spirit towards our fellow men. […] I believe that, besides the mentioned moral obligations and prayer, Christ dictated the religious acts of christening and the Last Supper, but no further obligatory customs.[70]

In the last line, Kinkel denies the custom of confession, by which she distances herself from the Catholic denomination. Kinkel's credo and her letters emphasise her own and Gottfried's faith in God. The reference to God as a rescuer in 'Rette Vater, Dein geliebtes Kind!' is therefore not surprising. This joint work

---

ein Feuer entzünden" in Ihnen sein unwiderstehliches Werk beginnt. Und ich habe mein festes Zeichen, daß Sie auf dem rechten Wege sind, denn Sie wollen versöhnlich werden, wollen den Bruder nicht mehr verachten und von sich stoßen, sondern nur die Sünde hassen, die in ihm ist.'

[69] See Klaus, *Johanna Kinkel,* 342.

[70] Johanna Kinkel, *Mein Glaubensbekenntnis,* 1842, ULB 2406, n.p. 'Ich glaube an Einen Gott, der die Welt geschaffen hat und regiert, der jeden Menschengeist mit seinem Leben durchdringt, und die Fähigkeit und den Trieb in ihn gelegt hat, zur Wahrheit und Tugend hinzustreben, der mit Liebe und Gerechtigkeit über allen Musen waltet und den Welthruf zu dem Ziele lenkt, daß Liebe und Gerechtigkeit über Hass und Sünde den Sieg davontragen. […] Ich glaube, daß keine menschliche Autorität uns die Form vorschreiben und gebieten darf, in der wir ihn äußerlich verehren und anbeten sollen; daß zwischen ihm und den einzelnen Seelen keine priesterliche Vermittlung nothwendig ist, und daß er vor Allem durch reinen Wandel, heilige Liebe zu ihm und Brudersinn gegen unsern Nächsten geehrt seyn will. […] Ich glaube, daß außer den erwähnten sittlichen Verpflichtungen und dem Gebete Christus noch die religiösen Handlungen der Taufe und des Abendmahls, außer diesen aber keine verpflichtenden Gebräuche vorgeschrieben hat.'

could be seen as an attempt at overcoming borders between Catholicism and Protestantism. Furthermore, Johanna might have used this Lied as a means of publicly demonstrating her close bond with Gottfried.

The Lied incorporates diverse harmony. A German sixth chord features towards the end of the first verse (E-flat major–Ger6–D major, second half of bar 15). In bar 24, A-flat major is reached via an interrupted cadence (G major⁷–[expected: C major]–A-flat major). This harmonic surprise could be interpreted as a symbol of the lyrical I's struggle (Ex. 4.6).

Ex. 4.6: Change of harmonic rhythm in 'Rette Vater, Dein geliebtes Kind!' (bars 15–24)

While 'Rette Vater, Dein geliebtes Kind!' grapples with issues surrounding Johanna and Gottfried Kinkel's personal lives, the Geibel setting 'Abendfeier' (Evening Ceremony, op. 8, no. 4) is more generic. The poem deals with the different stages of a religious ceremony: the sounding of the bells, the prayer to the Virgin Mary and her son, and the sacred devotions.

Abendfeier (op. 8, no. 4)		**Evening Ceremony[71]**
Emanuel Geibel (published 1838)		Translation by Sharon Krebs

Ave Maria! Meer und Himmel ruh'n,	*a*	Ave Maria! Sea and heaven are resting,
Von allen Türmen hallt der Glocken Ton,	*b*	From every tower echoes the sound of bells,
Ave Maria! Laßt vom ird'schen Tun,	*a*	Ave Maria! Leave off your earthly endeavours,
Zur Jungfrau betet, zu der Jungfrau Sohn,	*b*	Pray to the Virgin, to the Virgin's son,
Der Engel Scharen selber knieen nun[72]	*a*	The hosts of the angels themselves are now kneeling
Mit Lilienstäben vor des Vaters Thron,	*b*	With staves of lilies before the Father's throne,
Und aus den Rosenwolken wehn die Lieder[73]	*c*	And out of the rosy clouds the songs
Der sel'gen Geister feierlich hernieder.	*c*	Of the blessed spirits waft solemnly down [toward earth].
O heil'ge Andacht, welche jedes Herz	*d*	Oh holy devotion, which marvellously penetrates
Mit leisen Schauern wunderbar durchdringt!	*e*	Every heart with a quiet shiver!
O sel'ger Glaube, der sich himmelwärts	*d*	Oh holy faith that soars toward heaven
Auf des Gebetes weißem Fittig schwingt!	*e*	On the white wings of prayer!
In milde Tränen löst sich da der Schmerz,	*d*	There pain dissolves into mild tears,
Indes der Freude Jubel sanfter klingt.	*e*	While the rejoicing of happiness rings out more gently.
Ave Maria! Erd' und Himmel scheinen	*f*	Ave Maria! It seems that earth and heaven
Bei diesem Wort sich liebend zu vereinen.[74]	*f*	At this word love each other and become one.

In bar 18, a chromatic progession emphasises an important atmospheric turn where the exclamations 'Ave Maria!' (first verse) and 'O sel'ger Glaube' (Oh holy faith, second verse) are heard. Here, an F minor chord is followed by the tritone C-sharp, which, as dominant seventh chord, establishes the new tonal context of F-sharp minor – the initial tonic key was A minor (Ex. 4.7).

[71] <http://www.lieder.net/lieder/get_text.html?TextId=38707> (accessed 30 March 2020).

[72] Geibel's original poem reads 'Des Himmels Scharen' (heaven's hosts). Emanuel Geibel, 'Abendfeier in Venedig', in Geibel, *Gedichte*, 90.

[73] Geibel's original reads 'und durch die' (and through). The translation is adjusted by the author.

[74] Like Schumann, Kinkel uses this version, while Geibel's original reads 'Ave Maria! Wenn die Glocke tönet, | So lächeln Erd' und Himmel mild versöhnet' (When the bell sounds, earth and heaven smile, reconciled).

Ex. 4.7: Enharmonic progression in 'Abendfeier' (bars 17–20)[75]

Linda Siegel observes that the formal design of this Lied features five seven-bar sections, interrupted by two two-bar sections: 7–7–2–7–2–7–7. She explains that Kinkel might have chosen this division on account of the importance of the number seven within religious contexts.[76] It might have been the unusual harmonic progression and the melodic division adhering to the individual aspects of the ceremony that led Rellstab to draw the following conclusion:

No. 4, 'Abendfeier', is undoubtedly the most distinctive Lied in the collection, but it is possibly the hardest to understand. The music distances itself from the purely religious idea of the poem, and relates to the formal appearance of the ceremony. This is not intended as criticism, but the observation that 'she is giving us an image rather than a thought'.[77]

Rellstab's interpretation of Kinkel giving the listener an image rather than a thought can be developed further. Kinkel accentuates the line 'In milde Thränen löst sich da der Schmerz' (There pain dissolves into mild tears, second verse, Ex. 4.8) by changing the piano accompaniment. Furthermore, the enharmonic

---

[75] Considering the harmonic progression and the placing of accidentals in the rest of the bar, the first 'c♯' in the piano right-hand part in bar 19 was added by myself although the original publication includes 'c♮' here. This is likely to be an editorial mistake.

[76] Siegel, *Johanna Kinkel*, i, iv.

[77] Ludwig Rellstab, review of Johanna Mathieux, *Sechs Gedichte von Emanuel Geibel für eine Singstimme mit Begleitung des Pianoforte: Opus 8* (1838), *Iris im Gebiete der Tonkunst*, 3 August 1838, 121–22. 'Nr. 4, "Abendfeier", ist unstreitig das eigenthümlichste Lied der Sammlung, kommt aber vielleicht am schwersten zur Verständnis. Die Musik geht von der reinen religiösen Idee des Gedichts ab, und wendet sich mehr auf die äußere Gestalt der gottesdienstlichen Feier. Dies soll hier kein Tadel sein; vielmehr das: "Sie giebt uns mehr ein Bild, als einen Gedanken".'

Ex. 4.8: Changing piano accompaniment in 'Abendfeier' (bars /24–26)

progression at the words 'Ave Maria' and 'Oh Holy faith' contradicts the purity often associated with belief. Although Kinkel published this Lied in 1838, before her philosophical grappling with religiosity, the disappointment of her first marriage and in the Rhenish Catholic conventions might have provoked critical thoughts.

Published in Johanna and Gottfried Kinkel's year of marriage, 1843, the Lied 'Stürmisch Wandern' (Stormy Ramble, op. 18, no. 6) can be interpreted as processing the lovers' ordeal by means of an allegory of nature. In this through-composed setting of Gottfried's verse, the lyrical I wanders through the mountains and meets such natural barriers as storms, rivers, snow, and rain with determination and courage.

Stürmisch wandern (op. 18, no. 6) Gottfried Kinkel (published 1843)		**Stormy Ramble**
Felsen steigen herauf, herab,	*a*	Rocky cliffs lead up and down,
Fliegt es zum Himmel?	*b*	Ascending to heaven?
Steigt es ins Grab?	*a*	Descending into the grave?
Über die Felsen hinab, hinauf,	*c*	Over the rocks, down and up,
Geht ungehalten mein steter Lauf.	*c*	My steady ramble leads.
Oben umwandelt der Sturm mich rund,	*d*	On top of the mountain a storm surrounds me,
Los mich zu reißen vom festen Grund.	*d*	Attempting to tear me away from the firm ground.
Unten aber der Ströme Grausen,	*e*	But in the valley there are terrifying rivers
Die grimmig schwellend zum Meere brausen;	*e*	Which bluster grimly to the sea;
Schnee auf den Höhn, Regen im Tal,	*f*	Snow on the top, rain in the valley,
Grausen und Schrecken allzumal.	*f*	Horror and fright everywhere.

Nimmer verzagt, nimmer geklagt und gejammert,	*g*	I never give up, I never complain or moan,
Sprung da gewagt, fest an den Fels dich geklammert.	*g*	I risk a jump, holding tightly onto the rocks.
Und dem Sturm zuwider mit trotziger Lust	*h*	Against the storm, with bold happiness,
Jauchz ich aus wild arbeitender Brust.	*h*	I cheer wildly out of my hard-working chest.
Und dem brausenden Gießbach,	*i*	In response to the roaring stream
dem eisigen Regen,	*k*	And the icy rain,
Ruf ich ein fröhliches Lied entgegen!	*k*	I sing a happy song!

The irregular rhyme scheme and uneven division of lines per poetic strophe (5–6–4–3) support the impression of an unpredictable course of events. The first stanza, which introduces the natural barriers, is set in G minor, 4/4 metre, and is played *forte*. The second part, poetic strophes two and three, incorporates the brighter major tonic key of G major, is set in a lighter 6/8 metre and its dynamics increase from *piano* to *fortissimo*. These changes turn the Lied into an optimistic and positive reassurance of the lyrical I's confidence. The melody includes many leaps, which support the textual content. For instance, the first word, 'Felsen' (rocks), is set to a descending minor sixth ('d²–'f♯¹', Ex. 4.9) – a melodic feature which is found relatively rarely in Kinkel's compositions, as she did not have much confidence in her own singing. This Lied's vocal range spans a diminished twelfth ('c♯¹'–'g²'); thus, Kinkel, as an alto singer, might not have composed this song with her own performance in mind.

Ex. 4.9: Melodic symbolism in 'Stürmisch Wandern' (bars 5–6)

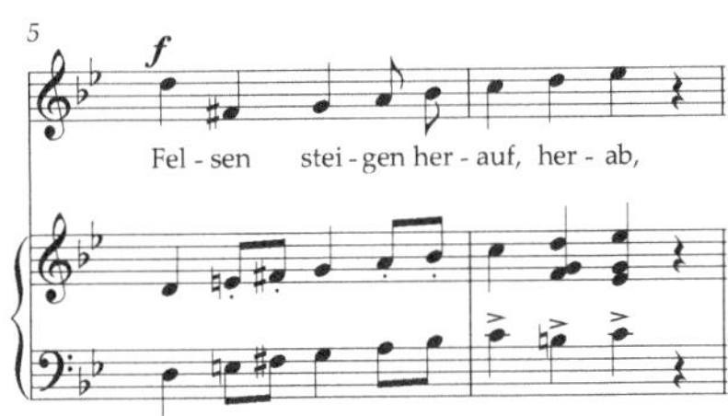

Considering the date of publication, 1843, one is tempted to interpret the lyrical I's hurdle race and his/her optimism as an allegory of Gottfried and Johanna Kinkel's own socio-political struggles which preceded their marriage. But Kinkel was aware of women's struggles and their hesitation to fight for their rights more generally, as is reflected in her memoirs, where she states that:

> My first marriage is the story of thousands of my sisters, and the logical consequence of our social situation. Numerous women collapse under similar circumstances, while hardly anyone out of an entire generation has the courage to break free and rescue her better self.[78]

Besides gender and religion, Kinkel's songs cover other political themes. The words of 'Thurm und Fluth' (Tower and Floodwaters, op. 19, no. 6) were written by Gottfried in 1846; the Lied was published in 1848, one of the most eventful years in nineteenth-century German history.[79] The poem is laden with personification and metaphors, giving the reader the impression that the tower and the sea are acting like human beings. In the light of the semantically ambiguous chorus ('Die Wellen kennen nicht Rast noch Ruh', The waves know neither rest nor repose), the lyrics seem to criticise the German political status quo. Symbolising the Prussian emperor, the waterfront tower is destroyed by the raging sea as spirits sally in from the West, possibly an allusion to the strong democratic movement in the Western parts of Germany, such as the Rhineland, Baden, and the Palatinate, or to the French revolutions which preceded the German revolutionary upheavals.

Thurm und Fluth (op. 19, no. 6) Gottfried Kinkel (published 1848)		**Tower and Floodwaters**[80] Translation by Sharon Krebs
Auf starkem Klippenrande[81]	*a*	Upon a mighty cliff edge
Raget ein starker Turm	*b*	There looms a strong tower
Weitschauend über die Lande,	*a*	That gazes far across the land,
Und trotzt so stolz dem Sturm.	*b*	And defies the storm so proudly.
Unten so dumpf und schwer	*c*	Below so dully and heavily
Wälzt sich das ew'ge Meer.	*c*	Rolls the eternal sea;

Die Wogen kennen nicht Rast
    noch Ruh,
	d	The waves know neither rest
		    nor repose,

Sie wühlen und spülen immerzu.	*d*	They moil and swirl without end.

[78] Johanna Kinkel, 'Erinnerungsblätter aus dem Jahre 1848', *Deutsche Monatsschrift für Politik, Wissenschaft, Kunst und Leben*, 4 (1851), 39–108, 98. 'Meine erste Heirath ist die Geschichte von Tausenden meiner Schwestern, und das nothwendige Resultat unserer sozialen Zustände. Unzählige Frauen gehen an ähnlichen Verhältnissen zu Grunde, indeß von einer ganzen Generationen kaum eine den Muth hat, sich loszureissen und ihr besseres Selbst zu retten.'

[79] The year 1846 is included underneath the title in Gottfried Kinkel, 'Thurm und Flut', in *Gedichte*, 7th edn (Tübingen/Stuttgart: Cotta, 1872), 60–61. It is also included in the *Maikäfer* journal from 30 December 1845 (Brandt-Schwarze and others, *Der Maikäfer*, iv, 367–69).

[80] <http://www.lieder.net/lieder/get_text.html?TextId=98071> (accessed 6 May 2019).

[81] The original reads 'scharfem' (sharp) rather than 'starkem' (mighty).

Was frommt, o Flut, dein Tollen?	*e*	Of what use is, oh floodwaters, your agitation?
Dein tausendjährig Drohn?	*f*	Your thousand-year-long threatening?
Es spricht ja deinem Rollen	*e*	Your rolling waves are mocked
Der feste Zwinger Hohn!	*f*	By the sturdy ward [of the castle]!
Früh bis zum Abendroth	*g*	From early morning until sunset,
Rollst du in deinen Tod.	*g*	You [waves] break yourself into death;

Die Wogen kennen nicht Rast
    noch Ruh,
	d	The waves know neither rest
		        nor repose,

Sie wühlen und spülen immerzu.	*d*	They moil and swirl without end.

Todmuthig Well an Welle	*h*	Valiant unto death, wave after wave
Zerschellt ihr krauses Haupt,	*i*	Shatters its curly head,
Und hat doch von der Stelle	*h*	And has only managed to steal
Ein Sandkorn nur geraubt.	*i*	A grain of sand from that place.
Stolz noch das Schloß sich bläht,	*k*	Proudly the castle still stands,
Well' an Welle vergeht.	*k*	Wave upon wave passes away –

Die Wogen kennen nicht Rast
    noch Ruh,
	d	The waves know neither rest
		        nor repose,

Sie wühlen und spülen immerzu.	*d*	They moil and swirl without end.

Da kommt die Nacht. Es stürmen	*l*	Then comes the night. From the West
Vom West die Geister her,	*m*	The spirits storm forth;
Da hebt sich empor zu Türmen	*l*	Then the still, eternal sea lifts itself
Das stille, das ewige Meer.	*m*	Up to the height of towers.
Tief in die Luken zischt	*n*	Deep into the crevices hisses
Weiß und wütig der Gischt.	*n*	Whitely and angrily the spume –

Die Wogen kennen nicht Rast
    noch Ruh,
	d	The waves know neither rest
		        nor repose,

Sie wühlen und spülen immerzu.	*d*	They moil and swirl without end.

Die ihr vertraut den
    Riffen,[82]
	o	Those of you who have placed your trust
		        in the reefs:

Bebt, die ihr droben haust,	*p*	Tremble, you who live above!
Die Flut hat euch ergriffen	*o*	The floodwaters have seized you
Mit tausendfingriger Faust.	*p*	With a thousand-fingered fist.
Just um die Mitternacht	*q*	Precisely at midnight
Berstend der Turm zerkracht.	*q*	The tower cracks asunder –

Die Wogen kennen nicht Rast
    noch Ruh,
	d	The waves know neither rest
		        nor repose,

Sie wühlen und spülen immerzu.	*d*	They moil and swirl without end.

In a letter of 12 February 1850, Johanna Kinkel refers to the chorus of 'Thurm und Fluth' by using the line 'Die Wogen kennen nicht Rast noch Ruh' as a motto.[83] Here, she assures her husband that she is considering a plan for his

---

[82] The original reads 'Ihr habt' (you have) rather than 'Die ihr' (Those of you who).

[83] Johanna and Gottfried Kinkel, *Liebe treue Johanna! Liebster Gottit!*, ii, 852.

escape from prison. From prison, Gottfried suggested to Johanna on 29 July 1849 that she should try to print some of his recent poems in order to relieve their difficult financial situation.[84] Johanna, too, pursued a commercial interest with her song compositions, perhaps one reason why her setting of 'Thurm und Fluth' includes many simple folk-like elements.[85]

✃ *Direct political connotations*

While the revolutionary appeals in 'Thurm und Fluth' would have only been recognised by the Kinkels' like-minded friends and acquaintances, Johanna's 'Demokratenlied' (Democrats' Song) contains direct references to the revolution.

Demokratenlied		**Democrats' Song**[86]
Johanna Kinkel (published 1849)		Translation by Sharon Krebs
Genug der Schmähung habt Ihr uns geboten,	*a*	You have offered us enough of vilification,
Der Lüge und des Hohnes nur zu viel.	*b*	Of lies and ridicule only too much.
Nicht schürten wir den Hass den blutig roten,	*a*	We did not fan the flames of hate, the blood-red [flames],
Die Menschlichkeit war unser Ziel.	*b*	The goal of our battle was brotherliness.
Wer trägt des Blutes Zeichen am Gewande,	*c*	Who has the sign of blood upon his garments?
Wem sprüht der Bürgerhass aus gift'gem Blick.	*d*	From out of whose venomous gaze spews hatred of the populace?
Wer küßt den Staub von eines Thrones Rande,	*c*	Who kisses the dust from the edging of a throne,
Und zittert vor dem Namen Republik.	*d*	And trembles before the name 'republic'?
Und Ihr die mit der Fülle Eures Goldes,	*e*	And you, who with the abundance of your gold,
Mit süßem Wein und süßer Schmeichelei	*f*	With sweet wine and sweeter flattery
Jetzt kirrt die Knechte des Tyrannensoldes,	*e*	Now tame the servants in the tyrant's pay,
Es gilt auch Euch der Freiheit Racheschrei.	*f*	The revengeful scream of freedom pertains to you as well!

[84] Ibid., 578.

[85] For further thoughts on the compositional logic of Kinkel's Lied 'Thurm und Fluth' see my article 'Johanna Kinkel's *Thurm und Fluth*'.

[86] <http://www.lieder.net/lieder/get_text.html?TextId=98653> (accessed 22 April 2019).

Droht nur dem freien Mann mit Kerkermauern,	*g*	Only threaten the free man with prison walls,	
Wenn tückisch Ihr die Waffen erst geraubt;	*h*	When you have first sneakily taken away his weapons,	
Erfüllt der Mütter Herz mit Todesschauern,	*g*	Fill the hearts of mothers with the horrors of death,	
Begehrt als Geisel unsrer Kinder Haupt.	*h*	Desire the heads of our children as hostages.	

O Freiheit die der Arme sich erkoren,	*i*	Oh freedom that the poor man has chosen for himself,	
Ob all sein Gut in Schutt und Trümmer sank.	*k*	Though all his possessions sank into rubble and ruin.	
Dich grüßen wir, wenn nur zu unsern Ohren	*i*	We greet you, if only in death our ears	
Im Tod der Name Republik erklang.	*k*	Hear the name 'republic' ringing out.	

Chorus: Schaut ob Ihr unser Recht	*l*	Chorus: See if you can shatter our right	
Und unsre Wehr zerbrecht.	*l*	And our defence.	
Heran, heran, heran Demokratie,	*m*	Draw near, draw near, draw near, democracy,	
Dran auf die rote Monarchie.	*m*	Storm the red monarchy.	

Advocating a democratic republic, this simple strophic setting focuses on delivering a political message. Monica Klaus suggests that 'Demokratenlied' was received positively when Gottfried Kinkel recited it at a meeting in December 1848.[87] Announced in the *Bonner Zeitung* on 16 December 1848, its publication by Sulzbach facilitated its instant dissemination. The poem develops a tension by starting off with a peaceful mood ('The goal of our battle was brotherliness') and concluding with combative enthusiasm ('if only in death our ears | Hear the name 'republic' ringing out'). The use of such personal pronouns as 'we' and 'us' suggests a direct link with the Kinkels' own political ambitions. In a letter dated 24 February 1849 – Gottfried had moved to Berlin – Johanna assured Gottfried that 'even if I could not follow you, my glowing heart is with you, my mind and your mind aspire to the same aim'.[88]

---

[87] Klaus, *Johanna Kinkel*, 167.

[88] Johanna and Gottfried Kinkel, *Liebe treue Johanna! Liebster Gottit!*, I, 426. 'Wenn ich dir nicht folgen konnte, so ist doch mein volles glühendes Herz bei dir, mein Geist erstrebt mit deinem das gleiche Ziel.'

On 7 July, after Johanna Kinkel visited her husband in prison, she included in a letter to him her poem 'Der gefangene Freischärler' (The Imprisoned Voluntary Soldier), a manuscript of which is archived in Leipzig.[89]

Der gefangene Freischärler
Johanna Kinkel

The Imprisoned Voluntary Soldier

Was schaut ihr Kindlein traurig zu mir auf,	*a*	Why, children, are you looking at me sadly,
Und fragt, warum der Mutter Thränen rollen?	*b*	And ask why mother's tears are falling?
Hemmt nicht mit süßem Schmeicheln ihren Lauf	*a*	Do not block with sweet words their path
Der aus der Seele quillt, der schwerzvollen.	*b*	Which springs from the aching soul.
Der Vater, den wir lieben treu und rein,	*c*	The father, whom we love truly and purely,
Er weilt gefangen auf dem hohen Thurme,	*d*	He is kept in the high tower,
Und lauscht durch sein vergittert Fensterlein	*c*	He listens through his barred window
Dem fernen Schlachtendonner und dem Sturme.	*d*	To the remote battle-thunder and storms.
Er kämpfte für die deutsche Republik –	*e*	He fought for the German Republic –
Prophetisch sah sein Aug' die Zukunft tragen;	*f*	The future on his mind, like a prophet;
Zur Freiheit hingewandt den kühnen Blick,	*e*	With a brave view towards freedom,
Nicht mocht' er nach der Zahl der Feinde fragen.	*f*	He did not ask about the number of his enemies.
Es färbt sein edles Blut den Boden roth;	*g*	His noble blood colours the ground;
Er sank; doch hielt die Hand noch die Muskete.	*h*	He fell; but he kept the musket in his hand.
O darum nun verschont' ihn früher Tod	*g*	This is why he did not die early,
Daß er des Kerkers öden Raum betrete.	*h*	So that he was spared from stepping into the dull prison cell.

[89] Universitätsbibliothek Leipzig, signature: Kestner/II/A/IV/1087/Nr. 8; 1087; Nr. 8; Johanna and Gottfried Kinkel, *Liebe treue Johanna! Liebster Gottit!*, ii, 564–65; Willison Lemke, "'Alles Schaffen ist wohl eine Wechselwirkung von Inspiration und Willen'", 66. According to Willison Lemke, Kinkel also set her husband's 'Männerlied', which was included as a poem in the *Maikäfer* journal from 30 December 1845 (Brandt-Schwarze and others, *Der Maikäfer*, iv, 367–68). Willison Lemke dates Kinkel's setting of 'Männerlied' *c.* 1846, but as the manuscript is missing and there are no letters between Johanna and Gottfried Kinkel recorded from October 1845 to May 1847, it is difficult to make definite statements about this composition.

Ihr stolzen Sieger! Ehrt den tapfren Feind	*i*	Proud winners! Honour the brave enemy
Der bis zum Tod getreu blieb seiner Fahne,	*k*	Who never attempted desertion,
Deß Lippe nie mit falschem Wort verneint	*i*	Whose lips never denied
Was still sein Herz beschloß im heil'gen Wahn.	*k*	What his heart decided in blessed delusion.
Doch <u>wir</u> verhüllen wehmuthsvoll das Haupt,	*l*	But <u>we</u> sadly veil our faces,[90]
Und harren stumm dem finstern Schicksalsspruche.	*m*	And we wait quietly for destiny's dark verdict.
Noch grünt die Hoffnung! Weh, wenn sie entlaubt –	*l*	There is still hope! Alas, once the hope is gone –
Dann wird die Welt, das Leben uns zum Fluche.	*m*	Then the world, and life, will turn into a curse.

In the same letter, Kinkel explains that 'nobody will hold against me that I accept the necessity of keeping my hands off politics completely from now on. How easily could an incautious statement of mine imperil your rescue!'.[91] In the light of this, it is not surprising that both 'Der gefangene Freischärler' and 'Der letzte Glaubensartikel' (The Last Credendum) remained unpublished.[92]

Der letzte Glaubensartikel		**The Last Credendum**
Gottfried Kinkel		

Von Allem, was ich einst geglaubt,	*a*	Of everything I used to believe
Ist wenig mir geblieben,	*b*	Very little has remained,
Die Priester haben's weggeraubt,	*a*	The priests robbed it,
Die <u>Welt</u> hat's ausgetrieben.	*b*	The <u>world</u> took it.[93]
Mir blieb ein einz'ger Glaube,	*c*	I am left with one belief,
Der macht mir Alles wett;	*d*	That compensates for every loss.
Vernehmt's beim Saft der Traube:	*c*	Hear it over a glass of wine:
Ich glaube, ich glaube,	*c*	I believe, I believe,
Ich glaub' an's Bajonet!	*d*	I believe in the bayonet.

---

[90] Underlining in original.

[91] Johanna and Gottfried Kinkel, *Liebe treue Johanna! Liebster Gottit!*, ii, 561. 'Daß ich mich der Nothwendigkeit beuge, und von jetzt an die Finger von aller Politik fern halte, wird mir niemand verdenken. Wie leicht könnte eine unvorsichtige Äußerung meinerseits den Faden abschneiden, an dem deine Rettung hängt.'

[92] The manuscript of this Lied is missing. See Willison Lemke, "Alles Schaffen ist wohl eine Wechselwirkung von Inspiration und Willen'", 66.

[93] All underlining in original.

So herrlich hatt' ich mir gedacht	*e*	How beautiful I imagined
Den Friedenssieg der Liebe!	*f*	The peaceful victory of love would be!
Doch seh' ich's heut: der <u>Fürst</u> der Nacht	*e*	But now I see: the <u>ruler</u> of the night
Weicht nur dem Flammhiebe.	*f*	Only yields to fire.
So wird er uns zum Raube,	*c*	That way he becomes our victim,
Er stürzt aufs blut'ge Bett!	*d*	He falls into the bloody bed!
Vernehmt's beim Saft der Traube!	*c*	Hear it over a glass of wine:
Ich glaube, ich glaube,	*c*	I believe, I believe,
Ich glaub' an's Bajonet!	*d*	I believe in the bayonet.
Was schert mich alles Reden noch,	*g*	Who cares about all the talking,
Was scheren mich die Kammern?	*h*	Who cares about the law?
Wir brechen nimmermehr das Joch,	*g*	We will never win
Solang wir's nur bejammern!	*h*	As long as we are sorry for ourselves!
Setzt auf die Pickelhaube	*c*	Put on helmets,
Zum blutigen Bankett!	*d*	Come to the bloody banquet!
Vernehmt's beim Saft der Traube:	*c*	Hear it over a glass of wine:
Ich glaube, ich glaube,	*c*	I believe, I believe,
Ich glaub' an's Bajonet!	*d*	I believe in the bayonet.
Die <u>Feinde</u> sparen uns die Wahl,	*i*	The <u>enemies</u> spare us our choice,
Fahr hin, du feige Sünde!	*k*	Away with you, cowardly sin!
Die Kugel und der blanke Stahl,	*i*	The bullet and pure steel
Das sind die letzten Gründe.	*k*	Are the last chances.
Hinab zu <u>Dampf</u> und Staube	*c*	Down to <u>steam</u> and dust
Von Eurem schwanken Brett!	*d*	Get off your labile board!
Vernehmt's beim Saft der Traube:	*c*	Hear it over a glass of wine:
Ich glaube, ich glaube,	*c*	I believe, I believe,
Ich glaub' an's Bajonet!	*d*	I believe in the bayonet.
Es saust der Hieb, die Kugel pfeift,	*l*	Strokes roar, bullets fly,
Und die Tyrannen zittern!	*m*	And the tyrants shake!
Die <u>Frucht</u> der deutschen <u>Freiheit</u> reift	*l*	The <u>fruit</u> of German <u>freedom</u> ripens
Nur in der <u>Schlacht</u> Gewittern.	*m*	Only during the <u>thunderstorms</u> of battle.
Es lebe dieser Glaube,	*c*	Long live this belief,
Ein <u>Hoch</u> dem Bajonet!	*d*	<u>Here's</u> to the bayonet!
Vernehmt's beim Saft der Traube:	*c*	Hear it over a glass of wine:
Ich glaube, ich glaube,	*c*	I believe, I believe,
Ich glaub' an's Bajonet!	*d*	I believe in the bayonet.

Comparing the poems, two different approaches emerge. While 'Der gefangene Freischärler' takes Johanna Kinkel's personal perspective as she processes her own and the children's sorrows about their husband and father, 'Der letzte Glaubensartikel' reflects Gottfried Kinkel's political eagerness. The closing paragraph of Kinkel's letter from 7 July 1849 shows that she prioritised her family's well-being over the completion of Gottfried's political mission, as she wrote:

Should the war situation change, of which there is no likelihood at the moment, I beg you: stay firm, and consider your political mission as definitely finished. There are other spheres for you in which no one takes you out. Do not tempt fate! If your life is saved by a miracle now, let us quieten down from then on.[94]

Kinkel's Lied 'Abendlied nach der Schlacht' (Evening Song after the Battle, op. 21, no. 5), in which she set her husband's words, demonstrates a more thoughtful and defensive position. This Lied is part of Gottfried Kinkel's Singspiel *Die Assassinen*, which originates from the early 1840s. This song marks an important atmospheric turn. After a bloody battle between the Christian crusaders and the Muslim assassins, which is won by the Christians, the Templar Enguerrand de Coucy looks sadly over the battlefield.[95] Throughout the Singspiel, de Coucy is in search of his missing son, who, as it turns out, is supposed to fight against him on the battlefield as an assassin. Later in the Singspiel, the assassin Musa and de Coucy find out that they are son and father, which brings about a positive ending.[96] A Christian earl, who listened to de Coucy's thoughtful recital of 'Abendlied nach der Schlacht', asks him why he was so serious after a hard-won battle. Thinking of his lost son, de Coucy replies:

Whether won or lost, a battle is something that makes even a warrior serious. Imagine how many a heart has died today that used to lean against a beautiful woman's chest! How many a man fell whose father was hoping to rejoice in his son's life![97]

[94] Johanna and Gottfried Kinkel, *Liebe treue Johanna! Liebster Gottit!*, II, 562. 'Wenn irgend ein Wechsel des Kriegsglücks einträte, wozu kein Anschein ist, so flehe ich dich an: bleibe standhaft, und sieh deine politische Mission für definitiv beendet an. Es gibt andre Sphären für dich, worin dich kein Mensch überbietet. Frevle nicht! Wenn jetzt dein Leben durch ein Wunder errettet wird, so wollen wir uns über das Weitere beruhigen.'

[95] It is uncertain whether Gottfried Kinkel chose this name referring to the French earl of the same name, who, according to the 1858 *Pierer's Universal-Lexikon*, ruled the counties Soissons and Bedford, and voiced tenures in relation to the Western Rhineland region Elsaß-Lothringen. Pierer mentions that de Coucy died in 1397 during a crusade, which links to the plot of *Die Assassinen*. See *Pierer's Universal-Lexikon*, 4th edn, iv, 486.

[96] This plot, according to Monica Klaus, goes back to the 'Hildebrandlied', in which a son and a father fight against each other unrecognised. See Monica Klaus, '"Die Assassinen – Romantisches Singspiel mit Gesang": von Gottfried und Johanna Kinkel, 1843' (unpublished article, Bonn, 24 November 2014), 14.

[97] All references to the Singspiel *Die Assassinen* are taken from Gottfried Kinkel's own manuscript, archived at ULB (S 2686, n.d. [1842/1843]). There is no pagination in this manuscript; the date [1842/1843] was ascertained by ULB. 'Gewonnen oder

The fact that Johanna Kinkel did not mention the Singspiel in her op. 21 warrants its analysis separately from the interpretation of the Singspiel further below.[98] In the *Adagio* setting 'Abendlied nach der Schlacht', the lyrical I wanders over an abandoned battlefield, pleading for peace.

Abendlied nach der Schlacht (op. 21, no. 5) Gottfried Kinkel (published 1851)		**Evening Song after the Battle**
Auf weitem blut'gen Feld,	*a*	On the wide bloody field,
Wo sich die Heere trafen,	*b*	Where the armies met,
So manche, manche Braven	*b*	Some brave [soldiers]
schlafen.	*b*	Sleep.
Auf weitem blut'gen Feld.	*a*	On the wide bloody field.
Die Sonne geht zu Ruh,	*c*	The sun sets,
Des Todes Schatten schleichen	*d*	Death's shadows sneak
So langsam auf den bleichen	*d*	Slowly over the pale
Leichen.	*d*	Corpses.
Die Sonne geht zu Ruh.	*c*	The sun sets.
Schlaft wohl nun, Freund und Feind!	*e*	Sleep well now, friend and foe!
So viele heut gefallen,	*f*	So many died today,
Euch wünsch' ich Frieden allen,	*f*	I wish you all peace,
allen.	*f*	All of you.
Schlaft wohl nun, Freund und Feind.	*e*	Sleep well now, friend and foe.

Gottfried Kinkel's words consist of many soft internal assonances portraying the torpid post-battle atmosphere. The Lied captures this mood through long legato passages and a moving piano postlude (Ex. 4.10).

Contrary to the folk-like melodies of most of Kinkel's Rhineland songs and her 'Demokratenlied', 'Abendlied nach der Schlacht' incorporates linear dissonances in the vocal line, mainly minor seconds, and a tritone in bars 12–13 ('a¹'–'eb¹'). Furthermore, the German augmented sixth chord in bar 6 enriches the harmonic context. These characteristics increase this song's difficulty. As Kinkel aimed to sell her Lieder, she included more delicate songs in her collections rather than publishing them singularly, and her collections often feature a diverse range of complexity.

---

verloren, eine Schlacht ist ein Ding, das auch einen Krieger ernst macht. Wie manches Herz hat heute ausgeschlagen, das einst an eines schönen Weibes Brust klaffte! Wie mancher sank, dessen Vater noch hoffte, Freude an dem Sohn zu erleben!'

[98] Kinkel did include the remark 'Aus den *Assassinen*' ('From the *Assassinen*') for other songs from this Singspiel which were published as part of collections.

Ex. 4.10: 'Abendlied nach der Schlacht' (op. 21, no. 5)

Political optimism under the disguise of Exoticism

Many nineteenth-century writers, among whom Gottfried Kinkel was no exception, were attracted by settings in the Middle East. The Middle East was the second favourite location for operas and ballets in the mid-1840s, following the South of Spain.[99] Derek B. Scott warns of a Western European sense of

[99] Ralph P. Locke, 'Cutthroats and Casbah Dancers', in *The Exotic in Western Music*, ed. Jonathan Bellman (Boston: Eastern University Press, 1998), 104–36 (111). The Middle East, in the narrower sense, includes Turkey, Egypt, and the Arabian Peninsula (including Palestine and Israel), but in the broader sense it

superiority as described by Edward Said, but he also posits that Exoticism can manifest a form of social critique by inverting dominant values.[100] Likewise, Ralph P. Locke proposes that Exoticist settings may have the potential to criticise the writer's own homeland. He therefore suggests that the study of Exoticist works may prove useful in the examination of a writer's own socio-political background.[101] According to Locke, musical Exoticism is 'the process of evoking a place in or through music (people, social milieu) that is perceived as different from home by the people who created the Exoticist cultural product and by the people who receive it'. Compositional Exoticist features are modes and harmonies that were considered non-normative in the era or place where the work was composed; rhythmic or melodic patterns derived from dances; simple songs representing the folk; and departures from normative types of continuity (asymmetrical phrase structures, sudden pauses, long notes, repetition).[102] Many of these features only evoke Exoticist impressions when placed in context, and often 'national' and 'Exotic' styles can be hard to distinguish. What could be considered national in the composer's home country could be considered Exotic in a foreign country. Thus, Locke points to the market value of musical works incorporating a form of both Exoticism and nationalism during the nineteenth century.[103] This aspect also surfaces in Gottfried and Johanna Kinkel's artistic output.

Many typical Exoticist features are combined in Kinkel's settings 'Der spanische Zitherknabe' (op. 8, no. 1) and 'Römische Nacht' (op. 15, no. 1): patriotism, thinking in national categories, as well as longing for Southern countries and cultures. In Geibel's 'Der spanische Zitherknabe' (The Spanish Zither Player), the lyrical I regrets that he cannot be in his beloved home country, Spain. Instead, he rambles from house to house trying to make a living from his playing.

---

stretches westwards as far as the rest of the Islamic North Africa (referred to as the Maghreb), eastwards as far as Persia (Iran), or even India and Ceylon, and southwards as far as Madagascar.

[100] Derek B. Scott, 'Orientalism and Musical Style', in *Musical Style and Social Meaning*, ed. Derek B. Scott (Farnham: Ashgate, 2010), 137–64 (155–56).

[101] Ralph P. Locke, *Musical Exoticism: Images and Reflections* (Cambridge/New York: Cambridge University Press, 2009), 36. For alternative explanations of musical Exoticism see Jonathan Bellman, 'Introduction', in *The Exotic in Western Music*, ed. Jonathan Bellman (Boston: Eastern University Press, 1998), ix–xiii (ix), and Nadejda Lebedeva, 'Die Lieder des Mirza-Schaffy op. 34 von Anton Rubinstein: Zwischen Folklorismus, Oientalismus und Nationalismus', *Archiv für Musikwissenschaft*, 67, 4 (2010), 284–309 (301).

[102] Locke, *Musical Exoticism*, 47–50.

[103] Ibid., 78.

Der spanische Zitherknabe
    (op. 8, no. 1)
    Emanuel Geibel (published 1838)
	The Spanish Zither Player

Fern im Süd das schöne Spanien,	*a*	Beautiful Spain in the remote South,
Spanien ist mein Heimatland,	*b*	Spain is my home country,
Wo die schattigen Kastanien	*a*	Where the shady chestnut trees
Rauschen an des Ebro Strand,	*b*	Rustle at the banks of the river Ebro,
Wo die Mandeln rötlich blühen,	*c*	Where the almond trees are in red blossom,
Wo die süße Traube winkt	*d*	Where sweet grapes beckon
Und die Rosen schöner glühen	*c*	And where the roses are more beautiful
Und das Mondlicht gold'ner blinkt.	*d*	And where the moonlight is brighter.
Lang schon wandr' ich mit der Laute	*e*	For long I have been wandering with the lute
Traurig hier von Haus zu Haus,	*f*	Sadly, from house to house,
Doch kein helles Auge schaute	*e*	But not a single bright eye looked out
Freundlich noch nach mir heraus.	*f*	And greeted me in a friendly manner.
Spärlich reicht man mir die Gaben,	*g*	Sparingly they pass me my payment,
Mürrisch heißet man mich gehn;	*h*	Grumpily, I am asked to leave;
Ach den armen braunen Knaben	*g*	Alas, nobody will understand
Will kein einziger verstehn.	*h*	The poor dark-skinned boy.
Dieser Nebel drückt mich nieder,	*i*	This fog depresses me,
Der die Sonne mir entfernt,	*k*	Which keeps the sun away from me,
Und die alten lust'gen Lieder	*i*	And these old happy songs
Hab ich alle schon verlernt.	*k*	I have long forgotten.
Ach, in alle Melodien	*l*	Alas, the same longing sound
Schleicht der eine Klang sich ein:	*m*	Has entered all my melodies:
In die Heimat möcht ich ziehen,	*l*	I want to go home,
In das Land voll Sonnenschein!	*m*	To the land of sunshine.
Als beim letzten Erntefeste	*n*	When, at the latest Thanksgiving,
Man den großen Reigen hielt,	*o*	Dances were performed in a big circle,
Hab ich jüngst das allerbeste	*n*	I played the very best
Meiner Lieder aufgespielt.	*o*	Of my songs.
Doch, wie sich die Paare schwangen	*p*	But, even though couples were dancing
In der Abendsonne Gold,	*q*	In the golden evening sun,
Sind auf meine dunkeln Wangen	*p*	Hot tears ran down
Heiße Tränen hingerollt.	*q*	My dark cheeks.
Ach, ich dachte bei dem Tanze	*r*	Alas, I thought during the dance
An des Vaterlandes Lust,	*s*	Of the joys of my native land,
Wo im duft'gen Mondenglanze	*r*	Where in the filmy moonshine
Freier atmet jede Brust,	*s*	Every chest breathes freely.
Wo sich bei der Zither Tönen	*t*	Where, accompanied by the zither,
Jeder Fuß beflügelt schwingt	*u*	Every foot moves as if winged.
Und der Knabe mit der Schönen	*t*	And where the young man dances glowingly
Glühend den Fandango schlingt.	*u*	The fandango with the beautiful woman.

Nein! Des Herzens sehnend Schläge	*v*	No! The heart's longing beats –
Länger halt ich's nicht zurück;	*w*	I can no longer hold it back;
Will ja jeder Lust entsagen,	*x*	I want to suppress all my desire,
Laßt mir nur der Heimat Glück!	*w*	Please let me be happy in my home!
Fort zum Süden, fort nach Spanien!	*a*	Let me go down South to Spain!
In das Land voll Sonnenschein!	*m*	To the country full of sunshine!
Unterm Schatten der Kastanien	*a*	I want to be buried
Muß ich einst begraben sein!	*m*	Under the shady chestnut trees!

The energetic accompaniment accentuates both the composer's brilliant piano skills and the *style hongrois*, which is also noted by Ludwig Rellstab, who wrote about this song:

> The music enhances the poetic expression; it has selected the form of fandango, and thus Lied appears in a national costume. Clothes make the man; a woman always has better taste at that than men. She has had a lucky hand here as well.[104]

James Parakilas depicts two typical images of Spain: the smuggler and the dancer, more particularly the female dancer and the bolero, which embodies an Exotic eroticism.[105] Dorothea Link states that the fandango was received as sexually attractive and provocative at the end of the eighteenth century.[106] This connotation might have faded by the 1830s, when fandango rhythms were heard in both opera and song. But Rellstab's highlighting of the dance reveals that it was still considered something extraordinary.

Unlike Geibel's words, Gottfried Kinkel's poem 'Römische Nacht' (Roman Night) must have been relatively unknown at the beginning of the 1840s. However, the poem was exceptionally well received; other composers such as Georg Vierling, Eduard Lassen, and Felix Draeseke set these words. Drawing on the temporal displacement between 'now and then', the poem portrays the calm city of Rome, which remembers its glorious past.

---

[104] Ludwig Rellstab, review of Johanna Mathieux, *Sechs Gedichte von Emanuel Geibel für eine Singstimme mit Begleitung des Pianoforte: Opus 8* (1838), *Iris im Gebiete der Tonkunst*, 3 August 1838, 121–22 (122). 'Die Musik erhöht die Eindrücke des Gedichts; sie hat die Form eines Fandango gewählt, und erscheint daher sogleich in Nationaltracht. Kleider machen Leute; eine Frau hat darin immer bessern Geschmack als die Männer, und so hat sie es denn auch hier sehr gut getroffen.'

[105] James Parakilas, 'How Spain Got a Soul', in *The Exotic in Western Music*, ed. Jonathan Bellman (Boston: Eastern University Press, 1998), 137–93 (141–43) and Locke, *Musical Exoticism*, 160–61.

[106] Dorothea Link, 'The Fandango Scene in Mozart's Le nozze di Figaro', *Journal of the Royal Musical Association*, 33, 1 (2008), 69–92 (82–84).

Römische Nacht (op. 15, no. 1)
  Gottfried Kinkel (published 1841)

Roman Night[107]
  Translation by Sharon Krebs

Ringsum auf allen Plätzen	*a*	Motionless, the night sleeps
Schläft unbewegt die Nacht.	*b*	Above all squares.
Am blauen Himmel stehet	*c*	The glorious moon shines
Der Mond in voller Pracht.	*b*	Down from the blue sky.
So totenstill sind beide,	*d*	The old and new Rome
Das alt' und neue Rom,	*e*	Are deadly silent,
Und selbst ihr Riesenwächter	*f*	Even its giant guard
Nickt ein – Sankt Peters Dom.	*e*	Falls asleep – St. Peter's Basilica.
Nur wunderbar noch rauschen[108]	*g*	Only the fountains rustle
Die Brunnen nah und fern.	*h*	Beautifully near and far.
Die halten wach die Seele	*i*	They keep awake the soul
Die selbst entschliefe gern.	*h*	That is longing to sleep as well.
Die spülen aus dem Herzen	*k*	Quietly, they rinse the woe gone by
Leise das alte Leid.	*l*	Out of the heart.
Im blauen Mondlicht dämmert	*m*	The old times are dawning
Weit fort die alte Zeit!	*l*	In the blue moonlight!

'Römische Nacht' combines enthusiasm for the ancient world with an interest in German musical aesthetics. Thalheimer detects in it Kinkel's fondness for Spohr's compositional style. 'Römische Nacht' is a composition, she writes

> which breathes the spirit of Spohr, especially in its instrumental parts, which incorporate soft cantilenas. One is struck by a modulation (second verse over the words 'Das alte Leid' [the woe gone by]). Here, one expects a modulation via the cadential six-four chord back to the tonic key, but a musically and textually unmotivated modulation to E-flat major is employed instead; the 'old times dawning in the blue moonlight' are expressed very dramatically until, finally, the initial musical idea picks up the aforementioned line and thereby concludes the Lied.[109]

---

[107] <http://www.lieder.net/lieder/get_text.html?TextId=105819> (accessed 22 April 2019).

[108] Gottfried Kinkel's original includes the word 'wundersam' (strangely) rather than 'wunderbar' (beautifully). Kinkel, *Gedichte*, 97.

[109] Thalheimer, 'Johanna Kinkel als Musikerin', 72. '[Eine Komposition], die ganz Spohr'schen Geist atmet, vor allem in ihrem instrumentalen Teil, der weiche Cantilenen aufweist. Auffallend in diesem Liede ist eine Modulation (Text 2 Str. auf den Worten: Das alte Leid). Man erwartet an dieser Stelle die Modulation über den cadenzierenden Quartsextakkord zur Haupttonart zurück, statt dessen erfolgt eine sowohl textlich als auch musikalisch unmotivierte Ausweichung nach Es-Dur, ganz dramatisch wird hier die "im blauen Mondlicht fort dämmernde alte Zeit"

Kinkel uses this unexpected harmonic turn as a means of dramatic expression in order to emphasise the lines 'the woe gone by' and 'the old times are dawning in the blue moonlight'. Another noteworthy compositional device occurs at the phrase 'nickt ein' (falls asleep), where a German augmented sixth chord prolongs the cadence in response to the words.

As already mentioned, Johanna Kinkel set her husband's Singspiel *Die Assassinen,* four songs of which she published within her two last Lieder collections: 'Beduinen-Romanze', 'Durch Carthago's Trümmerhallen', 'Provencalisches Lied', and the aforementioned 'Abendlied nach der Schlacht'. In the light of Gramsci's and Said's theories on hegemony and superiority, Gottfried Kinkel's socio-political background deserves attention. As a Protestant theologian, Kinkel was well-read, but he had never travelled to the Middle East. Scrutinising contextual similarities between *Die Assassinen* and Johann Philip Lorenz Withof's 1765 publication *Das meuchelmörderische Reich der Assassinen* (The Assassins' Empire), Klaus deduces that much of the Singspiel's content must be based on Withof.[110]

The Singspiel is divided into three acts and is preceded by an overture. Although the overture will not be discussed here, the account of Kinkel's friend, the singer Leopold Kaufmann, is insightful. He wrote to his sister that:

> The overture is a highly interesting piece, which takes up the following idea: the first movement is dominated by a chorale-like melody in the strings, serious and solemn, alluding to Christianity, while it gets ready for the fight against paganism. The middle movement represents the Orient by means of Janissary music; it merges artistically yet clearly with the chorale melody which wins in the end.[111]

Kaufmann's conflation of the assassins with pagans reflects typical nineteenth-century views on religion and 'otherness'; to us it is a warning that both the plot and its reception should be considered with care. Nevertheless an analysis of *Die Assassinen* sheds light on the socio-cultural context of Kinkel's published songs. Set in the assassins' headquarters, the first act introduces the two Muslim assassins Musa and Nadir, who were delivered to the assassins' ruler in their sleep. In scene 1, the ruler, 'Alte vom Berge' (old man of the mountains), consecrates the two men, anticipating that love will strengthen the murderers. In scenes 2 and 3, Musa and Nadir wake up slowly and find themselves in a paradise, surrounded by beautiful women, known as 'Paradiesjungfrauen' (paradise virgins). This reflects the nineteenth-century perception that the assassins

---

angesungen, bis endlich der musikalische Eingangsgedanke wieder versöhnend die erwähnte Versreihe aufnimmt und so das Lied abschliesst.'

[110] Klaus, "'Die Assassinen – Romantisches Singspiel mit Gesang'", 2–3.

[111] Cited after Klaus, *Johanna Kinkel,* 127.

were brave warriors, because they longed to return to paradise which they experienced temporarily after their consecration.[112] While Nadir leaves with the virgin Zoraide, Musa meets Melisande, who encourages Musa to ignore her and follow the others. Melisande's monologue in scene 4 reveals that she is not originally a Muslim but a French Christian, who was kidnapped during the Children's Crusade in 1212.[113] In the fifth scene, Melisande remembers a song of her childhood, 'Provencalisches Lied'. This song was set by Johanna Kinkel and published within her op. 21.

In 'Provencalisches Lied' (Lied from Provence), the lyrical I praises her home, Provence. She regrets that she is forced to abet the men to kill and fears that her grief will never end.

Provencalisches Lied (op. 21, no. 4) Gottfried Kinkel (published 1851)		Lied from Provence
Am Strande der Dürançe	*a*	At the beach of the Durance river,
In blühender Provençe,	*a*	In the beautiful Provence,
Da ragt im Sonnenglanze	*a*	My father's castle towers
Des Vaters Schloß empor.	*b*	In the bright sunshine.
Mich hat der Sturm verschlagen,	*c*	The storm has carried me away,
Es bringt der Eltern Klagen	*c*	Of my parents' laments,
Kein Hauch aus West getragen	*c*	Not a breath is carried from the West
Zu der Gefangnen Ohr.	*b*	To the captive woman's ear.
Ob noch zu Kirchenhallen	*d*	Do the believers still
Die Frommen gläubig wallen,	*d*	Go to church,
Ob noch die Glocken schallen	*d*	Do the bells still announce
Ins Land den Festesgruß?	*e*	The solemn ceremony?
Weh mir, daß ich mit Tücken	*f*	Woe betide me, for I maliciously
Der Männer Herz berücken,	*f*	Have to bewitch the men's hearts,
Mit frevelndem Entzücken	*f*	With bad enchantment
Zum Mord sie locken muß.	*e*	I have to lure them to kill.
O grünt ihr noch, Oliven,	*g*	Oh olive trees are you still growing,
Wo wir am Mittag schliefen,	*g*	Where we used to sleep at midday,
Wenn kühl in blauen Tiefen	*g*	When the Rhone, cool,
Gerauscht der Rhone Flut?	*h*	In blue depths, rushed past?
Stumm ring ich meine Hände,	*i*	Silently, I pray,
Nie hat mein Gram ein Ende,	*i*	Never will my grief come to an end,
Es schmachtet Melisande	*i*	Melisande languishes
In Ostens Todesglut.	*h*	In the Eastern fervour of death.

[112] *Pierer's Universal-Lexikon*, 4th edn, i, 830–31.

[113] Klaus, "'Die Assassinen – Romantisches Singspiel mit Gesang'", 11.

In correspondence with the image of Melisande as a graceful woman, the melodic line is laden with ornamentation. The most meaningful words are stressed by means of melodic turns and stretches, for example 'Klagen' (regrets, first verse) and 'Ende' (end, third verse) in bar 19 (Ex. 4.11), as well as 'Gefangnen' (convict, first verse), 'locken' (lure, second verse), and 'Ostens' (Eastern, third verse) in bars 24–25 (Ex. 4.12). The *Allegretto* tempo and 6/8 metre highlight Melisande's light-hearted childhood memories, which are also captured in the richly decorated piano prelude, interlude and postlude.

Ex. 4.11: Melodic ornamentation in 'Provencalisches Lied' (bar 19)

Ex. 4.12: Melodic stretch in 'Provencalisches Lied' (bars 23–25)

When Melisande finishes her song, Musa turns towards her, as the singing attracts his interest. In scene 6, the following dialogue between Melisande and Musa establishes that Musa, like Melisande, is not a Muslim:

Musa: I heard the song and it warmed my heart. This is not an Arab song. It sounds to me like a tune of my earliest childhood!

Melisande: Then you are not a son of the East!

Musa: I do not know my origin; I only know weapons and battle songs. But this song, where is this from?

Melisande: They sing it in the beautiful country of France.

Musa: Then that is my homeland.[114]

Although Melisande does not tell Musa the whole truth, she reveals that he has been betrayed. She advises him to accept guidance from the moon and the river, should he wish to see her again. At the end of the first act, the assassins' ruler releases Musa and Nadir from paradise.

The second act is set in a Christian earl's castle. In scene 1, the Christian soldiers, led by their commander, Falco, bemoan that they have not been paid for three months. In the second scene, Falco asks the earl for money, who, after a while, agrees to obtain the soldiers' salary. In the following two scenes, the earl and the Templar Enguerrand de Coucy have a conversation over money and morals; they finally meet the wealthy Prince of Armenia and his daughter. It becomes clear that de Coucy is in Palestine because he is looking for his missing son, who was stolen when he was a baby. In the song 'Durch Carthago's Trümmerhallen' (Over Carthage's Battlefields), which Kinkel sets as op. 19, no. 2, de Coucy contemplates his unsuccessful search.

Durch Carthago's Trümmerhallen
   (op. 19, no. 2)
   Gottfried Kinkel (published 1848)

Over Carthage's Battlefields

Durch Carthago's Trümmerhallen	*a*	Over Carthage's battlefields
Suchend bin ich umgeschweift;	*b*	I rambled searching;
Wo in heissem Mittagwallen	*a*	Where in the hot midday's sun
Voll die gold'ne Ernte reift.	*b*	The golden corn ripens.
Und ich sah wie bunt zum Kranze	*c*	I saw how sea and earth
Meer und Erde sich verflicht	*d*	Merged to a colourful corona,
Unter klarem Himmelsglanze.	*c*	Beneath the clear sky.
Aber ach, ihn fand ich nicht,	*d*	But alas, I did not find him,
Aber ach, ihn fand ich nicht.	*d*	But alas, I did not find him.

---

[114] 'Musa: Ich hörte den Gesang und er wärmte mir das Herz in der Brust. Das ist kein arabisch Lied. Es klingt zu mir herüber aus meiner frühesten Kindheit! | Melisande: Dann bist du kein Sohn des Ostens! | Musa: Ich weiß meinen Stamm nicht, ich kenne nur Waffen und Schlachtgesang. Aber diese Weise, wo ist sie her? | Melisande: Sie singen die Weise im schönen Frankreich. | Musa: Dann ist das mein Vaterland.'

Durch Egyptens reiche Fluren	*e*	I pilgrimaged through
Zog ich an dem Pilgerstab;	*f*	Egypt's rich landscape;
Alter Grösse heil'ge Spuren	*e*	Many a glorious tomb
Trägt manch prächtig Königsgrab.	*f*	Carries the sacred traces of ancient greatness.
Auf den Pyramiden leuchtet	*g*	The sunlight shines under the clear sky
Unbewölkt der Sonne Licht,	*d*	On the pyramids,
Weit der Strom das Land befeuchtet,	*g*	The wide river waters the land,
Aber ach, ihn fand ich nicht,	*d*	But alas, I did not find him,
Aber ach, ihn fand ich nicht!	*d*	But alas, I did not find him!
Canaan! zu süsser Labe	*h*	Canaan! I entered your ground
Deinen Grund betrat ich nun,	*i*	For the sake of a sweet balm,
Wo an des Erlösers Grabe	*h*	Where all sorrows rest
Alle Erdensorgen ruhn.	*I*	At the Saviour's tomb.
Gläubig bin ich hingesunken	*k*	Faithfully, I kneeled down
Auf mein flammend Angesicht,	*d*	Onto my flaming face,
Himmelslust hab' ich getrunken.	*k*	I imbibed heavenly joy.
Aber ach, ihn fand ich nicht,	*d*	But alas, I did not find him,
Aber ach, ihn fand ich nicht!	*d*	But alas, I did not find him!

Like Kinkel's 'Provencalisches Lied', this song includes characteristic piano passages, whose stylistic diversity symbolises the father's restless search (bars 19–22 and 46–51; Exx. 4.13 and 4.14). The constant interchange between major and minor keys underlines de Coucy's uncertainty, which is also emphasised by means of a prolongation at the words 'Aber ach, ihn fand ich nicht' (But alas, I did not find him) at the end of each stanza.

In scenes 6 to 10, the Armenian Prince, convinced by de Coucy, the earl, Falco, and the warriors, agrees to provide the money for the crusade towards Tigado, the residence of the assassins' ruler. The warriors prepare themselves for battle. Simultaneously, in scenes 11 to 12, the assassins Musa and Nadir receive their final consecration by their ruler. Nadir is supposed to murder the Christian earl; Musa is asked to murder the Templar de Coucy. In scene 11, Nadir hopes for an early death as he is longing to be reunited with his beloved Zoraide. Musa, however, is terrified by the thought of having to murder someone:

> Murder, murder and murder does not bring any blessing. I should seek to throw the lance and send the arrow into my enemy's eye in an open valley in a hand-to-hand combat. But it seems easy to attack the enemy secretly with a poisoned arrow. The dead body's shadows lurk everywhere. All songs sound of the curse of murder. What does the wild song of the Bedouins sound like; the song that

Ex. 4.13: Piano interlude in 'Durch Carthago's Trümmerhallen' (bars 19–22)

Ex. 4.14: Piano postlude in 'Durch Carthago's Trümmerhallen' (bars 46–51)

tells of Yussuf, who secretly murdered his enemy? I often heard it overnight in the desert when the Arabs sang it in the far distance.[115]

The 'wild song' is entitled 'Beduinen-Romanze' (Bedouins' Romance), a setting of which was published by Kinkel as op. 19, no. 4.

[115] 'Mord, Mord und der Mord bringt keinen Segen. In offener Schlucht, wie Mann gegen Mann, wo Leben um Leben gekämpft wird, da hab ich die Lanze zu werfen und den Pfeil ins Auge des Feindes zu senden. Aber ungemerkt, mit Lehmungsgift, inmitten des Lebens den Gegner zu berücken, das ist gewiß leicht. Und die Schatten der Ermordeten lauern auf allen Wegen. In allen Liedern klingt der Fluch des Mordes. So, wie lautet das wilde Lied der Beduinen von Jussuf, der seinen Feind heimlich erschlug? Oft hört ichs nachts über den Wüstensand hintönen, wenns der Araber weggezogen erklingen ließ.'

Beduinen-Romanze (op. 19, no. 4)
  Gottfried Kinkel (published 1848)

Bedouins' Romance

Vorwärts mit des Vogels Fluge,	*a*	Onward with the bird's flight,
Fort!, fort, mein Roß in Sturmesflucht!	*b*	Onward!, onward, my horse in stormy escape!
Denn gemordet liegt der Feind	*c*	For the murdered enemy lies
Drunten in der Felsenschlucht.	*b*	Down there in the rocky gorge.
Halala leila halala!		Halala leila halala!
Mondlicht zittert! In der Wüste	*d*	Moonlight is trembling! In the desert
Bäumt ein Schatten sich empor.	*e*	A shadow rears up.
Und die Stute beißt den Zaum,	*f*	And the mare bites the bridle,
Schaudert, schnaubt und spitzt das Ohr.	*e*	It shudders, snuffles and strains its ears.
Halala leila halala!		Halala leila halala!
Jussuf senkt die Lanzenspitze	*g*	Yussuf lowers the lancehead
Spornt das Tier mit aller Macht.	*h*	With a vengeance, he cheers on the beast.
Doch der Schatten unbewegt	*i*	But motionless, the shadow
Steht im Weg ihm da und lacht	*h*	Stands in his way and laughs.
Halala leila halala!		Halala leila halala!
Rückwärts wendet sich die Stute,	*k*	The mare turns backwards
Braust dahin in Sturmesflucht,	*b*	Blusters in stormy escape.
Und der Mörder liegt zerschellt	*l*	And the shattered murderer lies
Bei dem Feind in tiefer Schlucht.	*b*	Besides the enemy in the rocky gorge.
Halala leila halala!		Halala leila halala!

Johanna Kinkel combines in this song Western and non-Western stylistic means, an approach which may have increased the song's marketability. According to Locke, many compositions of the 1830s and 1840s were based on authentic Islamic or non-European musical sources and included a range of compositional features derived from Middle Eastern folk music.[116] It is unlikely that Kinkel was familiar with original Middle Eastern music; rather, many of the means she used were simplified and/or based on prejudice. Locke finds different explanations for simplifications in pseudo-Exoticist music: the Western notation system and instruments lacked expressive power, nineteenth-century Western composers wrongly assumed that the non-Western world was less elaborate, and much of the music composed during the 1830s and 1840s was performed within amateur contexts.[117] These observations also apply to Kinkel. As a result, melodic progressions and rhythmicity in 'Beduinen-Romanze' step into the foreground. *Neue Zeitschrift für Musik* regrets that this Lied conveys

[116] Locke, 'Cutthroats and Casbah Dancers', 110.

[117] Ibid., 116–17.

'nothing of Bedouin wilderness'.[118] However, the upbeat creates a spurring impression and maintains the musical impetus. The accompaniment's first three bars, in which only one melodic line is recognisable, allude to another characteristic of Arab music: monophony. The homophonic voice-leading in parallel octaves in bar three hints towards oriental monophony (Ex. 4.15).

Ex. 4.15: Beginning of 'Beduinen-Romanze' (bars /1–3)

Apart from musical features reminiscent of Middle Eastern music, the impulsive chorus is evocative of pseudo-oriental music as composed by Mozart or Haydn, perhaps an indicator that Kinkel was a woman of her own time. Kinkel also used Western compositional techniques: traditional tempo and dynamic markings, as well as the 6/8 metre. The tempo, *molto allegro*, alongside several *forte* passages and *staccato* notes, add to the spurring rhythm. Finally, Kinkel's allusion to the so-called 'Devil's Mill' harmonic progression reflects her own Western education (bars 11–13, Ex. 4.16). Marie-Agnes Dittrich claims that the Devil's Mill in the nineteenth century was modified in order not to seem clichéd.[119] That said, Kinkel's application of an incomplete Devil's Mill – it only spans three bars – could be seen as a response to mid-nineteenth-century trends rather than a lack of compositional knowledge. The chromatic descent in the bass line supports an augmented sixth chord, which adds tension and diversity (bar 12).

After Musa's monologue, he takes note of the moon and the river. He remembers Melisande's advice to accept guidance from those two natural occurrences and, in scene 14, eventually meets her. During their brief encounter, Melisande and Musa discover that Musa was originally a Christian. Melisande tells Musa that she was kidnapped as a child and forced to obey the assassins' ruler as a

---

[118] [Anon.], review of Johanna Kinkel, *Opus 19* (1848), *Neue Zeitschrift für Musik*, 2 April 1849, 146. 'läßt [...] nichts von Beduinen-Wildheit erklingen'.

[119] Marie-Agnes Dittrich, '"Teufelsmühle" und "Omnibus"', *Zeitschrift der Gesellschaft für Musiktheorie*, 4, 1–2 (2007), 107–21 (121).

Ex. 4.16: Allusion to Devil's Mill in 'Beduinen-Romanze' (bars 11–14)

paradise virgin. She asks Musa to help her to escape, but their conversation is interrupted by the assassins' battle song 'Auf in den Kampf' (Let's Go to War, scene 15). The second act concludes with the battle.

The third act, which begins with de Coucy's song at the battlefield, 'Abendlied nach der Schlacht', resolves the dramatic plot in favour of the Christians. Moved by de Coucy's thoughtful remarks, the earl orders a ceasefire, as the Templars take up their weapons against Nadir. The latter had approached the Christians in order to free Musa, who had been caught by the Templars (scenes 3–5). De Coucy recognises Musa's ring, and in scene 6 they learn that they are father and son. Finally, Musa rescues Melisande, who is due to be murdered by the assassins for dishonesty (scenes 8–14). Musa, whose original name is Geoffrey, De Coucy and Melisande return to France. The assassins' ruler is defeated and the earl frees many Christians who had been kept in captivity by the assassins. Monica Klaus observes that the defeat of the Muslims by the Christians 'had to be achieved in order for the piece to be performable and effective according to the times'.[120] But Klaus suggests that Kinkel aimed to express a second thought, namely 'that the human being is more than a Christian', and that the struggles of a father trying to find his son, and of a beloved couple facing socio-cultural displacement, were at least as serious concerns as religious cruelty.[121] Finally, Locke points out that 'a work about the Middle East may touch on issues other than the Empire', for example sexual considerations, or questions concerned with individual psychology.[122] In *Die Assassinen,* all the leaders are male, but the plot is controlled almost entirely by female characters.

[120] Klaus, '"Die Assassinen – Romantisches Singspiel mit Gesang"', 7: 'denn ein Sieg musste das Stück, und zwar im Sinne der Zeit, bühnenwirksam zu Ende bringen'.

[121] Ibid., 8.

[122] Locke, 'Cutthroats and Casbah Dancers', 107.

A better-known representative of nineteenth-century Orientalism is Johann Wolfgang von Goethe's *West-Östlicher Divan*. Its title refers to the amalgamation of Western and Eastern strands. First published in 1819, the cyclic collection of poetry includes twelve books. The eighth book, *Book of Suleika,* inspired many nineteenth-century composers: for instance, Carl Banck, Carl Eberwein, Moritz Hauptmann, Fanny Hensel, Felix Mendelssohn, Franz Schubert, and Carl Friedrich Zelter.[123] While all of these composers set Suleika's poem 'Ach, um deine feuchten Schwingen' (Alas, I Envy You for Your Fresh Breezes), Johanna Kinkel chose a different passage from Suleika's and Hatem's conversation. In the Lied 'Traumdeutung' (Interpretation of Dreams, op. 10, no. 5), Suleika tells Hatem that she lost the ring which he once gave her. In response to her question what this omen might mean, Hatem refers to the Venetian legend that the elected Doge, as a symbol of loyalty, had to get married to his Venetian Republic by throwing a finger ring into the sea surrounding Venice.

Traumdeutung (op. 10, no. 5)
   Johann Wolfgang von Goethe
   (published 1839)

Interpretation of Dreams
   Translation by Emily Ezust

Suleika:		*Suleika:*[124]
Als ich auf dem Euphrat schiffte,	*a*	When I was sailing on the Euphrates,
Streifte sich der goldne Ring	*b*	The golden ring slid off
Finger ab, in Wasserklüfte,	*a*	My finger into the watery abyss –
Den ich jüngst von dir empfing.	*b*	The ring that I received from you recently.
Also träumt ich. Morgenröte	*c*	Thus I dreamed. The red dawn
Blitzt' ins Auge durch den Baum,	*d*	Blazed into my eyes down through the trees;
Sag, Poete, sag, Prophete!	*c*	Tell me, poet, tell me, prophet!
Was bedeutet dieser Traum?	*d*	What does this dream mean?
Hatem:		*Hatem:*[125]
Dies zu deuten bin erbötig!	*e*	I am willing to interpret this!
Hab ich dir nicht oft erzählt,	*f*	Have I not often recounted the story
Wie der Doge von Venedig	*e*	Of how the Doge of Venice
Mit dem Meere sich vermählt?	*f*	Married the sea?

[123] For considerations of the work's cyclic character see George F. Peters, 'Air and Spirit in Goethe's "West-Östlicher Divan"', *Rocky Mountain Review of Language and Literature*, 30, 4 (Autumn 1976), 216–28 (217).

[124] <http://www.lieder.net/lieder/get_text.html?TextId=6388> (accessed 30 March 2020).

[125] <https://www.lieder.net/lieder/get_text.html?TextId=6380> (accessed 29 March 2020).

So von deinen Fingergliedern	*g*	It was this way that your fingers
Fiel der Ring dem Euphrat zu.	*h*	Let the ring fall into the Euphrates.
Ach, zu tausend Himmelsliedern,	*g*	Ah, to a thousand flowery songs
Süßer Traum, begeisterst du!	*h*	You inspire me, sweet dream!
Mich, der von des Indostanen	*i*	I, who have been everywhere
Streifte bis Damaskus hin,	*k*	From the Indies to Damascus,
Um mit neuen Karawanen	*i*	And come with new caravans
Bis ans rote Meer zu ziehn,	*k*	All the way to the Red Sea:
Mich vermählst du deinem Fluße,	*l*	You have married me to your river,
Der Terrasse diesem Hain:	*m*	To the terrace of this grove;
Hier soll bis zum letzten Kuße	*l*	Here I shall, until the last kiss,
Dir mein Geist gewidmet sein.	*m*	Dedicate my soul.

Johanna Kinkel must have been unaware of the autobiographical scope of Goethe's *Book of Suleika*, but she might have been attracted by the parallels between her own unsettled love life and that of the lyrical protagonist.[126] Written in F major, the three-part strophic setting includes extensive piano passages whose arpeggios respond to Suleika's uncertainty. The moderate tempo supports the wisdom of Hatem, Suleika's poet and prophet. These words are stressed in the vocal part by means of large leaps, for instance in bar 19, 'f¹'–'d²', and bar 20, 'a¹'–'g²' (Ex. 4.17).

Ex. 4.17: Melodic leaps in 'Traumdeutung' (bars 19–20)

126 For details on the autobiographical scope of Goethe's work in relation to Marianne von Willemer see Dorothee Metlitzki, 'On the Meaning of "Hatem" in Goethe's West-Östlicher Divan', *Journal of the American Oriental Society*, 117, 1 (January–March 1997), 148–51 (148–150), and Carl Hammer, 'Goethe and Marianne: After the "Divan"', *The South Central Bulletin*, 28, 4 (Winter 1968), 134–38.

Another effective way of addressing revolutionary thoughts without voicing them directly was to praise the political achievements of foreign countries that were situated closer to home. Early Romantics were drawn towards foreign nations: wanderlust, longing for pre-industrialised regions, and sympathy with homesick vagabonds. Furthermore, the worship of antique heroes was a form of self-encouragement. The two Lieder 'Auf wohlauf ihr Candioten!' (op. 18, no. 3) and 'Hymne auf den Tod des Marco Botzaris' can be read as revolutionary appeals in the disguise of Greek heroism. Both Lieder can be linked with the German socio-political situation in the 1840s. However, while 'Auf wohlauf ihr Candioten' is a pseudo-foreign folk song, penned by Gottfried Kinkel, 'Hymne auf den Tod des Marco Botzaris' was originally Greek.

Reminiscent of German folk music, Johanna Kinkel's setting 'Hymne auf den Tod des Marco Botzaris' (Hymn in Memoriam Marco Botzaris) was composed for voice and guitar or piano accompaniment. The words originate from a Greek legend and were translated by Gottfried Kinkel. The poem tells the story of the Greek Marco Botzaris, who died in a battle against the Ottomans. His fate is used in order to encourage his fellow men to keep fighting for freedom.[127]

Hymne auf den Tod von Marco Botzaris	**Hymn in Memoriam Marco Botzaris**
Greek Folk Song: German by Gottfried Kinkel (published 1843)	

Männer von Hellas,	*a*	Men of Hellas,
Klagt um den Heroen!	*b*	Grieve for your hero!
Botzaris Heldengeist	*a'*	Botzaris' heroic spirit
Ist uns entflohen;	*b*	Has left us;
Uns zu erlösen, sank er auf's Blutfeld.	*c*	He died on the battlefield for our salvation.
Schaut auf sein Heldenbild,	*d*	Look at his heroic life,
Ihm nachzustreben,	*e*	And follow his example,
Wenn euch die Freiheit gilt	*d*	If freedom means
Mehr als das Leben!	*e*	More to you than life!
Bald dann zermalmen wir unsre Tyrannen.	*f*	Soon then will we defeat our tyrants.
Blutiger Türkenschwarm,	*g*	The bloody Turks
Der ihn geschlachtet,	*h*	Killed him,
Noch ist der Freiheit Stern	*g'*	The star of freedom
Uns nicht umnachtet;	*h*	Is not yet obscured for us.
Wilder nur braust heran griechische Kampfwuth.	*i*	Our Greek bloodlust has just become wilder.

[127] Marco Botzaris (1788–1823) was a hero of the Greek war of independence against the Ottomans; he died in a battle at Missolunghi in 1823. *Brockhaus' Kleines Konversations-Lexikon*, 5th edn, i, 248.

Nie von dir, Botzaris,	*k*	Never will your legend, Botzaris,
Schweigt die Kunde;	*l*	Fall silent;
Aller Hellenen Herz	*k'*	Your wound struck
Traf deine Wunde.	*l*	All Hellenic hearts.
Ruhet dein Staub im Grab, doch dein Ruhm nicht.	*m*	May your body rest in the grave, but not your fame.
Steig' ein, Unsterblicher,	*n*	Farewell, immortal hero,
Auf zu den Fernen,	*o*	Off you go to a remote place;
Wo dir die Hütte winkt	*p*	Where a refuge is waiting for you
Über den Sternen;	*o*	Above the stars;
Bitte den Herrn der Welt für deine Treuen.	*q*	Beg the Lord on behalf of your loyal friends.

Compositionally, the Lied is simple. The vocal range spans an octave ('d¹'–'d²') and the harmonic constitution consists of the tonic, D major, and its dominant and subdominant. In her *Lecture on Harmony*, Johanna Kinkel explains that such simple harmonic plans are usually found in national songs:

> The life of a harmless, quiet person, which moves daily in the same circle of family = [*sic*] relations, resembles the circle of the so called [*sic*] relative chords, in which all simple national songs move. No modulation surprises us; the attendant major and minor chords greet us like the familiar faces of father, mother, sister & brother, neighbours and cousins.[128]

While it is unclear whether Kinkel refers to folk-songs or songs featuring national characteristics, her choice of words is more precise in *Acht Briefe an eine Freundin über Clavier-Unterricht*. Here, she concludes humorously that 'almost all *Volkslieder* can be accompanied with [the tonic, the dominant, and the subdominant], and if you add a minor chord, you have almost enough material to compose an entire Italian opera'.[129] Kinkel was aware of folk-like simplicity, and her 'Hymne auf den Tod des Marco Botzaris' must have been composed with amateur performances in mind. The guitar and piano recede into the background, so performers could easily pick up an instrument and accompany themselves.

The three-part strophic Lied 'Auf wohlauf ihr Candioten' (Arise, Arise Well, Ye Residents of Crete, op. 18, no 3, Ex. 4.18), which is a setting of Gottfried Kinkel's words, is not as simple. The harmonic progression is slightly more diverse, as the tonic, dominant and subdominant are joined by the supertonic and mediants.

[128] Kinkel, *Lecture on Harmony*, n.d., ULB S S 2394, no pagination, original in English.

[129] Kinkel, *Acht Briefe*, 14. 'Fast die meisten Volkslieder lassen sich mit diesen drei Akkorden begleiten, und thut man gar einen Mollakkord hinzu, so ist ja beinahe der Stoff vorhanden, um eine ganze italienische Oper zu machen.'

Auf wohlauf ihr Candioten
(op. 18, no. 3)
Gottfried Kinkel (published 1843)

Arise, Arise Well, Ye Residents of Crete[130]
Translation by Sharon Krebs

Auf wohlauf, ihr Candioten,	*a*	Arise, arise well, ye residents of Crete,
Schwinget hoch das Kreuzpanier,	*b*	Raise high the banner of the cross,
Funkeln laßt die weißen Felsen	*c*	Let the white cliffs sparkle
In des Blutes Purpurzier.	*b*	In the crimson ornament of blood.
Unser ist das Land, das mächtig	*d*	Ours is the country that lifts itself
Aus dem Ozean sich hebt;	*e*	Mightily from the sea;
Unser sei es, bis es mörd'risch	*d'*	Ours shall it remain until murderously
Neu der Ozean begräbt,	*e*	The ocean buries it anew,
Unser ist des Kornes Fülle,	*f*	Ours is the plethora of wheat,
Unser ist des Weines Glut,	*g*	Ours the blazing of wine,
Unser die metall'ne Ader,	*h*	Ours the veins of minerals
Die in ew'gen Bergen ruht.	*g*	That lie in the eternal mountains.
Auf wohlauf, ihr Candioten,	*a*	Arise, arise well, ye residents of Crete,
Hoch das Kreuz und hoch den Speer,	*i*	Raise high the cross and high the spear,
Und der Roßhuf des Osmanli	*k*	And the horse-hooves of the Ottomans
Stampfe nie den Boden mehr.	*i*	Shall nevermore tread upon our soil.
Unser sind die hundert Städte	*l*	Ours are the hundred cities
Hoch mit Ruhme sonst genannt;	*m*	Named once with high praise;
Ach, es blieben wenig Dörfer,	*n*	Alas, there remain few villages,
Hingemordet und verbrannt.	*m*	[Their residents] murdered and [the villages] burned.
Unser sind die frischen Rosen	*o*	Ours are the fresh roses[131]
Rein aus Hellas Blut entstammt!	*p*	Which originate purely from Hellas's blood!
Soll sie der Barbare rauben	*q*	Should the barbarian steal them
Nur zu schnöder Lust entflammt?	*p*	Out of disdainful desire?
Steig herauf, gerechter Minos,	*r*	Arise, fair Minos,
Der des Orkus Waage hält,	*s*	Who balances Hades' scales,
Hilf du rechten Deinem Volke	*t*	Help your people fight for justice
Rechten mit der Christenwelt,	*s*	And fight for justice in the Christians' world,
Die des Kreuzes freien Kriegern	*u*	Where the free warriors of the cross
Schon mit neuen Ketten dräut.	*v*	Are being theatened with new chains.
Die verräth'risch uns gerathen,	*w*	And where we got betrayed
Unterwerfung uns gebeut.	*v*	As we were told to comply.
Wehe aber, dreifach wehe	*x*	But woe, threefold woe
Jedem, der des Volkes Schritt	*y*	To everyone, who hinders the steps
Hemmet auf dem Pfad der Freiheit,	*z*	Of the people on the path of freedom,
Ihn zermahlt der Rache Tritt!	*y*	May he be ground down by the footsteps of revenge!

---

[130] <http://www.lieder.net/lieder/get_text.html?TextId=110769> (accessed 26 April 2019).

[131] The following twelve lines are not included in Sharon Krebs's translation; therefore, the author has translated these lines.

Ex. 4.18: 'Auf wohlauf ihr Candioten' (op. 18, no. 3)

Ex. 4.18   *(continued)*

The poem aims to encourage the Candiots to fight against the Ottoman attempts to conquer their Greek island.[132] Striking are the common contextual features between Crete and Gottfried Kinkel's home, the Rhineland: white rocks, corn, wine, ore, mountains, and roses. Published in 1843, this Lied could be seen as a response to Nikolaus Becker's 'Der deutsche Rhein', which advocates the Rhenish resistance against the French conquerors. The march-like 4/4 metre disrupts the Romantic perception of the South which is carried by the words. The rhythm grants the Lied an energetic tone, similar to the spurring 'Demokratenlied' discussed earlier. Another parallel to 'Demokratenlied' is the use of such pronouns as 'we' and 'our' (bars 9, 13, 17, 19, 21), which are stressed through climactic emphases.

🎵 Epilogue: Kinkel's political art songs as cultural practice

In order to contextualise Kinkel's political songs, it is important to devote some thought to the emergence of popular music in the nineteenth century. Derek B. Scott refers to salon music as 'the stimulus behind the first flowering of the commercial popular music industry in Britain and North America'.[133] This observation also applies to German composers like Kinkel. David Gramit surmises that the Lied acquired a double nature as an artistic genre and a commercial product.[134] The latter aspect played a major role for Kinkel, because she

---

[132] The Candiots were the native people of Crete, which, in Italian, is called Candia. *Brockhaus' Kleines Konversations-Lexikon*, 5th edn, i, 305.

[133] Derek B. Scott, 'Music and Social Class in Victorian London', *Musical Style and Social Meaning*, ed. Derek B. Scott (Farnham: Ashgate, 2010), 205–18 (210).

[134] David Gramit, 'The Circulation of the Lied: The Double Life of an Artwork and a Commodity', in *The Cambridge Companion to the Lied*, ed. James Parsons (Cambridge: Cambridge University Press, 2004), 301–14 (301 and 306).

was financially dependent on her publications to complement her income as a teacher. James Deaville emphasises that texts and musical styles in mid-century Lieder collections were diverse, but all songs conformed to the demands of the time: singability, popularity, and simplicity.[135] In favour of variety, Kinkel published her political songs through different avenues: Dunst's *Rhein-Sagen und Lieder*, Schumann's *Neue Zeitschrift für Musik*, Trautwein, and other publishers for singular publications.

However, the Lied's significance transcends the commercial realm. David Gramit sees it as a 'national and nation-defining genre, circulating well beyond the local owing to its participation in print culture'.[136] The text-music combination attracted a wider audience than purely instrumental music would have done, and it enabled access to poetry that otherwise would have remained unknown. Kinkel's published ouevre was popular among her friends and her wider social environment, and it was also reviewed in public. Her unpublished works were performed and discussed within her circles. Thus, her artistic contribution to 'nation-building' had two dimensions: devotion to the Lied as a genre perceived as typically German, and the setting of poems with political agendas. Some of these poems were penned by herself or her husband, especially those ones which advocated a fight for democracy.

Kinkel's democratic values surface in the way she situated herself within the Bonner Gesangverein and the *Maikäferbund*. She considered herself equal to her fellow artists. Her input into the *Maikäfer* journals was based on democratic decisions, like that of every other member. Not only was the *Maikäferbund* a platform for the performance of Kinkel's Lieder, but it also generated political and aesthetic interaction. Much of the *Maikäfer* oeuvre was conceived by more than one person; some poems served Kinkel as inspirations for her songs. In 1841, Kinkel created a *Maikäfer Nationalhymne* (national anthem), based on the words of *Maikäfer* member Alexander Kaufmann.[137] Music must have played a powerful role as a means of identification, and Kinkel's political settings and

---

[135] James Deaville, 'A Multitude of Voices: The Lied at Mid Century', in *The Cambridge Companion to the Lied*, ed. James Parsons (Cambridge: Cambridge University Press, 2004), 142–67 (145).

[136] Gramit, 'The Circulation of the Lied', 306. See also Cook, 'Between Process and Product', 6.

[137] *Maikäfer* journal of 1 June 1841 (Brandt-Schwarze and others, *Der Maikäfer*, 484–85). The manuscript of the score is included in Paul Kaufmann's estate in the Stadtarchiv Bonn (SN 94/67, No. 10).

the songs that emerged from her activities within the *Maikäfer* would have contributed to the association's collective identity.[138]

Nevertheless, it would be wrong to assign the *Maikäfer's* political direction to Johanna Kinkel alone. Various poetic and prose contributions by other *Maikäfer* members and Nikolaus Becker's honorary membership reflect the group's collective political self-perception. On the other hand, it was also political discrepancies which forced the *Maikäferbund* to close towards the end of the 1840s. Nevertheless, and owing to her status as the association's co-founder and gatekeeper, Johanna Kinkel was presented as having a strong influence on both the *Maikäfer* association and Gottfried Kinkel's own political activities in nineteenth-century encyclopaedia entries. She was recognised as a key figure of the revolutionary democrats' movement, and her political Lieder must have contributed to this reception. Vice versa, Kinkel's political activities may have shaped the reception of her music, as her extraordinary socio-cultural standing was well-known to her friends, acquaintances and large parts of the public. It is doubtful whether Johanna Kinkel would have been associated with the nineteenth-century revolutionary movement had she not been married to Gottfried Kinkel, as one might be tempted to belittle her influence on the basis of typical nineteenth-century gender representations in marriages. However, it should be borne in mind that much of Gottfried Kinkel's popularity and media coverage only developed after his escape from prison – an event which was, by and large, Johanna Kinkel's achievement. Kinkel was a recognised Lieder composer before she moved back to Bonn in 1839, and the establishment of her musical reputation with the Bonner Gesangverein was in no way shaped by Gottfried. Undoubtedly, her personal and artistic biographies were influenced by Gottfried, a fact which is echoed in fifteen settings of his poetry and two Singspiele, *Die Assassinen* and *Friedrich der Rothbart in Suza*. However, Gottfried's political activities were encouraged by Johanna's support. The Kinkels' influence on each other's mindsets and identity was reciprocal in nature.

In what way did Kinkel's music contribute to this identity? Kinkel's Exocitist songs reflect musically imagined communities, and her patriotic Rhineland songs were driven by the cultural identity of the Rhineland already established in strands of art, education, and everyday life.[139] Outside of the realms of musical sound and language, Kinkel's songs were influenced by various parameters.

---

[138] On music and identity see Georgina Born and David Hesmondhalgh, 'Introduction', in *Western Music and Its Others: Difference, Representation, and Appropriation in Music*, ed. Georgina Born and David Hesmondhalgh (Berkeley/London/Los Angeles: University of California Press, 2000), 1–58 (31).

[139] On different types of musical identity see Born and Hesmondhalgh, 'Introduction', 35.

Her published Lieder were subject to self-censorship based on Kinkel's own socio-cultural anchoring, as publishability was an important aspect. Additionally, Kinkel's critics reviewed her works through a certain lens, depending on the editorial line and the socio-cultural conventions of the time. Finally, publication and dissemination strategies were geared towards the best possible positioning of Kinkel's music in the marketplace. All these aspects played a role in shaping Kinkel's music and thus contributed to her identity both in private and public.

CHAPTER 5

Songs in praise of nature

THE Romantic mind was torn constantly between system, fragment, and chaos, spirituality and reality, nature and industry, and knowledge and scepticism. This juxtaposition of dualisms is an important Romantic paradigm in itself, and harmony and reconciliation could be found in myth, tale, or an imagined dream.[1] Responding to the fast-paced socio-political reality, the Romantics turned to spiritual means in order to nourish a sense of identity and intensity of emotion among the Germans. Their themes focused on such sources as rivers, the Germanic past or buildings of historical significance. This aversion to modernity is also reflected in the popularity of Exoticist settings, as was outlined in the previous chapter, and in the idea of a regeneration of Europe by Asia, as voiced by Schlegel and Novalis. Mythology, even though it may seem like the promotion of religious chaos at first glance, was propagated by Schlegel in order to provide guidance in forming a unified whole and achieve greater social cohesion.[2] The Romantics' spiritual tendency within the context of nineteenth-century industrialisation and the rise of modern values posed ideological problems, which resulted in a strong sense of loneliness and a fear of isolation. The Romantic ideal of integration sought a sense of community by placing the *Bürger* (citizen) within a larger conglomeration of individualities, a view which reflects the German Romantic concept of nationalism.[3] However, the gap between Romantic ideal and reality was often too large. Thus another overarching theme of German Romanticism is the longing for release, to be achieved by way of contemplation and dreaming, by escaping to nature, by turning to mythology, by remembrance of the past, or through death.[4] It is therefore not surprising that art took up such themes as the Germanic – or indeed other peoples' – heroic past, myth, loneliness, wanderlust, and longing.

---

[1] Alan Menhennet, *The Romantic Movement* (London: Croom Helm, 1981), 22; Kramer, *Music and Poetry*, 22; Elizabeth Millàn-Zaibert, *Friedrich Schlegel and the Emergence of Romantic Philosophy* (New York: State University of New York Press, 2007), 16; Ernst Ribbat, 'Einleitung', in *Romantik: Ein literaturwissenschaftliches Studienbuch*, ed. Ernst Ribbat (Königstein: Athenäum, 1979), 1–6 (1); and Christopher A. Strathman, *Romantic Poetry and the Fragmentary Imperative: Schlegel, Byron, Joyce, Blanchot* (New York: State University of New York Press, 2006), 28.

[2] Millàn-Zaibert, *Friedrich Schlegel*, 161–62.

[3] Menhennet, *The Romantic Movement*, 35.

[4] Ibid., 37.

❧ *Dreamy images of foreign countries*

While the Greek and Spanish songs discussed in Chapter 4 deal with heroic imaginings of foreign pasts, the two Lieder 'Sehnsucht nach Griechenland' and 'Die Zigeuner' focus on the lyrical protagonists' dreamy images of Southern natural beauty. Kinkel's setting of Geibel's 'Sehnsucht nach Griechenland' (Longing for Greece, op. 6, no. 1) alludes to Romantic longing for the less industrialised South, along with a sense of transience, a strongly romanticised image of nature, and a desperate perspective on the self.

Sehnsucht nach Griechenland (op. 6, no. 1) Emanuel Geibel (published 1839)		Longing for Greece[5] Translation adapted from Allen Shearer
Ich blick' in mein Herz und ich blick' in die Welt,	*a*	I look into my heart and I look at the world
Bis vom schwimmenden Auge die brennende Träne mir fällt,	*a*	Till out of my moist eyes a burning tear falls.
Wohl leuchtet die Ferne im goldenen Licht,[6]	*b*	Though the distance glows in the golden light,
Doch hält mich der Nord, ich erreiche sie nicht.	*b*	The north holds me, I shall not reach it.
O die Schranken so eng, und die Welt so weit,	*c*	Ah! How narrow our confines, how wide the world,
Und so flüchtig die Zeit!	*c*	And how fleeting is time!
Ich weiß ein Land, wo aus sonnigem Grün,	*d*	I know a land where in sun-filled greenery
Um versunkene Tempel die Rosen glühn,[7]	*d*	Roses gleam among sunken temples,
Wo die purpurne Woge das Ufer beschäumt,	*e*	Where the purple wave covers the shore with foam
Und von kommenden Sängern der Lorbeer träumt.	*e*	And laurels dream of singers to come.
Fern lockt es und winkt dem verlangenden Sinn,	*f*	It lures from afar and beckons my longing soul,
Und ich kann nicht hin!	*f*	And I cannot go there!
O hätt' ich Flügel, durch's Blau der Luft	*g*	If I had wings to fly through the blue
Wie wollt' ich baden im Sonnenduft!	*g*	How I would wish to bathe in sun's fragrance!
Doch umsonst! Ach, Stunde auf Stunde entflieht;[8]	*h*	But in vain! Alas, hour flees upon hour;

[5] <https://www.lieder.net/lieder/get_text.html?TextId=6025> (accessed 30 March 2020).

[6] Geibel's original reads 'mit goldenem Licht' (with golden light). Emanuel Geibel, 'Sehnsucht', in Geibel, *Gedichte*, 130.

[7] Geibel's original reads 'Trauben glühn' (grapes gleam).

[8] The word 'Ach' (Alas) was added by Kinkel. The original poem reads 'Stund' um Stund' entflieht'. Kinkel changed 'Stund' to 'Stunde'.

Verträume die Jugend, begrabe das Lied! – [9]	*h*	Pass your youth in dreaming, bury your song.
O die Schranken so eng, und die Welt so weit,	*c*	Ah! How narrow our confines, how wide the world
Und so flüchtig die Zeit!	*c*	And how fleeting is time!

The first line 'Ich blick' in mein Herz und ich blick' in die Welt' (I look into my heart and I look at the world) reveals the lonesome lyrical protagonist's quarrel between him- or herself and the rest of the world. The hopeless longing for the South evokes a sense of Romantic unhappiness, also known as *Weltschmerz*. Kinkel intensifies the Romantic tone by modifying the poetry slightly: she adds the sighing word 'Ach' (Alas) and replaces the word 'Vertraure' (pass in mourning) with the word 'Verträume' (pass in dreaming) in the third stanza. In correspondence with the dualism carried by the words the vocal part creates a contrast between the 'narrow confines', set to repeated quavers ('b^1'), and the wide world, portrayed by way of a dotted ascent in crotchets ('a^1'–'c^2'–'f^2', bars 20 ff., Ex. 5.1). The changing piano accompaniment from one-bar arpeggios to groups of six arpeggio quavers per bar, in the middle section, supports the overall contrast between the melancholic first four lines of each verse and the desperate reality pictured in the final two lines. It is not until bar 20 that the piano accompaniment changes to pairs of *staccatissimo* quavers separated from each other by quaver rests. The *staccatissimo* expression and rests between each pair of quavers emphasise the corresponding words: 'O die Schranken so eng und sie Welt so weit, | Und so flüchtig die Zeit' (Ah! How narrow our confines, how wide the world | And how fleeting is time!). Moreover, the sudden inclusion of the D-sharp diminished seventh chord in bar 23, following the fermata on B-flat major, the Neapolitan sixth, stresses the lyrical I's sadness and sudden realisation of time passing quickly.

Unlike 'Sehnsucht nach Griechenland', and despite the clear reference to such Southern countries as Spain and Egypt, no particular country or landscape is praised in Kinkel's setting of Geibel's 'Die Zigeuner' (The Gypsies, op. 7, no. 6). Rather, a gypsy gathering at night time is portrayed. The last verse was not set by Kinkel. She never commented on this poem, so it is unclear whether she omitted this verse in accordance with the formal design of the Lied (each musical stanza covers two poetic verses) or whether she deliberately left out the allusion to the indefinite expressed in the last verse. The fast-flowing piano accompaniment and the distinct rhythm allude to the Southern temperament typically associated with gypsies in the nineteenth century (Ex. 5.2).

---

[9] The original poem reads 'Vertraure die Jugend' (pass your youth in mourning).

Ex. 5.1: Semantics in 'Sehnsucht nach Griechenland' (bars 20–29)

Die Zigeuner (op. 7, no. 6)
  Emanuel Geibel (published 1838)

Im Schatten des Waldes, im
  Buchengezweig,
Da regt sich's und raschelt's und flüstert's
  zugleich.[11]
Es flackern die Flammen, es gaukelt der
  Schein
Um bunte Gestalten, um Laub und
  Gestein.

Das ist der Zigeuner lebendige Schaar,[12]
Mit blitzenden Augen und nächtlichem
  Haar,[13]
Gesäugt an des Niles geheiligter Fluth,
Gebräunt von Hispaniens südlicher
  Gluth.[14]

The Gypsies[10]
  Translation by Martin Stock

a In the shady forest, between the beech
  trees,
a There's a hustling, bustling, and
  whispering.
b The flickering light of the fire
  dances
b Around colourful figures, leaves and
  rocks.

c This is where the restless gypsies gather,
c With flashing eyes and glowing
  hair,
d Suckled at the Nile's holy waters,
d Tanned by the blazing southern
  Hispanic sun.

[10] <http://www.lieder.net/lieder/get_text.html?TextId=6007> (accessed 28 April 2016).

[11] The original reads 'Da regt sich's und raschelt's und flüstert zugleich'. Emanuel Geibel, 'Zigeunerleben', in Geibel, *Gedichte*, 4–5.

[12] Geibel's original reads 'bewegliche' (lively) rather than 'lebendige' (restless).

[13] Geibel's original reads 'mit blitzendem Aug und wallendem Haar'. I keep the translation 'glowing hair' as 'glow' represents the atmosphere of this verse.

[14] Geibel's original reads 'gebrannt' (burnt) rather than 'gebräunt' (tanned).

Um's lodernde Feuer im schwellenden Grün,	*e*	Around the fire, amidst the lush green,
Da lagern die Männer verwildert und kühn,	*e*	The men lie, wild and brave.
Da kauern die Weiber und rüsten das Mahl,	*f*	The women squat, preparing the meal,
Und füllen geschäftig den alten Pokal.	*f*	Busily filling the old goblet.
Und Sagen und Lieder erklingen im Rund,	*g*	Folklore and tales are shared by the group,
Wie Spaniens Gärten so blühend und bunt,	*g*	Songs as fantastic and colourful as the gardens of Spain.
Und magische Sprüche für Not und Gefahr	*c*	Magic words for times of distress
Verkündet die Alte der horchenden Schaar.	*c*	Are told by the old woman.
Schwarzäugige Mädchen beginnen den Tanz.	*h*	Black-eyed maidens begin the dance.
Da sprühen die Fackeln im röthlichen Glanz.	*h*	Red-glowing torches are sparkling.
Heiß lockt die Guitarre, die Cymbel erklingt.	*i*	To the enticing sounds of guitars and cymbals
Wie wilder und wilder der Reigen sich schlingt.	*i*	The dancers are twirling in an ever wilder dance.
Dann ruhn sie ermüdet von nächtlichen Reih'n.	*k*	Then, exhausted by the night's dancing, they lie down and rest.
Es rauschen die Bäume in Schlummer sie ein.[15]	*k*	The beech trees are murmuring a lullaby.
Und die aus der glücklichen Heimat verbannt,[16]	*l*	Those once expelled from a homeland where they were happy
Sie schauen im Traume das südliche Land.[17]	*l*	See the Southern land in their dreams.
[not set]		[Not set]
Doch wie nun im Osten der Morgen erwacht,	*m*	When the morning awakes in the east
Verlöschen die schönen Gebilde der Nacht,	*m*	The beautiful images of the night fade away.
Laut scharret das Maultier bei Tagesbeginn,	*n*	At dawn the mule paws at the ground.
Fort ziehn die Gestalten. – Wer sagt dir, wohin?	*n*	The gypsies depart – who knows where they are going?

[15] Geibel's original reads 'Wipfel' (tree tops) rather than 'Bäume' (trees).

[16] Geibel's original reads 'sonnigen' (sunny) rather than 'glücklichen' (happy).

[17] Geibel's original reads 'im Traum das gesegnete Land' (blessed land) rather 'südliche Land' (Southern land).

Ex. 5.2: 'Die Zigeuner' (op. 7, no. 6)[18]

[18] In the original publication, the grace notes 'f♮' in the piano right hand in bars 7 and 8 are notated as 'f♯'; however, considering that upper auxiliary notes are usually diatonic notes, this is most likely an editorial mistake as it should be 'f♮' within the context of A minor rather than 'f♯'. Therefore, I have naturalised the 'f♯' in this example.

Ex. 5.2   (*continued*)

Ludwig Rellstab praised this Lied as one of the most characteristic Lieder included in Kinkel's op. 7 and pointed out that:

> The final Lied of this collection (Die Zigeuner von E. Geibel) has the most characteristic physiognomy of the entire opus. [...] The lively accompaniment contributes a great deal to the beauty of the Lied, although the melody is also significantly independent in places, especially at the words 'suckled at the Nile's holy waters'. However, the harmonisation of the line 'with flashing eyes and glowing hair' is almost too church-like to be singable, and here the melody loses its characteristic expression demanded by the words, although it keeps it throughout the rest of the Lied.[19]

Rellstab preferred the melodic leaps in bars 17–20 to the linear descent in the preceding line (bars 13–16). However, he seemed to ignore the overall formal design of this Lied. Bars 13–16 respond to their preceding phrase (bars 9–12) and thus form the middle section of the three-part structure, while bars 17–20, along with the following four-bar phrase (bars 21–24) mark the final section. Rellstab's phrasing is problematic in so far as it disregards the structural inter-relationships within each particular section. He did not comment on the Lied's formal design at all, although its division into a fast syllabic section (strophes 1, 3 and 5) and two melodically prolonged sections (strophes 2, 4 and 6) seems unusual, considering that each stanza covers two four-line poetic strophes (Table 5.1). Rellstab and Oswald Lorenz seemingly agreed on the effectiveness of the piano accompaniment.[20] Gottfried Wilhelm Fink did not refer to any of the songs in this opus in particular. However, he praised the entire opus for its character and its suitable declamations, the musical technical skills, fresh and natural rhythms, natural melodies, reasonable harmony and stable accompaniments.[21]

Thematically, this Lied incorporates a Romantically coloured admiration of the gypsies, imagery of the night and recognition of people who have been

---

[19] Ludwig Rellstab, review of Johanna Mathieux, *Sechs Lieder für eine Singstimme mit Begleitung des Pianoforte: Opus 7* (1838), 5–7. 'Das letzte Lied (Die Zigeuner von E. Geibel) hat die charakteristischste Physiognomie in der ganzen Sammlung. [...] Die bewegte Begleitung bildet einen wesentlichen Theil der Schönheit dieses Liedes, doch erhebt sich auch die Melodie an einigen Stellen besonders zur selbstständigen Bedeutsamkeit, zumal auf die Worte: "Gesäugt an des Niles geheiligter Fluth". Dagegen ist die Combination bei der Stelle: "Mit blitzenden Augen und nächtlichem Haar" fast zu sehr im kirchlich-harmonischen Stil gehalten um recht sangbar zu sein, auch verliert die Melodie hier, was sie sonst so festhält, den charakteristischen Ausdruck den die Worte fordern.'

[20] Oswald Lorenz, review of Johanna Mathieux, *Sechs Lieder für eine Singstimme mit Begleitung des Pianoforte: Opus 7* (1838).

[21] Gottfried Wilhelm Fink, review of Johanna Mathieux, *Sechs Lieder für eine Singstimme mit Begleitung des Pianoforte: Opus 7* (1838).

Table 5.1: Formal design of 'Die Zigeuner' (op. 7, no. 6)

Bar	1–8	9–16	17–24	25–28	29–32
Phrase	A	B	C	Postlude	Postlude
Stanza	1	2			
	3	4			
	5	6			

banned from their home countries. Considering Kinkel's own biographical background, she might have been drawn to Geibel's poem for different reasons. Besides her close friendship with Geibel, the thematic dimension of this Lied goes hand in hand with the Romantic fashion of the time and thus may have increased its marketability, and, on a psycho-biographical level, the words might point to Kinkel's own pride in, and longing for, her home, the Rhineland.

🙦 *Night songs*

In a similar way, Kinkel's night songs echo the Romantic tone and respond to the notion of *Besonnenheit*, a 'process of pausing and remembrance, which constitutes memory'.[22] In 'Abendruhe' (Evening Rest, op. 17, no. 3), set to Kinkel's own poetry, Kinkel describes how the thoughtful lyrical I, leaning against a tree, watches the approach of the night.[23] In the last verse, s/he wishes to rest like this 'day and night' and longs to dream of this very moment forever.

Abendruhe (op. 17, no. 3)
  Johanna Kinkel (published 1847)

Evening Rest[24]
  Translation by Sharon Krebs

Gelehnet lag ich an dem Baum,	*a*	I lay leaning against a tree,
Und lauscht' dem Wellensang;	*b*	And listened to the singing of the waves;
Versunken ganz in süssen Traum	*a*	Completely immersed in a lovely dream,
Ward mir die Zeit nicht lang.	*b*	Time did not hang heavy on my hands.
Die Sonne lenkt den Strahlenlauf	*c*	The sun took its beaming journey
Zum tiefen Horizont,	*d*	To the low horizon,
Das Abendroth stieg mild herauf,	*c*	The glow of sunset gently arose,
Es folgt der Silbermond.	*d*	The silvery moon followed suit.

---

[22] Alexander J. Cvetko, '… *Durch Gesänge lehrten sie …' Johann Gottfried Herder und die Erziehung durch Musik: Mythos – Ideologie – Rezeption* (Frankfurt: Peter Lang, 2005), 57.

[23] Kinkel's poem is included in the *Maikäfer* journal of 23 March 1841 (Brandt-Schwarze and others, i, 384–85).

[24] <http://www.lieder.net/lieder/get_text.html?TextId=109402> (accessed 13 March 2019).

Der Mond ging endlich auch zur Ruh'	*e*	The moon, too, finally went to rest,
Rings um mich ward es Nacht;	*f*	Round about me night fell;
Mir fielen nicht die Augen zu	*e*	My eyes did not fall shut
Auf einsam stiller Wacht.	*f*	During my solitary, silent watch.
So möchte' ich ruhen Tag und Nacht,	*f*	Thus would I like to rest day and night,
Und überschau'n mein Glück,	*g*	And survey my happiness,
Und ewig, ewig träumen nach	*f*	And ever, ever dream again
Dem einen Augenblick.	*g*	That one moment.

Throughout the Lied, the harmonic design centres on the tonic D major, but the German augmented sixth chord in bar 28 causes a meaningful halt before the concluding line, supported by the *rallentando* (Ex. 5.3). Large parts of the piano accompaniment expose broken semi-quaver triplets in the right hand and broken quaver triads in the left hand. Supporting the calm, dreamy and contented mood, the left-hand piano part is slowed down in the last eight-bar phrase of each musical stanza. Unlike her Berlin Lieder, in many of which Kinkel prioritised the piano accompaniment over the vocal part, this song focuses on the voice. The vocal range is unusually large ('c¹' to 'f²') and includes a great deal of ornamentation, by means of which Kinkel stresses such Romantic

Ex. 5.3: 'Abendruhe' (op. 17, no. 3)

Ex. 5.3   (*continued*)

key words as 'süssen Traum' (lovely dream), 'Abendroth' (glow of sunset), and 'Silbermond' (silvery moon). Notated as a varied strophic setting, the vocal lines of both musical stanzas differ from each other only in two places (in bars 5–8, and 21–26). In both instances, Kinkel responds musically to the words. While the movement of the waves in bar 7 is portrayed by means of a dotted descending motif, a held note ('c¹') characterises the night in the second strophe (also bar 7). In a similar way, the word 'horizon' in bar 23 is approached via a stepwise descent ('a¹'–'e¹'), while the word 'Glück' (happiness) in the second strophe is emphasised by an octave variation, which brings both the melody and the poem's semantic content to a climax.

The second nature setting of op. 17, 'In der Bucht' (In the Bay, op. 17, no. 5), in which the lyrical I praises the quietness and calmness of the night, is characterised by a wide vocal range similar to that of 'Abendruhe'. It spans a major ninth ('d¹'–'e²'). 'In der Bucht' is the only poem of Kinkel's friend and *Maikäfer* member Alexander Kaufmann set by Kinkel.[25] This Lied bears strong parallels to Kinkel's love songs of the early 1840s, many of which deal with nature and watery landscapes and were produced within the context of the *Maikäferbund*.

In der Bucht (op. 17, no. 5)		**In the Bay[26]**
Alexander Kaufmann (published 1847)		Translation by Sharon Krebs
Es schließt der dunkle Wald uns ein;	*a*	The dark forest encloses us;
Die Ruder plätschern matt und leise;	*b*	The oars splash tiredly and quietly;
Kaum, daß von oben noch herein	*a*	Faintly, from above,[27]
Der Mond bescheint die stille Reise.	*b*	The moon illuminates the quiet journey.
Die Blume träumt in stiller Pracht,	*c*	The flower dreams in quiet splendour,
Es singen leis die schönen Frauen –	*d*	The beautiful women sing softly --
Wer möchte wohl nach solcher Nacht	*c*	After such a night as this, who would
Noch wünschen je den Tag zu schauen!	*d*	Yet wish ever to see day!

While the first part of this two-part song suggests a simple eight-bar phrasal structure, the second part (Ex. 5.4) covers eleven bars and a three-bar piano postlude, and is phrased irregularly.

The second phrase is striking on account of its prolongation of the words 'Mond bescheint' (moon illuminates, first verse), and 'noch wünschen je' (yet wish ever, second verse). Contrary to the setting as a whole, which features a dense harmonic pattern, the harmonic progression at the prolonged line stagnates and rests over the tonic key of C major, which suggests that Kinkel wanted the listener to focus on the words. Atypically, the final chord of this Lied is reached via a melodic rise, which symbolises the longing for eternity and almost works as a literal interpretation of the rhetoric question asked at the end of the Lied ('Wer möchte wohl nach solcher Nacht | Noch wünschen je den Tag zu schauen!', After such a night as this, who would | Yet wish ever to see day!).

---

[25] The poem is included in the *Maikäfer* journal and is dated 20 September 1840. Brandt-Schwarze and others, i, 124.

[26] <http://www.lieder.net/lieder/get_text.html?TextId=110338> (accessed 18 March 2019).

[27] While I respectfully acknowledge the fine translation by Sharon Krebs, I have translated lines three and four of this verse more literally in order for the word order in the translation to match that of the original, since I elaborate on these two lines in the following paragraph.

Ex. 5.4: Part B of 'In der Bucht' (bars 9–22)

The duet 'Der Sommerabend' (The Summer Evening, op. 12, no. 2), a setting by Kinkel's friend Wolfgang Müller, evokes a similar mood. The lyrical I praises a quiet evening at the river Rhine and dreams away after the girls' singing has faded. The mountains and stars have a calming effect on the lyrical protagonist. Kinkel changed some of the words in favour of a slightly brighter and less gloomy conclusion of this poem.

Der Sommerabend (op. 12, no. 2) Wolfgang Müller von Königswinter (published 1840)		**The Summer Evening**[28] Translation by Sharon Krebs
Der Sommerabend schauet	*a*	The summer evening gazes
So still auf's Erdenreich,	*b*	So quietly upon the earthly realm,
Tiefer der Himmel blauet,	*a*	The sky is becoming a deeper blue,
Des Westens Rot wird bleich.	*b*	The red of the west is becoming pale.
An den Bergen verglühet	*c*	And the golden glow of evening
Der goldne Abendschein,	*d*	Dims upon the hills,
Still heimlich rauschend ziehet	*c*	Quietly, secretly rushing
Drunten der tiefe Rhein.	*d*	The deep Rhine flows below.

[28] <https://www.lieder.net/lieder/get_text.html?TextId=101582> (accessed 31 March 2020).

Es duften Orangen und Rosen	*e*	Scent rises from the orange trees and roses
Um das freundliche Haus,	*f*	About the friendly house,
Rosige Mädchen kosen[29]	*e*	Rosy maidens are flirting
Von dem Balkon heraus.	*f*	From the balcony.
Scherzend sie sich umschlingen,[30]	*g*	They jokingly embrace
Ringend im süßen Spiel,	*h*	Each other, wrestling in sweet play,
Saiten und Lieder erklingen,	*g*	Strings and songs ring out
Ich sinne und träume viel.	*h*	I ponder and dream many things.
Ich wandle auf und nieder	*i*	I wander up and down
In süßem seligen Traum;	*k*	In sweet blissful dreams;
Verklungen sind längst die Lieder,	*i*	The songs have long since died away,
Ich weiß es selber kaum.	*k*	I hardly know it myself.
Und wie ich erwache, blicket[31]	*l*	And when I awaken, the night
So groß mich an die Nacht,	*m*	Gazes at me so hugely,
Der Himmel sternendurchsticket,[32]	*l*	The sky all embroidered through with stars,
Und der Berge ruhige Pracht.	*m*	And the peaceful splendour of the hills.

Musically, this duet is divided into three sections, each of which covers two poetic verses. While the outer sections centre on the tonic key A major, the middle section includes modulations to the two mediants: F major and C major. As a means of harmonic variety, part C includes an augmented sixth chord at the line 'ich weiß es selber kaum' (I hardly know it myself), followed by a stabilising piano interlude in A major. The piano accompaniment, the flowing character of which Ludwig Rellstab acknowledges as a 'nutty seasoning of the melody', unifies the three musical stanzas.[33]

In a similar manner as 'Abendruhe', 'In der Bucht', and 'Der Sommerabend', Kinkel's setting of her husband's poem 'Es ist so still geworden: Geistliches Abendlied' (It Has Become so Quiet: Sacred Evening Song, op. 18, no. 1) reflects the quiet and thoughtful atmosphere at night-time as something inspiring and appealing. Both the title 'Geistliches Abendlied' and the link between the spiritual and nature evoke the impression that nature was Gottfried and Johanna

---

[29] Müller's original reads 'lieblich' (lovely) rather than 'rosig' (rosy). Wolfgang Müller, *Junge Lieder* (Düsseldorf: Schreiner, 1841), 3–4.

[30] The original reads 'Sie ringen und umschlingen Sich scherzend im süßen Spiel'.

[31] The original reads 'dunkelt' (darkens) rather than 'blicket' (gazes).

[32] The original reads 'sternendurchfunkelt' rather than 'sternendurchsticket'.

[33] Ludwig Rellstab, review of Johanna Mathieux, *Drei Duette für weibliche Stimmen mit Begleitung des Pianoforte: Opus 12* (1849), 46: 'pikante Würze durch die fortlaufende [melodische] Figur'.

Kinkel's religion, perhaps an intended turn of perspective considering the Kinkels' complicated religious background. The lyrics were quite popular during the nineteenth century and were also set by the Berlin composers Martin Blumner (1827–1901) and Eduard Grell (1800–1886), the Czech composer and music pedagogue Jan Bedřich Kittl (1806–1868), Ernst Methfessel (1811–1881), and Robert Schumann, to name but a few.

Es ist so still geworden: Geistliches Abendlied (op. 18, no. 1) Gottfried Kinkel (published 1843)		**It Has Become so Quiet: Sacred Evening Song**[34] Translation by Sharon Krebs
Es ist so still geworden,	*a*	It has become so quiet,
In Tiefen und auf Höh'n,[35]	*b*	In the valleys and the mountains,
Nun hört man allerorten	*a*	Now one hears everywhere
Der Engel Füße gehn,	*b*	The footsteps of the angels.
Rings in die Thale senket[36]	*c*	All around darkness sinks
Sich Finsterniß mit Macht –	*d*	Powerfully into the depths;
Wirf ab, Herz, was dich kränket	*c*	Cast off, heart, what grieves you
Und was dich traurig macht![37]	*d*	And what makes you sad!
Es ruht die Welt im Schweigen,	*e*	The world rests silently in peace,
Ihr Tosen ist vorbei,	*f*	The excitement is over,
Stumm ihres Jauchzens Reigen[38]	*e*	Joys have turned silent
Und stumm ihr Schmerzensschrei.	*f*	And so has the cry of pain.
Was sie von Rosen schenket,	*c*	[The world] has brought you roses
Von Dornen hat gebracht,[39]	*d*	It brought you thorns –
Wirf ab, Herz, was dich kränket	*c*	Cast off, heart, what grieves you
Und was dich traurig macht!	*d*	And what makes you sad!

[34] <http://www.lieder.net/lieder/get_text.html?TextId=42244> (accessed 31 March 2020); the second and third stanzas are translated by the author.

[35] Gottfried Kinkel's original reads 'Verrauscht des Abends Wehn' (the evening has gone past). Gottfried Kinkel, 'Ein geistlich Abendlied', in Kinkel, *Gedichte*, 191–92. It is uncertain whether Johanna Kinkel changed the lyrics, or whether this Lied reflects an original unpublished version of Gottfried Kinkel's poem.

[36] The published original reads 'Berge' (mountains) rather than 'Thale' (valleys).

[37] The published original reads '[dir] bange' (anxious) rather than '[dich] traurig' (sad).

[38] The published original poem reads 'Freude' rather than 'Jauchzen'.

[39] The published original poem reads 'Hat Rosen sie geschenket | Hat Dornen sie gebracht'.

Und hast du heut gefehlet,	*g*	If you failed today,
Und trübt die Schuld den Blick;[40]	*h*	If conscience clouds your view;
Empfinde dich beseelet	*g*	Rejoice
In freier Gnade Glück.[41]	*h*	In your freedom.
Auch des Verirrten denket	*c*	The guardian shepherd shall
Der Hirt auf hoher Wacht –	*d*	Also think of the confused ones –
Wirf ab, Herz, was dich kränket	*c*	Cast off, heart, what grieves you
Und was dich traurig macht!	*d*	And what makes you sad!
Nun stehn im Himmelskreise	*i*	Now all about the heavens
Die Stern' in Majestät;	*k*	The stars stand in majesty.
In gleichem festem Gleise	*i*	Along the old, firm pathway
Der goldne Wagen geht.	*k*	The golden carriage [the moon] is travelling.
Und gleich den Sternen lenket	*c*	And like the stars, it directs
Er deinen Weg durch Nacht –	*d*	Your way through the night.
Wirf ab, Herz, was dich kränket,	*c*	Cast off, heart, what grieves you
Und was dir bange macht!	*d*	And what makes you anxious!

'Es ist so still geworden: Geistliches Abendlied' is a varied strophic setting and the vocal range is quite wide ('d^1' to 'e^2'). The piano accompaniment incorporates a latent second voice in the right-hand part and such Romantic expressive means as tremolo (bar 13), a trill (bar 20) and a piano postlude (Ex. 5.5). Although the harmonic range does not exceed the commonly used third relations and dominant/subdominant representatives, the harmonic progression is strikingly dense with harmonic changes and abrupt shifts within single bars. It also includes Italian augmented sixth chords (bars 7 and 8) and a diminished seventh chord (bar 12).[42] Thus, this Lied seems more challenging than others, an aspect which might reveal the special attention with which Kinkel approached the compositional challenge of setting her husband's words.

Geibel's 'Nachtlied' (Nightly Song, op. 7, no. 1) is set in a simple harmonic pattern and harmonic changes mostly occur at the beginning of each bar. Oswald Lorenz of the *Neue Zeitschrift für Musik* praises the song for its 'most coherent and correct' harmonisation, while Rellstab compliments Kinkel on the original conclusion of each section.[43] Although not overly difficult, the vocal line is unusually wide-ranging for an early composition of Kinkel's ('c^1' to 'f^2').

---

[40] The published original poem reads 'O schaue nicht zurück' (Oh do not look back).

[41] The published original reads 'Von' (by) rather than 'in' (in).

[42] The manuscript of a later version of this Lied, which Kinkel dated 21 August 1857, does not include the Italian sixth chord in bar 7. It is uncertain whether Kinkel made a mistake in this manuscript as she places a '♮' before the note 'd' in the left hand piano in bar 7 even though it would have been 'd♭' without the accidental as the later version is set in B-flat major. Kinkel, manuscript of 'Es ist so still geworden: Geistliches Abendlied', ULB E 4° 756/6 Rara:15, 27–28.

[43] Oswald Lorenz, review of Johanna Mathieux, *Sechs Lieder für eine Singstimme mit Begleitung des Pianoforte: Opus 7* (1838), 77–78: 'am folgerichtigsten und

Ex. 5.5: 'Es ist so still geworden: Geistliches Abendlied' (op. 18, no. 1)

*) Die oberen Noten gelten für die erste und vierte Strophe.

Rellstab detects a horn-like melody, which he appreciates because of its simple and independent character, and calls the melody 'gesangvoll und gemüthlich'

---

korrektesten harmonisiert'; Rellstab, review of Johanna Mathieux, *Sechs Lieder für eine Singstimme mit Begleitung des Pianoforte: Opus 7* (1838), 5–7.

(singable and comfortable).[44] The positive reception of this Lied by two renowned music reviewers of the time reflects Kinkel's sense of marketability. Not only do both reviewers praise Kinkel's compositional style, they also acknowledge her choice of poetry. Thematically, the poem combines two paradigms, nightly thoughtfulness and the mystification of the beloved, and creates a dualism between the observer (the lyrical I) and the observed (the beloved).

Nachtlied (op. 7, no. 1)		Nightly Song[45]
Emanuel Geibel		Translation adapted from David
(published 1838)		Kenneth Smith

Der Mond kommt still gegangen	*a*	The moon rises so peacefully
Mit seinem gold'nen Schein,	*b*	With all its golden light,
Da schläft in holdem Prangen	*a*	Here sleeps in lovely glitter
Die müde Erde ein.	*b*	The weary earth below.
Im Traum die Wipfel weben,	*c*	In the dream, the tree tops sweep,
Die Quellen rauschen sacht;	*d*	The springs rustle softly;
Singende Engel durchschweben	*c*	Singing angels hover
Die blaue Sternennacht.	*d*	Through the blue starry night.
Und auf den Lüften schwanken	*e*	From many a faithful heart
Aus manchem treuen Sinn	*f*	Many thousand loving thoughts
Viel tausend Liebesgedanken	*e*	Waft on the breezes
Über die Schläfer hin.	*f*	Upon the sleeping ones.
Und drunten im Tal, da funkeln[46]	*g*	And down in the valley, there twinkle
Die Fenster von Liebchens Haus;	*h*	The lights from my lover's house;
Ich aber blicke im Dunkeln	*g*	But I in darkness still look out –
Still in die Welt hinaus.	*h*	Calmly – into the world.

The moon is the focus of the following two Goethe Lieder. In both settings the lyrical I asks the moon for advice in relation to his/her beloved. Published in 1770, 'An Luna' (To Luna, op. 6, no. 4) was the first of Goethe's poems dealing with the moon.[47] The first four verses describe a Romantic setting in the countryside where the moon overlooks a 'boundless expanse' and a knight tries to catch a glimpse of

---

[44] Rellstab, review of Johanna Mathieux, *Sechs Lieder für eine Singstimme mit Begleitung des Pianoforte: Opus 7.*

[45] <http://www.lieder.net/lieder/get_text.html?TextId=5994> (accessed 31 March 2020).

[46] Geibel's original reads 'Tale' rather than 'Tal'. Emanuel Geibel, 'Nachtlied', in Geibel, *Gedichte*, 13–14.

[47] Gerhard Sauder, in *Johann Wolfgang Goethe: Sämtliche Werke nach Epochen seines Schaffens (Münchner Ausgabe)*, i.1, 825. There are two versions of this poem. The first version, published in Breitkopf's *Neue Lieder in Melodien gesetzt*, reflects a mixture of styles: while the first verse takes on a Romantic colouring, the second and third verses acquire the style of the Rococo. Goethe and Breitkopf had agreed to the Lieder collection while Goethe still lived in Leipzig, but the second version of 'An Luna', written in 1815, was added after Goethe's return to Frankfurt.

his beloved's bedroom. In the final punchline, 'Ei, da schieltest du dich blind' (Ei, you have leered at her until you have turned blind) the (k)nightly spectator is ridiculed and the Romantic atmosphere replaced with anacreontic light-heartedness. In 1815, Goethe replaced this last verse with a more Romantically-coloured one, in which the love motif is mystified with the relationship between Selene (Luna, goddess of the moon) and Endymion, Luna's beloved.[48] Kinkel set this 1815 version.

An Luna (op. 6, no. 4) Johann Wolfgang von Goethe (published 1839)		**To Luna**[49] Translation by Briony Williams

Schwester von dem ersten Licht,	*a*	Sister of the sun,
Bild der Zärtlichkeit in Trauer!	*b*	Picture of tenderness in mourning!
Nebel schwimmt mit Silberschauer	*b*	Mist swims in silver shimmers
Um dein reizendes Gesicht;	*a*	Around your lovely face.
Deines leisen Fußes Lauf	*c*	The tread of your soft foot
Weckt aus tagverschloßnen Höhlen	*d*	Awakens from caves that shut out the day
Traurig abgeschiedne Seelen,	*d*	Sad isolated souls,
Mich und nächt'ge Vögel auf.	*c*	Me, and nocturnal birds.
Forschend übersieht dein Blick	*e*	Your glance searchingly surveys
Eine großgemeßne Weite.	*f*	A boundless expanse.
Hebe mich an deine Seite!	*f*	Raise me to your side!
Gib der Schwärmerei dies Glück.	*e*	Grant my zeal this happiness.
Und in wollustvoller Ruh'	*g*	And in peaceful ecstasy
Säh der weitverschlag'ne Ritter	*h*	The knight, driven far, would, through
Durch das gläserne Gegitter	*h*	The glass barriers, keep watch over
Seines Mädchens Nächten zu.	*g*	His lady as she slept.

1770:

Dämmrung, wo die Wollust thront,	*i*	Twilight, in which desire rules,[50]
Schwimmt um ihre runden Glieder.	*k*	Swims about her rounded limbs.
Trunken sinkt mein Blick hernieder.	*k*	Intoxicated, my gaze moves downward.
Was verhüllt man wohl dem Mond?	*i*	What does she hide from the moon?
Doch was das für Wünsche sind!	*l*	But what kind of desires am I thinking of!
Voll Begierde zu genießen,	*m*	Full of desire to enjoy,
So da droben hängen müssen;	*m*	You have to hang up there in the sky;
Ei, da schieltest du dich blind.	*l*	Ei, you have leered at her until you have turned blind.

---

[48] <http://www.goethezeitportal.de/wissen/dichtung/schnellkurs-goethe/klein-paris-studium-in-leipzig-und-frankfurter-rekonvaleszenz.html> (28 April 2016).

[49] Briony Williams, 'Maker, Mother, Muse: Bettina von Arnim, Goethe and the Boundaries of Creativity', in *Goethe: Musical Poet, Musical Catalyst*, ed. Lorraine Byrne (Dublin: Carysfort, 2004), 185–202 (195–96).

[50] As the 1770 version of this poem is not included in Williams's article, the two corresponding strophes are translated by the author.

1815:		1815:
Des Beschauens holdes Glück	*e*	The sweet happiness of contemplation
Mildert solcher Ferne Qualen,	*n*	Assuages the torments of such distance
Und ich sammle deine Strahlen,	*n*	And I gather your rays
Und ich schärfe meinen Blick;	*e*	And I focus my gaze;
Hell und heller wird es schon	*i'*	It becomes bright and brighter already
Um die unverhüllten Glieder,	*k*	Around the unveiled limbs
Und nun zieht sie mich hernieder,	*k*	And she draws me down to her
Wie dich einst Endymion.	*i'*	As once Endymion did to you.

Ex. 5.6 shows that the eight lines of each stanza, held together by the continuous piano accompaniment, differ from each other in terms of tonality. Set in A-flat major, the first part's conclusion in A-flat minor underlines the lyrical I's sad mood. The harmonic turn in the second part (bars 17–20) evokes a sense of tonal and emotional uncertainty. The range of expressive means – including changing dynamics and pace, a flowing piano accompaniment and a graceful vocal line rich in ornamentation – reflects a Romantic musical colouring. However, Kinkel's personal touch is revealed in the chromatic vocal line and the unusual tonal design.

Ex. 5.6: 'An Luna' (op. 6, no. 4)[51]

[51] Considering the latent second voice in the piano right hand in bar 22, it would make more sense if the last note in the right hand were 'e♭' rather than 'd'. That way, the upper and lower melodic lines in the piano right hand in bars 21–22 would both be 'c'–'c'–'d♭'–'e♭'–'f'. As the original publication suggests 'd' rather than 'e♭' and it is uncertain whether Kinkel intended the upper and lower voices to move in analogy to each other, I have followed the original publication here.

Ex. 5.6   *(continued)*

Ex. 5.6   (*continued*)

Kinkel's second Goethe moon setting, 'An den Mond' (To the Moon, op. 7, no. 5), reflects the Romantic perception of nature as a powerful influence on humanity's well-being even more obviously than 'An Luna'. There are three versions of 'An den Mond', all of which were written within the context of Goethe's relationship with Charlotte von Stein (1776–1778). Goethe wrote two versions of this poem, and another one was created by von Stein, but the chronology of the three versions is unclear.[52] Kinkel set Goethe's second version but omitted the second verse.

An den Mond (op. 7, no. 5)		To the Moon[53]	
Johann Wolfgang von Goethe (published 1838)		Translation adapted from Scott Horton	
Füllest wieder Busch und Thal	*a*	Once more you fill bush and valley	
Still mit Nebelglanz,	*b*	With your misty light,	
Lösest endlich auch einmal	*a*	At last also you bring	
Meine Seele ganz;	*b*	Rest to me;	

[52] Hartmut Reinhardt, in *Johann Wolfgang Goethe: Sämtliche Werke nach Epochen seines Schaffens (Münchner Ausgabe)*, ii.1, 559.

[53] <http://harpers.org/blog/2010/02/goetheschubert-_an-den-mond_/> (accessed 28 April 2019).

[not set]		[not set]
Breitest über mein Gefild	*c*	With calm you spread your brilliant gaze
Lindernd deinen Blick,	*d*	Over the fields around me
Wie des Freundes Auge mild	*c*	Like my loved one watching my fate
Über mein Geschick.	*d*	With his gentle eyes.
Jeden Nachklang fühlt mein Herz	*e*	Every echo fills my heart
Froh und trüber Zeit,	*f*	With memories of glad and sad times,
Wandle zwischen Freud' und Schmerz	*e*	I pass between happiness and pain
In der Einsamkeit.	*f*	In loneliness.
Fließe, fließe, lieber Fluß!	*g*	Flow on, flow on my beloved river!
Nimmer werd' ich froh;	*h*	Happiness will not return to me;
So verrauschte Scherz und Kuß	*g*	Thus passed from me
Und die Treue so.	*h*	Laughter, kisses and fidelity.
Ich besaß es doch einmal,	*a*	Though once I held
Was so köstlich ist!	*i*	What is so precious!
Daß man doch zu seiner Qual	*a*	What one to his torment
Nimmer es vergißt!	*i*	Will never forget!
Rausche, Fluß, das Tal entlang,	*k*	Rumble, oh river, along the valley,
Ohne Rast und Ruh,	*l*	Without rest or silence,
Rausche, flüstre meinem Sang	*k*	Rumble and whisper melodies
Melodien zu!	*l*	For my song.
Wenn du in der Winternacht	*m*	When on winter nights you
Wütend überschwillst	*n*	Rage and spill your banks,
Oder um die Frühlingspracht	*m*	Or when you surge around
Junger Knospen quillst.	*n*	The springtime glory of young buds.
Selig, wer sich vor der Welt	*o*	Blessed are we who withdraw
Ohne Haß verschließt,	*p*	From the world without hate,
Einen Freund am Busen hält	*o*	Holding a friend to the breast,
Und mit dem genießt,	*p*	And with him enjoy
Was, von Menschen nicht gewußt	*q*	That which is not known to man
Oder nicht bedacht,	*m*	Or not contemplated
Durch das Labyrinth der Brust	*q*	Wandering in the night
Wandelt in der Nacht.	*m*	Through the labyrinth of the heart.

'An den Mond' is characterised by tonal unconventionality, an aspect which was noted by Oswald Lorenz in 1838 when, in a gender-biased way, he stressed the unusual tonal excursion to A major in bars 12–13:

> [Compared to the 'Lorelei', a different Lied], 'An den Mond' makes a friendlier impression and will be appreciated by many female friends. The tonal modulation to A major, where the 'e♭' (instead of 'd♯') enters bravely among all the sharps, and

the naïve return to G major allude to the female hand just as much as the grace-ful character of the setting in general.[54]

As the vocal line in bar 12 suggests a parallelism to bar 4, the listener – in anal-ogy to bar 4 – would expect an A minor chord rather than an A major chord here. However, considering the seemingly more sedate textual content deliv-ered in bars 12–13, the offset to A major as opposed to A minor makes sense. Lorenz did not comment on the original introduction of the A major chord in question. This introduction demonstrates Kinkel's compositional versatility by applying a diminished seventh chord (bar 9), which introduces a harmonic state of uncertainty in the following bars. Bar 10 touches on a completely new tonal thought (F-sharp minor), followed by a remote progression (F major⁷– A major) in bar 11 (Ex. 5.7).

Thus, the 'eb', which was bemoaned by Lorenz, constitutes the minor sev-enth in F major. It is interesting that Lorenz suggests the German augmented sixth chord ('f'–'a'–'c'–'d♯') instead of the dominant seventh chord, because Kinkel used augmented sixth chords in many other Lieder and must have been familiar with this progression. It seems that Kinkel deliberately chose the dominant seventh chord here, followed by an incorrect resolution of the seventh by means of an ascending semitone ('eb'–'e', making it sound like an augmented sixth chord). In light of her affinity for semitones and enharmonic progressions, it can be imagined that she chose this progression on purpose in order to achieve a surprising harmonic turn. On the other hand, this Lied was part of Kinkel's first published and reviewed opus, so it is possible that her awareness of the augmented sixth chord and its correct resolution was raised through this review.

[54] Oswald Lorenz, review of Johanna Mathieux, *Sechs Lieder für eine Singstimme mit Begleitung des Pianoforte: Opus 7* (1838), 77–78. '"An den Mond" von Goethe hat dagegen ein recht freundliches und gewinnendes Ansehn und wird sich namentlich viele Freundinnen erwerben. An der Ausweichung aber nach A-Dur, bei der das es (statt dis) sich so furchtlos unter die vielen Kreuze hineingewagt hat, und an der naiven Rückkehr nach G-Dur ist, wie an der zarten Haltung des ganzen Liedes vor allem die weibliche Hand zu erkennen.'

Ex. 5.7: 'An den Mond' (op. 7, no. 5)[55]

 The sixth quaver in the piano right hand in bar 13 is notated as 'g#'' – 'a'' rather than 'g'' – 'a#''. This is an editorial mistake; in the score, a previous library user has written underneath this quaver the words 'ais+g♮'; the mistake was corrected in this example.

❧ *Mystic songs*

The Heine duet 'Die Geisterinsel' (Phantom Island, op. 11, no. 2) deals with a loving couple in a boat at sea. The couple float past a beautiful foggy phantom island, where lovely sounds are heard. The last two lines turn the melancholic mood into one of desperation, or even fear, as the boat floats past the island and drifts onto the wide sea, an atmospheric turn which reflects Heine's use of Romantic irony.

Die Geisterinsel (op. 11, no. 2)
    Heinrich Heine (published 1839)
		Phantom Island[56]
		    Translation adapted from Robert
		    McFarland and Emily Ezust

Mein Liebchen, wir saßen beisammen,	*a*	My darling, we sat together,
Traulich im leichten Kahn.	*b*	Comfortably in the light tub;
Die Nacht war still, und wir schwammen	*a*	The night was silent, and we floated
Auf weiter Wasserbahn.	*b*	On the broad watery road.
Die Geisterinsel, die schöne,	*c*	The phantom island, the lovely one,
Lag dämm'rig im Mondenglanz;	*d*	Lay duskily in the moonlight;
Dort klangen liebe Töne,	*c*	Sweet tones were sounding there,
Dort wogte der Nebeltanz.[57]	*d*	The dancing mists heaved up and down.
Dort klang es lieb und lieber,	*e*	It sounded lovely and lovelier,
Und wogt' es hin und her;	*f*	Dances heaved back and forth,
Wir aber schwammen vorüber,	*e*	But we floated past,
Trostlos auf weitem Meer.	*f*	Comfortless on the wide sea.

The romantic atmosphere, which is evoked by such key words as 'Wasserbahn' (watery road, bars 11–12); 'Geisterinsel' (Phantom island, bar 19); 'dämmrig' (duskily, bar 21); and 'Nebeltanz' (dancing mists, bar 29), is supported by the piano accompaniment. Suggesting the movement of the water, a barcarole rhythm is applied at the line 'wogt' es hin und her' (heaved back and forth), which Kinkel repeats several times. Although Rellstab, in his review from August 1839, praised the expressive accompaniment, he criticised the repetitiveness of this particular line in his review:

> The second duet benefits from its suitable accompaniment expressing the romantic background of the poem, the filmy night over the calm sea, the moonlight, the phantom island. However, the poem does not strike us as appropriate for a duet as it expresses a single mood. As a result, there are some drawbacks, such as the

---

[56] <http://sophie.byu.edu/?q=texts/die-geisterinsel> (accessed 13 March 2016) and <http://www.lieder.net/lieder/get_text.html?TextId=17777> (accessed 13 March 2019).

[57] Heine's original reads 'Und wogte der Nebelglanz' rather than 'Dort wogte der Nebelglanz'. Heine, 'XLIII', in *Buch der Lieder von Heinrich Heine* (Hamburg: Hoffmann und Campe, 1827), 147, cited after *Heinrich Heine: Historisch-Kritische Gesamtausgabe*.

weakening compositional treatment of the line 'heaved back and forth', indeed, an almost meaningless line.[58]

Bearing in mind Kinkel's affinity with nature and considering the great number of Rhineland myths and love stories, the line describing a romantic setting on the water was certainly not 'meaningless' to Kinkel. In the next paragraph of his review, Rellstab criticises the seemingly incomprehensible conclusion of Heine's poem, which reflects Rellstab's and Kinkel's different emotional approaches to the words. Rellstab bemoans that:

> We have never been able to bring the ending of the poem in line with its beginning. While Heine often purposely completes a wonderful painting with a bizarre question, here he seems to have been at a loss for a pathetic ending, for a definite thought in order to vitalise the graceful picture [...]. He, who, arm in arm with his beloved, floats in a boat on the calm sea, does not go past the foggy phantom island in a state of debility but in a state of blessedness.[59]

The employment of numerous compositional means at the corresponding line, 'Wir aber schwammen vorüber | Trostlos auf weitem Meer' (But we floated past | Comfortless on the wide sea), suggests that Kinkel granted special attention to the atmospheric turn in the poem – for personal and aesthetic reasons, and/ or for reasons of fashion. The tempo changes from *Andantino* to *Adagio*; the dynamics change from *mf* to *f*; the rhythm changes from lively repeated semi-quavers to heavier alternating crotchets and quavers; and the line opens with an unexpected dramatic E minor chord within the tonal context of E major (Ex. 5.8). The word 'trostlos' (comfortless, bar 57) is harmonised with a German augmented sixth chord, and is set as a melodic tritone ('e²'–'a♯¹'), which is emphasised by means of a fermata on both syllables (bar 58).

[58] Ludwig Rellstab, review of Johanna Mathieux, *Drei Duetten für Sopran und Alt: Opus 11* (1839), 123. 'Das zweite Duett drückt den romantischen Hintergrund des Gedichts, die duftige Nacht auf dem still ruhenden Meere, den Mondenschimmer, die Geisterinsel, sehr glücklich im Accompagnement aus. Doch das Gedicht selbst scheint uns zum Duett nicht geeignet, sondern nur der Ausdruck der einzelnen Seelenstimmung zu sein. Daher kommen denn manche Übelstände, z. B. die den Eindruck des Ganzen schwächende Ausführung der Worte 'dort wogt es hin und her', eine in der That fast bedeutungslose Zeile.'

[59] Ibid. 'Den Schluß des Gedichts haben wir nie mit dem Anfang in Einklang bringen können; wie Heine oft absichtlich bizarr ein wundervoll angelegtes Gemälde mit einer Frage vollendet, so scheint er hier, um einen pathetischen Schluß, um einen sicheren Gedanken, um dem reizenden Bilde Leben zu geben, verlegen gewesen zu sein [...] Wer mit der Geliebten Arm in Arm, auf leichtem Nachen auf ruhigem Meere schwimmt, treibt nicht kraftlos, sondern seelig an der nebligen Geisterinsel vorüber.'

Ex. 5.8: 'Die Geisterinsel' (bars /50–63)

So far, Rellstab's dislike of this duet has been explained on the basis of his disapproval of Heine's words. However, the next section of Rellstab's review calls into question whether the lack of comprehension was the only reason for his harsh critique. Ulrich Tadday posits that Rellstab's political background was, at first, republican, although he changed to a monarchist mindset after the 1848/49 revolutions.[60] Thus, already in 1839, Rellstab, being an advocate of German nationalism, must have regretted Heine's expatriation to Paris in 1831, which becomes evident in the following passage, and which might have triggered Rellstab's unconscious search for negative aspects in Heine's poetry:

> The unfortunate close relation to the words leads us to a number of critical asides. But they should not distract us from the third duet, which has a delightful, innocent charm, and in which nothing disturbs us, but in which everything delights us. The poem is a jewel among the many genre portraits and reverently, harmoniously depicted states of being, in which Heine is so successful, or in which he once was so successful. For now being immersed in the immoral Parisian mire, he seems to be lost to all more lovely creativity.[61]

Rellstab's reference to Heine's residency draws upon nineteenth-century Rhineland patriotism and the consideration of the Rhineland as a fruitful area for artistic creativity. Kinkel conforms to this fashion in her *Lecture on Beethoven*, in which she praises Beethoven's 'merry rhythms' and concludes that:

> A few of them are of a particular colour, which I might believe that only a native of the Rhine could impart to music. It is that despising of affected dignity, which the grand genius likes to express in a sort of bold rhythm, full of health and liberty.[62]

---

[60] Ulrich Tadday, 'Rellstab, (Heinrich Friedrich) Ludwig', in *Die Musik in Geschichte und Gegenwart*, 2nd edn, xiii, Personenteil, 1547–49 (1549). The nationalist impact of Rellstab's Lieder reviews is discussed in Hopkins Porter, 'The "Rheinlieder Critics"'.

[61] Ludwig Rellstab, review of Johanna Mathieux, *Drei Duetten für Sopran und Alt: Opus 11* (1839), 123–24. 'Der unglückselige zu innige Zusammenhang mit dem Text verführt uns zu allerlei kritischen Nebenbetrachtungen. Sie sollen uns aber wenigstens nicht von dem dritten Duo abziehen, welches eine reizende, unschuldige Lieblichkeit hat, und uns durch Nichts stört, sondern durch Alles erfreut. Das Gedichtchen ist ein Juwel unter den vielen zarten Genrebildern und ehrend, harmonisch dargestellten Zuständen, in denen Heine so glücklich ist, oder einst so glücklich war, da er, jetzt im unsittlichen Schlamme von Paris versunken, für jedes schönere Wirken verloren zu sein scheint.'

[62] Kinkel, *Lecture on Beethoven's Earliest Sonatas*. Original in English.

That Rellstab approved of Kinkel's second Heine duet, 'Der Seejungfern Gesang' (The Mermaids' Singing, op. 11, no. 3) might be related to its thematic and musical Romantic colouring. Additionally, the reviewer of the *Allgemeine Musikalische Zeitung* notes the 'feminine choice of words'.[63]

Der Seejungfern Gesang (op. 11, no. 3) Heinrich Heine (published 1839)		**The Mermaids' Singing**[64] Translation by James Thomson
Der Mond ist aufgegangen	*a*	The moon is fully risen
Und überstrahlt die Wellen;	*b*	And shineth o'er the sea;
Ich halte mein Liebchen umfangen,	*a*	And I embrace my darling,
Und unsre Herzen schwell'n.	*b*	Our hearts are swelling free.
Im Arm des holden Kindes	*c*	In the arms of the lovely maiden
Ruh' ich allein am Strand;	*d*	I lie alone on the strand;
Was horchst du beim Rauschen des Windes?	*c*	What sounds in the breeze's sighing?
Was zuckt deine weiße Hand?	*d*	Why trembles your white hand?
Das ist kein Rauschen des Windes,	*c*	That is no breezes sighing,
Das ist der Seejungfern Gesang,	*e*	That is the mermaids' song,
Und meine Schwestern sind es,	*c*	The singing of my sisters
Die einst das Meer verschlang!	*e*	Whom the sea hath drowned so long.

This poem reflects such Romantic paradigms as loneliness, the ideal of deep emotional love, and mysticism. Compositionally, this duet meets Rellstab's ideal of simplicity. Taking on a supportive function, the piano imitates the noise of the wind with lively semiquavers and symbolises the rise of the moon by means of calm minims in the left-hand part in the first section.

❧ *Nature as an allegory for love and the beloved*

Whereas Thalheimer considers Kinkel's melodic progressions monotonous, Rellstab's criticism in the first duet of op. 11, 'Das Lied der Nachtigall' (The Song of the Nightingale, op. 11, no. 1), is that the natural melodic flow is interrupted by unexpected accentuations:

> Like the other duets [of Op. 11], we would like to imagine this duet without its sharp accentuations which are supposed to stress a single feature at the expense of the nice melodic flow. For instance, the first 'e♭' (C minor) at the word 'spring' ('spring out of my tears') in the first line. It is true: at this point, the expression becomes bitter, but the melody does not remain natural. One can, one should

[63] [Anon.], review of Johanna Mathieux, *Drei Duetten für Sopran und Alt: op. 11* (1840), 340: 'weiblich ausgewählte Texte von H. Heine'.

[64] James Thomson, 'Der Mond ist aufgegangen', in *Poems Selected from Heinrich Heine*, ed. Kate Freiligrath Kroeker (London: Walter Scott, 1887), 91.

apply such means, but one should introduce them in a more natural way; the preparation of the dissonances occurs here at an aesthetic level higher than required by strict composition.[65]

Rellstab argues that the melodic progression 'b'–'c'–'d'–'eb'–'c' (bars 9–10, Ex. 5.9) interrupts the natural flow of the melody. However, he admits that the 'eb' matches the bitter mood. Although Rehm considers Rellstab's view as distinctively regressive, the reviewer's criticism of semitones was neither singular nor uncommon during the first half of the nineteenth century.[66] Kinkel referred to the employment of chromaticism in her music-historical writing *Zur Geschichte der Musik* (On Musical History). She comments on this novelty in Chopin's compositional style, a perspective which reflects Kinkel's broad understanding of the music-historical discourse:

Chopin dares to bring together the intervals by a semitone; for example, he applies the minor second where we expect the major second, and thereby achieves completely new and much more subtle expressions, which also causes unforeseen harmonic turns. With this adventure, he approaches the mysteriously locked region of the quarter tones, which, in later centuries, will be received like the semitones in our generation or the third in the generation of our ancestors.'[67]

Kinkel never entered the compositional realms of Chopin in her Lieder, but in Rellstab's opinion, the unprepared introduction of the dissonance and mode mixture in bars 9–10 is inappropriate – perhaps he would have preferred an earlier preparation or the omission of this chromatic inflection.

[65] Thalheimer, *Johanna Kinkel*, 70; Ludwig Rellstab, review of Johanna Mathieux, *Drei Duetten für Sopran und Alt: Opus 11* (1839), 123. 'Nur die zu scharfen Accentuationen, die ein Einzelnes auf Kosten des schönen Flusses in der Melodie hervorheben wollen, möchten wir aus diesem Duett wie aus den andern hinwegwünschen. Z.B. gleich das Es (C-Moll) auf das Wort 'spriessen' (Aus meinen Thränen spriessen) in der ersten Zeile. Es ist wahr, der Ausdruck dieser Stelle wird herb, aber die Melodie bleibt nicht natürlich. Dergleichen kann, soll angebracht werden, allein man muß natürlicher darauf hinleiten; es tritt hier eine Vorbereitung der Dissonanzen in einem höhern ästhetischen Sinne ein, als der strenge Satz dieselbe fordert.'

[66] Jürgen Rehm, *Zur Musikrezeption im vormärzlichen Berlin: Die Präsentation bürgerlichen Selbstverständnisses und biedermeierlicher Kunstanschauung in den Musikkritiken Ludwig Rellstabs* (Hildesheim: Olms, 1983), 77.

[67] Kinkel, *Zur Geschichte der Musik*, 16. 'Chopin wagt es die Intervalle wieder um 1/2 Ton näher zu rücken, z.B. die kleine Sekunde da anzuwenden, wo wir die große erwarten; und bringt dadurch ganz neue und viel feinere Ausdrücke hervor, welche die Harmonie ebenfalls zu völlig ungeahnten Wendungen veranlaßen. Mit diesem Wagestück rüttelt er an der noch geheimnisvoll verschloßnen Pforte der Vierteltöne, die dereinst späteren Jahrhunderten das sein werden, was uns der kleine Sekundschritt, und was unsern Vorfahren die Terz war.'

Ex. 5.9: 'Das Lied der Nachtigall' (bars 1–18)

In 'Das Lied der Nachtigall', Heine embraces different Romantic topoi side by side. While it is clearly a love song, nature is used as an allegory for the longing for love. In the first verse, the lyrical I compares his/her emotions with natural phenomena: tears are associated with flowers and the nightingales' singing is interpreted as sighing. In the second verse, the lyrical protagonist offers the flowers to his/her beloved and the nightingales are supposed to sing underneath the beloved's window. The bitter mood of the corresponding line, which was emphasised in Rellstab's review, is stressed by means of chromaticism, and the allegory of the lyrical I's emotions as powerful natural instances lends more weight to the heartache thematised in the poem.

Das Lied der Nachtigall (op. 11, no. 1)
Heinrich Heine (published 1839)

Aus meinen Tränen sprießen	*a*	
Viel blühende Blumen hervor,	*b*	
Und meine Seufzer werden	*c*	
Ein Nachtigallenchor.	*b*	
Und wenn du mich lieb hast, Kindchen,	*d*	
Schenk' ich dir die Blumen all',	*e*	
Und vor deinem Fenster soll klingen	*f*	
Das Lied der Nachtigall.	*e*	

The Song of the Nightingale[68]
Translation by J. E. Wallis

Where e'er my bitter teardrops fall,
The fairest flowers arise;
And into choirs of nightingales
Are turned my bosom's sighs.

And wilt thou love me, thine shall be
The fairest flowers that spring,
And at the window evermore
The nightingales shall sing.

In the Goethe setting 'Gegenwart' (Presence, op. 16, no. 4) the beloved is associated with such natural phenomena as the sun, the roses and lilies in the garden, the stars, and the moon. The sun serves as an overall allegory when the lyrical I requests that it 'be also to me | The creator of majestic days' ('sei du auch mir | Die Schöpferin herrlicher Tage').

Gegenwart (op. 16, no. 4)[69]
Johann Wolfgang von Goethe
(published 1841)

Alles kündet dich an!   *a*
Erscheinet die herrliche Sonne,   *b*
Folgst du, so hoff' ich es, bald.   *c*
Trittst du im Garten hervor,   *d*
So bist du die Rose der Rosen,   *e*
Lilie der Lilien zugleich.   *f*

Wenn du im Tanze dich regst,   *g*
So regen sich alle Gestirne   *h*
Mit dir und um dich umher.   *i*

Nacht! und so wär es denn Nacht!   *k*
Nun überscheinst du des Mondes   *l*
Lieblichen, ladenden Glanz.   *m*

Presence[70]
Translation by Emily Ezust

Everything announces your presence!
When the majestic Sun appears,
I hope you will follow soon.
When you walk in the garden,
You are the rose of roses
And the lily of lilies at the same time.

When you move in dance,
All the stars move
With you and about you.

Night! and so it is then night!
Now you outshine the moon's
Lovely, inviting gleam.

[68] J. E. Wallis, 'Aus meinen Tränen sprießen', in Freiligrath-Kroeker, ed., *Poems Selected from Heinrich Heine*, 55.

[69] This poem was published in 1815 and was probably written in 1812 when Goethe listened to a Lieder performance by Mamsell Engels at his home. As he disliked the words of one of the songs, he wrote a different poem to the melody of this song (which was composed by Ludwig Berger). See Christoph Siegris, in *Johann Wolfgang Goethe: Sämtliche Werke nach Epochen seines Schaffens (Münchner Ausgabe)*, ix, 1100.

[70] <http://www.lieder.net/lieder/get_text.html?TextId=6422> (accessed 31 March 2020).

Ladend und lieblich bist Du,	*n*	You are attractive and lovely
Und Blumen, Mond und Gestirne	*o*	And the flowers, moon and stars
Huldigen, Sonne, nur Dir.	*p*	Worship only you, my sun!
Sonne! so sei du auch mir	*p*	My sun! be also to me
Die Schöpferin herrlicher Tage;	*q*	The creator of majestic days;
Leben und Ewigkeit ist's.	*r*	This is life and eternity.

Unusually for a nineteenth-century poem, the verses do not rhyme, although coherence is created by way of assonance and alliteration. Kinkel's setting is characterised by regularity and unity: each of the two phrases occupies six bars, the text-setting is syllabic, and each phrase is divided into two-bar motives, each of which corresponds with one line of the poem. Unlike most of Kinkel's songs, this does not have a piano introduction, interlude or postlude, an aesthetic feature which holds together the verses even more eloquently.

'Gegenwart' exhibits a peculiar melody with some challenging turns, the most striking example of which is the note 'f♮' rather than 'f♯' in bar 8 (Ex. 5.10). It precedes a harmonic change to A minor within the context of A major. The return to A major in the last two bars confirms the positive impression of the lyrical I's beloved.

Ex. 5.10: Melodic extravaganza in 'Gegenwart' (bars 7–12)

🎵 *Lullabies in praise of nature*

Kinkel's lullabies carry autobiographical links on different levels. Although three of the four lullabies are settings of Kinkel's own words, not all were composed for her own children. It is uncertain for whom Kinkel composed 'Wiegenlied' op. 10, no. 4, published in 1839, but its Berlin references reveal that she must have had one of her Berlin friends in mind. Written for someone other than the mother or father of the child, this lullaby calms down and entertains an upset child. Each of the three stanzas introduces specific characters – the wind, the horse, and the musicians – who are envious of the child for having delicious food and a warm bed. Praising its unusual style, Rellstab acknowledges this song as a children's song rather than a lullaby and calls it 'one of the nicest compositions'.[71]

Wiegenlied (op. 10, no. 4) Johanna Kinkel (published 1839)		**Lullaby[72]** Translation by Sharon Krebs
Refrain:		Chorus:
O du hast es gar zu gut, lieb Herzenskind,	*a*	Oh you are completely spoiled, dear child of my heart,
Drum gib dich zufrieden und schlafe geschwind.	*a*	So be contented and go to sleep quickly.
Schlaf, schlaf, schlaf, schlaf.	*b*	Sleep, sleep, sleep, sleep.
Wie bist du so glücklich,	*c*	How happy you are,
Wie bist du so reich,	*d*	How rich you are,
Der Vater, die Mutter tun alles	*e*	Your father, your mother do everything
Dir nach deinem Sinn;	*f*	That you want;
Liegst warm in dem Bettchen	*g*	You lie in a warm little bed
Von Flaume so weich,	*d*	So soft and downy,
Kriegst köstliches Süppchen	*h*	You are given delightful soups
Mit zuckersüßem Zucker drin.	*f*	With sweet sugar in them.
Eia, ei, weint das Kind, eia, ei.	*i*	Wah, wa, cries the child, wah, wa.
Refrain		Chorus
Da draußen da heulet	*k*	There outdoors howls
Der eiskalte Wind,	*l*	The ice-cold wind,
Er weinet und bläst durch Berlin,	*m*	It cries and blows through Berlin,
Die große, große Stadt;	*n*	The great, great city;
Der Sturmwind ist neidisch	*o*	The storm-wind is jealous
Auf dich, mein lieb Kind,	*l*	Of you, my dear child,
Weil er nicht wie du	*p*	Because, unlike you,
Ein warm Flaumenfederbettchen hat.	*n*	He doesn't have a downy feather bed.
Susu, su, bläst der Wind, susu su.	*p*	Whoosh, whoosh, blows the wind, whoosh, whoosh.
Refrain		Chorus

[71] Ludwig Rellstab, review of Johanna Mathieux, *Op. 10* (1839), 92: 'eines der gelungensten'.

[72] <http://www.lieder.net/lieder/get_text.html?TextId=109218> (accessed 29 April 2019).

Da draußen da ziehet	*q*	There outdoors a horse
Den Schlitten das Pferd,	*r*	Is pulling a sled,
Es läuten die Schellen,	*s*	The sleigh bells are ringing,
Das Pferdchen aber ist betrübt;	*t*	The little horse, however, is sad;
Mit Schnauben und Wiehern	*u*	With snorting and neighing
Es laut sich beschwert,	*r*	It complains loudly
Daß niemand ihm Zucker	*v*	That no one gives him sugar
Und delikates Süppchen gibt.	*t*	Or dainty soups.
Klingi, ling, schellt das Pferd, klingi, ling.	*w*	Jingle jing, ring [the bells on] the horse, jingle jing.

Refrain

Chorus

Da draußen da stehn	*x*	There outdoors in the snow
Musikanten im Schnee,	*y*	Stands a group of musicians,
Die Frau singt ein Liedchen,	*z*	The woman sings a song,
Die Fiedel spielt der Mann dazu;	*A*	The man plays the fiddle in accompaniment;
Ob ihnen der Hals		Even if their throats
Und die Finger tun weh,	*B*	And their fingers hurt,
Doch müssen sie singen	*y*	They must sing
Und fiedeln ohne Rast und Ruh.	*C*	And fiddle without rest or repose.
Lala la, singt die Frau,	*A*	Lala, la sings the woman,
Vidividi bum, spielt der Mann, vidividi bum.	*D*	Feedeefeedee boom, plays the man,
	E	Feedeefeedee boom

Refrain

Chorus

As the song is in strophic form, all three characters are portrayed musically in the same way, a simplification which makes the lullaby more memorable. Both the vocal part and the piano accompaniment are extraordinarily fast-paced, which seemingly contradicts the purpose of the lullaby. Only the chorus, 'Schlaf, schlaf, schlaf, schlaf' (Sleep, sleep, sleep, sleep), creates a calm and soothing atmosphere by way of dotted minims. Perhaps Kinkel wanted to portray the eventful and fast-paced city life of Berlin, and, as Rellstab pointed out, aimed to entertain the child as much as soothing him/her.

In a letter to her friend Emilie von Henning's daughter Laura, dated 2 September 1841, Kinkel mentions her lullaby op. 15 ('Wiegenlied', op. 15, no. 3), which she had composed for Laura's daughter Maria Johanna.[73] It is organised in strophic form with a regular pattern of eight bars per phrase. The even rhythm and straightforward structure create a flowing momentum within this song. The lyrical observer reminds the child of such phenomena as the wind, small mosquitoes, and bees, all of which are given human traits. That way, the child's fear of the wind's loud noise, and of bees, is eliminated. In the last verse, the child is reassured of his/her safety: angels are watching and guarding him/her.

[73] Maria Johanna von Henning was born on 18 April 1839; Kinkel dated her composition 15 April 1839. Klaus, *Johanna Kinkel*, 55.

Wiegenlied (op. 15, no. 3)
  Johanna Kinkel (published 1841)

Lullaby

Schlaf Du holdes süsses Kind!	*a*	Sleep well, you lovely child!
Draussen weht der Frühlingswind,	*a*	Outside, the spring wind is blowing,
Flüstert leis dir Märchen zu,	*b*	And softly whispers fairy tales to you,
Wiegt dich sanft damit zur Ruh.	*b*	It cradles you to sleep gently.
Lula leila lilalu	*b*	Lula Leila lilalu
Schlummre sanft, mein Liebchen du.	*b*	Sleep well, my sweetheart.

Schlummre ein zu meiner Weis,	*c*	Sleep now, with me singing,
Draussen summt ein Bienchen leis,	*c*	Outside a bee is softly humming,
Honig bringt's dem Kind herein	*d*	It brings honey to the child
Wenn's will still und artig sein.	*d*	If it is quiet and well-behaved.
Lula leila lilalu	*b*	Lula Leila lilalu
Schlummre sanft, mein Liebchen du.	*b*	Sleep well, my Sweetheart.

Schlummre süss die ganze Nacht,	*e*	Sleep well all night long,
Muttertreue für dich wacht,	*e*	The mother is watching you,
Scheucht von deiner Wiege still	*f*	She shoos away the midges
Mückchen, das dich stechen will.	*f*	That want to sting you.
Lula leila lilalu	*b*	Lula Leila lilalu
Schlummre sanft, mein Liebchen du.	*b*	Sleep well, my Sweetheart.

Englein drückt zu jeder Stund	*g*	An angel kisses you
Sanften Kuss auf deinen Mund,	*g*	At every hour,
Ist zum Hüter dir bestellt	*h*	It is guarding you
Von dem Herrn der ganzen Welt.	*h*	At the behest of the Lord.
Lula leila lilalu	*b*	Lula Leila lilalu
Schlummre sanft, mein Liebchen du.	*b*	Sleep well, my Sweetheart.

Also the addressee of the third of Kinkel's lullabies ('Wiegenlied', op. 21, no. 2) is soothed by way of natural phenomena: the wind, the river Rhine, the garden, the moon, and the mountains. It is slow-paced and calm.

Wiegenlied (op. 21, no. 2)
  Johanna Kinkel (published 1851)

Lullaby[74]
  Translation by Sharon Krebs

Die milden Sterne scheinen,	*a*	The mild stars are shining,
Sanft rauscht der Abendwind.	*b*	The evening wind is soughing gently.
Hör' endlich auf zu weinen,	*a*	Stop crying at last,
Du mein geliebtes Kind!	*b*	You my beloved child!
Dein Bettchen ist bereitet,	*c*	Your little bed is prepared,
O ruhe sanft darin;	*d*	Oh sleep softly therein;
Den weichsten Teppich breitet	*c*	The softest blanket over it
Die Mutter drüber hin.	*d*	Your mother is spreading.
Schlaf wohl, gut Nacht, gut Nacht.	*e*	Sleep well, good night, good night.

[74] <https://www.lieder.net/lieder/get_text.html?TextId=77473> (accessed 1 April 2020).

Die sieben Berge schauen	*f*	The seven mountains are gazing
In unser Kämmerlein,	*g*	Into our little chamber,
Bestrahlt vom silberblauen	*f*	Illuminated by the silvery blue
Verklärten Vollmondschein.	*g*	Transfigured glow of the full moon.
Sie stehn an Rheines Borden,	*h*	They stand on the banks of the Rhine;
Wir wandeln hin dereinst,	*i*	We shall go there someday,
Wenn du bist gross geworden	*h*	When you have grown up
Und wenn du nicht mehr weinst.	*i*	And when you no longer cry.
Schlaf wohl, gut Nacht, gut Nacht.	*e*	Sleep well, good night, good night.
Ein Garten ist da drunten,	*k*	A garden is down there,
Voll Blumen rot und weiss.	*l*	Full of red and white flowers.
Es schlingen drum die bunten	*k*	Weaving their circles about it
Nachtfalter ihren Kreis.	*l*	Are the colourful moths of the night.
Die Blumen woll'n wir pflücken,	*m*	We shall pick the flowers
Sobald der Tag erwacht,	*e*	As soon as the day awakes,
Dein Bettchen damit schmücken.	*m*	In order to adorn your bed with them.
Doch nun, schlaf wohl, gut Nacht.	*e*	But now, sleep well, good night.
Schlaf wohl, gut Nacht, gut Nacht.	*e*	Sleep well, good night, good night.

Contrary to the two lullabies discussed previously, this lullaby is set at the river Rhine, which suggests that Kinkel might have composed it for one of her own children. The late opus number (op. 21) supports this idea. Like the other lullabies, this *andante* setting is in strophic form, which enables the singer to foster a calming atmosphere and to memorise the melody easily. In light of Kinkel's own biographical background, her dependency on the marketability of her Lieder, and the topicality of lullabies at the time, it is not surprising that Kinkel published a number of works within this sub-genre.

The fourth song included in this group, 'Nachtgesang' to words by Goethe (Night Song, op. 12, no. 3), is not devoted to a specific person and it is unclear whether the addressee is a child or a beloved. The third and fourth verses suggest a romantic relationship between the lyrical protagonists, as the lyrical I admits eternal feelings ('ewige Gefühle', stanzas two and three) to the addressee. Moreover, s/he feels that the addressee separates him/her from the 'earthly throng' ('irdischem Gewühle', stanzas three and four), which suggests an uplifting, almost spiritual imaginary relationship.

Nachtgesang (op. 12, no. 3)[75]
  Johann Wolfgang von Goethe
  (published 1840)
		Night Song[76]
		  Translation by Richard Wigmore

O! gib, vom weichen Pfühle,	*a*	O lend, from your soft pillow,
Träumend, ein halb Gehör!	*b*	Dreaming, but half an ear!
Bei meinem Saitenspiele	*a*	To the music of my strings
Schlafe! was willst du mehr?	*b*	Sleep! What more can you wish?
Bei meinem Saitenspiele	*a*	To the music of my strings
Segnet der Sterne Heer	*b*	The host of stars
Die ewigen Gefühle;	*a*	Blesses eternal feelings;
Schlafe! was willst du mehr?	*b*	Sleep! What more can you wish?
Die ewigen Gefühle	*a*	These eternal feelings
Heben mich, hoch und hehr,	*b*	Raise me high and glorious
Aus irdischem Gewühle;	*a*	Above the earthly throng;
Schlafe! was willst du mehr?	*b*	Sleep! What more can you wish?
Vom irdischen Gewühle	*a*	From this earthly throng
Trennst du mich nur zu sehr,	*b*	You separate me only too well,
Bannst mich in deine Kühle,[77]	*a*	You spellbind me to this coolness,
Schlafe! was willst du mehr?	*b*	Sleep! What more can you wish?
Bannst mich in diese Kühle,	*a*	You spellbind me to this coolness,
Gibst nur im Traum Gehör.	*b*	Giving ear only in your dream.
Ach! auf dem weichen Pfühle	*a*	Ah, on your soft pillow
Schlafe! was willst du mehr?	*b*	Sleep! What more can you wish?

The compositional realisation as a duet might point to an equal relationship between the lyrical I and the addressee. It evokes a more artistic impression than the three simple lullabies designed to be sung by a worried parent or caretaker. The duet's complex harmonic pattern with many tonal shifts and sudden changes was criticised by the reviewer of the *Allgemeine Musikalische Zeitung*.[78] The piano accompaniment, which includes arpeggios and ornamentation, adds to the challenging compositional fabric. The most striking feature, however, is the formal structure (Table 5.2), which was also acknowledged by Rellstab:

[75] This poem is dated 1802. See *Johann Wolfgang Goethe: Sämtliche Werke*, ix, 74 and 899.

[76] Richard Wigmore, in *Franz Schubert: The Complete Songs*, transl. Richard Wigmore (London: Hyperion, 2005), 32–33.

[77] Goethe's original reads 'diese Kühle' instead of 'deine Kühle'.

[78] [Anon.], review of Johanna Mathieux, *Drei Duetten für weibliche Stimmen: Opus 12* (1840), 904.

By linking the verses melodically, the composer has musically taken up the plaiting of the [poetic] stanzas, which is achieved through a repetition of the last line of each verse in the first line of each following verse – a very happy thought. Every finesse of form increases the value of a musical work, of an artistic work in general; the same applies here.[79]

Table 5.2: Formal design of 'Nachtgesang' (op. 12, no. 3)

Stanza	Prelude	1	2		3			4		5	Coda	
Poetic Strophe		1	2		3			4		5		
Phrase		A	B	B	C	C	D	D	E	E'	B'	B'
Bar	1–4	5–8	9–12	13–16	17–20	21–24	25–28	29–32	33–36	37–40	41–44	45–47
Chord	a	a–E	E–A	D–G	C–E	E–G♯	C♯–F♯–F	F–a	E	a–E	E–A	Ger6– a–E–a
Function	i	i-V	V-I	harmonic uncertainty				VI-i	V	i-V	V-I	Ger6– V-i

As Table 5.2 shows, the duet's formal sketch corresponds with the harmonic pattern. Each stanza's four-bar opening phrase is a rhythmic repetition of the concluding phrase heard in the preceding stanza, arranged on a different degree of the scale. This technique increases the harmonic variety. Kinkel concludes by reinserting the B phrase initially heard in bars 9–12 in order to create overall unity (bars 41–47).

❧ Epilogue: Kinkel's Lieder and nineteenth-century Romanticism

Kinkel's Lieder contain many Romantic features: tone-painting in the piano accompaniment and simplicity in piano accompaniment and voice-leading. The majority of Kinkel's solo Lieder are strophic settings, although she employs small variations and irregularities. Her combination of both conventional and unconventional form, for instance in 'Die Zigeuner' and 'In der Bucht', confirms

---

[79] Ludwig Rellstab, review of Johanna Mathieux, *Drei Duette für weibliche Stimmen mit Begleitung des Pianoforte: Opus 12* (1849), 46. 'Die Verschlingung der Strophen, durch die gleichlautenden Zeilen der alten, an denen die neue Strophe angeknüpft wird, hat die Componistin, ein sehr glücklicher Gedanke, in der Musik wiedergegeben, indem sie ihre Melodie ebenso fortspinnt. Jede Feinheit der Form erhöht den Werth eines Musikstückes, eines Kunstwerkes überhaupt; so auch hier.'

her sense for tradition and her attempt to situate herself as an individual artist within her own time. All of Kinkel's duets are through-composed. Even though the through-composed form challenges Herder's preference for simplicity and naïveté, its musical modulation and variety respond directly to his notion of sensual power, comprehensibility, and complexion, all three of which were popular Romantic features. Additionally, Kinkel's choice of poems by Geibel and Heine conforms to general nineteenth-century fashion. With regard to Heine's special role within the nineteenth-century literary canon, Sonja Gesse-Harm points out that:

> [His] folk-like Romantic subjects, bizarre dream worlds, poetic musicality and folk-like tone, which, according to him, he adopted from the poems of Wilhelm Müller, triggered the musical ambitions of the composers just as much as the irony and disparity of his themes.[80]

Although Heine's themes attracted many nineteenth-century composers, Kinkel was one of the first to have set 'Die Geisterinsel', which might explain Rellstab's criticism of the unexpected thematic turn in the last verse.[81]

It is worth noting that Kinkel's choice of poets by no means limits her Lieder to the Romantic genre. Although Kinkel set poems by Heine and Goethe – the latter of whose relationship to the Romantic movement was complex and partially ambivalent – Kinkel never set such popular Romantics as Joseph von Eichendorff, Ludwig Tieck, or Clemens Brentano, for instance, although she must have been aware of their poetry. Kinkel chose poets who were less established within the musico-literary discourse of the time: Alexander Kaufmann, Wolfgang Müller, and her husband Gottfried Kinkel, to name but a few. Yet Kinkel was cautious about whose lyrics to pick, as she criticised Franz Schubert for his choice of words in her 1843 essay 'Über die modernen Liederkomponisten' (On the Modern Lieder Composers):

<hr>

[80] Sonja Gesse-Harm, 'Heine, Heinrich, Harry', in *Die Musik in Geschichte und Gegenwart*, 2nd edn, xiii, Personenteil, 1167–76 (1169). 'Die volkstümlich-romantischen Sujets, bizarre Traumbilder, die Sprachmusikalität und der Volkston, den Heine nach eigener Angabe wesentlich den Gedichten Wilhelm Müllers abgelauscht hat, motivierten die Vertonungsansätze der Komponisten ebenso wie die Ironie und die Disparität seiner Themen.' See also Sonja Gesse-Harm, *Zwischen Ironie und Sentiment: Heinrich Heine im Kunstlied des 19. Jahrhunderts* (Stuttgart/Weimar: Metzler, 2006).

[81] Johann Vesque von Püttlingen set the poem in 1838 as a solo song (op. 36). Moritz Hauptmann's and Felix Mendelssohn's settings of the Heine poem were published in 1844 and 1846 respectively.

Franz Schubert, who only created a few large-scale compositions, poured the rich resources of his heart into the Lied, which he usually set as an expanded form of a through-composed melody and which gained him the uncontested name of Germany's first musical lyricist. No one can compete with him for inventive passion and depth, wealth of imagination as well as rhythmic and melodic originality and beauty. (It is understood that we are referring only to Lieder composers here.) Unfortunately, Schubert often wasted his lovely melodies on the worst poetry. One can hardly ascribe these blunders to a lack of taste, for he also set a great number of excellent poems, which, compositionally, are treated with more passion and thoughtfulness. But his dedications reveal that, sometimes out of gratitude, sometimes for other reasons, he aimed to introduce to the public his friends' and aristocratic patrons' poetic attempts.[82]

Not only does this quotation offer an insight into Schubert's contemporary reception, but it also reflects Kinkel's aesthetic and economic awareness, and the sincerity with which she must have selected the poetry of her friends.

Her chosen themes represent such typical Romantic features as a longing for pre-industrialised landscapes and the South ('Sehnsucht nach Griechenland' and 'Die Zigeuner'); the praise of night scenes and the healing powers of the moon ('Abendruhe', 'In der Bucht', 'Der Sommerabend', 'Es ist so still geworden: Geistliches Abendlied', and the moon settings); the dualism between the inner self and the outside world ('Nachtlied' and 'Sehnsucht nach Griechenland'); mystifications of nature and the spiritualisation of reality ('Die Geisterinsel' and 'Der Seejungfern Gesang'); nature as an allegory for love and the beloved in combination with the Romantic ideal of pure-hearted emotions ('Das Lied der Nachtigall' and 'Gegenwart'); and the belief in nature as a powerful influence on humanity's well-being (lullabies and 'Nachtgesang'). Despite Kinkel's fondness

---

[82] Kinkel, 'Über die modernen Liederkomponisten', 34. 'Franz Schubert, welcher nur wenig größere Compositionen geschaffen, ergoß seine ganze reiche Seelenfülle in dem Lied, dem er meist die erweiterte Form eines durchkomponierten Gesanges gab, und erwarb sich so den unbestrittenen Namen des ersten musikalischen Lyrikers in Deutschland. An Gluth und Tiefe der Erfindung, Reichtum der Phantasie, Originalität und Schönheit des Rhythmus wie der Melodie kann keiner mit ihm wetteifern. (Es versteht sich daß hier ausschließlich von Liederkomponisten die Rede ist.) Leider hat Schubert seine Weisen allzu oft an die schlechtesten Texte verschwendet. Einer Geschmacklosigkeit von seiner Seite ist dieser Misgriff schwer zuzutrauen, denn er hat ebenfalls eine große Zahl trefflicher Gedichte in Musik gesetzt und diese sind zugleich in der Composition mit mehr Liebe und Aufmerksamkeit behandelt. Aus den Worten seiner Dedikationen geht eher hervor daß er theils aus Dankbarkeit theils aus andern Rücksichten die poetischen Versuche seiner Freunde und vornehmen Gönner in's Publikum zu bringen strebte.'

for Romantic themes her Lieder exhibit a unique style made up of harmonic variety, melodic peculiarity and partially challenging piano accompaniments. That these features were unusual within the gendered discourse of the time can be deduced from the reviews of Ludwig Rellstab and Gottfried Wilhelm Fink, both of whom found Kinkel's chromaticism and dissonances unfavourable. On the other hand, some Lieder confirm that Kinkel's biography, musical taste, and choice of topoi merged with the Romantic mindset.

CHAPTER 6

Compositional aesthetics

N OT unlike Kinkel's thematic scope, her compositional aesthetics range from simple to quite challenging. In a similar way to the works of some of Kinkel's contemporaries who set the same words, Kinkel's style embraces such typical principles as recourses to previous compositional techniques; Romantic colouring including rhythm, tone, and time; harmonic and melodic spontaneity; characteristic beginnings and endings; and the use of Romantic irony.[1]

✎ *Recourses to previous compositional techniques*

Siegmund Freiherr von Seckendorff (1744–1785), whose Goethe setting 'An den Mond' is dated 1778, employs a four-bar phrasal structure, and harmony, melody, and piano accompaniment are straightforward, owing to the compositional ideals of his own time.[2] The setting by Andreas Romberg (1767–1824) is characterised by modesty of expressive means.[3] His composition, dated 1793, differs from von Seckendorff's in so far as it offers some more challenges in the vocal line through suspensions. Like those of von Seckendorff and Romberg, Carl Friedrich Zelter's 1812 setting of 'An den Mond' utilises a four-bar phrasal

---

[1] For further considerations of Romantic compositional features see Wehnert, 'Romantik', 501.

[2] Siegmund Freiherr von Seckendorff, 'Füllest wieder's liebe Thal', in *Gedichte von Goethe in Compositionen seiner Zeitgenossen*, ed. Max Friedlaender (Weimar: Verlag der Goethe-Gesellschaft, 1896), 55. Siegmund Freiherr von Seckendorff was a German composer and writer. From December 1775, he was involved as a director, actor, singer, instrumentalist, and composer at the Weimar Musenhof (Court of Muses). In 1785, he was appointed Prussian minister in the Frankish area; however, he died from tuberculosis during his first travels as a Prussian minister. Undine Wagner, 'Seckendorff, eigentl. Karl, *Carl*, (Friedrich) Siegmund, *Sigismund*, Freiherr von Seckendorff-Aberdar', in *Die Musik in Geschichte und Gegenwart*, 2nd edn, xv, Personenteil, 500–02.

[3] Andreas Romberg, 'An den Mond', in Friedlaender, *Gedichte von Goethe*, 55. Andreas Romberg was a German violinist and composer. He made his debut as a violinist in 1774 and was considered a child prodigy. In 1815, he took over Spohr's position as Hofkapellmeister in Gotha. Klaus G. Werner, 'Romberg, Andreas', in *Die Musik in Geschichte und Gegenwart*, 2nd edn, xiv, Personenteil, 331–35.

206

pattern and a strophic formal plan.[4] The harmonic progression in his Lied is slightly more diverse than in those discussed previously. The second four-bar phrase of each musical stanza includes a descending circle of fifths sequence in combination with two diminished triads. Furthermore, Zelter employs a two-bar piano postlude. Friedrich Heinrich Himmel (1765–1814), too, develops the notion of solo piano passages in his 'An den Mond' (1806), which includes a three-bar piano prelude and a four-bar piano postlude.[5] Himmel's setting is also characterised by a four-bar phrasal pattern, but the harmonic design is slightly more varied, as the second line of each stanza is set to a tonal enclave reached by a mediant progression (E major within the tonal context of C major). Like Himmel, Václav Jan Tomášek (1774–1850), who published his version of Goethe's 'An den Mond' around 1818, emphasised the piano more.[6] The harmonic design is still straightforward throughout the vocal parts though more diverse than the pre-1818 versions, as a number of diminished seventh chords enrich his piano postlude. Tomášek structures his setting in a different way: by grouping three poetic strophes as one musical stanza, each musical stanza is in ternary form (ABA'). As the original version of this poem includes nine strophes, Tomášek's setting repeats the musical stanza (ABA') three times.

By comparison, Kinkel's Lied is in binary form, and she omits the second strophe of the poem. Wilhelmine von Schwertzell (1787–1863), too, combines two poetic strophes in each musical stanza.[7] She omits the seventh strophe.

---

[4] Carl Friedrich Zelter, 'An den Mond', in Friedlaender, *Gedichte von Goethe*, 56.

[5] Friedrich Heinrich Himmel, 'An den Mond', in Friedlaender, *Gedichte von Goethe*, 56. Friedrich Heinrich Himmel was a German composer and pianist. From 1787 onwards, Himmel served Prussia and was appointed chamber composer by the Prussian king in 1792. He toured Europe as a pianist, music director, and composer many times; his last opera *Der Kobold* was first premiered in Vienna on 23 March 1814. Karsten Mackensen, 'Himmel, Friedrich Heinrich', in *Die Musik in Geschichte und Gegenwart*, 2nd edn, ix, Personenteil, 1–4.

[6] Wenzel Johann Tomaschek, *Gedichte von Goethe mit Begleitung des Piano-Forte*, 9 vols (self-published, c.1818), iv. Václav Jan Tomášek was a Bohemian composer, pianist and pedagogue. Markéta Kabelková, 'Tomášek, *Tomaschek*, Václav Jan, *Wenzel Johann* (Křitel)', in *Die Musik in Geschichte und Gegenwart*, 2nd edn, xvi, 900–06.

[7] Wilhelmine von Schwertzell, 'An den Mond', in *Zwölf Lieder von Göthe, Fouque, Hebel, Tiek, und Uhland* (Leipzig: Probst, n.d.), 18. Staatsbibliothek zu Berlin (DMS O.25274). It is unknown when this setting was composed and/or published. Very little is known about Wilhelmine von Schwertzell, who was the daughter of Georg von Schwertzell and his wife Luise. Wilhelmine's brother, who was employed as the chief administrator of the royal hunt in Hesse, was a friend of the Grimm brothers who visited the Schwertzells' house on a regular basis. Hermann Rebel, *When Women Held the Dragon's Tongue and Other Essays on Historical Anthropology* (Oxford/New York: Berghahn, 2013), 106.

Von Schwertzell's version is characterised by a large vocal range ('d¹–'g²') and some chromatic movement in the vocal line; she prioritised the voice over the piano, while, as in the settings above, structural regularity serves as a stabilising element.

Franz Schubert set this poem twice. His first version is simple: a strophic setting, two poetic strophes form one musical stanza based on a four-bar phrasal pattern. In *Schubert's Werke*, it is dated 19 August 1815 and the fifth strophe is printed in brackets.[8] However, Lorraine Byrne explains that Schubert had not initially intended this version to be performed like this, as, instead of omitting strophe 5, Schubert had omitted strophes 5, 6 and 7, an arrangment which corresponds with Goethe's *Urgestalt*.[9] The harmonic progression in this first version is straightforward; the only harmonic peculiarity occurs at the word 'mild', where a diminished seventh chord based on the sharpened tonic (E diminished seventh) creates harmonic variety (bar 14). Schubert's second version features more complex characteristics.[10] Byrne dates this second version 1819/20. She provides a close reading of the harmonic complexity of this Lied, asserting that 'the use of strophic variation allows for an uneven number of verses and captures the changing tones in Goethe's verse'.[11] Additionally, Table 6.1 shows that the strophic variation in Schubert's setting, besides the uneven number of strophes, also allows for an uneven number and irregular division of bars per stanza.

Table 6.1: Formal design of Schubert's second version of 'An den Mond'

Poetic strophe	Lyrics		Formal design			Musical stanza
			Bar	Motive	Number of bars	
			1–5	Piano prelude	5	
1	Füllest wieder Busch und Thal	*a*				
	Still mit Nebelglanz,	*b*	6–11	A	6	1st
	Lösest endlich auch einmal	*a*				stanza
	Meine Seele ganz;	*b*				
			12–13	Piano interlude	2	

[8] Franz Schubert, 'An den Mond', in *Franz Schubert's Werke, Serie XX: Sämtliche Lieder und Gesänge, No.116*, ed. Eusebius Mandyczewski (Leipzig: Breitkopf & Härtel, 1894–95), 40–41.

[9] Lorraine Byrne, *Schubert's Goethe Settings* (Aldershot: Ashgate, 2003), 116.

[10] Franz Schubert, 'An den Mond II', in *Franz Schubert's Werke, Serie XX: Sämtliche Lieder und Gesänge, No.176*, 195–97.

[11] Byrne, *Schubert's Goethe Settings*, 117.

2	Breitest über mein Gefild Lindernd deinen Blick, Wie des Freundes Auge mild Über mein Geschick.	*c* *d* *c* *d*	14–20	B	7	2nd stanza
			21–22	Piano interlude	2	
3	Jeden Nachklang fühlt mein Herz Froh- und trüber Zeit, Wandle zwischen Freud' und Schmerz In der Einsamkeit.	*e* *f* *e* *f*	6–11 (rep.)	A	6	3rd stanza
			12–13 (rep.)	Piano interlude	2	
4	Fließe, fließe, lieber Fluß! Nimmer werd' ich froh; So verrauschte Scherz und Kuß Und die Treue so.	*g* *h* *g* *h*	14–20 (rep.)	B	7	4th stanza
			21–22 (rep.)	Piano interlude	2	
5	Ich besaß es doch einmal, Was so köstlich ist! Daß man doch zu seiner Qual Nimmer es vergißt!	*a* *i* *a* *i*	23–28	A	6	5th stanza
			29–30	Piano interlude	2	
6	Rausche, Fluß, das Tal entlang, Ohne Rast und Ruh, Rausche, flüstre meinem Sang Melodien zu!	*k* *l* *k* *l*	31–38	B/C (first 2 bars of B in minor key)	8	6th stanza
7	Wenn du in der Winternacht Wütend überschwillst Oder um die Frühlingspracht Junger Knospen quillst.	*m* *n* *m* *n*	39–43	D	5	7th stanza
			44	Piano interlude		
8	Selig, wer sich vor der Welt Ohne Haß verschließt, Einen Freund am Busen hält Und mit dem genießt,	*o* *p* *o* *p*	45–50	A	6	8th stanza
9	Was, von Menschen nicht gewußt Oder nicht bedacht, Durch das Labyrinth der Brust Wandelt in der Nacht.	*q* *m* *q* *m*	51–59	E/B (B accompaniment)	7+2 (rep)	9th stanza
			60	Piano coda		

Although, poetically, all lines contain the exact same number of syllables (twelve), Schubert's stanzas differ in length and duration. By breaking away from a regular phrasal pattern, Schubert responds to the concept of changing paces of life as is suggested by the different paces of the stream and the irregular 'labyrinth of the heart'.

As discussed in Chapter 5, Kinkel's Goethe setting 'An den Mond' (op. 7, no. 5) includes unusual tonal excursions (Ex. 5.7). While Kinkel applies diverse and sometimes unexpected harmony, the formal structure is very regular. Four bars equal one phrase, and two phrases form one musical stanza. Two musical phrases set two poetic strophes (Table 6.2). As this Lied is a strophic setting, each musical stanza (sixteen bars long) is repeated four times. While the words, the expressive piano accompaniment, and the tonal meanderings in the second eight-bar phrase point to Romantic aesthetics, the strophic phrasal patterns are reminiscent of eighteenth-century aesthetics.[12] The simple form creates unity and enables a focus on the harmonic progression and the piano accompaniment. Compared to other composers, it appears that Kinkel's approach was not unique. However, her harmony and pianistic expressiveness are more advanced than those of many other settings of the same words.

Finally, Ferdinand Hiller (1811–1885) employs an even more diverse formal structure in his through-composed setting of 'An den Mond' (Table 6.3).[13] No motivic material recurs in its original shape, except for stanzas 8 and 9, which are repeated at the end of this setting. As in Schubert's second version, Hiller's stanzas differ in length. The harmonic and melodic progressions are diverse. Furthermore, the piano seems to respond more directly to the words than for example in Johanna Kinkel's strophic setting, which does not allow for individual treatments of each stanza. This is especially notable in stanzas 4, 5 and 6 of Hiller's setting, all three of which deal with movement as symbols of the

---

[12] For further details on the division of musical works into periods and phrases, see Heinrich Christoph Koch, *Versuch einer Anleitung zur Composition: Studienausgabe*, ed. Jo Wilhelm Siebert (Hanover: Siebert, 2007), 424.

[13] Ferdinand Hiller, 'An den Mond', in *Sechs Lieder für eine Singstimme mit Begleitung des Pianoforte: Op. 204* (Leipzig: Kahnt, n.d.), 2–11. Staatsbibliothek zu Berlin (28598). This opus is announced by Hofmeister in February 1885 <http://anno.onb. ac.at/cgi-content/anno-buch?apm=0&aid=1000001&bd=0001885&teil=0203&seit e=00000048&zoom=1> (accessed 4 March 2019). Ferdinand Hiller was a German composer, music pedagogue, writer, pianist, conductor, and music organiser; he was born in Cologne and is considered one of the most representative nineteenth-century musical characters. Klaus Wolfgang Niemöller, 'Hiller, Ferdinand (von)', in *Die Musik in Geschichte und Gegenwart*, 2nd edn, viii, Personenteil, 1581–87; for details on Kinkel's and Hiller's acquaintanceship see Rittershaus, 'Felix Mendelssohn und Johanna Kinkel: Ungedruckte Tagebuchblätter und Briefe'; *Felix Mendelssohn Bartholdy: Sämtliche Briefe*, iv, 48–51, and Reinhold Sietz, *Aus Ferdinand Hillers Briefwechsel (1826–1861)* (Cologne: Arno Volk, 1958), 73.

Table 6.2: Formal design of Kinkel's Lied 'An den Mond'

Poetic strophe	Lyrics		Formal design			Musical stanza
			Bar	Motive	Phrase	
1	Füllest wieder Busch und Thal	*a*	1–4	a		
	Still mit Nebelglanz,	*b*	5–8	a'	A	
	Lösest endlich auch einmal	*a*				
	Meine Seele ganz;	*b*				
2	Breitest über mein Gefild	*c*	(not set by Kinkel)			1st stanza
	Lindernd deinen Blick,	*d*				
	Wie des Freundes Auge mild	*c*				
	Über mein Geschick.	*d*				
3	Jeden Nachklang fühlt mein Herz	*e*	9–12	b		
	Froh- und trüber Zeit,	*f*	13–16	c	B	
	Wandle zwischen Freud' und Schmerz	*e* *f*				
	In der Einsamkeit.					
4	Fließe, fließe, lieber Fluß!	*g*				2nd stanza
	Nimmer werd' ich froh;	*h*				
	So verrauschte Scherz und Kuß	*g*	same as 1st stanza			
	Und die Treue so.	*h*				
5	Ich besaß es doch einmal,	*a*				
	Was so köstlich ist!	*i*				
	Daß man doch zu seiner Qual	*a*				
	Nimmer es vergißt!	*i*				
6	Rausche, Fluß, das Tal entlang,	*k*				3rd stanza
	Ohne Rast und Ruh,	*l*				
	Rausche, flüstre meinem Sang	*k*	same as 1st stanza			
	Melodien zu!	*l*				
7	Wenn du in der Winternacht	*m*				
	Wütend überschwillst	*n*				
	Oder um die Frühlingspracht	*m*				
	Junger Knospen quillst.	*n*				
8	Selig, wer sich vor der Welt	*o*				4th stanza
	Ohne Haß verschließt,	*p*				
	Einen Freund am Busen hält	*o*	same as 1st stanza			
	Und mit dem genießt,	*p*				
9	Was, von Menschen nicht gewußt	*q*				
	Oder nicht bedacht,	*m*				
	Durch das Labyrinth der Brust	*q*				
	Wandelt in der Nacht.	*m*				

Table 6.3: Formal design of Hiller's 'An den Mond'

Poetic strophe	Lyrics		Formal design			Musical stanza
			Bar	Motive	Number of bars	
			1–3	Piano prelude	3	
1	Füllest wieder Busch und Thal	*a*				
	Still mit Nebelglanz,	*b*	4–16	A	13	1st stanza
	Lösest endlich auch einmal	*a*		(a[6]+b[7])		
	Meine Seele ganz;	*b*				
			17	Piano interlude	1	
2	Breitest über mein Gefild	*c*				
	Lindernd deinen Blick,	*d*	18–32	B	15	2nd stanza
	Wie des Freundes Auge mild	*c*		(c[6]+a[6]+b'[3])		
	Über mein Geschick.	*d*				
			33–35	Piano interlude	3	
3	Jeden Nachklang fühlt mein Herz	*e*	36–41			3rd stanza
	Froh- und trüber Zeit,	*f*		C	6	
	Wandle zwischen Freud' und Schmerz	*e*				
	In der Einsamkeit.	*f*				
			42–47	Piano interlude	6	change of key and metre
4	Fließe, fließe, lieber Fluß!	*g*	48–57			
	Nimmer werd' ich froh;	*h*		D	10	4th stanza
	So verrauschte Scherz und Kuß	*g*				
	Und die Treue so.	*h*				
5	Ich besaß es doch einmal,	*a*	58–65			
	Was so köstlich ist!	*i*		E	8	5th stanza
	Daß man doch zu seiner Qual	*a*				
	Nimmer es vergißt!	*i*				
6	Rausche, Fluß, das Tal entlang,	*k*				
	Ohne Rast und Ruh,	*l*	66–72	F	7	6th stanza
	Rausche, flüstre meinem Sang	*k*				
	Melodien zu!	*l*				
7	Wenn du in der Winternacht	*m*				
	Wütend überschwillst	*n*	73–81	G	9	7th stanza
	Oder um die Frühlingspracht	*m*				
	Junger Knospen quillst.	*n*				
			82–89	Piano interlude	8	change of key and expressive character

8	Selig, wer sich vor der Welt	*o*				
	Ohne Haß verschließt,	*p*	90–97	H	8	8th stanza
	Einen Freund am Busen hält	*o*				
	Und mit dem genießt,	*p*				
9	Was, von Menschen nicht gewußt	*q*				
	Oder nicht bedacht,	*m*	98–104	I	7	9th stanza
	Durch das Labyrinth der Brust	*q*				
	Wandelt in der Nacht.	*m*				
			105	Piano interlude	1	
			106–113	H (repetition of strophe 8)	8	8 (rep.)
			114–120	I' (repetition of strophe 9; a tone below original I)	7	9 (rep.)
			121–126	I" (repetition of second part of strophe 9)	6	9 (rep.)

passing of love. Here, the semi-quaver figuration in the piano part symbolises the flow of the stream.

A similar pianistic feature is evident in the corresponding stanzas of Franz Schubert's second version of these words; although Schubert's passage is shorter and thus its impression is more temporary.

As can be seen, the late eighteenth-century and early nineteenth-century composers discussed here were quite modest as regards harmonic, melodic, and pianistic challenges. Schubert's first version and Kinkel's setting, even though both of them adhere to the traditional eighteenth-century phrasal regularity, employ a greater harmonic range. The recourse to a structural pattern originating from the previous epoch serves as a unifying parameter in these settings. Schubert's second version and Hiller's setting point to a further developed aesthetic ideal. Considering Kinkel's financial dependency on the marketability of her compositions (especially during her time in Berlin, during which she published this Lied) it is imaginable that Kinkel purposely avoided overly challenging compositional features so as to ensure performability within amateur circles. After all, Kinkel aimed to place herself among 'those contemporary popular Lieder composers who have serious artistic ambitions and who mainly try to follow in Mendelssohn's and Schubert's footsteps', although this endeavour did not always surface in her compositions.[14]

---

[14] Kinkel, 'Über die modernen Liederkomponisten', 37. 'Unter den in neuester Zeit beliebt gewordenen Liederkomponisten von ernsterem künstlerischen Bestreben,

❧ *Rhythm, tone and time*

Kinkel's 'Die Zigeuner' (op. 7, no.6) and 'Der spanische Zitherknabe' (op. 8, no. 1) were received positively by critics, who praised Kinkel's use of *couleur locale* and tempo changes. In both Lieder, the spirited tone is created by means of rhythmic characteristics, which respond directly to the textual content and the overall theme. Linda Siegel states that 'Kinkel's two Spanish songs appear to be the first to introduce Spanish culture and pseudo-Spanish music to the realm of the German *lied*', although other composers too felt attracted by Spanish themes.[15] Carl Gottlieb Reissiger (1798–1859) set Geibel's 'Der Zigeunerbube im Norden' (The Gypsy Boy in the North) for guitar and voice.[16] This setting is characterised by a recognisable 'fandango motif' in the accompaniment, which predominates in the entire strophic Lied (Ex. 6.1).

Ex. 6.1: Fandango in Reissiger's 'Der Zigeunerbube im Norden' (bars 1–3)

The composition is striking on account of its folk-like character enhanced by its simple harmony and melody (the vocal line ranges from 'f♯¹' to 'f²'). The rhythm creates a distinct tone associated with Spanish music and temperament.

Like most of Kinkel's Lieder, her 'Der spanische Zitherknabe' (The Spanish Zither Player) is a strophic setting. Each musical stanza consists of four parts

---

welche meist vorzugsweise in Mendelssohns und Schuberts Fußstapfen einzutreten bemüht sind, wären noch Bank, Dessauer, Hiller, L. Huth, Lachner, J. Mathieux, Speier, Taubert, Truhe zu erwähnen.'

[15] Siegel, *Johanna Kinkel*, i, 3.

[16] Carl Gottlieb Reissiger, 'Der Zigeunerbube im Norden', in *Auswahl beliebter Lieder und Gesänge* (Dresden: Paul, [1838]), Staatsbibliothek zu Berlin (76495). This opus is announced by Hofmeister in March 1838 <http://anno.onb.ac.at/cgi-content/ anno-buch?apm=0&aid=1000001&bd=0001838&teil=0203&seite=00000046&z oom=1> (accessed 4 March 2019). Carl Gottlieb Reissiger was a German composer and conductor. Christoph Dohr, 'Reissiger, Carl, Karl, Gottlieb', in *Die Musik in Geschichte und Gegenwart*, 2nd edn, xiii, Personenteil, 1539–42.

which are separated by piano interludes. The piano accompaniment includes motivic material which recurs throughout the Lied (Ex. 6.2). These rhythmic figures create unity within the Lied, because they also sound in the solo piano passages embracing the vocal parts (Ex. 6.3). Kinkel, occasionally, contrasts the fandango motif with a one-bar melodic gesture in the right-hand piano part (Ex. 6.4).

Ex. 6.2: Rhythmic figures in Kinkel's 'Der spanische Zitherknabe'[17]

Ex. 6.3: Piano prelude of Kinkel's 'Der spanische Zitherknabe' (bars 1–4)

Ex. 6.4: Rhythmic contrast in Kinkel's 'Der spanische Zitherknabe' (bar 16)

[17] The 'e♭' in the piano left hand in bar 19 was notated as 'e♮' in the original publication. Considering the 'e♭' in the piano right hand and the harmonic progression in the same bar this is likely to be an editorial mistake. Therefore, the 'e♭' has been added to the piano left hand in this example.

Elise Schmezer employs a similar aesthetic concept. Although her Lied is notated as a through-composed setting, each stanza features the same (or slightly varied) melodic motif in the vocal line.[18] However, frequent key, tempo and dynamic changes create tension throughout this Lied, which is unified by a recurring fandango motif in the piano. The only rhythmic change occurs in the piano postlude, where the characteristic rhythmic figure is abandoned and replaced by a descent comprising leaps, which evokes the impression of the Lied fading away slowly (Ex. 6.5, bar 94). This impression is supported by the reduction of double octaves to a single-part melody in the right-hand piano part (bar 95). The reviewer of Schmezer's 'Zigeunerlied' in the *Neue Zeitschrift für Musik* is full of criticism for this setting. S/he criticises the accompaniment, which 'torments us with its monotony and its vexed decoration', and s/he believes to discover in this Lied the 'inadequate education which turns a simple and innocent folk song into a monster full of morbid modern salon sensibility'.[19] Although Kinkel applied the same fandango motif as Schmezer, Kinkel's setting was received more positively than Schmezer's, which might be attributed to the dates: Kinkel's Lied was reviewed in 1838, while Schmezer's review dates from 1851. The reviewer of Schmezer's setting might have approached this Lied with much more listening experience in relation to compositional aesthetics surrounding Southern themes than would have been the case with the critique of Kinkel's composition, and the theme itself was less of a novelty in 1851.

[18] Elise Schmezer, 'Zigeunerbube', in *Romanzen und Balladen für Tenor: Op. 5* (Magdeburg: Heinrichshofen, [1850]). This opus was announced by Hofmeister in July 1850 <http://anno.onb.ac.at/cgi-content/anno-buch?apm=0&aid=100000 1&bd=0001850&teil=0203&seite=00000105&zoom=1> (accessed 4 March 2019). Very little is known about Elise Schmezer, née Kratky. She was born around 1810; her birthplace is unknown. Her father was the music pedagogue Josef Kratky, who taught trumpet, trombone, and horn in Graz (1819–1830). Elise Schmezer most likely received lessons in piano and singing; she performed as a singer in Graz during the first half of the nineteenth century. She married Friedrich Schmezer in the 1830s; in 1836, Friedrich Schmezer was appointed in Braunschweig as a singer and director. In Braunschweig, Elise Schmezer established herself as a composer; she is now considered one of the most influential Braunschweig (female) composers of the nineteenth century. Between 1848 and 1856, Schmezer had a great deal of Lieder issued by such renowned publishers as Mayer (Braunschweig), Heinrichshofen (Magdeburg), Schlesinger (Berlin), Damköhler (Berlin), Bachmann (Hanover), and Luckhardt (Kassel). Silke Wenzel, 'Elise Schmezer', in *MUGI: Musikvermittlung und Genderforschung: Lexikon und multimediale Präsentationen*, ed. Beatrix Borchard (Hochschule für Musik und Theater Hamburg, 2003–) <https://mugi.hfmt-hamburg.de/Artikel/Elise_Schmezer.pdf> (accessed 3 April 2020).

[19] [Anon.], review of Elise Schmezer, *Lieder, Romanzen und Balladen* (1850), *Neue Zeitschrift für Musik*, 3 January 1851, 4. '[die] uns [...] peinigt mit ihrer Monotonie und leiden Verbrämtheit'; 'die mangelhafte Bildung, die aus einem schlichten und treuherzigen Volksliedchen ein Ungethüm voller krankhafter, moderner Salonempfindung macht'.

Ex. 6.5: Fandango motif and motivic changes in the piano part of
Schmezer's 'Zigeunerlied' (bars 87–97)

Carl Krebs (1804–1880) also employs the fandango rhythm in his strophic
setting in order to achieve rhythmic coherence.[20] This coherence is contrasted
in the piano postlude, which sounds after each of the individual musical stanzas
except for the last one (Ex. 6.6). This feature creates tension and emphasises the

Ex. 6.6: Postlude of Krebs's 'Der Zigeunerknabe im Norden' (bars 21–29)

[20] Carl Krebs, *Der Zigeunerknabe im Norden: deutsches Lied für eine Singstimme mit
Begleitung des Pianoforte: Op. 50* (Hamburg/Leipzig: Schuberth, n.d.). Carl Krebs
was a German composer and conductor. SL [Richard Schaal], 'Krebs, Karl August',
in *Die Musik in Geschichte und Gegenwart,* 2nd edn, x, Personenteil, 649–50.

rhythmic distinctiveness by way of contrast. It occurs in the right hand piano and is juxtaposed with the fandango motif in the left hand.

Carl Ludvig Lithander (1773–1843) uses a similar rhythmic figure as Kinkel. However, Lithander uses this motif only in the fifth stanza of his setting, which refers directly to the couple dancing the fandango.[21] The quick change of metre and rhythm in this stanza constitutes a major contrast to the rest of Lithander's Lied. Lithander's song incorporates numerous changes of key and tempo. In a similar way, the setting of the same words by Friedrich Hieronymus Truhn (1811–1886) is characterised by diverse compositional aesthetics

Ex. 6.7: Fandango in Truhn's 'Der Zigeunerbube im Norden' (bars 60–71)

---

[21] Carl Ludvig Lithander, *Der Zigeunerknabe im Norden* (Leipzig: Breitkopf & Härtel, n.d.). Staatsbibliothek zu Berlin (O.25191). Carl Ludvig Lithander was born in Estonia to a Finnish pastor who served a Swedish-speaking community. Carl Ludvig Lithander moved to Sweden when his parents and one of his ten siblings died. He combined his musical career as a pianist, composer, and violinist with the military; he was a teacher for maths (at a military school from 1795 onwards) and geometry (at an arts academy from 1807 to 1824). Ruth-Esther Hillila and Barbara Blanchard Hong, *Historical Dictionary of the Music and Musicians of Finland* (Westport: Greenwood, 1997), 231.

(Ex. 6.7).[22] It is a varied strophic setting – the Lied begins in 3/4 metre and switches to 6/8 metre at the fourth and fifth stanzas. At the end of the fifth stanza, when the metre changes back to 3/4, Truhn includes the fandango motif, which is used sparingly in this song.

Rhythm, more specifically the 'fandango motif', was an important means to evoke associations with Spain – or, more generally, the South. In terms of complexity, however, the Lieder discussed here differ from each other. While Reissiger's setting for guitar and voice is undoubtedly the simplest, those by Krebs, Schmezer and Kinkel are more diverse. All three of them employ the same rhythmic features throughout the Lied and use a contrasting figure in selected passages in order to raise awareness to the importance of rhythm. Lithander and Truhn apply more complex concepts, which are characterised by changes of metre, tempo, key, and dynamics.

However, Kinkel's second setting dealing with the South, 'Die Zigeuner' (The Gypsies), exposes similar complex characteristics. While the first strophe is set in eight fast-moving bars, the second strophe equals sixteen slow-moving bars, which are divided into two eight-bar phrases (see Ex. 5.2). The rhythmic variation, which is achieved through melodic prolongation, creates atmospheric tension between the first and second sections. By changing the piano accompaniment and the rhythm in the vocal line, Kinkel creates a sense of inner peace and ease which acts as a foil to the preceding bars. The two excerpts in Ex. 6.8 demonstrate the contrasting expressive characters of these sections.

Unlike Kinkel, Charlotte von Bülow (1817–1908), in her setting of the same words, applies the same rhythm in the vocal line throughout the Lied (Ex. 6.9).[23] However, von Bülow employs a change of piano accompaniment in the

---

[22] Friedrich Hieronymus Truhn, 'Der Zigeunerbube im Norden', in *Lieder aus Spanien: Op. 38, Nr. 1* (Berlin: Schlesinger, [1840]), 3–7. This opus is announced by Hofmeister in December 1840 <http://anno.onb.ac.at/cgi-content/anno-buch?apm =0&aid=1000001&bd=0001840&teil=0203&seite=00000174&zoom=1> (accessed 4 March 2019). Friedrich Hieronymus Truhn was a German composer, conductor and writer. Emanuel Scobel, 'Truhn, Friedrich Hieronymus', in *Die Musik in Geschichte und Gegenwart*, 2nd edn, xvi, Personenteil, 1086–87.

[23] Charlotte von Bülow, 'Zigeunerleben', in *Lieder und Gesänge für eine Singstimme mit Begleitung des Pianoforte* (Berlin: Bahn, n.d.), 3–5. Although the publication date of this opus is unknown, it is certain that it was published after Kinkel's, as the title page reads 'M. Bahn Verlag (früher Trautwein)' (M. Bahn Publishers [formerly Trautwein]). When Kinkel published her op. 7, which includes 'Die Zigeuner', the publishing company was still called Trautwein. Charlotte von Bülow was born in Erfurt and lived in Berlin from 1832 (at the latest), where she died in 1908. She was

Ex. 6.8: Contrasting motives in Kinkel's 'Die Zigeuner' (bars 1 and 9)

middle section of the second part of this strophic setting, which evokes a calm atmosphere (bars 19–22).

Thus, both Kinkel's and von Bülow's settings create a distinct atmosphere using rhythmic features as an expressive vehicle. Kinkel's rhythmic change confuses the listener's sense of symmetrical structure, while von Bülow plays with the expressive potential of rhythm as a stylistic means.

musically educated by Karl Friedrich Rungenhagen and she was a member of the Berlin Singakademie from 1832 to 1847. She was also a founding member of the Berlin Sternsche Gesangverein, founded in 1847. From the mid-1850s onwards, von Bülow published Lieder with several publishers (Schott, Heinrichshofen, Breitkopf & Härtel, and Trautwein/Bahn). Silke Wenzel, 'Charlotte von Bülow', in *MUGI: Musikvermittlung und Genderforschung: Lexikon und multimediale Präsentationen*, ed. Beatrix Borchard (Hochschule für Musik und Theater Hamburg, 2003–) <https://mugi.hfmt-hamburg.de/artikel/Charlotte_von_Bülow.pdf> (accessed 3 April 2020).

Ex. 6.9: Second part of von Bülow's 'Zigeunerleben' (bars 16–29)

❧ *Harmonic and melodic spontaneity*

Another effective way of portraying changes of atmosphere is the inclusion of spontaneous breakouts and interjections, sudden interruptions, and/or fragments, and the abrupt abandonment of ideas. Such means can occur in many different ways, for instance on melodic, harmonic, and pianistic levels. Kinkel's Lied 'An Luna' is a strophic setting and employs the traditional four-bar phrasal pattern. In Chapter 5, I discussed the quite progressive concept of tonality in this Lied; and I explained that the contrasting harmonic patterns are held together by the piano accompaniment, which does not change throughout the entire Lied. Melodically, this Lied is striking on account of its chromatic technique and its vocal ornamentation in bars 14–16. These three bars interrupt the evenly flowing vocal line via a *rallentando* and through the melodic figure, a six-note cambiata and turn, which provokes an unexpected shift of style (see Ex 5.6 in the previous chapter). This passage also prepares the change of tonality in the following bars.

Compared to Kinkel's Lied, Bettina von Arnim's setting features a rather simple piano accompaniment, but it also stands out for its undefined structure, which Briony Williams explains by referring to von Arnim's perception of the poem as a cyclic work. In her analysis of this Lied, Williams states that:

> The almost constant use of the dominant seventh chord removes any feeling of climax and repose. [...] Despite the harmonic stasis, however, 'An Luna' is tonally ambiguous. Because there is no introduction and no postlude, the ambiguity of the final chord of each verse blurs the strophic boundaries until the very end, when the questioning half-close becomes at last apparent. This makes the music almost glide, and the rests in both voice and piano seem a particularly poignant cessation of movement. [...] It is as if all the accepted defining components have been removed – harmonic direction, formal symmetry – so that we are left with what is, in a sense, a return to the original lyric.[24]

However, von Arnim makes an exception to her structural neutrality when she changes the metre and marks the tempo 'schneller' (faster) at the beginning of the second verse of each stanza (bar 17). Like Kinkel, she seemingly wanted to stress the lyrical I's change of mood at the corresponding passage (Ex. 6.10).

Bettina von Arnim applies this surprising change of style by means of rhythmic, metric, and pianistic variety. The melodic progression seems straightforward, although some fermatas interrupt the regular sense of time. Both Kinkel and von Arnim treat 'An Luna' in unconventional (though very different) ways.

---

[24] Williams, 'Maker, Mother, Muse', 197.

Ex. 6.10: Bettina von Arnim's 'An Luna'

While Kinkel applies a complex harmonic progression, an unexpected melodic figure and a slow-down of pace, von Arnim uses sudden changes in time and pace. Considering Kinkel's financial dependency on her Lieder on the one hand and her outstanding skills as a pianist as well as her well-grounded music-theoretical knowledge on the other, it is not surprising that Kinkel took a subtler direction than von Arnim. Indeed, perhaps von Arnim's unconventional style mirrors her misguided ignorance of music theory rather than her decision to try out something new. In her memoirs, Kinkel, who was also Bettina von Arnim's music teacher in 1836, remembers that:

> In her [Bettina's] opinion, music theory spoilt the arts, and she had the strange belief that 'Beethoven never cared about figured bass'. In order to prove that theoretical background knowledge is dispensable, she showed me her own compositional attempts. She was convinced that the beautiful melodies and ingenious peculiarities of these musical fragments outdid all structured compositions, which drag behind them the chinking chain of figured bass. I looked at these pieces, and I thought that they really revealed a great musical talent, but they were wild and incoherent. A piece could begin with an A minor chord and conclude in E flat major. In another piece *one* bar contained five crotchets and another bar contained three quavers. She had confused the key signatures and played completely different notes than she had written down.[25]

While Kinkel makes fun of Bettina von Arnim's understanding of harmony, her own concept of tonality was occasionally quite diverse, too.

In her setting 'Abendfeier', Kinkel employs a distant progression leading from F major to F-sharp minor, reached via F minor and C-sharp major. The new tonal context is retained for two bars (bar 18). This tonal interjection to F-sharp minor is surprising and seems to question metaphorically the 'ird'schen Thun' (earthly endeavours, first stanza) which is set in the corresponding bars (Ex. 4.7).

---

[25] Kinkel (jun.), 'Aus Johanna Kinkels Memoiren', 245. Italics in original. 'In ihren Augen war Theorie der Musik das Verderben jedes Künstlers, und sie lebte in dem seltsamen Irrthum, der "Beethoven habe nicht nach Generalbaß gefragt". Zum Beweise für ihre Behauptung von der Entbehrlichkeit theoretischer Vorstudien holte sie ein Packet lose Notenblätter herbei, auf denen ihre eigenen Kompositionsversuche geschrieben standen. Sie war davon überzeugt, daß diese Bruchstücke musikalischer Einfälle an Schönheit der Melodie und genialer Eigenthümlichkeit jede geordnete Komposition, welche die Kette des Generalbasses nachschleppte, weit überböten. Ich betrachtete diese Stücke und fand, daß sie wirklich ein großes Talent zur Musik verriethen; aber sie waren wild und zusammenhangslos. Hier fing ein Stück mit einem A-moll-Akkord an und endete in Es-Dur. Dort hatte *ein* Takt fünf Viertel und ein anderer drei Achtel. Sie hatte die Vorzeichnungen verwechselt und spielte ganz andere Noten, als sie geschrieben hatte.'

Like Kinkel, Carl Amand Mangold (1813–1889) applied a harmonic excursion at the line 'Ave Marie! Lasst vom ird'schen Thun'.[26] Within the context of C major, Mangold sets this line in E minor, which is reached via a mediant progression (Ex. 6.11).

Ex. 6.11: Mediant progression in Mangold's 'Abendfeier in Venedig' (bars 8–15)

[26] Carl Amand Mangold, 'Abendfeier in Venedig', in *Drei Lieder gedichtet von Emanuel Geibel, für eine Singstimme mit Begleitung des Pianoforte: Op. 43* (Mainz: Schott, [1855]). This opus was announced by Hofmeister in June 1855 <http://anno.onb.ac.at/cgi-content/anno-buch?apm=0&aid=1000001&bd=0001855&teil=0203&seite=00000782&zoom=1> (accessed 4 March 2019). Carl Amand Mangold was a German composer and conductor. Ursula Kramer, 'Mangold, Carl [Ludwig] Amand', in *Die Musik in Geschichte und Gegenwart*, 2nd edn, xi, Personenteil, 973–75.

While Kinkel chose a distant relationship for her progression (F minor–C-sharp major), Mangold's choice of the upper mediant creates less friction. Furthermore, Mangold prepares the modulation to E major in the preceding bars. By contrast, Kinkel's introduction of the new key is more sudden.

Unlike Mangold, Heinrich Marschner employs numerous harmonic interjections in his setting of the same words, which makes the harmonic design of his Lied much more diverse.[27] He also stresses the line 'Ave Maria! lass vom ird'schen Thun', which he harmonises with a half-diminished seventh chord, surrounded by harmonically unstable seventh chords (bars 14 and 15, Ex. 6.12). The parallel fifths in the piano right and left hands in bar 17 lead to the belief that Marschner prioritised diverse harmony over voice-leading, as such block parallels were considered inelegant.

Ex. 6.12: Seventh chords in Marschner's 'Abendfeier in Venedig' (bars 12–17)

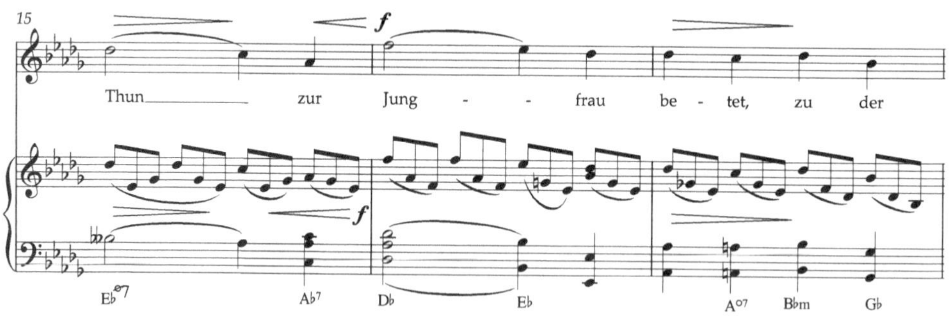

[27] Heinrich Marschner, 'Abendfeier in Venedig', in *Drei Gesänge für eine Singstimme mit Begleitung des Pianoforte: Op. 179* (Hamburg: Cranz, [1857]), 2–7. Hofmeister announced this opus in June 1857 as a novelty by the Vienna publisher Spina. It is not certain whether the Vienna edition was published first, or whether the Hamburg edition by Cranz predates the Vienna edition <http://anno.onb.ac.at/cgi-content/anno-buch?apm=0&aid=1000001&bd=0001857&teil=0203&seite=000000 94&zoom=1> (accessed 4 March 2019).

Furthermore, Marschner applies an Italian augmented sixth chord at the line 'welche jedes Herz | Mit leisen Schauen wunderbar durchdringt' ([Oh holy devotion], which marvellously penetrates | Every heart with a quiet shiver, bars 38 and 39, Ex. 6.13). These augmented sixth chords are embedded within a modulating passage. While Mangold does not stress this line at all, Kinkel applies two diminished seventh chords (C-sharp diminished seventh, bar 12; and B diminished seventh, bar 13) at the corresponding line(s) (Ex. 6.14).

Ex. 6.13: Italian sixth chord in Marschner's 'Abendfeier in Venedig' (bars 34–41)

Ex. 6.14: Diminished seventh chords in Kinkel's 'Abendfeier' (bars 11–13)

Compared to those by Marschner, Mangold and Kinkel, Joachim Raff's (1822–1882) through-composed setting exhibits a more dense harmonic design, which might be attributed to its later date.[28] Because the harmonic design in Raff's setting is diverse throughout this Lied, he uses a different feature in order to put emphasis on the line 'Ave Maria! Lasst ab vom irdischen Thun': following a fermata, the piano accompaniment changes completely. The characteristic rhythmic figure above a pedal point established in the prelude and the first section is replaced by a chorale-like four-part passage moving in crotchets in church style (from bar 20, Ex. 6.15).

Ex. 6.15: Changing atmosphere in Raff's 'Abendfeier in Venedig' (bars 18–27)[29]

---

[28] Joachim Raff, 'Abendfeier in Venedig', in *Fünf Lieder für eine Singstimme mit Begleitung des Pianoforte: Opus 51* (Leipzig: Kistner, [1853]), 14–17. Staatsbibliothek zu Berlin (28289). Hofmeister announced this opus in February 1853 <http://anno. onb.ac.at/cgi-content/anno-buch?apm=0&aid=1000001&bd=0001853&teil=0203& seite=00000274&zoom=1> (accessed 4 March 2019). Joachim Raff was a German composer and pedagogue. Rainer Bayreuther, 'Raff, Joachim', in *Die Musik in Geschichte und Gegenwart*, 2nd edn, xiii, Personenteil, 1191–99.

[29] The triplet numbers '3' in bars 18 and 19 were not originally printed in the publication. However, in order to enable a better orientation for the pianist, these numbers have been added in this example.

All four composers emphasise the same line of the poem (Ave Maria! Lasst ab vom ird'schen Thun!). However, the ways in which these emphases are achieved are diverse. Kinkel's setting incorporates interjections of sudden harmonic turns, while Mangold's setting features a similar tonal escape; however, the harmonic relationships are less distant in Mangold's. Marschner and Raff both use a more complex harmonic framework, partly owing to their later dates of composition and thus the progression of compositional-aesthetic ideals.

Kinkel uses stylistic diversity in the piano accompaniment in different Lieder, one of which is 'Der Runenstein'. Similarly to 'Abendfeier in Venedig', 'Der Runenstein' incorporates one significant line stressed by many different composers. It is the line 'Wo sind sie hin?' (Where have they gone?), which refers to the lyrical I's regrets that his/her beloved and acquaintances are gone. Typically for Heine's poetry, this line constitutes an ironic turn. Kinkel employs a tremolo in the piano accompaniment besides an abrupt insertion of the note d' natural in the vocal line, which counteracts an E-sharp dimished seventh chord within the temporarily established context of C-sharp major (bar 18, Ex. 4.1). By contrast, Ferdinand Gumbert (1818–1896) employs tremolos in the piano accompaniment throughout the first and third parts of his setting, so he uses broken triads followed by repeated quavers in order to set apart the middle section (bars 11–14, Ex. 6.16).[30]

Julius Becker (1811–1859) emphasises the line 'Wo sind sie hin?' by means of a minim and fermata in the piano left-hand part.[31] However, Becker's pianistic change does not occur quite as surprisingly, as it is prepared gradually in the two preceding bars by way of rhythmic augmentation in the accompaniment (bar 25, Ex. 6.17).

[30] Ferdinand Gumbert, *Es ragt in's Meer der Runenstein: Op. 3* (Berlin: Schlesinger, [1843]), 4–5. This opus was announced by Hofmeister in December 1843 <http:// anno.onb.ac.at/cgi-content/anno-buch?apm=0&aid=1000001&bd=0001843&teil =0203&seite=00000190&zoom=1> (accessed 4 March 2019). Ferdinand Gumbert was a German Lieder composer, singer, music pedagogue, and writer. Linda Maria Klodau, 'Gumbert, Ferdinand', in *Die Musik in Geschichte und Gegenwart,* 2nd edn, viii, Personenteil, 272–73.

[31] Julius Becker, 'Es ragt in's Meer der Runenstein', in *Fünf Lieder für eine Stimme mit Begleitung des Pianoforte: Op. 4* (Leipzig: Hofmeister, [1837]),. 2–3. This opus was announced by Hofmeister in September/October 1837 <http://anno.onb.ac.at/cgi- content/anno-buch?apm=0&aid=1000001&bd=0001837&teil=0203&seite=0000012 5&zoom=1> (accessed 4 March 2019). Julius Becker was a German music critic and composer. Konstanze Freudenberg, [Peter Schmiedel], 'Becker, (Constantin) Julius', in *Die Musik in Geschichte und Gegenwart,* 2nd edn, ii, Personenteil, 625–26.

Ex. 6.16: Emphasis in Gumbert's 'Es ragt in's Meer der Runenstein' (bars 10–19)[32]

Robert Franz (1815–1892) chose a slow-paced piano accompaniment for this poem, which climaxes at the line 'Wo sind die hin?'.[33] He superscribes this bar 'poco rit.[ardando]'; furthermore, he employs a momentary swelling of sound in bar 14 (Ex. 6.18).

[32] Considering that the last note in the vocal line of bar 13 is 'g♭', the octave on 'g♮' in the left hand of the piano in the same bar might be intended to be a 'g♭'. However, I have kept the original notes, as I am uncertain whether the chromatic technique is intended there or whether this is an editorial error.

[33] Robert Franz, 'Es ragt ins Meer der Runenstein', in *Sechs Lieder von Heinrich Heine für eine Singstimme mit Begleitung des Pianoforte: Op. 39* (Leipzig: Breitkopf & Härtel, [1867]), 6. This date is given by Staatsbibliothek zu Berlin. Hofmeister announced it for the first time in June 1872; however, in this announcement, op. 39 is part of a larger collection of Franz's Lieder and it is imaginable that the composition was published as an individual opus before. <http://anno.onb.ac.at/

Ex. 6.17: Pianistic feature in Becker's 'Der Runenstein' (bars 19–27)

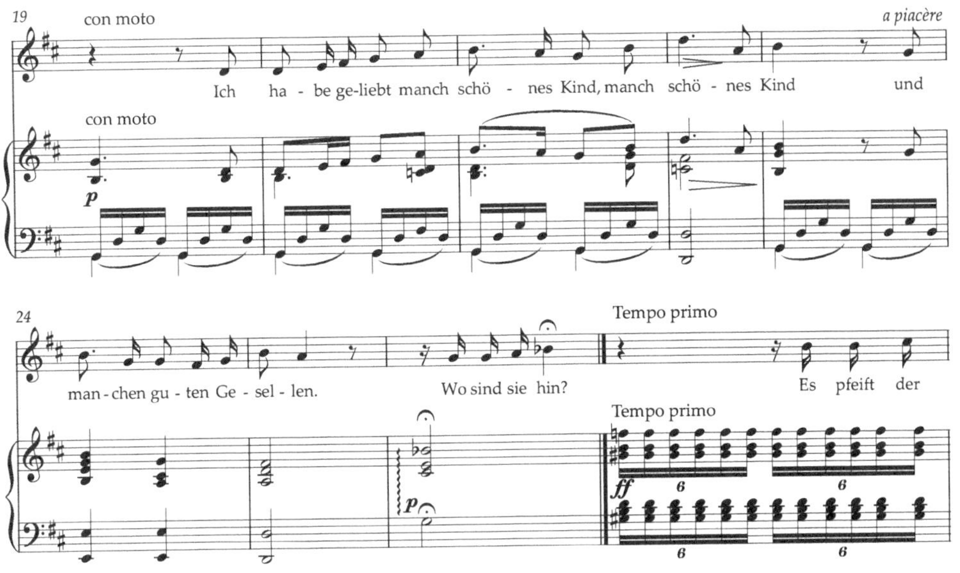

Ex. 6.18: Diversity in Franz's 'Es ragt in's Meer der Runenstein' (bars /13–15)

Gumbert, Kinkel, and Becker portray the fast movements of the wind and waves similarly, whereas Franz uses such means at very specific bars in order to emphasise the corresponding words. He employs a four-note semi-quaver motive at the words 'Wind' (wind), 'schäumen' (foam), and 'Wellen' (waves). Furthermore, Gumbert and Kinkel make use of tremolos in the piano accompaniment. However, while Kinkel treats this feature as a special means in order to

cgi-content/anno-buch?apm=0&aid=1000001&bd=0001872&teil=0203&seite=00 000134&zoom=1> (accessed 4 March 2019). Robert Franz was a German composer and conductor. Ulrike Kienzle, 'Franz, ursprüngl. Knauth, Robert (Franz Julius)', in *Die Musik in Geschichte und Gegenwart*, 2nd edn, vii, Personenteil, 26–36.

emphasise the most meaningful line, Gumbert applies it throughout his setting. Featuring semi-quaver figures and a latent second voice in some places, Kinkel's piano accompaniment overall is more challenging than Franz's and Gumbert's (and no less challenging than Becker's), which testifies to her pianistic skills.

❧ *Piano preludes and postludes*

Kinkel's focus on the piano accompaniment is also reflected in many of her preludes and postludes. The elaborate piano prelude in Johanna Kinkel's Rückert setting 'So wahr die Sonne scheinet' (Ex. 6.19) points to both Kinkel's skills as a pianist and her use of the piano as a means of free expression to place music within a larger context. While the prelude is challenging, the accompaniment throughout this Lied is straightforward. The prelude establishes the tonic key of G major. However, it seems detached from the vocal part, which begins without any motivic preparation (bar 5). As regards the ending of this Lied, the piano postlude serves, at the same time, as prelude (and interlude), which creates unity between the piano parts and the musical stanzas.

Ex. 6.19: Piano prelude in Kinkel's 'So wahr die Sonne scheinet' (bars /1–4)

Because the prelude, interlude and postlude are the same piano passages it seems hard to know whether or not the Lied is finished or whether another strophe will follow after the appearance of the piano solo. This structural feature might allude to the reciprocal exchange of love between the poem's two lovers. Within a larger context, this repetitive feature portrays the cyclical rhythm of life including the sunrise, the sunset, and the seasons. The contrast between the piano parts, i.e., the spiritual cycle of life, and the words, i.e., the reality of life, could be interpreted as an attempt to highlight the dualism between the inner self and its environment. On a less abstract level, however, this contrast can also be explained by means of practical reasons. By eclipsing the piano part whenever the voice is present, Kinkel puts more emphasis on the words.[34]

---

[34] This Lied was reviewed by Ludwig Rellstab in *Iris im Gebiete der Tonkunst*, 7 June 1839, 91–92.

Like Kinkel, Leopold Lenz (1804–1862) provides a prelude and a postlude in his setting for piano, cello, and voice.[35] However, Lenz's prelude differs from Kinkel's in so far as it introduces the motif which then occurs in the vocal part. Prelude and vocal part thus form one entity (Ex. 6.20). In a similar way, the piano and cello postludes recapitulate motivic material that first sounded in the second section of this through-composed Lied.

Unlike Kinkel and Lenz, Robert Schumann employs no piano prelude in his duet to Rückert's words.[36] Voice-leading is clearly a priority of Schumann's in this setting, as the entire duet is reminiscent of a chorale: the two voices and the piano accompaniment are in rhythmic unison and the accompaniment consists of multi-note chords, which accentuates the harmonic progression. At the end, following a repetition of the last vocal line with a *ritardando*, the piano has a codetta in which the last motif is echoed, which clearly indicates the end of this Lied.

In a similar way, Kinkel's Lied 'Gegenwart', a strophic setting to words by Goethe, does not incorporate any solo piano passages. Here, however, this avoidance constitutes one of the main characteristics, as it responds directly to the words by way of contradiction. As the Lied launches straight into the first line ('Alles kündet dich an!', Everything announces your presence!) in *forte* dynamics, the spontaneous beginning draws attention to the strong feelings the lyrical I has for his/her beloved (Ex. 6.21).

The rather abrupt ending exposes another contrast to the words: the last line reads 'Leben und Ewigkeit ist's' (This is life and eternity), but the lack of a postlude contradicts the notion of eternity. In comparison, Fanny Hensel employs a one-bar piano prelude as well as interludes and a postlude in her

---

[35] Leopold Lenz, 'So wahr die Sonne scheinet', in *Zwölf Gedichte von Friedrich Rückert für eine Singstimme mit Pianoforte und obligatem Cello, auch mit Pianoforte allein: Op.36* (Munich: Falter & Sohn, [1844]), 31–38. This opus was announced by Hofmeister in January 1844 <http://anno.onb.ac.at/cgi-content/anno-buch?apm= 0&aid=1000001&bd=0001844&teil=0203&seite=00000011&zoom=1> (accessed 4 March 2019). An anonymous note in the *Allgemeine Musikalische Zeitung* from 23 June 1841 (503) reveals that Lenz was a member of the Munich Kapelle and was stage director at the opera. The note mentions that Lenz travelled with his pianist brother to Lausanne where he performed some of his own compositions including the Goethe setting 'Kennst du das Land', the Heine setting 'Die beiden Grenadiere', and a setting of Victor Hugo's words.

[36] Robert Schumann, 'So wahr die Sonne scheinet', in *Zwölf Gedichte aus Friedrich Rückerts Liebesfrühling: Op. 37*, in *Robert Schumanns Werke, Serie XIII: Für eine Singstimme, mit Begleitung des Pianoforte*, ed. Clara Schumann (Leipzig: Breitkopf & Härtel, 1879–1912), 26–27.

Ex. 6.20: Opening of Lenz's 'So wahr die Sonne scheinet' (bars /1–6)

Ex. 6.21: Beginning of Kinkel's 'Gegenwart' (bars 1–2)

through-composed setting of these words.[37] Hensel's version is more complex than Kinkel's. It features abrupt rhythmic changes, tonal enclaves, modifications in the piano accompaniment, and melodic decoration. The one-bar introduction forms a contrast to the beginning of the vocal line in the following bar. It is set *piano*, while the vocal part begins *forte*, and the piano introduction is an octave linear ascent while the vocal line incorporates leaps and descends (Ex. 6.22). Furthermore, Hensel's setting takes away the listener's sense of regularity. As soon as the listener has become used to one differentiated structure, a completely new feature replaces the established pattern and thereby creates surprise.

Ex. 6.22: Opening of Hensel's 'Gegenwart' (bars 1–6)

Kinkel and Hensel respond to the words in this poem in completely different ways. While Kinkel chooses a strophic setting and plays with the abrupt beginning and ending, Hensel plays with the listener's expectations of certain compositional patterns. Both techniques are effective, although Hensel's Lied is more challenging.

By way of contrast, Kinkel's setting of her husband's words 'Römische Nacht' begins with a long piano prelude. The motivic material introduced in the prelude recurs frequently and also concludes the Lied. The vocal conclusion is followed by a very short but expressive piano postlude, which, played softly, incorporates a *rallentando*, then a *diminuendo* and then a fermata, evoking the impression that the Lied dies away slowly. 'Römische Nacht' generates a thoughtful atmosphere and places the characterisation of the 'alte Zeit' (old times) within the larger historical context. Both Eduard Lassen and Felix Draeseke, who set the same words, employ a similar calm ending as Kinkel.[38] All three composers

[37] Fanny Hensel, 'Gegenwart', in *Fanny Hensel: Ausgewählte Lieder für Singstimme und Klavier*, ed. Annette Maurer, 2 vols (Leipzig: Breitkopf & Härtel, 1993), i, 57–61.

[38] Eduard Lassen, 'Nacht in Rom', in *Sechs Lieder für eine Singstimme mit Begleitung des Pianoforte: Op. 92* (Leipzig: Otto Junne, [1893]), 16–18; Felix Draeseke, 'Nacht in Rom', in *Landschaftsbilder: Sechs Gesänge für eine Bariton- oder Mezzo-Sopran-Stimme mit Begleitung des Pianoforte: Op. 20* (Dresden: Hoffarth, 1880/81), 12–13.

complete the last word of the vocal part with a *legato* and conclude with a *piano* (Kinkel), *pianissimo* (Draeseke), or even *pianississimo* dynamic (Lassen). At the opening, however, all three composers use different techniques. While Lassen employs a two-bar prelude in cantabile style, Draeseke opens his setting with three staccato crotchet chords. Lassen's piano accompaniment is hugely diverse, and his harmonic progression is also more complex than Draeseke's and Kinkel's, which might be attributed to the later publication date.

₧ *(Romantic) irony*

That Kinkel conversed in different musical styles is also evident in her duet 'Die Geisterinsel', which responds to Heinrich Heine's use of Romantic irony. I discussed Kinkel's musical response to Heine's ironic ending in Chapter 5 (Ex. 5.8): by applying a sudden change of rhythm in the piano accompaniment, voice-leading, dynamics, tempo, and harmony, Kinkel emphasises the unexpected textual turn of atmosphere. Fanny Hensel and Peter Emilius Hartmann (1805–1900), like Kinkel, employ a 6/8 metre and broken chords in the piano accompaniment, which portray the movement of the water.[39] Hensel's setting is challenging on account of harmony and voice-leading, but, by replacing the word 'trostlos' (comfortless) with the word 'ruhig' (quiet), she erases the irony intended by Heine. Hartmann plays with the ambiguity of the key signature (Ex. 6.23). While his Lied opens in B minor, the harmonic progression hints at D major several times (bars 6, 10) and finally establishes D major in bar 22. In bar 30, however, which is where the final two lines begin, the Lied returns to the initial key of B minor. Interestingly, Hartmann, like Hensel, changes the words. He replaces the word 'weitem' (wide) with 'meinem' (my).

Unlike Hensel and Hartmann, Johann Vesque von Püttlingen (1803–1883) responds to Heine's ironic turn very effectively.[40] He sets apart harmonically the

---

Lassen's op. 92 was announced by Hofmeister in November 1893 <http://anno.onb. ac.at/cgi-content/anno-buch?apm=0&aid=1000001&bd=0001893&teil=0203&seite =00000496&zoom=1> (accessed 4 March 2019).

[39] Fanny Hensel, 'Mein Liebchen, wir saßen beisammen', in *Fanny Hensel, geb. Mendelssohn Bartholdy: Duette: Gesamtausgabe in 5 Bänden*, ed. Willi Gundlach, 5 vols (Kassel: Furore, 1999), ii; (Johan) Peter Emilius Hartmann, 'Die Trostlosen', in *Sechs Gesänge: Op. 35* (Leipzig: Kistner, 1839), 2–8. Staatsbibliothek zu Berlin (29518). (Johan) Peter Emilius Hartmann was a Danish composer, organist and conductor. Inger Sørensen, 'Hartmann, Johan Peter Emilius', in *Die Musik in Geschichte und Gegenwart*, 2nd edn, viii, Personenteil, 736–40.

[40] Johann Vesque von Püttlingen, 'Die Geisterinsel', in *Album der Neuen Zeitschrift für Musik* (1838), 43–44. Johann Vesque von Püttlingen was a lawyer, composer and tenor. His most important musical genre was the Lied; he set almost 120 poems of Heine's. Ludwig Finscher, [Reinhold Sietz], 'Vesque von Püttlingen, Johann

Ex. 6.23: Last stanza of Hartmann's 'Die Trostlosen' (bars 24–39)

middle section of his song from the two outer sections, all three of which cover one poetic strophe. While the two outer sections are in E-flat major, the second stanza is in the raised tonic (E major). The return of the tonic key at the beginning of the third stanza evokes the impression of a different atmosphere, which is emphasised by the return to *pianissimo* dynamics (as opposed to *fortissimo* in the preceding bars, Ex. 6.24). Furthermore, Vesque von Püttlingen plays with minor–major relations and inserts the minor tonic key of E-flat minor when the last line is repeated at the end of his setting (bars 36–40). As the rhythmic patterns of the piano accompaniment and vocal part do not change throughout this Lied, however, the final two lines are not as clearly stressed as in Kinkel's setting.

Freiherr, Pseud. *J. Hoven, Hans Hoven*', in *Die Musik in Geschichte und Gegenwart,* 2nd edn, xvi, Personenteil, 1520–23.

Ex. 6.24: Last stanza of Vesque von Püttlingen's 'Die Geisterinsel' (bars 26–45)

Julius Becker uses a partly strophic structure for these words, setting the first and second stanzas to the exact same music.[41] The third stanza begins with the same melodic phrase in the vocal part and the same rhythmic pattern in the piano. However, in order to stress the final two lines of the poem, this last stanza is notated separately. Like Kinkel, Becker changes the piano accompaniment in order to create a more sedate atmosphere here (Ex. 6.25). Furthermore, arpeggio figures in the right-hand piano part and harmonic variation emphasise the negative atmospheric turn.

Ex. 6.25: Conclusion of Becker's 'Mein Liebchen, wir sassen beisammen' (bars 11–23)

[41] Julius Becker, 'Mein Liebchen, wir sassen beisammen', in *Fünf Lieder für eine Stimme mit Begleitung des Pianoforte; Op. 4* (Leipzig: Hofmeister, [1837]), 6–7. Like 'Der Runenstein', which is part of the same opus number, this Lied was announced by Hofmeister in September/October 1837.

Like Kinkel, Hartmann, and Hensel, Moritz Hauptmann arranges his setting of the same words, 'Meerfahrt', in 6/8 metre.[42] His composition for voice, violin and piano accompaniment differs from the other songs introduced above in many ways. Besides the different instrumentation, Hauptmann sets Heine's entire poem twice in one and the same Lied. While, in the first section, the poem's final two lines experience a change of piano accompaniment and are harmonised with diminished seventh chords (bars 36–38, Ex. 6.26a), the second section differs in terms of piano accompaniment and melody (bars 61–71, Ex. 6.26b).

Ex. 6.26a: Bars 31–40 of Hauptmann's 'Meerfahrt'

<hr>

[42] Moritz Hauptmann, 'Meerfahrt', in *Drei Lieder für eine Singstimme mit Pianoforte- und Violinbegleitung: Op. 31* (Leipzig: Peters, [1844]), 2–5. This opus was announced by Hofmeister in November 1844 <http://anno.onb.ac.at/cgi-content/anno-buch?apm=0&aid=1000001&bd=0001844&teil=0203&seite=00000168&zoom=1> (accessed 4 March 2019).

Ex. 6.26b: Bars 61–71 of Hauptmann's 'Meerfahrt'

All composers here seem to capture the sea and the image of a loving couple floating on the water by means of a 6/8 (or 9/8) metre and a light-hearted piano accompaniment. However, their responses to Heine's use of irony are different. While Hensel and Hartmann defused the ironic sharpness through minor changes to the words, Vesque von Püttlingen, Hauptmann, Becker, and Kinkel responded musically to this irony. However, Kinkel is the only composer discussed here to use at the same time several surprising expressive means, including dynamics, tempo, rhythm, harmony, melody, and voice-leading, some features of which remind us of previous musical epochs.

❧ *Epilogue: Kinkel's compositional style*

Musical responses to poetic content differ depending on many aspects including personal preference, compositional ability, and educational background, but also target groups, performance, and conception contexts. Kinkel made use of such typical Romantic stylistic features as recourses to earlier compositional techniques; differentiated structures of tone and time; spontaneous outbursts, interjections and sudden interruptions; the embedment of music within a larger context; and the musical response to Romantic irony. However, Kinkel's style is diverse, as her songs feature different levels of harmonic and melodic progressiveness and technical demands, some of which earned her critical – not always positive – reviews in the nineteenth-century print media.

Kinkel's complexity and degrees of difficulty do not change in a chronological order. The reasons for this are manifold: Kinkel only published Lieder within a period of thirteen years (1838–1851); most of them were published between 1838 and 1848. This period of time is quite short – and perhaps too short to make observations as regards a chronological development. Furthermore, Kinkel, at all stages of her career, composed for herself and for others, as she depended financially on her publications. Therefore, it is imaginable that she aimed to include Lieder of different degrees of difficulty in her collections in order to attract as many performers (i.e. consumers) as possible. Compared to the settings of other nineteenth-century composers, many of Kinkel's Lieder are striking because of their challenging piano accompaniments, diverse harmonic designs, distinct rhythms, and relatively simple melodic lines. These may echo Kinkel's music-biographical identity, as she preferred the piano to singing and felt that she was a good pianist but an untalented singer. This self-perception is partly confirmed in the recollections of Kinkel's contemporaries.

Kinkel was aware of music-aesthetic developments in history, as is shown in several of her writings, but she did not necessarily apply the full range of her comprehension of harmony to her own compositions. For instance, she praised Chopin's treatment of successive dissonances and chromaticism on many occasions, although her own compositions rarely transcend common mediant relationships. While the use of augmented sixths and diminished seventh chords was no longer a novelty during the 1840s, this is not to say that all Lieder of the 1840s feature those chords. In this regard, perhaps Kinkel's Lieder are positioned somewhere among the more progressive ones – in line with her self-identification in her essay on modern Lieder composers, especially when considering that Kinkel did not publish any large-scale works which would have enabled her to show her full compositional-aesthetic knowledge.

It is impossible to make a definite statement about Kinkel's Lieder *compositions* as opposed to her Lieder *publications*, because it is unknown how many Lieder she may have composed which were not published. We do know, however, that Kinkel set the words of her husband's and her own Singspiele, all of which remained unpublished. Those surviving documents that are available, however, testify to compositional aesthetics which transcend those that surface in Kinkel's Lieder. Familiarity with the poet might be a factor here: while Kinkel did not know Goethe or Heine in person, she was friendly with Emanuel Geibel, and was in love with and married to Gottfried Kinkel. She might have felt strongly about Gottfried's poems and therefore employed more elaborate formal designs in some of her settings of these, especially her unpublished large-scale works. Perhaps Kinkel was a woman of her own time in so far as she did not publish her large-scale stage works but focused on popular genres, always with one eye to marketability and her image as a nineteenth-century female composer and performer.

Afterword

C ONSIDERING the nineteenth-century socio-political discourse, Johanna Kinkel's biography is extraordinary. Kinkel's persistent fight for a divorce from her first husband, her conversion from Catholicism to Protestantism, her second marriage with the Protestant theologian and later revolutionary Gottfried Kinkel, and her escape to and exile in London bear witness to her strong and emancipated personality. Her own involvement in socio-politics through journalistic activities, her leadership of the *Maikäferbund,* her constant juggling of family, household, and the public domain, and her directorship of the Bonner Gesangverein reveal her democratic and proactive mindset. Finally, her broad artistic affinity surfaces in her composition, teaching, and writing.

While Kinkel's musical engagement, considered in isolation, is a relatively common nineteenth-century phenomenon, the combination of all biographical facets of Kinkel's is astonishing. The nineteenth-century print media testify to a great number of Lieder composed by women, many of whom have long been forgotten: Charlotte Bauer (dates unknown), Isabella Behr (dates unkown), Jeanette Bürde (1799–?), Fanny Hensel, Marie Hinrichs, Marie König (1831–1859), Elise Müller (1782–1849), Elise Schmezer, Clara Schumann, Bettina von Arnim, Ingeborg von Bronsart (1849–1913), Charlotte von Bülow, Wilhelmine von Schwertzell, to name but a few.[1] Likewise, women writers were not uncommon.[2] Such salon gatherings as Kinkel's *Maikäferbund* in Poppelsdorf were a fashionable phenomenon throughout the eighteenth and nineteenth centuries and across the length and breadth of Europe. Some examples of salonnières are Ingeborg von Bronsart, Marie d'Agoult (1805–1876), Fanny Hensel, Jessie

---

[1] This list of names is the result of a four-week research visit to the Berlin Staatliches Institut für Musikforschung, during which I examined systematically the *Neue Zeitschrift für Musik, Allgemeine Musikalische Zeitung,* and *Neue Berliner Musikzeitung.* I am very grateful to the Stiftung Preußischer Kulturbesitz for this four-week research scholarship in February/March 2015.

[2] For example Louise Aston, Caroline de la Motte Fouqué, Henriette Frölich, Ida Hahn-Hahn (1805–1888), Fanny Lewald, Sophie Mereau (1770–1806), Rahel Varnhagen, Bettina von Arnim, Emilie von Binzer, Annette von Droste-Hülshoff (1797–1848), Malwida von Meysenbug, and Karoline von Woltmann (1782–1842). Kinkel was friendly with many of those women.

Hillebrand (1827–1905), Malla Silfverstolpe (1782–1861), Bettina von Arnim, and Elisabeth von Staegemann (1761–1835).[3] In terms of teaching, Kinkel herself took precise record of her impression of the job market for music teachers in her memoirs and her *Briefe aus London*. Both documents reveal that Kinkel was one of many who tried to make a living from teaching and that the job market was extremely competitive in both Berlin and London. It is the combination and nature of all those activities that grant Kinkel an extraordinary standing within her own context. Kinkel was a woman of her own time with regard to her socio-cultural restrictions and her national views, but her biography also reflects her quite progressive mindset in terms of gender roles and socio-cultural conventions.

As much as Kinkel was a woman of her own time, her generation is also a reflection of women like Kinkel. In the light of Kinkel's largely positive reception by the media, her own public appearance with the Bonner Gesangverein, the *Maikäfer*, and her published compositions, fictional and non-fictional writings, Kinkel's artistic output can be considered a significant contribution to the nineteenth-century literary and musical canon. Not only did Kinkel reiterate the cultural and compositional-aesthetic significance of such popular poets as Goethe, Heine, Platen, and Geibel, but she also set her own, her husband's, and her friends' poems, all of which reflect typical Romantic, and in part post-Romantic, thought. Corresponding to the quite small and intimate settings in which most of Kinkel's songs were performed, these compositions carry autobiographical content and are thus linked to Kinkel's socio-political background and environment. The poetry Kinkel set in her Lieder reveals autobiographical detail on different levels: in her correspondence, Kinkel refers to specific songs; some of the poems she set are clearly associated with key moments of Johanna and Gottfried's courtship and relationship; Kinkel's doubts and sorrows voiced in her letters to friends recur in her songs. On a technical level, Kinkel's compositional style and the poets she set changed in accordance with her personal development and environment. Not only do Kinkel's Lieder illustrate musically her letters, memoirs, and writings by underlining certain life events and states of mind, but Kinkel's love songs serve as biographical evidence of emotions to which she only alluded by way of passing remarks in her literary works. A close reading of Kinkel's love songs thus enables her audience to gain insight into her biography and her inner life at a time when the socio-political conventions did not allow for an open and uncensored exposure of one's feelings about marriage, faith, and politics.

---

[3] I am grateful to all speakers at the international bilingual conference *The European Salon: Nineteenth-Century Salonmusik* (Maynooth University, 2–4 October 2015) who shed light on many different salons throughout Europe.

Kinkel's political songs allude to the socio-political climate of the time. The small salon-like performance context and Kinkel's democratic involvement in the *Maikäferbund* reveal that Kinkel considered her own songs as quite personal. In light of this, it is not surprising that many of Kinkel's political Lieder carry strong political content, including criticism of religious and socio-political conventions as well as the encouragement of revolutionary activities. By setting her own and her husband's words, Kinkel placed herself within the male domain of politics and indicated her fondness for and her affiliation with the democratic revolutionary movement of the first half of the nineteenth century. Although it is questionable whether Kinkel's Lieder and poetry alone would have been powerful enough to qualify the *Maikäferbund* as a democratic movement, it is obvious that her gatekeeping as the leader of this association, her drawings, and her numerous reminders to fellow writers to contribute to the weekly *Maikäfer* journal influenced the tone predominating this group. In terms of creative innovation, many of Kinkel's political settings are joint works and thus Johanna and Gottfried Kinkel are joint identifiers of the revolutionary movement. Not only did Johanna Kinkel set a great number of Gottfried's and their mutual friends' words, but, in a similar way to Kinkel's love songs, Gottfried Kinkel's political activities served as an inspiration for Johanna's own creative process of writing poetry and prose throughout their marriage. Thus, her political settings had a significant impact on the socio-political environment surrounding Kinkel, as those settings were distributed, bought, and performed by Kinkel's contemporaries.

Many of Kinkel's Lieder feature such Romantic themes as the longing for pre-industrialised landscapes and the South; the praise of night-time atmospheres and the moon; dualisms between the inner self, its spiritual and surrounding worlds; mystical nature; nature as an allegory for love and the beloved; and strong emotions. In light of this, Kinkel's Lieder in praise of nature give an excellent account of the Romantic period both paradigmatically and compositionally, especially as many of her Lieder were received with great enthusiasm by renowned music critics of the time. Some aspects of Kinkel's compositional style, however, also attracted negative criticism. The reviewers deemed Kinkel's prominence of the piano accompaniment and some of her harmonic progressions too difficult, considering the performance purposes of Kinkel's Lieder. This negative criticism (or – in some cases – lack of criticism) reflects the general tenor of the time just as arrestingly as the positive criticism of Kinkel's Lieder. Therefore, a more careful consideration of those works which were not reviewed by the public print media might be especially worthwhile; for instance, Kinkel's Heine ballad 'Don Ramiro' was never reviewed by the public media.

In a similar way, it seems that the print media disregarded Kinkel's compositional diversity and her ability to adapt styles and compositional features to certain themes, moods, purposes, and target groups. The works of eighteenth- and nineteenth-century composers feature a great degree of diversity depending on the words they set. While Kinkel employed typical Romantic means, her style differs depending on the textual content, the poet, and the performance context. Considering Kinkel's complex and unusually diverse biographical facets, the thematic range of her Lieder, the variety of her compositions, her reception history and her personal correspondence, it seems difficult and perhaps impossible to generalise about her compositional style. However, her use of diverse harmonic progressions including augmented sixth chords, diminished and half-diminished seventh chords and enharmonic progressions, as well as challenging piano passages, places some of her Lieder among such artful and canonical compositions as Schumann's, Schubert's, and Vesque von Püttlingen's.

Kinkel's works were received with suspicion by contemporary reviewers, because she was a woman who produced noteworthy Lieder. Thus, Kinkel's contemporary reception was typical in so far as most women composers were treated with caution, as is reflected in Ludwig Rellstab's reviews. On the other hand, however, Kinkel is one of a few exceptions within this context, as most women composers were either criticised for their rather simple styles or were not reviewed at all. Kinkel's works, by contrast, were reviewed quite positively.

Finally, in terms of twentieth-century reception, Kinkel might be more typical than it may seem at first glance. Viewed within context, only a small number of nineteenth-century composers are performed on a regular basis today, as many have long been forgotten and consequently abandoned in both the research canon and the performance repertoires. Most of the composers performed today stand out for their stylistic distinctiveness or because of other unusual features (e.g., family background) and are therefore considered epoch-making representatives. Despite (or because of) her typical nineteenth-century aesthetics on the one hand and her stylistic diversity and unusual biography and reception on the other, it almost seems to be the case that Kinkel's oeuvre is not usual enough to be considered within the context of typical nineteenth-century composers and the history of ideas; and her work is not unusual enough to be considered within the context of epoch-making profound works and thinkers.

To date, the only context within which Kinkel's literary and musical works have been explored (although in limited depth) is the context of gender, an approach which – at least to a certain extent – enabled Kinkel's Lieder to enter the canon, but also limits the lens through which these Lieder have been received and examined. It was the aim of this book to explore Kinkel's published music beyond the particular aspect of Kinkel's gender, namely via such other frameworks as autobiographical composition, cultural identity, and Romanticism. This approach might inspire further research on Kinkel's unpublished Singspiele and Scottish songs, or similar projects on her lesser-known contemporaries. To this effect, I hope to encourage a reconsideration of current trends in performance and third-level education in favour of a broader variety of nineteenth-century Lieder, because, when explored within its own reception and performance contexts, the nineteenth-century Lied has much more to offer than the few canonical figures featured prominently in most concert programmes and university curricula. It is up to us – musicologists, performers, cultural agents, and audiences – to rectify the image of Johanna Kinkel and her lesser-known contemporaries as significant nineteenth-century cultural protagonists, and to celebrate their socio-cultural impact by way of detailed examination and performances of their artistic output.

Johanna Kinkel's compositions

Op.	Title	Composition Title	First Line	Poet	Publisher	Dedicatee	Date	Source
Published compositions								
7	*Sechs Lieder für eine Singstimme mit Begleitung des Pianoforte*	1 Nachtlied	Der Mond kommt still gegangen	E. Geibel	Trautwein (Berlin)	Bettina von Arnim	March 1838	Hofmeister
		2 Wunsch	Im Meere möcht' ich fahren	A. Kopisch				
		3 Vorüberfahrt	Ihr Liebesflüsternden Linden	J. Kinkel				
		4 Die Lorelei	Ich weiss nicht was soll es bedeuten	H. Heine				
		5 An den Mond	Füllest wieder Busch und Thal	J. W. von Goethe				
		6 Die Zigeuner	Im Schatten des Waldes	E. Geibel				
8	*Sechs Gedichte von Emanuel Geibel für eine Singstimme mit Begleitung des Pianoforte*	1 Der spanische Zitherknabe	Fern im Süd das schöne Spanien	E. Geibel	Trautwein (Berlin)	Emilie von Henning	July 1838	Hofmeister
		2 Rheinsage	Am Rhein, am grünen Rheine	E. Geibel				
		3 Gondellied	O komm zu mir	E. Geibel				
		4 Abendfeier	Ave Maria! Meer und Himmel	E. Geibel				
		5 Trennung	In meinem Garten die Nelken	E. Geibel				
		6 Abreise	Es kommt ein Schiff gezogen	E. Geibel				
/	*Trinklied für Männerchor*	Trinklied für Männerchor	Lasst uns trinken, lasst uns singen	J. Kinkel	Musical Supplement to *Neue Zeitschrift für Musik* (Leipzig)	/	September 1838	*Neue Zeitschrift für Musik*, 28 September 1838, 106
/	*Der Runenstein*	Gedicht von Heine	Es ragt ins Meer der Runenstein	H. Heine	Trautwein (Berlin)	/	November 1838	Hofmeister

Op.	Title	Composition Title	First Line	Poet	Publisher	Dedicatee	Date	Source
9	*Das Schloss Boncourt: Gedicht von Adelbert von Chamisso für eine Singstimme mit Begleitung des Pianoforte*	Das Schloß Boncourt	Ich träume als Kind mich zurücke	H. Heine	Trautwein	Adelbert von Chamisso	November 1838	Hofmeister
/	*Rhein-Sagen und Lieder*, i	Kölln	Im Rhein, im heiligen Strome	H. Heine	Dunst (Bonn)	/	December 1838	Announcement in supplement to *Allgemeine Zeitung*, 16 December 1838, 2668; Hofmeister announced this in January 1840
		Der Rheinstrom	Berg und Burgen schau'n herunter	H. Heine				
1	*Die Vogelkantate*	*Die Vogelkantate*; comic cantata		J. Kinkel	Trautwein (Berlin)	Prof. Lucas in Bonn	1838	Klaus, *Johanna Kinkel*, 50; Hofmeister announced this in January 1839; composed in 1829 (Klaus, *Johanna Kinkel*, 342)

Op.	Title	Composition			Publisher	Dedicatee	Date	Source
		Title	First Line	Poet				
10	*Sechs Lieder für eine Singstimme mit Begleitung des Pianoforte*	1 Nachgefühl	Wenn die Reben wieder blühen	J. W. von Goethe	Trautwein (Berlin)	/	May 1839	Hofmeister
		2 Der Kuss	Ich will meine Seele tauchen	H. Heine				
		3 So wahr die Sonne scheinet	So wahr die Sonne scheinet	F. Rückert				
		4 Wiegenlied	O du hast es gar zu gut	J. Kinkel				
		5 Traumdeutung	Als ich auf dem Euphrat schiffte	J. W. von Goethe				
		6 Der Müllerin Nachbar	Die Mühle die dreht ihre Flügel	A. von Chamisso				
/	*Rhein-Sagen und Lieder*, iii	Die beiden Brüder	Oben auf der Bergesspitze	H. Heine	Dunst (Bonn)	/	May 1839	Hofmeister
6	*Sechs Lieder mit Begleitung des Pianoforte*	1 Sehnsucht nach Griechenland	Ich blicke in mein Herz	E. Geibel	Kistner (Leipzig)	Angela Oppenhoff	July 1839	Hofmeister
		2 Wasser und Wein	Freunde sagt, was wollt ihr trinken?	A. Kopisch				
		3 Die Geister haben's vernommen	Da hab' ich viel blasse Leichen	H. Heine				
		4 An Luna	Schwester von dem ersten Licht	J. W. von Goethe				
		5 Verlornes Glück	Sitze hier an lieber Stelle	J. Kinkel				
		6 Die Sprache der Sterne	Es stehen unbeweglich	H. Heine				

Op.	Title	Composition Title	First Line	Poet	Publisher	Dedicatee	Date	Source
11	*Drei Duetten für Sopran und Alt mit Begleitung des Pianoforte*	1 Das Lied der Nachtigall	Aus meinen Thränen spriessen	H. Heine	Trautwein	Nanny Müller	July 1839	Hofmeister
		2 Die Geisterinsel	Mein Liebchen, wir sassen beisammen	H. Heine				
		3 Der Seejungfern Gesang	Der Mond ist aufgegangen	H. Heine				
12	*Drei Duetten für weibliche Stimmen mit Begleitung des Pianoforte*	1 Die Fischerkinder	Hast du von den Fischerkindern	W. Müller von Königs-winter	Trautwein	Adele and Emily Thormann	September 1840	Hofmeister
		2 Der Sommerabend	Der Sommerabend schauet so still	W. Müller von Königs-winter				
		3 Nachtgesang	O gieb vom weichen Pfühle	J. W. von Goethe				
13	*Don Ramiro: Ballade von H. Heine für Alt oder Bariton mit Begleitung des Pianoforte*	Don Ramiro	Donna Clara, Donna Clara! Heissgeliebte langer Jahre	H. Heine	Eck & Lefebvre (Cologne)	Sophie Schloß	September 1840, 2nd edition 1846	Hofmeister
/	*Der deutsche Rhein*	Der deutsche Rhein	Sie sollen ihn nicht haben, den freien deutschen Rhein	N. Becker	Kistner (Leipzig)	/	December 1840	Hofmeister

Op.	Title	Composition		Poet	Publisher	Dedicatee	Date	Source
		Title	First Line					
15	*Sechs Lieder für Alt oder Bariton mit Begleitung des Piano-Forte*	1 Römische Nacht	Ringsum auf allen Plätzen	G. Kinkel	Eck & Lefebvre / (Cologne and Amsterdam)		September 1841 (2nd edition 1846)	Hofmeister
		2 Du nah'st	Du nah'st! und wie Morgenröthe	J. Kinkel				
		3 Wiegenlied	Schlaf du holdes süsses Kind	J. Kinkel				
		4 Lust und Qual	Knabe sass ich, Fischerknabe	J. W. von Goethe				
		5 Rette Vater, Dein geliebtes Kind!	Einem Ruf hab' ich gelauschet	G. Kinkel				
		6 Allegretto	War hinaus gezogen	J. Kinkel				
16	*Sechs Lieder für eine Singstimme mit Begleitung des Pianoforte*	1 Die Gefangenen	Der erste Tagesschimmer	J. Kinkel	Hofmeister (Leipzig)	Emilie von Binzer	December 1841	Hofmeister; Text to 'Die Gefangenen': 25 August 1840 (*Maikäfer*); Text to 'Klage': 21 July 1840 (*Maikäfer*)
		2 Nächtliche Fahrt	Wenn über Wellen und Land	J. Kinkel				
		3 Abschied von Italien	Fort nun, o Schiff!	G. Kinkel				
		4 Gegenwart	Alles kündet dich an	J. W. von Goethe				
		5 Rheinfahrt	Die Nacht kommt still gezogen	S. Longard				
		6 Klage	Ach dass da doch so ferne bist	S. Longard				
14	*Hymnus in Coena Domini*	*Hymnus in Coena Domini*; choral work		Words from the seventh century; poet unknown	F. W. Arnold (Elberfeld)	Franz Ries	May 1843	Hofmeister

Op.	Title	Composition Title	First Line	Poet	Publisher	Dedicatee	Date	Source
18	*Sechs Lieder für eine Singstimme mit Piano*	1 Es ist so still geworden: Geistliches Abendlied	Es ist so still geworden	G. Kinkel	Schlesinger (Berlin)	Fräulein Forstheim	May 1843	Hofmeister; Text to 'Am Ufer': 29 September 1840 (*Maikäfer*); Text to 'Seelige Nacht': 12 April 1841 (*Maikäfer*); Johanna Kinkel's letter to Emilie von Henning, 6 May 1843, cited in Goslich, 'Schluß', 406.
		2 Am Ufer	Erblick' ich dort	J. and G. Kinkel				
		3 Auf wohl auf ihr Candioten	Auf wohl auf ihr Candioten	G. Kinkel				
		4 Seelige Nacht	Noch einmal erklingt	J. Kinkel				
		5 Wolle keiner mich fragen	Wolle keiner mich fragen	E. Geibel				
		6 Stürmisch wandern	Felsen steigen herauf, herab	G. Kinkel				
/	*Hymne auf den Tod des Marco Botzaris*	Hymne auf den Tod des Marco Botzaris	Männer von Hellas, klagt um den Heroen	Greek folk song, transl. by G. Kinkel	Eisen (Cologne); also: 1849 Sulzbach (Bonn)	/	June 1843	Both announced by Hofmeister

Op.	Title	Composition Title	First Line	Poet	Publisher	Dedicatee	Date	Source
17	*Sechs Lieder für eine tiefe Stimme mit Begleitung des Pianoforte*	1 Blaue Augen	In ahnungsvollem Glanze	G. Kinkel	Bote & Bock (Berlin)	Josephine Hubar	December 1847	Hofmeister; Text to 'In der Bucht': 20 September 1840 (*Maikäfer*); Texts to 'Schwarze Augen' and 'Blaue Augen': June 1840 (*Maikäfer*)
		2 Schwarze Augen	Ach, in dem funkelnden, träumerisch dunkelnden	S. Longard				
		3 Abendruhe	Gelehnet lag ich an dem Baum	J. Kinkel				
		4 Die Stimme der Geliebten	Lass tief in dir mich lesen	A. von Platen				
		5 In der Bucht	Es schliesst der dunkle Wald uns ein	A. Kaufmann				
		6 Welt, o Welt! Wie liegst du so weit!	Auf einsam hohem Thurme	G. Kinkel				
19	*Sechs Lieder für Alt oder Bariton mit Clavierbegleitung*	1 Die Mandoline	Ich bin der Mandoline gleich	W. Seibt	Schloss (Cologne)	Heinrich Dorn	August 1848	Hofmeister; Text to 'Thurm und Fluth': 30 December 1845 (*Maikäfer*); *Neue Zeitschrift für Musik* on 23 September 1848, 144
		2 Aus dem Singspiel 'Die Assassinen'	Durch Carthago's Trümmerhallen	G. Kinkel				
		3 Liebesmacht	Das Bächlein magst du dämmen	J. Kinkel				
		4 Beduinen-Romanze	Vorwärts mit des Vogels Fluge	G. Kinkel				
		5 Abschied	Schöne Wiege meiner Leiden	H. Heine				
		6 Thurm und Fluth	Auf starkem Klippenrande	G. Kinkel				
/	*Demokratenlied*	Demokratenlied	Genug der Schmähung habt ihr uns geboten	J. Kinkel	Sulzbach (Bonn)		September/ October 1849	Hofmeister

Op.	Title	Composition		Poet	Publisher	Dedicatee	Date	Source
		Title	First Line					
20	*Anleitung zum Singe, Übungen und Liedchen für Kinder von drei bis sieben Jahren*	1 Vom guten Vater und der lieben Mutter 2 Vom Grossvater 3 Von der Grossmutter 4 Von der Pathinn und der Tante 5 Vom Doktor Velten 6 Vom weissen Kätzchen 7 Vom Osterhääschen 8 Von der Katze Stuppstetz 9 Von der Lerche 10 Von der Bürgerwache 11 Vom Spektakel 12 Vom dicken Mops und braven Pudel 13 Vom Juni 14 Von der Tante Antonie 15 Geburtstagsliedchen für die Grossmama 16 Geburtstagsliedchen für den Vater 17 Von der Tante Maria 18 Vom zukünftigen Brudermann 19 Vom Haselnüsschen 20 Von der Hummel 21 Vom Federvieh 22 Vom Hääschen höp höp höp 23 Von der Eisenbahn 24 Von den Nummern 25 Vom Christkindchen 26 Vom Brummställchen		J. Kinkel	Schott (Mainz)		January 1849	January 1849 is noted in the original publication; Hofmeister announced this in September/Oc-tober 1849

Op.	Title	Composition Title	First Line	Poet	Publisher	Dedicatee	Date	Source
21	*Sechs Lieder für eine tiefe Stimme mit Pianoforte-Begleitung*	1 Lied aus dem 'Spessarttraum'	Welle, darfst du nimmer weilen	G. Kinkel	Schott (Mainz)	/	March 1851	Hofmeister
		2 Wiegenlied	Die milden Sterne scheinen	J. Kinkel				
		3 Jugenderinn'rung	Altverscholl'ne Lieder steigen	J. Kinkel				
		4 Provencalisches Lied	Am Strande der Dürance	G. Kinkel				
		5 Abendlied nach der Schlacht	Auf weitem blut'gen Feld	G. Kinkel				
		6 Des Lehnsmanns Abschied	Weh dass wir scheiden müssen	G. Kinkel				
22	*Tonleitern und Solfeggien für die Altstimme*	Solfeggios for the Contralto-Voice		no words	Schott (Mainz)		1852	1852 is noted in the original publication; Hofmeister announced this in August 1853
/	*Ritters Abschied (Sololied)*	Ritters Abschied	Weh dass wir scheiden müssen	G. Kinkel	Schott (Mainz)	/	date unknown	

Op.	Title	Composition Title	First Line	Poet	Publisher	Dedicatee	Date	Source
/	*Ritters Abschied* (Male Choir)	Ritters Abschied	Weh dass wir scheiden müssen	G. Kinkel	various publishers	/	dates unknown; 1880s	Hofmeister

Unpublished compositions

	Schottische Lieder	1 Farewell to Lochaber	Farewell to Lochaber, and farewell my Jean		[no date], Stadtarchiv Bonn			
		2 Lady Anne Bothwell's Lament	Balow, my babe, lye still and sleep					
		3 Gilderoy	Oh! Chloris could I now but sit as unconcerned as when					
		4 O the Broom	How blyth ilk morn was I to see					
		5 The Boatman	Ye gales that gently wave the sea					
		6 Johny Fa	The gypsies came to our lord's gate					
		7 The Banks of Forth	Awake, my love, with genial ray					
		8 Logan Water	Forever, fortune wilt thou prove					
		9 The Lass of Patie's Mill	The lass of Patie's mill					
		10 Auld Rob Morris	There's auld Rob Morris that win's in yon glen					
		11 Busk You, Busk You, my Bonny Bonny Bride	Weep not, weep not, my bonny bonny bride					
		12 Oh Open the Door Lord Gregory	Oh! Open the door, Lord Gregory					

Op. Title	Composition Title	First Line	Poet	Publisher	Dedicatee	Date	Source
Sechs Duette für zwei weibliche Stimmen, ohne Klavierbegleitung	1 Späte Liebe	Es lag ein junger deutscher Held	G. Kinkel	[no date], Stadtarchiv Bonn			
	2 Ständchen	Leise flehen meine Lieder	L. Rellstab				
	3 Täuschung	Blütenweiß bestreuet schaute	W. Müller von Königs-winter				
	4 Trinklied im Sommer	Ei sagt mir doch ihr Leute	E. Geibel				
	5 Der Musensohn	Durch Feld und Wald zu schweifen	J. W. von Goethe				
	6 Ich wandelte unter den Bäumen	Ich wandelte unter den Bäumen	H. Heine				

Op. Title	Composition Title	First Line	Poet	Publisher	Dedicatee	Date	Source
Fragment eines Liederheftes	1 Kathleen Mavourneen	Kathleen Mavourneen! The grey dawn is breaking	F. N. Crouch			[1856–1857]	ULB
	2 Der Musensohn; Composition by F. Schubert	Durch Feld und Wald zu schweifen	J. W. von Goethe			[1856–1857]	ULB
	3 Französische Melodie; Composition by F. Silcher	Das Thal ruht still im Dunkeln	poet unknown; French original			March 1856 (Kinkel's own date)	ULB
	4 Matrosenlied; Composition by F. Silcher	Auf dem Meer bin ich geboren	poet unknown			June 1856 (Kinkel's own date)	ULB
	5 Mein Herz ist im Hochland; Composer unknown	Mein Herz ist im Hochland	R. Burns (My Heart is in the Highland)			5 July 1856 (Kinkel's own date)	ULB
	6 The Highland Watch; Composition by L. van Beethoven	Old Scotia wake thy mountain strain	J. Hogg (1770–1835)			24 December 1856 (Kinkel's own date)	ULB
	7 Lied aus Friedrich in Suza	Du gabst dem Mann des Schwertes	G. Kinkel			1 May 1857 (Kinkel's own date)	ULB
	8 Lied von Bernhard Klein; Composition by B. Klein	Rauschendes Bächlein, so silbern und hell	poet unknown			5 July 1857 (Kinkel's own date)	ULB
	9 Geistliches Abendlied	Es ist so still geworden	G. Kinkel			21 August 1857	ULB
	10 Der Pilgrim; Composition by F. Schubert	Noch in meines Lebens Lenze	F. Schiller			[1857]	ULB

Op. Title	Composition Title	First Line	Poet	Publisher	Dedicatee	Date	Source
Vineta	Vineta; fragment manuscript; final fifteen bars	Und der Schiffer	W. Müller	[no date] Staatsbibliothek zu Berlin			
Der gefangene Freischärler	Der gefangene Freischärler	Was schaut ihr Kindlein traurig zu mir auf	J. Kinkel	[1849] Willison Lemke, 'Kinkel, Johanna', p. 611, Universitätsbibliothek Leipzig, signature: Kestner/II/A/IV/1087/Nr. 8; 1087; Nr. 8			
	Geburtstagslied für Emilie von Henning		J. Kinkel	date unknown, S 2954			

Unpublished works (manuscripts untraceable)

Op. Title	Composition Title	First Line	Poet	Publisher	Dedicatee	Date	Source
Dampfwagen-Komödie	*Dampfwagen-Komödie*; [words: Johanna Kinkel]			[1836–1839] Johanna Kinkel to Philipp von Nathusius on 26 February 1841, UB Kassel, 4° Ms. hist. litt. 15[151]			
Landpartie nach Pichelswerder	*Landpartie nach Pichelswerder*; [Johanna Kinkel]; comic operetta			[1836–1839] Johannes Werner, ed., *Maxe von Arnim: Tochter Bettinas/ Gräfin Oriola: 1818–1894: Ein Lebens- und Zeitbild aus alten Quellen geschöpft* (Leipzig: Köhler and Amelang: 1937), 54–60, Württembergische Landesbibliothek Stuttgart (Cod.mus.II fol. 111a–c)			
Savigny und Themis oder die Olympier in Berlin	*Savigny und Themis oder die Olympier in Berlin*; [Johanna Kinkel]			[1836–1839] Werner, ed., *Maxe von Arnim*, 54–60			
Tröderln und Ziepern	*Tröderln und Ziepern*; [Johanna Kinkel]			[1836–1839] Werner, ed., *Maxe von Arnim*, 54–60			

Op. Title	Composition Title	First Line	Poet	Publisher	Dedicatee	Date	Source
Verrückte Komödien aus Berlin: Der Wettstreit der schottischen Minstrels	Verrückte Komödien aus Berlin: Der Wettstreit der schottischen Minstrels; [Johanna Kinkel]			[1836–1839] Willison Lemke, 'Kinkel, Johanna', 611.			
Gelbi's Liebe	Gelbi's Liebe; Lied; [Gisela von Arnim]			[1838] Willison Lemke, 'Kinkel, Johanna', 611.			
[Chor der strickenden Damen]	[Chor der strickenden Damen]; choir for SSA with solo soprano and piano; [Johanna Kinkel]			[1838] Melanie Ayaydin, 'Kinkel, Johanna', Musik und Gender im Internet, ed. by Beatrix Borchard <http://mugi.hfmt-hamburg.de/artikel/Johanna_Kinkel.pdf>			
Hänneschen als Wunderkind	Hänneschen als Wunderkind; [Johanna Kinkel]			[1840] Willison Lemke, 'Kinkel, Johanna', 611.			
Das Malztier	Das Malztier; Lustspiel; [Johanna Kinkel]			Premiered on 18 March 1840 (Klaus, Johanna Kinkel, 342)			
Friedrich der Rothbart in Suza, oder Vasallentreue	Friedrich der Rothbart in Suza, oder Vasallentreue; Liederspiel; [Gottfried Kinkel]			1841 Willison Lemke, 'Kinkel, Johanna', 611.			
Otto der Schütz	Otto der Schütz; Liederspiel; [Johanna Kinkel]			Premiered at Maikäfer Stiftungsfest on 29 June 1841 (Klaus, Johanna Kinkel, 342); Württembergische Landesbibliothek Stuttgart (Cod.mus.II fol. 111a-c)			
Die Assassinen	Die Assassinen; Singspiel; [Gottfried Kinkel]			Premiered on 26 July 1843 (Klaus, Johanna Kinkel, 128)			
Männerlied	Männerlied; Lied; [Gottfried Kinkel]			[1846] Willison Lemke, 'Kinkel, Johanna', 611.			
Jubiläum des Großvaters	Jubiläum des Großvaters; Singspiel; [Johanna Kinkel]			1849 Ayaydin, 'Kinkel, Johanna', also Brand and others, Komponistinnen in Berlin, 91.			
Der letzte Glaubensartikel, T.: Gottfried Kinkel.	Der letzte Glaubensartikel; Lied; [Gottfried Kinkel]			[1850] Willison Lemke, 'Kinkel, Johanna', 611.			

Op. Title	Composition			Publisher	Dedicatee	Date	Source
	Title	First Line	Poet				
[Duetten Arrangements]	Duet arrangements					[1853]	Willison Lemke, 'Kinkel, Johanna', 611.
The Baker and the Mice: Cantata for Children	*The Baker and the Mice: Cantata for Children*; comic cantata; [Johanna Kinkel]					1854	Willison Lemke, 'Kinkel, Johanna', 611.
Katzenkantate 'Aus meiner Kindheit'	*Katzenkantate 'Aus meiner Kindheit'*; [Johanna Kinkel], also *Mäusekantate*					[no date]	Brand and others, *Komponistinnen in Berlin*, 91.
Die Fürstin von Paphos	*Die Fürstin von Paphos*; opera in two acts with an overture; [Johanna Kinkel]					[no date]	Ayaydin, 'Kinkel, Johanna', also Willison Lemke, 'Kinkel, Johanna', 611.
Gelegenheitsstücke	*Gelegenheitsstücke*; [Lieder?]; manuscripts in parts lost; Ayaydin might be referring to the fragment of a songbook (Fragment eines Liederbuches) archived in Bonn					[no date]	Ayaydin, 'Kinkel, Johanna'.

Discography

Anklänge: Lieder von Komponistinnen des 19. und 20. Jahrhunderts, Lan Rao (soprano) and Micaela Gelius (piano) (Salto Records, 2000). Includes: 'Wunsch', op. 7.2; 'Stürmisch wandern', op. 18.

Johanna Kinkel: An Imaginary Voyage through Europe: 32 Songs, Ingrid Schmithüsen (soprano) and Thomas Palm (piano) (cpo, 2007). Includes 32 Lieder.

Johanna Kinkel: Lieder, Felicitas Bergmann (mezzo-soprano) and Véronique Pélisséro (piano) (Rognes: Media Sound Art, 1999). Includes 16 Lieder.

Josephine Lang, Johanna Kinkel: Ausgewählte Lieder, Claudia Taha (soprano) and Heidi Kommerell (piano) (CD Bayer Records, 1995). Includes: 'Wunsch', op. 7.2; 'An den Mond', op. 7.5; 'Die Zigeuner', op. 7.6; 'Verlornes Glück', op. 6.3; 'Vorüberfahrt', op. 7.3; 'Nachtlied', op. 7.1.

Komponistinnen der Romantik, Tuule Nienstedt (alto) and Uwe Wegner (piano) (CD Christophorus, 1994). Includes: 'An den Mond', op. 7.5; 'Die Zigeuner', op. 7.6; 'Die Lorelei', op. 7.4; 'Die Geister haben's vernommen', op. 6.3.

Rhein-Sagen und Lieder, Günther Massenkeil (bass-baritone), Monica Hofmann (piano) and Werner Kämmerling (guitar) (Aulos Schallplatten, 1987). Includes: 'Rheinsage', op. 8.2; 'Der Rheinstrom'; 'Kölln'; 'Die beiden Brüder'.

Robert Schumann: Sammlung von Musik-Stücken alter und neuer Zeit: Collection of Compositions from Old and New Times: Supplements to the Neue Zeitschrift für Musik, Vol. 1–16, various performers (Radio Bremen/Universität Bremen/cpo, 2010). Includes 'Trinklied für Männerchor'.

Traum der eignen Tage: Lieder von Carl Löwe, Johanna Kinkel, Clara Schumann, Robert Schumann, Dorothée Burkert (soprano) and Patrick Francis Chestnut (piano) (CD Sonopress, 2007). Includes: *Sechs Lieder*, op. 10; 'Das Schloss Boncourt', op. 9.

Wie ein Cherub aus den Wolken: Hommage an Bettina von Arnim, Verena Rein (soprano) and Axel Bauni (piano) (CD Dreyer Gaido, 2003). Includes: 'Nachtlied', op. 7.1; 'Wunsch', op. 7.2; 'Vorüberfahrt', op. 7.3; 'Die Lorelei', op. 7.4

Bibliography

&. *Primary sources*

[Anon.], announcement of Dunst, *Rhein-Sagen und Lieder* (1838), supplement of *Allgemeine Zeitung*, 16 December 1838, 2668

[Anon.], announcement of Johanna Kinkel, *Anleitung zum Singen: Opus 20* (1849), *Neue Berliner Musikzeitung*, 29 August 1849, 280

[Anon.], announcement of Johanna Kinkel, *Anleitung zum Singen: Opus 20* (1849), *Neue Berliner Musikzeitung*, 5 September 1849, 287

[Anon.], announcement of Johanna Kinkel, *Anleitung zum Singen: Opus 20* (1849), *Neue Zeitschrift für Musik*, 9 September 1849, 111

[Anon.], announcement of Johanna Kinkel, *Opus 19* (1848), *Neue Zeitschrift für Musik*, 23 September 1848, 144

[Anon.], announcement of Johanna Mathieux, *Opus 17* (1847), *Neue Zeitschrift für Musik*, 2 December 1847, 270

[Anon.], announcement of Johanna Mathieux, *Opus 8* (1838), *Neue Zeitschrift für Musik*, 13 July 1838, 18

[Anon.], concert announcement, *Vossische Zeitung*, 24 November 1838, 7–8

[Anon.], concert announcement, *Vossische Zeitung*, 26 November 1838, 8

[Anon.], concert review of a concert at Berlin Königliches Schauspielhaus (26 November 1838), *Iris im Gebiete der Tonkunst*, 30 November 1838, 192

[Anon.], concert review of a concert at Berlin Königliches Schauspielhaus (26 November 1838), *Vossische Zeitung*, 28 November 1838, 9

[Anon.], note on Leopold Lenz's concert in Paris, *Allgemeine Musikalische Zeitung*, 23 June 1841, 503

[Anon.], review of Elise Schmezer, *Lieder, Romanzen und Balladen* (1850), *Neue Zeitschrift für Musik*, 3 January 1851, 4

[Anon.], review of Johanna Kinkel, *Acht Briefe* (1852), *Neue Wiener Musik-Zeitung*, 28 August 1856, 152

[Anon.], review of Johanna Kinkel, *Opus 19* (1848), *Neue Zeitschrift für Musik*, 2 April 1849, 146

[Anon.], review of Johanna Kinkel, *Opus 21* (1851), *Neue Zeitschrift für Musik*, 4 April 1851, 151–52

[Anon.], review of Johanna Mathieux, *Die Vogelkantate* (1838), *Allgemeine Musikalischer Anzeiger*, 17 September 1840, 149–50

[Anon.], review of Johanna Mathieux, *Die Vogelkantate* (1838), *Allgemeine Musikalische Zeitung*, 1 May 1839, 346–47

[Anon.], review of Johanna Mathieux, *Drei Duetten für Sopran und Alt: op. 11* (1840), *Allgemeine Musikalische Zeitung*, 15 April 1840, 340

[Anon.], review of Johanna Mathieux, *Drei Duetten für weibliche Stimmen: Opus 12* (1840), *Allgemeine Musikalische Zeitung*, 28 October 1840, 904

[Anon.], review of Johanna Mathieux, *Opus 17* (1847), *Neue Zeitschrift für Musik*, 19 February 1848, 87–88

[Anon.], review of Johanna Mathieux, *Opus 6* (1839), *Allgemeine Musikalische Zeitung*, 8 December 1841, 1044

[Anon.], review of Johanna Mathieux, *Sechs Gedichte von Emanuel Geibel: Opus 8* (1838), *Allgemeine Musikalische Zeitung*, 26 September 1838, 637–38

[Anon.], review of Silphin vom Walde, *Drei Salon-Trio für Pianoforte, Violine und Violoncello* (1847), *Allgemeine Musikalische Zeitung*, 1 December 1847, 834

Becker, Julius, 'Es ragt in's Meer der Runenstein', in *Fünf Lieder für eine Stimme mit Begleitung des Pianoforte: Op. 4* (Leipzig: Hofmeister, [1837]), 2–3

—, 'Mein Liebchen, wir sassen beisammen', in *Fünf Lieder für eine Stimme mit Begleitung des Pianoforte: Op. 4* (Leipzig: Hofmeister, [1837]), 6–7

Begas, Carl, letter to Johanna Kinkel on 2 June 1838, Stadtarchiv Bonn (SN 98/165)

Beyschlag, Willibald, *Aus meinem Leben: Erinnerungen und Erfahrungen der jüngeren Jahre* (Halle/Saale: Strien, 1896)

Brandt-Schwarze, Ulrike and others, eds, *Der Maikäfer: Zeitschrift für Nichtphilister*, 4 vols (Bonn: Stadtarchiv, 1982–85)

Burckhardt, Jacob, *Briefe Jacob Burckhardts an Gottfried (und Johanna) Kinkel*, ed. Rudolf Meyer-Kraemer (Basel: Schwabe, 1921)

Draeseke, Felix, 'Nacht in Rom', in *Landschaftsbilder: Sechs Gesänge für eine Bariton- oder Mezzo-Sopran-Stimme mit Begleitung des Pianoforte: Op. 20* (Dresden: Hoffarth, 1880/81), 12–13

Dunst, J. M., ed., *Rhein-Sagen und Lieder* (Bonn: Dunst, 1838)

Fink, G. W., review of Johanna Mathieux, *6 Lieder für eine Singstimme mit Begleitung des Pianoforte: Op. 7* (1838), *Allgemeine Musikalische Zeitung*, 8 August 1838, 524–25

Franz, Robert, 'Es ragt ins Meer der Runenstein', in *Sechs Lieder von Heinrich Heine für eine Singstimme mit Begleitung des Pianoforte: Op. 39* (Leipzig: Breitkopf & Härtel, [1867/72]), 6

G., C., review of Johanna Kinkel, *Anleitung zum Singen: Opus 20* (1849), *Neue Zeitschrift für Musik*, 'Gesangschulen', 30 September 1849, 141–42

Geibel, Emanuel, *Emanuel Geibels Jugendbriefe: Bonn – Berlin – Griechenland*, ed. Karl Curtius (Berlin: Curtius, 1909)

—, *Gedichte*, ed. Emanuel Geibel, 39th edn (Berlin: Duncker, 1855)

Goethe, Johann Wolfgang, *Sämtliche Werke nach Epochen seines Schaffens (Münchner Ausgabe)*, ed. Karl Richter and others, 33 vols (Munich: Hanser, 1985–98)

Grönke, Kadja and Alexander Staub, eds, *Felix Mendelssohn Bartholdy: Sämtliche Briefe*, 11 vols (Kassel: Bärenreiter, 2008–)

Gumbert, Ferdinand, *Es ragt in's Meer der Runenstein: Op. 3* (Berlin: Schlesinger, [1843])

Hartmann, (Johan) Peter Emilius, 'Die Trostlosen', in *Sechs Gesänge: Op. 35* (Leipzig: Kistner, 1839), 2–8, Staatsbibliothek zu Berlin (29518)

Hauptmann, Moritz, 'Meerfahrt', in *Drei Lieder für eine Singstimme mit Pianoforte- und Violinbegleitung: Op. 31* (Leipzig: Peters, [1844]), 2–5

Heine, Heinrich, *Buch der Lieder von Heinrich Heine* (Hamburg: Hoffmann und Campe, 1827)

Hensel, Fanny, 'Gegenwart', in *Fanny Hensel: Ausgewählte Lieder für Singstimme und Klavier*, ed. Annette Maurer, 2 vols (Leipzig, Wiesbaden, Paris: Breitkopf & Härtel, 1993), I, 57–61

—, *Duette: Gesamtausgabe in 5 Bänden*, ed. Willi Gundlach, 5 vols (Kassel: Furore, 1999)

—, letter to Johanna Kinkel on 2 December 1838, Stadtarchiv Bonn (SN 98/163)

Hiller, Ferdinand, 'An den Mond', in *Sechs Lieder für eine Singstimme mit Begleitung des Pianoforte: Op. 204* (Leipzig: Kahnt, [1885]), 2–11, Staatsbibliothek zu Berlin (28598)

—, *Aus Ferdinand Hillers Briefwechsel (1826–1861)*, ed. Reinhold Sietz (Cologne: Arno Volk, 1958)

Himmel, Friedrich Heinrich, 'An den Mond', in *Gedichte von Goethe in Compositionen seiner Zeitgenossen*, ed. Max Friedlaender (Weimar: Verlag der Goethe-Gesellschaft, 1896), 56

Kinkel, Gottfried (jun.), ed., 'Aus Johanna Kinkels Memoiren', *Internationales Jahrbuch der Bettina von Arnim-Gesellschaft*, 8/9 (1996/97), 239–71

Kinkel, Gottfried, *An die Mitglieder des Gesangvereins unter Leitung der Frau Kinkel*, 1846, ULB (S2374)

—, *Die Assassinen*, n.d., ULB (S 2686)

—, *Gedichte* (Stuttgart/Tübingen: Cotta, 1843)

—, *Gedichte*, 7th edn (Tübingen/Stuttgart: Cotta, 1872)

Kinkel, Johanna and Gottfried Kinkel, eds, *Erzählungen* (Stuttgart: Cotta, 1849)

—, *Liebe treue Johanna! Liebster Gottit!: Der Briefwechsel zwischen Gottfried und Johanna Kinkel: 1840–1858*, ed. Norbert Schloßmacher, comp. Monica Klaus, 3 vols (Bonn: Stadtarchiv und Stadthistorische Bibliothek, 2008)

Kinkel, Johanna, 'Der gefangene Freischärler', Universitätsbibliothek Leipzig, signature: Kestner/II/A/IV/1087/Nr. 8; 1087; Nr. 8

—, 'Der Runenstein', anonymous manuscript copy, Stadtbibliothek Lübeck (Mus. P 1433 Ex. 1)

—, 'Erinnerungsblätter aus dem Jahre 1848', *Deutsche Monatsschrift für Politik, Wissenschaft, Kunst und Leben*, 4 (1851), 39–108

—, 'Es ist so still geworden', version dated 21 August 1857, ULB (E 4' 756/6 Rara:15), 27–28

—, 'Vineta', autograph fragment, Staatsbibliothek zu Berlin, Preußischer Kulturbesitz, Musikabteilung mit Mendelssohn-Archiv (Mus.ms.autogr. Kinkel, J. 1 M)

—, *Acht Briefe an eine Freundin über Clavier-Unterricht* (Stuttgart/Tübingen: Cotta, 1852)

—, *Anleitung zum Singen, für Kinder von drei bis sieben Jahren: Opus 20* (Mainz: Schott, 1849)

—, *Briefe aus London*, n.d., ULB (S 2390)

—, *Demokratenlied* (Bonn: Sulzbach, 1848)

—, *Endenicher Modejournale*, Stadtarchiv Bonn (SN 94/253)

—, Fragment eines Liederbuches, ULB (E 4' 756/6 Rara:15)

—, *Friedrich Chopin als Komponist*, 1855, ULB (S 2399)

—, *Gesuch an die Prinzessin von Preußen*, 4 July 1849, ULB (S 2407)

—, *Hans Ibeles in London*, 2 vols (Stuttgart: Cotta, 1860)

—, *Lecture on Beethoven's Earliest Sonatas, including Opus 10*, n.d., ULB (S 2397)

—, *Lecture on Harmony*, n.d., ULB (S 2394)

—, *Lecture on Mendelssohn*, n.d., ULB (S 2398)

—, *Lecture on Mozart*, n.d., ULB (S 2396)

—, letter to Bote and Bock, 2 January 1839, Berlin Staatsbibliothek, Mus.ex.Johanna Kinkel 2

—, letter to Felix Mendelssohn on 25 February 1843, Oxford Bodleian Library, GB-Ob, M.D.M.d.43/100–101

—, letter to Fräulein A. Dorn on 31 March 1838, Stadtarchiv Bonn (SN 98/77)

—, letter to Gretchen Biesing, 26 October 1854, ULB (S 2424)

—, letters to Ferdinand Mendheim, Berlin Staatsbibliothek, Mus.ex. Johanna Kinkel 5–10

—, *Maikäfer* national anthem, score manuscript, Paul Kaufmann's estate, Stadtarchiv Bonn (SN 94/67, No. 10)

—, manuscript book including parts of *Die Assassinen*, twelve Scottish songs, and six duets, Stadtarchiv Bonn (SN 098/95)

—, *Mein Glaubensbekenntnis*, 1842, ULB (S 2406)

—, *Musical History*, n.d., ULB (S 2393)

—, *Musikalisches aus London*, n.d., ULB (S 2391)

—, *Notizen den Gesangverein betreffend*, n.d., ULB (S 2400)

—, *Notizen zum Klavier- und Gesangsunterricht und zur Ästhetik der Musik*, n.d., ULB (S 2394)

—, *Sechs Lieder für Alt oder Bariton: Op. 19* (Cologne: Schloss, 1848)

—, *Sechs Lieder für eine tiefe Stimme mit Pianoforte-Begleitung: Op. 21* (Mainz: Schott, [1851])

—, *Songs for Little Children: English Words Adapted to Madame Kinkel's German "Kindergesangsschule"* (London, 1852)

—, *Tonleitern und Solfeggien für die Altstimme/Solfeggios for Contralto-Voice: Op. 22* (London: Schott, 1852)

—, *Zur Geschichte der Musik*, n.d., ULB (S 2393)

Krebs, Carl, *Der Zigeunerknabe im Norden: deutsches Lied für eine Singstimme mit Begleitung des Pianoforte: Op. 50* (Hamburg/Leipzig: Schuberth, n. d.)

Lange, Otto, review of Johanna Kinkel, *Anleitung zum Singen* (1849), *Neue Berliner Musikzeitung*, 21 November 1849, 372

Lassen, Eduard, 'Nacht in Rom', in *Sechs Lieder für eine Singstimme mit Begleitung des Pianoforte: Op. 92* (Leipzig: Otto Junne, [1893]), 16–18

Lenz, Leopold, 'So wahr die Sonne scheinet', in *Zwölf Gedichte von Friedrich Rückert für eine Singstimme mit Pianoforte und obligatem Cello, auch mit Pianoforte allein: Op.36* (Munich: Falter & Sohn, [1844]), 31–38

Lewald, Fanny, *Zwölf Bilder nach dem Leben: Erinnerungen von Fanny Lewald* (Berlin: Otto Janke, 1888)

Lithander, Carl Ludvig, *Der Zigeunerknabe im Norden* (Leipzig: Breitkopf & Härtel, n.d.), Staatsbibliothek zu Berlin (O.25191)

Loos, Helmut and Wilhelm Seidel, eds, *Felix Mendelssohn Bartholdy: Sämtliche Briefe*, 12 vols (Kassel: Bärenreiter, 2008–)

Lorenz, Oswald, review of Johanna Mathieux, *Sechs Lieder für eine Singstimme mit Begleitung des Pianoforte: Op. 7* (1838), *Neue Zeitschrift für Musik*, 9 March 1838, 77–78

—, review of Johanna Mathieux, *Sechs Lieder: Op. 6* (1839), *Neue Zeitschrift für Musik*, 3 January 1840, 7–8

—, review of *Rhein-Sagen und Lieder* (1840), *Neue Zeitschrift für Musik*, 7 February 1840, 47

Lübke, Wilhelm, *Lebenserinnerungen* (Berlin: Fontane, 1891)

Mangold, Carl Amand, 'Abendfeier in Venedig', in *Drei Lieder gedichtet von Emanuel Geibel, für eine Singstimme mit Begleitung des Pianoforte: Op. 43* (Mainz: Schott, [1855])

Marschner, Heinrich, 'Abendfeier in Venedig', in *Drei Gesänge für eine Singstimme mit Begleitung des Pianoforte: Op. 179* (Hamburg: Cranz, [1857?]), 2–7

Mathieux, Johanna, *Das Schloss Boncourt: Gedicht von Adelbert von Chamisso: Op. 9* (Berlin: Trautwein, [1838])

—, *Don Ramiro: Ballade von H. Heine für Alt oder Bariton mit Begleitung des Pianoforte: Op. 13* (Cologne: Eck & Co., [1840])

—, *Drei Duetten für Sopran und Alt: Op. 11* (Berlin: Trautwein, [1839])

—, letter to Philipp von Nathusius, 26 February 1841, UB Kassel (4° Ms. hist. litt. 15[151])

—, *Sechs Gedichte von Emanuel Geibel für eine Singstimme mit Begleitung des Pianoforte: Op. 8* (Berlin: Trautwein, [1838])

—, *Sechs Lieder für Alt und Bariton: Op. 15* (Cologne/Amsterdam: Jacob Eck & Lefebvre, [1841])

—, *Sechs Lieder für eine Singstimme mit Begleitung des Pianoforte: Op. 7* (Berlin: Trautwein, [1838])

—, *Sechs Lieder für eine Singstimme mit Begleitung des Pianoforte: Op. 10* (Berlin: Trautwein, [1839])

—, *Sechs Lieder für eine Singstimme: Op. 16* (Leipzig: Hofmeister, [1841])

—, *Sechs Lieder für eine Singstimme: Op. 18* (Berlin: Schlesinger, [1843])

—, *Sechs Lieder für eine tiefe Stimme mit Begleitung des Pianoforte: Op. 17* (Berlin: Bote & Bock, [1847])

—, *Sechs Lieder mit Begleitung des Pianoforte: Op. 6* (Leipzig: Kistner, [1839])

Müller von Königswinter, Wolfgang, *Junge Lieder* (Düsseldorf: Schreiner, 1841)

—, ed., *Dichtungen eines rheinischen Poeten*, 4th edn, 6 vols (Leipzig: Brockhaus, 1871–76)

R. S., review of Johanna Kinkel's 'Trinklied für Männerchor' (1838), *Neue Zeitschrift für Musik*, 28 September 1838, 106

Raff, Joachim, 'Abendfeier in Venedig', in *Fünf Lieder für eine Singstimme mit Begleitung des Pianoforte: Op. 51* (Leipzig: Kistner, [1853]), 14–17, Staatsbibliothek zu Berlin (28289)

Reissiger, Carl Gottlieb, 'Der Zigeunerbube im Norden', in *Auswahl beliebter Lieder und Gesänge* (Dresden: Paul, [1838]), Staatsbibliothek zu Berlin (76495)

Rellstab, Ludwig, review of Johanna Mathieux, *Die Vogelkantate* (1838), *Iris im Gebiete der Tonkunst*, 4 January 1839, 2–3

—, review of Johanna Mathieux, *Drei Duette für weibliche Stimmen mit Begleitung des Pianoforte: Op. 12* (1849), *Iris im Gebiete der Tonkunst*, 19 March 1841, 45–46

—, review of Johanna Mathieux, *Drei Duetten für Sopran und Alt: Op. 11* (1839), *Iris im Gebiete der Tonkunst*, 2 August 1839, 122–24

—, review of Johanna Mathieux, *Op. 10* (1839), *Iris im Gebiete der Tonkunst*, 7 June 1839, 91–92

—, review of Johanna Mathieux, *Sechs Gedichte von Emanuel Geibel für eine Singstimme mit Begleitung des Pianoforte: Op. 8* (1838), *Iris im Gebiete der Tonkunst*, 3 August 1838, 121–22

—, review of Johanna Mathieux, *Sechs Lieder für eine Singstimme mit Begleitung des Pianoforte: Op. 7* (1838), *Iris im Gebiete der Tonkunst*, 12 January 1838, 5–7

Romberg, Andreas, 'An den Mond', in *Gedichte von Goethe in Compositionen seiner Zeitgenossen,* ed. Max Friedlaender (Weimar: Verlag der Goethe-Gesellschaft, 1896), 55

Rückert, Friedrich, *Friedrich Rückert's gesammelte poetische Werke in zwölf Bänden: neue Ausgabe,* ed. Heinrich Rückert, 12 vols (Frankfurt: Sauerländer, 1882)

Schlegel, Friedrich, *Kritische Friedrich-Schlegel-Ausgabe,* ed. Ernst Behler and others, 36 vols (Paderborn: Schöningh, 1979–)

Schmezer, Elise, 'Zigeunerbube'; in *Romanzen und Balladen für Tenor: op. 5* (Magdeburg: Heinrichshofen, [1850])

Schubert, Franz, 'An den Mond', in *Franz Schubert's Werke, Serie XX: Sämtliche Lieder und Gesänge, No.116,* ed. Eusebius Mandyczewski (Leipzig: Breitkopf & Härtel, 1894–95), 40–41

—, 'An den Mond II', in *Franz Schubert's Werke, Serie XX: Sämtliche Lieder und Gesänge, No.176,* ed. Eusebius Mandyczewski (Leipzig: Breitkopf & Härtel, 1894–95), 195–97

Schumann, Robert, 'So wahr die Sonne scheinet', in *Zwölf Gedichte aus Friedrich Rückerts Liebesfrühling, Op. 37, No. 12,* in *Robert Schumanns Werke, Serie XIII: Für eine Singstimme, mit Begleitung des Pianoforte,* ed. Clara Schumann (Leipzig: Breitkopf & Härtel, 1879–1912), 26–27

—, *Robert Schumann Tagebücher,* ed. Gerd Nauhaus, 4 vols (Stroemfeld/ Roter Stern, Basel & Frankfurt am Main: VEB Deutscher Verlag für Musik, 1971–87)

Schurz, Carl, *Lebenserinnerungen bis zum Jahre 1852* (Berlin: Reimer, 1906/11)

Tomaschek, Wenzel Johann, 'An den Mond', in *Gedichte von Goethe mit Begleitung des Piano-Forte,* 9 vols (self-published, c1818), IV

Truhn, Friedrich Hieronymus, 'Der Zigeunerbube im Norden', in *Lieder aus Spanien: Op. 38* (Berlin: Schlesinger, [1840]), 3–7 von Bülow, Charlotte, 'Zigeunerleben', in *Lieder und Gesänge für eine Sing-stimme mit Begleitung des Pianoforte* (Berlin: Bahn, n.d.), 3–5

von Chamisso, Adelbert, *Gedichte von Adelbert von Chamisso*, ed. Wilhelm Rauschenbusch (Berlin: Grote, 1874)

—, *Sämtliche Werke in zwei Bänden*, ed. Jost Perfahl, 2 vols (Munich: Winkler, 1975)

von Meysenbug, Malwida, *Gesammelte Werke*, ed. Berta Schleicher, 5 vols (Stuttgart: Deutsche Verlags-Anstalt, 1922)

von Püttlingen, Johann Vesque, 'Die Geisterinsel', in *Album der Neuen Zeitschrift für Musik* (1838), 43–44

von Schwertzell, Wilhelmine, 'An den Mond', in *Zwölf Lieder von Göthe, Fouque, Hebel, Tiek, und Uhland* (Leipzig: Probst, n.d.), 18, Staatsbibliothek zu Berlin (DMS O.25274)

von Seckendorff, Siegmund Freiherr, 'Füllest wieder's liebe Thal', in *Gedichte von Goethe in Compositionen seiner Zeitgenossen*, ed. Max Friedlaender (Weimar: Verlag der Goethe-Gesellschaft, 1896), 55

Weiss., Jul., announcement of Johanna Mathieux, *Opus 17* (1847), *Neue Berliner Musikzeitung*, 29 March 1848, 97

Zelter, Carl Friedrich, 'An den Mond', in *Gedichte von Goethe in Compositionen seiner Zeitgenossen*, ed. Max Friedlaender (Weimar: Verlag der Goethe-Gesellschaft, 1896), 56

Secondary sources

Ackermann, Peter, 'Palestrina', in *Die Musik in Geschichte und Gegenwart*, ed. Ludwig Finscher and others, 2nd edn, 29 vols (Kassel: Bärenreiter, 1994–2008), xiii, Personenteil, 7–46

Agawu, Kofi, 'Theory and Practice in the Analysis of the Nineteenth-Century "Lied"', *Music Analysis*, 11, 1 (1992), 3–36

Ashton, Rosemary, *Little Germany: Exile and Asylum in Victorian England* (Oxford: Oxford University Press, 1986)

Baini, Giuseppe, *Memorie storico-critiche della vita e delle opere di G. P. da Palestrina*, 2 vols (Rome: Societa Tipografica, 1828)

Ballstaedt, Andreas, 'Salonmusik', in *Die Musik in Geschichte und Gegenwart*, ed. Ludwig Finscher and others, 2nd edn, 29 vols (Kassel: Bärenreiter, 1994–2008), viii, Sachteil, 854–67

Barricelli, Jean-Pierre, 'Musical Forms of Romantic Irony', in *Romantic Irony*, ed. Frederick Garber (Budapest: Akadémiai Kiadó, 1988), 310–22

Bayreuther, Rainer, 'Raff, Joachim', in *Die Musik in Geschichte und Gegenwart*, ed. Ludwig Finscher and others, 2nd edn, 29 vols (Kassel: Bärenreiter, 1994–2008), xiii, Personenteil, 1191–99

Bellman, Jonathan, 'Introduction', in *The Exotic in Western Music*, ed. Jonathan Bellman (Boston: Northeastern University Press, 1998), ix–xiii

Binder, Benjamin, 'The Lied from the Inside Out', in 'Colloquy: Studying the Lied: Hermeneutic Traditions and the Challenge of Performance', convened by Jennifer Ronyak, *Journal of the American Musicological Society*, 67, 2 (2014), 543–82 (553–55)

Boetcher Joeres, Ruth-Ellen, *Respectability and Deviance: Nineteenth-Century German Women Writers and the Ambiguity of Representation* (Chicago: University of Chicago Press, 1998)

Born, Georgina and David Hesmondhalgh, eds, *Western Music and Its Others: Difference, Representation, and Appropriation in Music* (Berkeley: University of California Press, 2000)

Botstein, Leon, 'Listening through Reading: Musical Literacy and the Concert Audience', *19th-Century Music*, 16, 2 (1992), 129–45

Brand, Bettina, '"…wie die Stimme, die aus ihrer innersten Seele spricht": Johanna Kinkels "Vortrag über Beethovens früheste Sonaten inkl. op.10"', in *Maßstab Beethoven?: Komponistinnen im Schatten des Geniekults*, ed. Bettina Brand and Martina Helmig (Munich: TextUndKritik, 2001), 159–74

—, 'Johanna Kinkel (1810–1858)', in *Komponistinnen in Berlin*, ed. Bettina Brand and others (Berlin: Bender Schnelldruck, 1987), 74–95

Bröcker, Marianne, 'Johanna Kinkels schriftstellerische und musikpädagogische Tätigkeit', *Bonner Geschichtsblätter*, 29 (1977), 37–48

Büchter-Römer, Ute, '"Ein rheinisches Musikfest muß man erlebt haben": Johanna Kinkel, Clara Schumann, Fanny Hensel und die Rheinromantik', in *Romantik, Reisen, Realitäten: Frauenleben am Rhein*, ed. Bettina Bab and Helga Arend (Bonn: Lempertz, 2002)

Bunzel, Anja and Barbora Kubečková, 'Václav Jan Tomášek (1774–1850): A Versatile Lieder Composer?: A Comparative Analysis of Selected Goethe Settings by Carl Friedrich Zelter, Václav Jan Tomášek and Johanna Kinkel', *Musicologica Olomucensia*, 20 (2014), 15–36

Bunzel, Anja, 'Johanna Kinkel (1810–1858) within the Context of Nineteenth-Century Music Criticism', in *Nineteenth-Century Music Criticism*, ed. Teresa Cascudo García-Villaraco (Turnhout: Brepols, 2017)

—, 'Johanna Kinkel's Pedagogical Approaches as a Socio-Political Mirror of Her Time', *Musicological Explorations*, 14 (2014), 27–58

—, 'Johanna Kinkel's Political Art Songs as a Contribution to the Socio-Cultural Identity of the German Democratic Movement during the Late 1840s', *Focus on German Studies*, 22 (2015), 1–20

—, 'Johanna Kinkel's Social Life in Berlin (1836–39): Reflections on Historiographical Sources', in *Musical Salon Culture in the Long Nineteenth Century*, ed. Anja Bunzel and Natasha Loges (Woodbridge: Boydell, 2019), 13–26

—, 'Johanna Kinkel's *Thurm und Fluth* (Opus 19, No. 6): Revolutionary Ideas and Political Optimism in a 19th-Century Art Song', in *The National Element in Music: Conference Proceedings*, ed. Nikos Maliaras (Athens: Athens University, 2014), 18–25

Burnham, Scott, 'The Role of Sonata Form in A. B. Marx's Theory of Form', *Journal of Music Theory*, 33, 2 (1989), 247–71

Byrne, Lorraine, *Schubert's Goethe Settings* (Aldershot: Ashgate, 2003)

Carr, Bruce, 'Crouch, Frederick Nicholls', in *The New Grove Dictionary of Music and Musicians*, ed. Stanley Sadie, 2nd edn, 29 vols (London: Macmillan, 2001), xxiii, 733–34

Cook, Nicholas, 'Between Process and Product: Music and/as Performance', *The Online Journal of the Society for Music Theory: Music Theory Online*, 7, 2 (2001), 1–31 <http://www.mtosmt.org/issues/mto.01.7.2/mto.01.7.2.cook.html> (accessed 12 June 2019)

Cvetko, Alexander J., '… *Durch Gesänge lehrten sie …' Johann Gottfried Herder und die Erziehung durch Musik: Mythos, Ideologie – Rezeption* (Frankfurt: Peter Lang, 2005)

Dahlhaus, Carl, *Die Musik des 19. Jahrhunderts* (Laaber: Laaber Verlag, 1996)

Davis, Deanna C., 'The Veil of Fiction: Pedagogy and Rhetorical Strategies in Carl Czerny's *Letters on the Art of Playing the Pianoforte*', in *Beyond the Art of Finger Dexterity: Reassessing Carl Czerny*, ed. David Gramit (New York: University of Rochester Press, 2008), 67–81

Deaville, James, 'A Multitude of Voices: The Lied at Mid Century', in *The Cambridge Companion to the Lied*, ed. James Parsons (Cambridge: Cambridge University Press, 2004), 142–67

—, 'A Star Is Born?: Czerny, Liszt, and the Pedagogy of Virtuosity', in *Beyond the Art of Finger Dexterity: Reassessing Carl Czerny*, ed. David Gramit (New York: University of Rochester Press, 2008), 52–66

—, 'This Is (Y)our Life: (Re)Writing Women's Autobiographies in Music in Nineteenth-Century Germany', in *Musical Biography: Towards New Paradigms*, ed. Jolanta T. Pekacz (Aldershot: Ashgate, 2006), 135–58

Diethe, Carol, *Towards Emancipation: German Women Writers of the Nineteenth Century* (Oxford: Berghahn, 1998)

Dittrich, Marie-Agnes, '"Teufelsmühle" und "Omnibus"', *Zeitschrift der Gesellschaft für Musiktheorie*, 4, 1–2 (2007), 107–21

Dohr, Christoph, 'Reissiger, Carl, Karl, Gottlieb', in *Die Musik in Geschichte und Gegenwart*, ed. Ludwig Finscher and others, 2nd edn, 29 vols (Kassel: Bärenreiter, 1994–2008), xiii, Personenteil,1539–42

Eatock, Colin Timothy, *Mendelssohn and Victorian England* (Farnham: Ashgate, 2009)

Finscher, Ludwig, [Reinhold Sietz], 'Vesque von Püttlingen, Johann Freiherr, Pseud. *J. Hoven, Hans Hoven*', in *Die Musik in Geschichte und Gegenwart*, ed. Ludwig Finscher and others, 2nd edn, 29 vols (Kassel: Bärenreiter, 1994–2008), xvi, Personenteil, 1520–23

Freudenberg, Konstanze, [Peter Schmiedel], 'Becker, (Constantin) Julius', in *Die Musik in Geschichte und Gegenwart*, ed. Ludwig Finscher and others, 2nd edn, 29 vols (Kassel: Bärenreiter, 1994–2008), ii, Personenteil, 625–26

Freund, Marion, *'Mag der Thron in Flammen glühn!': Schriftstellerinnen und die Revolution von 1848/49* (Königstein: Helmer, 2004)

Friedrich, Karin, 'Cultural and intellectual trends', in *Nineteenth-Century Germany: Politics, Culture and Society: 1780–1918*, ed. John Breuilly (London: Arnold, 2001), 96–116

Gesse-Harm, Sonja, 'Heine, Heinrich, Harry', in *Die Musik in Geschichte und Gegenwart*, ed. Ludwig Finscher and others, 2nd edn, 29 vols (Kassel: Bärenreiter, 1994–2008), xiii, Personenteil, 1167–76

—, *Zwischen Ironie und Sentiment: Heinrich Heine im Kunstlied des 19. Jahrhunderts* (Stuttgart: Metzler, 2006)

Glahn, Daniela, *Johanna Kinkel – Bilder einer Autorschaft* (Munich: Allitera, 2017)

Goslich, Marie, 'Biefe von Johanna Kinkel', *Preußische Jahrbücher*, 97 (1899), 185–222

—, 'Briefe von Johanna Kinkel: Schluß', *Preußische Jahrbücher*, 97 (1899), 398–433

Gramit, David, 'The Circulation of the Lied: The Double Life of an Artwork and a Commodity', in *The Cambridge Companion to the Lied*, ed. James Parsons (Cambridge: Cambridge University Press, 2004), 301–14

—, 'Unremarkable Musical Lives: Autobiographical Narratives, Music, and the Shaping of the Self', in *Musical Biography: Towards New Paradigms*, ed. Jolanta T. Pekacz (Farnham: Ashgate, 2006), 159–78

—, ed., *Beyond the Art of Finger Dexterity: Reassessing Carl Czerny* (New York: University of Rochester Press, 2008)

Grout, Donald J., J. Peter Burkholder and Claude Palisca, *A History of Western Music*, 7th edn (New York: W. W. Norton & Company, 2006)

Hahn, Barbara, 'Der Mythos vom Salon', in *Salons der Romantik: Beiträge eines Wiepersdorfer Kolloquiums zu Theorie und Geschichte des Salons*, ed. Hartwig Schulz (Berlin: de Gruyter, 1997), 213–34

Hammer, Carl, 'Goethe and Marianne: After the "Divan"', *The South Central Bulletin*, 28, 4 (Winter, 1968), 134–38

Henseler, Theodor Anton, *Das musikalische Bonn im 19. Jahrhundert* (Bonn: Universitäts-Buchdruckerei, 1959)

Herder, Bartholomä, 'Kinkel', in *Herders Conversations-Lexikon*, ed. Bartholomä Herder, 5 vols (Freiburg: Herder, 1854–57), iii, 591

Hillila, Ruth-Esther and Barbara Blanchard Hong, *Historical Dictionary of the Music and Musicians of Finland* (Westport: Greenwood, 1997)

Hochradner, Thomas, 'Probleme der Periodisierung von Musikgeschichte', *Acta Musicologica*, 67, 1 (January–June 1995), 55–70

Hopkins Porter, Cecelia, 'The "Rheinlieder Critics": A Case of Musical Nationalism', *The Musical Quarterly*, 63, 1 (January 1977), 74–98

Iitti, Sanna, *The Feminine in German Song* (New York: Peter Lang, 2006)

Kabelková, Markéta, 'Tomášek, *Tomaschek*, Václav Jan, *Wenzel Johann* (Křitel)', in *Die Musik in Geschichte und Gegenwart*, ed. Ludwig Finscher and others, 2nd edn, 29 vols (Kassel: Bärenreiter, 1994–2008), XVI, Personenteil, 900–06

Kaufmann, Paul, 'Johanna Kinkel: Neue Beiträge zu ihrem Lebensbild', *Preußische Jahrbücher*, 221 (1930), 290–304

—, 'Johanna Kinkel: Neue Beiträge zu ihrem Lebensbild: Schluß', *Preußische Jahrbücher*, 222 (1930), 48–67

—, 'Noch einmal auf Johanna Kinkels Spuren', *Preußische Jahrbücher*, 229 (1932), 263–68

Kenny, Aisling, 'Josephine Lang's Goethe, Heine and Uhland Lieder: Contextualizing Her Contribution to Nineteenth-Century German Song' (unpublished PhD dissertation, National University of Ireland, Maynooth, 2010)

Kienzle, Ulrike, 'Franz, ursprüngl. Knauth, Robert (Franz Julius)', in *Die Musik in Geschichte und Gegenwart*, ed. Ludwig Finscher and others, 2nd edn, 29 vols (Kassel: Bärenreiter, 1994–2008), vii, Personenteil, 26–36

Kier, Herfried, 'Kiesewetter', in *Die Musik in Geschichte und Gegenwart*, ed. Ludwig Finscher and others, 2nd edn, 29 vols (Kassel: Bärenreiter, 1994–2008), x, Personenteil, 87–91

Klaus, Monica and Ingrid Bodsch, eds, *Johanna Kinkel: eine Auswahl aus ihrem literarischen Werk* (Bonn: StadtMuseum, 2010)

Klaus, Monica, '"Die Assassinen – Romantisches Singspiel mit Gesang": von Gottfried und Johanna Kinkel, 1843' (unpublished article, Bonn, 24 November 2014)

—, '"Die Nachtigall hat etwas detoniert!": Johanna Kinkels Vogelkantate – eine Komposition und ihre Geschichte', *Bonner Geschichtsblätter*, 53/54 (2004), 289–300

—, *Johanna Kinkel: Romantik und Revolution* (Cologne: Böhlau, 2008)

Klodau, Linda Maria, 'Gumbert, Ferdinand', in *Die Musik in Geschichte und Gegenwart*, ed. Ludwig Finscher and others, 2nd edn, 29 vols (Kassel: Bärenreiter, 1994–2008), viii, Personenteil, 272–73

Koch, Heinrich Christoph, *Versuch einer Anleitung zur Composition: Studienausgabe*, ed. Jo Wilhelm Siebert (Hanover: Siebert, 2007)

Kraemer, Florian, *Entzauberung der Musik: Beethoven, Schumann und die romantische Ironie* (Munich: Fink, 2014)

Kramer, Lawrence, *Music and Poetry: The Nineteenth Century and After* (Berkeley: University of California Press, 1984)

Kramer, Ursula, 'Mangold, Carl [Ludwig] Amand', in *Die Musik in Geschichte und Gegenwart*, ed. Ludwig Finscher and others, 2nd edn, 29 vols (Kassel: Bärenreiter, 1994–2008), xii, Personenteil, 973–75

Krebs, Harald and Sharon Krebs, *Josephine Lang: Her Life and Songs* (Oxford: Oxford University Press, 2007)

Lampert, Vera, 'Nationalism, Exoticism, or Concessions to the Audience?: Motivations behind Bartók's Folksong Settings', *Studia Musicologica Academiae Scientiarium Hungaricae*, 47 (March 2006), 337–43

Lebedeva, Nadejda, 'Die Lieder des Mirza-Schaffy op. 34 von Anton Rubinstein: Zwischen Folklorismus, Oientalismus und Nationalismus', *Archiv für Musikwissenschaft*, 67, 4 (2010), 284–309

Link, Dorothea, 'The Fandango Scene in Mozart's Le nozze di Figaro', *Journal of the Royal Musical Association*, 33, 1 (2008), 69–92

Löbe, Julius, 'Kinkel', in *Pierer's Universal-Lexikon*, ed. Julius Löbe, 4th edn, 19 vols (Altenburg: Pierer, 1857–65), ix, 494

Locke, Ralph P., 'Cutthroats and Casbah Dancers', in *The Exotic in Western Music*, ed. Jonathan Bellman (Boston: Eastern University Press, 1998), 104–36

—, *Musical Exoticism: Images and Reflections* (Cambridge/New York: Cambridge University Press, 2009)

Longyear, Rey M., *Nineteenth-Century Romanticism in Music*, 3rd edn (New Jersey: Prentice Hall, 1988)

Mackensen, Karsten, 'Himmel, Friedrich Heinrich', in *Die Musik in Geschichte und Gegenwart*, ed. Ludwig Finscher and others, 2nd edn, 29 vols (Kassel: Bärenreiter, 1994–2008), ix, Personenteil, 1–4

Manea, Norman, *On Clowns: The Dictator and the Artist* (New York: Grove Weidenfeld, 1992)

Marretta-Schär, Luise, 'Silcher, Philipp Friedrich', in *The New Grove Dictionary of Music and Musicians*, ed. Stanley Sadie, 2nd edn, 29 vols (London: Macmillan, 2001), vi, 386

Menhennet, Alan, *The Romantic Movement* (London: Croom Helm, 1981)

Metlitzki, Dorothee, 'On the Meaning of "Hatem" in Goethe's West-Östlicher Divan', *Journal of the American Oriental Society*, 117, 1 (January–March 1997), 148–51

Millàn-Zaibert, Elizabeth, *Friedrich Schlegel and the Emergence of Romantic Philosophy* (New York: State University of New York Press, 2007)

Nieberle, Sigrid, 'Kinkel, Johanna', in *Die Musik in Geschichte und Gegenwart*, ed. Ludwig Finscher and others, 2nd edn, 29 vols (Kassel: Bärenreiter, 1994–2008), x, Personenteil, 131–34

Niemöller, Klaus Wolfgang, 'Hiller, Ferdinand (von)', in *Die Musik in Geschichte und Gegenwart*, ed. Ludwig Finscher and others, 2nd edn, 29 vols (Kassel: Bärenreiter, 1994–2008), viii, Personenteil, 1581–87

Pahncke, Max, 'Briefe von Johanna Kinkel an Willibald Beyschlag', *Preußische Jahrbücher*, 122 (1905), 77–112

Parakilas, James, 'How Spain Got a Soul', in *The Exotic in Western Music*, ed. Jonathan Bellman (Boston: Eastern University Press, 1998), 137–93

Pasler, Jann, *Writing through Music: Essays on Music, Culture, and Politics* (Oxford: Oxford University Press, 2008)

Perrey, Beate Julia, *Schumann's* Dichterliebe *and Early Romantic Poetics* (Cambridge: Cambridge University Press, 2002)

Peters, George F., 'Air and Spirit in Goethe's "West-östlicher Divan"', *Rocky Mountain Review of Language and Literature*, 30, 4 (Autumn 1976), 216–28

Plantinga, Leon, 'The Piano and the Nineteenth Century', in *Nineteenth-Century Piano Music*, ed. Larry Todd, 2nd edn (New York/London: Routledge, 2004), 1–15

Raynor, Henry, *Music and Society Since 1815* (London: Barry & Jenkins, 1976)

Rebel, Hermann, *When Women Held the Dragon's Tongue and Other Essays on Historical Anthropology* (Oxford/New York: Berghahn, 2013)

Rehm, Jürgen, *Zur Musikrezeption im vormärzlichen Berlin: Die Präsentation bürgerlichen Selbstverständnisses und biedermeierlicher Kunstanschauung in den Musikkritiken Ludwig Rellstabs* (Hildesheim: Olms, 1983)

Ribbat, Ernst, 'Einleitung', in *Romantik: Ein literaturwissenschaftliches Studienbuch*, ed. Ernst Ribbat (Königstein: Athenäum, 1979),1–6

Ritte, Hans, *Das Trinklied in Deutschland und Schweden: Vergleichende Typologie der Motive* (Munich: Fink, 1973)

Rittershaus, Adeline, 'Felix Mendelssohn und Johanna Kinkel: Ungedruckte Tagebuchblätter und Briefe', *Neue Freie Presse: Morgenblatt*, 19 April 1900, 1–4

Rösch-Sondermann, Hermann, 'Johanna Kinkel: Emanzipation und Revolution einer Bonnerin', in *Bonn: 54 Kapitel Stadtgeschichte*, ed. Joseph Matzerath (Bonn: Bouvier, 1989), 179–88

Rosen, Charles, *The Romantic Generation* (London: Fontana, 1999)

Rupp, Heinz and Carl Ludwig Lang, *Deutsches Literatur-Lexikon*, 3rd edn, 35 vols (Bern: Francke/ Munich: Saur/ Berlin: de Gruyter, 1966–)

Schmidt, Klaus, *Gerechtigkeit – das Brot des Volkes: Johanna und Gottfried Kinkel: Eine Biographie* (Stuttgart: Radius, 1996)

Scobel, Emanuel, 'Truhn, Friedrich Hieronymus', in *Die Musik in Geschichte und Gegenwart*, ed. Ludwig Finscher and others, 2nd edn, 29 vols (Kassel: Bärenreiter, 1994–2008), xvi, Personenteil, 1086–87

Scott, Derek B., 'Music and Social Class in Victorian London', in *Musical Style and Social Meaning*, ed. Derek B. Scott (Farnham: Ashgate, 2010), 205–18

—, 'Orientalism and Musical Style', in *Musical Style and Social Meaning*, ed. Derek B. Scott (Farnham: Ashgate, 2010), 137–64

Siegel, Linda, 'Johanna Kinkel's "Chopin als Komponist" and Other Musical Writings: Untapped Source Readings in the History of Romantic Music Author(s)', *College Music Symposium*, 43 (2003), 105–25

—, ed., *Johanna Kinkel: Lieder*, 2 vols (Mount Airy: Hildegard, 2000)

SL [Richard Schaal], 'Krebs, Karl August', in *Die Musik in Geschichte und Gegenwart*, ed. Ludwig Finscher and others, 2nd edn, 29 vols (Kassel: Bärenreiter, 1994–2008), x, Personenteil, 649–50

Solomon, Maynard, 'Thoughts on Biography', *19th-Century Music*, 5, 3 (Spring 1982), 268–76

Sonntag, Brunhilde, *Annäherung an sieben Komponistinnen* (Kassel: Furore, 1997)

Sørensen, Inger, 'Hartmann, Johan Peter Emilius', in *Die Musik in Geschichte und Gegenwart*, ed. Ludwig Finscher and others, 2nd edn, 29 vols (Kassel: Bärenreiter, 1994–2008), viii, Personenteil, 736–40

Strathman, Christopher A., *Romantic Poetry and the Fragmentary Imperative: Schlegel, Byron, Joyce, Blanchot* (New York: State University of New York Press, 2006)

Strodtmann, Adolf, *Gottfried Kinkel: Wahrheit ohne Dichtung: Biographisches Skizzenbuch*, 2 vols (Hamburg: Hoffmann und Campe, 1850/51)

Suurpää, Lauri, 'Schumann, Heine, and Romantic Irony: Music and Poems in the First Five Songs of "Dichterliebe"', *Intégral*, 19 (1996), 93–123

Tadday, Ulrich, 'Rellstab, (Heinrich Friedrich) Ludwig', in *Die Musik in Geschichte und Gegenwart*, ed. Ludwig Finscher and others, 2nd edn, 29 vols (Kassel: Bärenreiter, 1994–2008), xiii, Personenteil, 1547–49

Taruskin, Richard, *The Oxford History of Western Music: The Nineteenth Century* (New York: Oxford University Press, 2005)

Thalheimer, Else, 'Johanna Kinkel als Musikerin' (unpublished PhD dissertation, University of Bonn, 1922)

Thomson, James, translation of Heinrich Heine, 'Der Mond ist aufgegangen', in *Poems Selected from Heinrich Heine*, ed. Kate Freiligrath Kroeker (London: Walter Scott, 1887), 91

Unseld, Melanie, *Biographie und Musikgeschichte: Wandlungen biographischer Konzepte in Musikkultur und Musikhistoriographie* (Cologne: Böhlau, 2014)

von Winterfeld, Carl, *Johannes Pierluigi von Palestrina: Seine Werke und deren Bedeutung für die Geschichte der Tonkunst: Mit Bezug auf Baini's neueste Forschungen* (Wroclaw: Adelholz, 1832)

Wagner, Undine, 'Seckendorff, eigentl. Karl, *Carl*, (Friedrich) Siegmund, *Sigismund*, Freiherr von Seckendorff-Aberdar', in *Die Musik in Geschichte und Gegenwart*, ed. Ludwig Finscher and others, 2nd edn, 29 vols (Kassel: Bärenreiter, 1994–2008), xv, Personenteil, 500–02

Wallis, J. E., translation of Heinrich Heine, 'Aus meinen Tränen sprießen', in *Poems Selected from Heinrich Heine*, ed. Kate Freiligrath Kroeker (London: Walter Scott, 1887), 55

Wehnert, Martin, 'Romantik und romantisch', in *Die Musik in Geschichte und Gegenwart*, ed. Ludwig Finscher and others, 2nd edn, 29 vols (Kassel: Bärenreiter, 1994–2008), viii, Sachteil, 464–506

Weissweiler, Eva, 'Die stille Opposition: Heine-Vertonungen von Frauen am Beispiel von Johanna Kinkel und Clara Schumann', in *Komponistinnen in Berlin*, ed. Bettina Brand and others (Berlin: Bender Schnelldruck, 1987), 96–108

Werner, Klaus G., 'Romberg, Andreas', in *Die Musik in Geschichte und Gegenwart*, ed. Ludwig Finscher and others, 2nd edn, 29 vols (Kassel: Bärenreiter, 1994–2008), xiv, Personenteil, 331–35

Whittle, Ruth and Debbie Pinfold, *Voices of Rebellion: Political Writings by Malwida von Meysenbug, Fanny Lewald, Johanna Kinkel and Louise Aston* (Bern: Peter Lang, 2005)

Whittle, Ruth, 'Modes of Exile: Revisiting Johanna Kinkel', *Colloquia Germanica*, 34, 2 (2001), 97–119

Wigmore, Richard, translation of Johann Wolfgang von Goethe, 'Nachtgesang', in *Franz Schubert: The Complete Songs*, transl. Richard Wigmore, intr. Graham Johnson (London: Hyperion, 2005), 32–33

Wilhelmy, Petra, *Der Berliner Salon im 19. Jahrhundert (1780–1914)* (Berlin: de Gruyter, 1989)

Williams, Briony, 'Maker, Mother, Muse: Bettina von Arnim, Goethe and the Boundaries of Creativity', in *Goethe: Musical Poet, Musical Catalyst*, ed. Lorraine Byrne (Dublin: Carysfort, 2004), 185–202

Williamson, George S., *The Longing for Myth in Germany: Religion and Aesthetic Culture from Romanticism to Nietzsche* (Chicago: University of Chicago Press, 2004)

Willison Lemke, Ann, '"Alles Schaffen ist wohl eine Wechselwirkung von Inspiration und Willen": Johanna Kinkel als Komponistin', in

Annäherungen an sieben Komponistinnen, ed. Clara Mayer (Kassel: Furore, 1998), 55–67

—, 'Kinkel, Johanna', in *The New Grove Dictionary of Music and Musicians*, ed. Stanley Sadie, 2nd edn, 29 vols (London: Macmillan, 2001), xiii, 611

—, 'Robert Schumann und Johanna Kinkel: Musikalische Stimmen der Revolution von 1848/49, *Internationales Jahrbuch der Bettina-von-Arnim-Gesellschaft*, 11/12 (1999/2000), 179–206

❧ Online sources

[Anon.], Stadtarchiv Bonn, Findbuch Johanna Kinkel, Stadtarchiv Bonn, <http://www.archive.nrw.de/LAV_NRW/jsp/findbuch.jsp?archivNr=20&klassId=20&tektId=115&id=296&expandId=18> (accessed 26 November 2018)

Ayaydin, Melanie, 'Kinkel, Johanna', Musik und Gender im Internet, ed. Beatrix Borchard, <http://mugi.hfmt-hamburg.de/artikel/Johanna_Kinkel.pdf> (accessed 18 April 2018)

Brandt-Schwarze, Ulrike, *Nachlass Gottfried und Johanna Kinkel: Findbuch* (Bonn: n.p., 2001), <https://www.ulb.uni-bonn.de/de/sammlungen/nachlaesse/findbuecher-und-inhaltsverzeichnisse/kinkel> (accessed 25 November 2018)

Heinrich Heine: Historisch-Kritische Gesamtausgabe, ed. Manfred Winfuhr, <http://hhp.uni-trier.de/Projekte/HHP/Projekte/HHP/werke/baende/D07/index_html> (accessed 4 May 2019)

Hofmeister catalogue: <http://www.hofmeister.rhul.ac.uk/2008/index.html> (accessed 4 May 2019)

Kinkel, Johanna, digitised scores, ULB <http://digitale-sammlungen.ulb.uni-bonn.de/ulbbnhans/content/titleinfo/2148925> (accessed 5 January 2019)

MUGI: Musikvermittlung und Genderforschung: Lexikon und multimediale Präsentationen, ed. Beatrix Borchard (Hochschule für Musik und Theater Hamburg, 2003–), <https://mugi.hfmt-hamburg.de> (accessed 14 April 2019)

Multiple poetry translations: *The LiederNet Archive*, hosted by Emily Ezust, <http://www.lieder.net/lieder/> (accessed 10 September 2019)

Sophie: A Digital Library of Works by German-Speaking Women <http://sophie.byu.edu/?q=texts/die-geisterinsel> (accessed 13 March 2019)

Index

Page numbers in **bold** include musical examples or an analytical table. The index covers the main text and the Appendix. (Bibliographic references in the footnotes have not been indexed.)